Trance and Modernity in the Southern Caribbean

NEW WORLD DIASPORAS

UNIVERSITY PRESS OF FLORIDA

Florida A&M University, Tallahassee
Florida Atlantic University, Boca Raton
Florida Gulf Coast University, Ft. Myers
Florida International University, Miami
Florida State University, Tallahassee
New College of Florida, Sarasota
University of Central Florida, Orlando
University of Florida, Gainesville
University of North Florida, Jacksonville
University of South Florida, Tampa
University of West Florida, Pensacola

Trance and Modernity
in the Southern Caribbean

African and Hindu Popular Religions
in Trinidad and Tobago

Keith E. McNeal

University Press of Florida
Gainesville / Tallahassee / Tampa / Boca Raton
Pensacola / Orlando / Miami / Jacksonville / Ft. Myers / Sarasota

Copyright 2011 by Keith E. McNeal
Printed in the United States of America. This book is printed on Glatfelter Natures Book, a
paper certified under the standards of the Forestry Stewardship Council (FSC). It is a recycled
stock that contains 30 percent post-consumer waste and is acid-free.

16 15 14 13 12 11   6 5 4 3 2 1

Library of Congress Cataloging-in-Publication Data
McNeal, Keith E.
Trance and modernity in the southern Caribbean : African and Hindu popular religions in
Trinidad and Tobago / Keith E. McNeal.
p. cm. — (New World diasporas)
Includes bibliographical references and index.
ISBN 978-0-8130-3736-3 (alk. paper)
1. Trinidad and Tobago—Religion. 2. Yoruba (African people)—Trinidad and Tobago—
Religion. 3. Hindus—Trinidad and Tobago—Religion. I. Title.
BL2566.T7M36 2011
200.972983—dc23   2011028135

The University Press of Florida is the scholarly publishing agency for the State University
System of Florida, comprising Florida A&M University, Florida Atlantic University, Florida
Gulf Coast University, Florida International University, Florida State University, New College
of Florida, University of Central Florida, University of Florida, University of North Florida,
University of South Florida, and University of West Florida.

University Press of Florida
15 Northwest 15th Street
Gainesville, FL 32611-2079
http://www.upf.com

In Memoriam

Joan & Vernon "Keloy" Lue Shue
"Auntie Cynthia" Seegobin
Ricardo Niles
Cynthia Maharaj
Peter Seegobin

*

Iyalorisha Melvina Rodney
Babalorisha "Baja" Sam Phills
Pujari Naziph Ali

*

Keith E. McNeal Jr.

Funding to assist in publication of this book
was generously provided by
the Wenner-Gren Fund for Anthropological Research.

Contents

Figures

Acknowledgments

My work has been dependent upon the bountiful kindness, generosity, thoughtfulness, and support of many informants, teachers, and friends, most of whom belong to more than one of these categories. My gratitude is therefore vast.

This project grows from seeds planted by many teachers and mentors, especially Elizabeth Ewalt and William Puka (Rensselaer Polytechnic Institute); Livia Kohn and Charles Lindholm (Boston University); Robert Paul and Bradd Shore (Emory University). I would also like to acknowledge (in alphabetical order) Mark Auslander, Donald Donham, Carla Freeman, Bruce Knauft, Charles Nuckolls, Dianne Stewart, and Carol Worthman.

I share something with Mark Padilla and Donna Murdock that will nourish me forever. Katherine Frank and Michael Hill have also always been there with verve and acumen. Others—all precious, smart, or fabulous in ways too numerous to mention—are (in alphabetical order) John Bing, Mary Katherine "Tassi" Crabb, Jason DeCaro, Lara Deeb, Alexa Dietrich, Kendra Hatfield-Timajchy, Alex Hinton, Yanique Hume, Ben Junge, Chris Kuzawa, Daniel Lende, Thom McDade, Hal Odden, Gayatri Reddy, Elaine Salo, Rebecca Seligman, and Saul Tobias.

I ate keskadoo in Trinidad in 1997 and—in line with its legendary ethnobiology—have kept returning and returning. My connections in "T and T" have grown auspiciously over the years and continue to permutate like a pumpkin vine.

At the University of the West Indies (UWI), I received critical assistance from Patricia Mohammed and Rhoda Reddock of Gender and Development

Studies, Selwyn Ryan of the Institute for Social and Economic Research, as well as Brinsley Samaroo, Bridget Brereton, Funso Aiyejina, and Kusha Haraksingh in the Humanities and Social Sciences. Kim Gransaull, Kathleen Helenese-Paul, and the helpful staff of the West Indiana Archive helped enormously as well. Beyond the sphere of UWI, I received videographic assistance from Christopher Laird and invaluable access to the video archives at Banyan, Ltd. My research has also been well facilitated at both the National Archives and the Heritage Library in Port-of-Spain.

I hereby express my gladness and gratitude to Frances Henry—professor emerita at York University—for collaboration and transgenerational camaraderie along the way. Moreover, though not based in the Caribbean, Kevin Yelvington, Aisha Khan, Viranjini Munasinghe, and Daniel Segal have all offered vitalizing specialist feedback at important junctures. Cheryl Levine and Vincent Goldberg also carried out fieldwork in the twin islands that overlapped fortuitously with mine; I greatly appreciate their friendship and remember our cerebral "limes" fondly.

Diana "Damcho" Finnegan began working her magic before I had even stepped foot onto terra firma in the isle of the hummingbird. Stephen Lue Shue—my "guardian angel" as well as guide to Blanchisseuse—will always be golden to me. He, Uncle Lester, and the Lue Shue family took phenomenal care of me in the summer of 1997, and I will never forget their extraordinary kindness.

The following people also deserve mention with my sincerest gratitude (in no particular order): Burton Sankeralli, Brian James, Tyrone Mohammed, Father Carlyle Fortune, Paul Prudent and Errol James, the late Ricardo Niles, Nola and Danica Daniel, darling Nikolaus Jennings and Wayne Mohammed, Ken Hunt, the late "Auntie" Cynthia Seegobin, the late Peter "Petey-pie" Seegobin, Peter "Julie" Sheppard and the one and only Nazeer Gopaul, Derek "Doo Doo" Williams, the late Cynthia Maharaj and extended Maharaj family, Father Stephen Doyle, Geeta Maharaj, Kumar Mahabir, Ravi Rampersad, Vernon Ramesar, Merlene Samlalsingh, Meiling, Peter Minshall, Yvonne and Susie Morgan, Steve Lewis (Trinidad's most polydexterous car mechanic), Marlon and Yvette of Santa Cruz, Dev Ramlal, Mark Pereira, Orlando Smith, Robert Lee, Grace and Winston Carr, "Redman" Philip, Dale, the late Gary Poon, Terence John, Garvin Gonzalez, Rudy Persad, Gabrielle Hossein, Shawn Rocke, Jacqueline Gregoire, Roger and Aulrica McFarlane, John Donation and Mother Joan, Raghoonath Chaboo, Garth Wilson, David Tindall, Pamela Franco, Abigail Hadeed, Randy Mohammed, Roland and Ann Duncan, Rajnie Ramlakhan, Selma Flood, Judith Johnston, Mrs. Maniyam, Jackie and Terence and the kids,

Larry and Sarah McIntosh, Lars and Regina Øyan, and Tammy. Ah does miss allyuh too bad.

On the Hindu side, I would especially like to mention the following people and institutions for their astonishing assistance (in no particular order): Tanti, Deanne, Saga, Shamma, Boom, their families, and the members of Maha Kali Mata Devi Mandir; Pujari Krishna Angad and the members of the Divine Maha Kali Shakti Temple; Pujari Tony and Susan Rampersad of Shiv Shankar Shakti Temple; Pujari Brian Bachulal and the members of the Bhawanie Shankar Sewa Sankh; the late Pujari Naziph Ali (Kali Charan Dass), Ramesh Maraj, and members of the Sai Sadhana Shakti Temple; Kartic Jangalee and the Prem Jyoti Shakti Mandir; Varun Narinesingh; Prematie Soodeen; Ravi-Ji of the Hindu Prachar Kendra; Jaishima Lelladarsingh; Mrs. Capildeo and Pandit Persad of the St. James Hindu Mandir; Auntie Kae; Pandit Vijay Ramroop, his family, and members of Shri Bandi Hanuman Shakti Mandir; Chattargoon and Elizabeth Moonsammy; Shamma Moonsammy of the Mariamman Kovil; Rajendra and Rani Jadoo and family; Lallo Sammy and the Streatham Lodge Shakti Temple; Derek Madray and Linda Brown; Tanti Beitin; Ramdeo Murugan; Emmanuel Nelson; Satnarayan Maharaj of the Sanatan Dharma Maha Sabha and the Bomb; Suresh Sookdeo and family of Sangre Grande; Dhanraji Sam and Ramdanie of El Dorado; Basdeo Mallian and Bissoondaye; Marla Gangadeen; the late Pandit Sam Parasaram; and Max Sulty.

There are many on the African side who have also assisted in equally amazing ways, including (again in no particular order) Dexter Oxley; the late "Baja" Sam Phills; the late Iyalorisha Rodney and Egbe Orisa Ile Wa; Iyalorisha Amoye Valerie Stephenson Lee Chee, Franklin, and members of Enia Wa; Mother Joan of D'Abadie; Boysie Ben, his family, and members of his shrine; Rhoma Spencer; Pearl Eintou Springer; Michael Cyrus, Mother Joan Cyrus, Valerie Foster, and all the members and friends of Kenny Cyrus Alkebu Lan Ile Ijebu Shrine; Zakiya Wadada, Queen Mother Kali, Babaluwa, and the shrine at La Canoa; Julianna Sutton; Pat McCleod (Iya Sangowumi), her family, and the Abiadamma community; Olori Jeffrey Biddeau and family; Oludari Massetungi and Egbe Onisin Eledumare; the late Babalorisha Clarence Forde and sons; Henry White; Aaron and Rhonda Jones; Marjorie Anderson; and James Houk.

I have a special place in my heart for Rabindranath Maharaj, who not only kept me going in very good company during the longest period of fieldwork, but also gave me the honor of sharing in one of the unfathomably difficult things life brings. Thomas LePere has cherished my work for a long while, spanned the transition to San Diego with an encouraging twinkle in his eye, cared in countless ways, and generously shared his love for travel. Felipe Zúñiga waltzed into my life in SoCal and never fails to make me smile. Jacinto Delgado-Guizar kept me on my toes and graciously midwifed the first complete draft of this manuscript. I thank each of you for being and becoming with me.

My family also deserves credit for whatever I have been able to make of myself, especially my mother, Katheryn McNeal Pennington. I appreciate everyone's love and support—emotional, spiritual, material—in ways not always enough expressed. I dedicate this work in part to the memory of my father, Keith E. McNeal Jr., who would have been the only one of the clan to highlight extensively in his personal copy.

In San Diego, I have the cherished, ever-unfolding friendship of Erin Dwyer, which began so long ago in upstate New York. Ian Abramson—a more recently acquired guardian angel as well as plant guru extraordinaire—has bent over backwards to make life easier as well as share love for the life of mind (not to mention help take care of Bibi). The move to SoCal also brought the auspicious and stimulating friendships of Nancy Postero and Jeff Harkness; Elana Zilberg and Matthew Elgart; Jodie, Marivi, and Sofia Blanco; Nayan Shah and Ken Foster; Barbara Bamberger; Roberto Tejada; and David Perlmutter. I also thank Michael Kimmel for caring and keeping me sane.

My students Brendan Thornton, Noga Shemer, and Joshua "Elvis" Nordin have taught me more than they realize and made being a Caribbeanist even more pleasurable. I acknowledge support from the Department of Anthropology at the University of California–San Diego (UCSD) as well as intellectual sustenance from Joel Robbins in particular. Time at UCSD also made possible a very special relationship with one of my anthropological heroes, Melford E. Spiro, with whom I have been able to felicitously sidestep the disciplinary oedipal bottleneck. Last, but certainly not least, there is Esra Özyürek, who immeasurably enriches my soul with royal pomegranate seeds and also brought the miraculous Azize and Firuze Özyürek-Baer—as well as the indubitable Marc David Baer—into the center of my life.

Research and publication have been made possible through the generous support of the Fulbright-Hays Foundation; the Social Science Research Council; the Wenner-Gren Foundation; the Emory University Fund for Internationalization; the Center for the Study of Race and Ethnicity at UCSD; the Hellman Fellowship Program at UCSD; a UCSD Humanities Center Transborder Interventions, Transcontinental Archives Fellowship; and the UCSD Faculty Career Development Program, for all of which I am most grateful.

Kevin Yelvington benevolently ensured that this project found the right home in the University Press of Florida's New World Diasporas series. At UPF, Amy Gorelick's steady hand made publishing this book a less daunting endeavor.

Finally, I want to heartily "big up" Erin Dwyer and Felipe Zúñiga for their masterly transformations of my hand-drawn diagrams into such delightful schematic illustrations for publication; Katherine Frank for superheroic editing assistance; and Bobby Drake for solving a last-minute technical glitch and therefore saving the images presented in this book.

Prologue

Ecstasy

The Mother Intervenes

"Watch me! Put this in the first line of your book: the purpose of being human
is to realize God. Worshipping the Mother—Great Mother Kali—is a good thing,
not *obeah*! [a colloquial reference to black magic]"

It was a Sunday in September of 2000, and I was standing in a shakti temple in
southern Trinidad. Dressed in white ceremonial garments, a Hindu spirit medium—who was also the temple's leader and known affectionately as "Guru"—
had singled me out during his trance and, as Kali, proclaimed the words above.
His eyes were closed and his head moved in unison with the intensive drumming that had driven the action for more than an hour. The medium punctuated his interactions with short periods of trance dancing, attended by a small
posse of *pujaris* (assistant ritualists). The temple's largest Kali *murti* (statuary
icon)—threw a meaningful shadow on the ecstatic performance.[1]

I appreciated the divinely ordained attention to my research and by that
point had become comfortable interacting with what practitioners of spiritual
mediumship in Trinidad and Tobago call "manifestations." However, I had only
recently made contact with this particular temple, and though the Guru and
I had conversed in other settings, that Sunday was my first time attending its
weekly Shakti Puja. I had not anticipated such an intense personal interaction
with the Guru's "manifestation" of Mother Kali.

I had been watching attentively that morning as offerings were made to the other *deotas* (colloquial term for a deity) at their murtis, following as the round of puja activity made its way to Kali. The drumming had intensified, and the Guru's body began to quiver and spasm. He spun in place several times, then circled three times around the large, colorful icon of Kali, all the while gyrating in trance dance. A handful of the temple's assistant pujaris closed rank around the medium, singing loudly and passionately to the Mother. Before approaching me, the Guru had already conducted healing ministrations on a number of devotees and had offered a discourse on sexual morality. Next was my turn.

After finishing with the imperative regarding my research, Kali continued, "Did yuh tell anyone in de temple dat you are an anthropologist?"

"You," I replied, pointing to the Guru. His assistants immediately corrected me, clarifying that it was the Goddess—not the Guru—with whom I was speaking.

The Guru's Kali continued: "Do you want to experience *shakti*?" I hesitated, as I had expressed my agnostic and nonparticipatory stance regarding ecstasy in earlier conversations with him. "You're afraid," Kali countered, "but yuh have no reason to be—don't be scared!"

Shakti refers to the cosmic energy of the universe and is especially associated with the goddesses of Hinduism. In the local practice of mediumship, shakti is temporarily "raised" or "elevated" in the bodies of Hindu mediums. In this context, it is conceptualized as a potent spiritual "energy" capable of doing superhuman "work" through the vehicle of the votary's body. Shakti is also referred to as "power" and may come in generalized as well as highly specific forms. My rationale for keeping my participant-observation nonecstatic—a decision I am more skeptical of in hindsight—was a naïve belief that doing so would enable me to remain more objective. And given the comparative nature of my research on both African and Hindu spiritisms, I believed it would be problematic to personally cultivate the ecstasy of one tradition and not the other. I was apprehensive about "catching power" but playing the fool. And I was concerned, as well, about acquiring spiritual obligations that would become impracticable upon my return to the United States.

In one of our earlier conversations, the Guru and his pujaris had argued that I should allow them to help me undergo the experience of shakti, given the centrality of ceremonial ecstasy within this Hindu tradition. "Yuh cyan' [can't] jus' talk about it," they said, "yuh have tuh feel it." Conceding their point, I nonetheless countered that anthropology is a human science and therefore concerned primarily with social and cultural dynamics, not theological ones. To experiment with ecstasy myself would flirt too closely with theology, I thought. I had no interest in disparaging the beliefs of the people with whom my research brought me into contact, but I also could not sincerely claim that I fully shared their beliefs, and extending my participant-observation into the arena of ecstasy would seem to require doing so. Further, I did not want to come across as yet another charlatan on the spiritistic circuit—albeit a rather peculiar one in the form of the foreign anthropologist—and thought a faux pas in this regard would prove more insulting than the decision to steer clear of any trance praxis altogether.

In retrospect, I appreciate how much space there is for experimentation within local ecstatic circles and fear my reticence may have been more patronizing than intended. Though cultivating any degree of ecstasy in myself would raise problems with both documentation and epistemology, I probably should have been more open to the lead of practitioners. After all, since I wanted to understand their experiences, why not let them lead me all the way into the heart of the matter? Aren't anthropologists inclined to grasp the "native's" point of view? Why could I not simply keep up an anthropological—rather than theological—mode of investigation?

Under the shadow of the Kali murti, with the eyes of the devotees on me, I barely had time to run through these arguments in my head before Kali engaged me again. "Here," she said, "take this camphor!" An assistant pujari took me by the wrist and held it so the Guru's Kali could drop a burning cube of camphor onto my upturned palm. Fiery cubes of camphor are ubiquitous items of puja praxis of all kinds within West Indian Hinduism and are also utilized specifically in ecstatic puja to authenticate the reality of manifestations. Mediums cup flaming camphor in their hands or pop it into their mouths as a performative sign of divine presence.

I reflexively pulled my hand away, dropping the camphor almost as soon as the sizzling cube met my skin. It rolled several inches along the ground and then snuffed itself out. "See," Kali proclaimed, "yuh does need the shakti in order to take de camphor, eh!"

The Mother's medium made one final attempt. "This may be yuh las' opportunity tuh get the shakti and it important fuh yuh study." With this, the manifesting medium took me by the arm himself and tried to spin me round in circles. "Get de shakti and then yuh will understand." I felt awkward under the watchful eyes of the temple audience but continued to abstain in the face of what had begun to feel like Trini-style harassment. Part of me wanted to comply, but I could not. The Guru's Kali finally gave up, quipping in some exasperation, "Well, what do anthropologists really know anyway?"

Before she moved on, Kali called for a moonstone *mala* (string of prayer beads) and gave them to me as a token of insight, wishing me luck with my studies. It seemed like a consolation prize, but I was glad for our interchange to conclude on a more positive note. And though I attended more services at this temple in the ensuing period, no one there—neither pujari nor deota—attempted to ignite the spark of shakti in me again.

From Agony to Ecstasy and a Passage to India

Naziph Ali—the man known as Guru to his congregation—was born into a Muslim family and grew up even farther south from where his temple and residence were later located in Penal. He was "very spiritual" in his youth and active at the mosque. Yet he experienced a series of enigmatic "fits and trances" while growing up that troubled him and his parents. They believed he was "possessed" by some wayward force and took him to a number of seer-men as well as medical doctors, though the issue was never resolved. Naziph felt so bad about the problem and the burden it presented that, at times, he flirted with suicide.[2]

"I was in love with Hinduism from a tender young age," he recalled. Growing up in a predominantly Hindu area, Naziph was enchanted by the images and rituals to which he was exposed. However, it was not until living in central Trinidad during his university years—when his fits and trances resurfaced after a period of teenage latency—that he began to actively seek out Hindu religious activity.

Naziph sought intervention at the largest shakti temple in the area after having gotten nowhere in consultation with a *pandit* (priestly specialist). He only wanted "tuh get dis ting off 'uh me" at the time. But the temple couldn't "*shanti* it off" (*shanti* means "peace" in Hindi and is used idiomatically in ecstatic puja to refer to the process of deactivating manifestations by pressing upon one's third eye, mystically located just behind the middle of the forehead). Instead, to Naziph's surprise, he experienced powerful waves of shakti while attending this temple's services and began rather quickly to "*jharay* and see about people" (jharay is a South Asian–derived term that refers to blessing, purifying, and healing people with a sanctified implement such as *neem* [margosa] leaves in Shakti Puja, or other items such as dried palm spines or peacock feathers among other Indian healers). This went on for several months, yet he remained ambivalent and then dropped out of the shakti temple as quickly as he had taken it up.

Not long thereafter, however, the push of what he was beginning to understand as the "power" of shakti returned again. One day, feeling "haunted," he jumped in his car and sped to the Sunday services of yet another prominent temple. He remembers arriving and stepping out of the car: "All I know is that I lost my senses—it just knocks you out." The temple's leader approached him afterward, inquiring who he was and inviting him to take part in the temple's annual Big Puja, including its "fire dance," which was coming up the following week. Naziph protested that he had not been fasting in preparation, but the leader assured him that it would not matter, since he clearly had the "real shakti." Naziph turned out to be a star of their firepass ceremony that year, "the onliest person who was able to do such justice to the fire."

This debut gained him some popularity. He stayed with the temple for a time but was a quick study and, in 1990, founded his own temple back down south. As his capacity as a medium matured and he gained momentum with independent spiritual work, Naziph came to manifest the shakti of Durga, Lakshmi, and Ganesha primarily—solidly orthodox Hindu deities within the West Indian Hindu imagination. He manifested Kali too, when her uniquely potent energy was needed. His entire family became involved in the activities of the temple, and his father now claims, "Muslims are Hindus anyway." Naziph married a Hindu woman and credits her influence upon his progress within the religion as well. He believes others may look askance because of his Muslim background but knows that hiding it would make no difference. He is who he is. And besides, God knows only the "temple of your heart" and, if you serve him with sincerity and devotion, that is all that matters.

Naziph traveled to India after beginning his formal engagement with Shakti Worship in order to investigate the nature of the work there—where it is "true"— as well as to visit the late Sai Baba at his renowned ashram in Puttaparthi. His experience in India taught him that Kali Worship is not just a "Madrassi ting" (i.e., south Indian thing, via the port city of Madras—a common belief in Trinidad) but in fact a pan-Hindu phenomenon of great significance. And he learned from Sai Baba that Kali is a higher, more esoteric form of Durga, which recuperates the "bad reputation" Kali has come to garner in Trinidad. "I was very much taken up by this fact," he said.

His experience within Sai Baba's orbit not only influenced his understanding of Shakti Worship, but also brought him into the fold of devotion to Sai as well. This is reflected in the name of his temple—Sai Sadhana Shakti Temple—as well as its weekly services featuring Sai *satsang* (nonecstatic devotional gathering) and ecstatic Shakti Puja. This confluence of Sai and Shakti is facilitated by the universalism of Sai philosophy and the fact that the Baba is considered an avatar of Shiva, who is associated with Shakti as mythical consort. The Sai-Shakti interconnection is signified on the walls of the temple by three large photographic images of Sai Baba dressed in red, white, and yellow robes, respectively, the three primary colors of Shakti Worship in this area of the West Indies. Indeed, in line with the philosophy of Shri Sathya Sai Baba, the Guru believes Sai and Shakti are in fact two dimensions of the same esoteric reality.

Naziph's subsequent travels to India and Puttaparthi are reflected in other photographs displayed on inner temple walls, including one of him with Sai Baba. The first time I visited the temple's innermost sanctum, I was shown a large devotional image from India of Sai Baba sitting on a golden chariot-throne. Miraculous honey from Sai's "body" dripped down to the bottom of the poster, where it was being collected in a *taria* (brass puja plate). In addition to his physical travels, Naziph also demonstrated a capacity for visions and an ability to "travel spiritually" to India for mystical audiences with Sai Baba.

The temple's devotion to Sathya Sai Baba reaches a liturgical climax every year on his birthday, the twenty-third of November. When I attended this event in 2000, the temple was decorated with strings of blinking Santa Claus lights, a fully adorned Christmas tree, a large Nativity scene, and a spectacular wreath hung over Sai Baba's main devotional alcove. A meal was served, lauded as a "lavish Chinese feast." Afterwards, the celebrants sang "Happy Birthday" over a large cake, with the children of the temple blowing out the candles.

The Guru's congregation not only embodies wider trends in the transformation of ecstatic Hinduism in postcolonial Trinidad, it also represents a unique facet of this terrain. How such a temple with this profile came into being in the Caribbean—with a ceremonial life revolving around both ecstatic Shakti Puja and a decidedly nonecstatic form of *satsang* for Sai Baba, along with an auxiliary Christmas celebration at the end of the year—is one of the questions I address.

Ecstasy

Nowadays, any form of ecstatic local Hinduism takes place within heterodox temples primarily dedicated to Mother Kali. The term "ecstasy" describes a spectrum of dynamic states of experience referred to as "trance," "dissociation," or "altered states of consciousness" in the scholarly literature, in which everyday consciousness is intentionally displaced and temporarily transformed through specific ritual practices. This experience of ecstasy is central to the Hindu and African ritual traditions examined in this study.

Psychoanalyst Michael Eigen (2001) believes there is an ecstatic core at the center of existence, involving both creative and destructive energies. Ecstasy, he says, is as basic and yet as elusive as breathing. The English word *ecstasy* derives from the Greek *ekstasis*, meaning to stand outside oneself: based on *ek*, "out," and *stasis*, "to stand," *ecstatic* therefore points to mystical experiences associated with trance and dissociation as well as visions and meditation. The word also pertains to peak experiences of excitement or enthusiasm in English. Here I take ecstatic traditions to be characterized by their involvement in the cultivation of altered states of consciousness for a range of expressive, devotional, and therapeutic purposes. The result in the cases examined here is the ability to achieve a paradoxical mode of being combining self-transcendence with divine immanence: the phenomenological projection of self outside of self on behalf of self and others in the quest for competence and well-being.

While addressing me at the temple that morning, the Guru "vibrated" with Kali's shakti, spasms moving continually through his body. There is something electric and mesmerizing about observing the power—or shakti—of Kali temporarily manifest within the body of her servant, what people refer to as "kyetching powah" (catching power). When I questioned mediums about manifesting, they had difficulty describing their experiences, which involve the displacement of mundane consciousness by that of a higher, "spiritual" force. The more intensely one catches power, or manifests, the more completely one's worldly self is temporarily vanquished. "I don't remember," a medium would tell me. Or "It impossible tuh know wha' happen to yuh when de power an' dem does come on yuh, unless dey don' come fuh true" (it's impossible to know what happens to you when the powers [literally, the power and them] come on you, unless they aren't real). Indeed, by definition, to manifest is to become a worldly vessel for an otherworldly power, a conceptualization operative within both traditions considered here. This is what makes trance ceremonialism so distinctive. In the West Indies, it is a vision of the sacred based on popular contact with the spirit world. One senior pujari characterized catching power as "the oldest way of helping people." An elderly Iyalorisha told me that she "dances out" her troubles, including the aches and pains of aging.

The complexity of ecstatic mediumship is exemplified by the problem of identifying the speaker during interactions. It was not simply the Guru who spoke to me that morning, but also—simultaneously—Mother Kali, whose presence Naziph temporarily embodied and whose voice found a channel through his own. Most practitioners would emphasize that it was Kali—the Mother herself—who materialized during the puja and held court that day. It was *she* who blessed devotees, healed seekers, and taught the anthropologist his lesson about experiencing shakti, not the Guru. Indeed, theologically speaking, Kali and her spiritual associates are paramount for devotees; her history and mythology preceded and encompassed Naziph's personal efforts, making his manifestation possible. And yet, anthropologically speaking, Kali depends upon the energies and efforts of her devotees, who cradle her puja in their hearts and ceremonial life and who regularly—albeit temporarily—conjure her forth in sacred dramaturgy. The locution "Guru's Kali" therefore signifies the Mother speaking through her medium as well as Kali as an idiom for Naziph's own revelations, a bifocal form of sacred vision and action.

Hardly incidentally, Naziph—now, tragically, deceased—was a civil servant in the Ministry of Education for many years, and he was the medium who most explicitly addressed my research while in the ecstatic mode. Other manifestations spoke now and then of my "studies," but these references were vague and meant simply to be supportive of me personally rather than pedagogically oriented. Only Naziph referred to my "book," and it was *his* Kali who went as far as to offer an imperative about its first line. Naziph's knowledge of academia informed his mystical consciousness and the interaction his Kali had with me, hence not just Kali, but the Guru's Kali.

A dynamic tension in the interplay of humanity and divinity pulsates at the heart of this form of religious practice, generating a remarkable capacity for responsivity and flexibility across space and through time. These processes are evident in Naziph's evolution from an everyday Muslim into a Hindu guru with his own Sai-Shakti temple. The intimate immediacy of trance performance within heterodox popular religions in the southern Caribbean not only grants these traditions their most compelling characteristics, but also presents them with their greatest challenges in relation to wider social and political affairs.

Meeting Erile

In the summer of 1997, a few years before my encounter with the Guru's Kali, I found myself on the corner of Park and Charlotte streets in downtown Port-of-Spain. I was a graduate student on my first trip to Trinidad, beginning pilot research on African traditions and anxiously waiting for someone I'd never met to "carry" me—as West Indians say—to my first *orisha* feast. I leaned against the outside wall of Republic Bank in the glow of the streetlights, my attention shifting between the imposing presence of the Roman Catholic church across the street and intermittent pedestrians, who were trying not to stare too overtly at the white guy loitering on the sidewalk after dark. As headlights streamed by, I looked for the automobile Mr. McFarlane had described to me earlier on the telephone. McFarlane, a deep-voiced man of few words, was a contact I'd made through an American colleague, and most generous in his willingness to escort a young, new student researcher to the first of what would become a countless number of orisha feasts.

I had no idea what to expect when I slipped into the back seat of the car next to the silent but bright-eyed McFarlane children. The family was dressed in fashionably African-styled clothing that indexed their socioeconomic status and political orientation, I would later come to learn. Likewise, there was no way I could have known that the orisha "yaad" (yard) to which we were going belonged to the sister of an important Afro-Trinidadian spiritist who had died about a decade before and whose own, much larger, shrine lay just a stone's throw away. Most significantly, I could not have anticipated the dramatic encounter I was to have many hours later, deep in the night, with an ecstatically manifesting orisha medium, one who—in the imagery so commonly invoked in the Caribbean and beyond—became a temporary "horse" for her patron spirit "rider." Though I had spent a summer studying Pentecostalism in the southern United States and had attended a Vodou ceremony in the Dominican Republic the year before, this was to be my first interaction with an ecstatic medium in Trinidad.

As we began making our way southward toward Oropouche, the car began sputtering, slowing down on hills and spewing fumes into the cabin where the McFarlanes, their two kids, and I all choked and rubbed our burning eyes. Mr. McFarlane would pull over on the side of the highway, calmly tinker with the engine, and then restart the car for another jaunt. I wondered if we would ever make it.

But arrive we did, after midnight. By then, the first major manifestation had already materialized within the *palais* (French patois for "palace")—the most public ceremonial structure and main performance space—though many people still milled around on the road next to the house-and-shrine compound. The voices of those inside the palais singing liturgical song-chants to the orishas rang out into the night, propelled by percussion more spectacular and magnetic than anything I had ever heard. Most women wore head wraps, some made of colored dashiki cloth. More dressed up than the men, women also wore dresses or skirts instead of pants. Though I would find that women were involved in much of the ceremony, only men drummed and, later, slew the sacrificial animals in the wee hours of the morning.

Mr. McFarlane introduced me to a few people, and we stood on the street for a long while. As I was still having trouble understanding the local dialect within the stratified continuum of Creole English spoken by Trinbagonians, I felt confused and self-conscious. Finally, we made our way through the gate and into the palais, where a ceremonial vortex had formed around the central pole. I loitered by the concrete wall until Mrs. McFarlane beckoned me inside, then I settled into a spot against the outer wall of the palais, feeling the song and percussion begin to resonate in my body. Though I knew none of the chants, the energetic pulsations were irresistible and I started to move and keep time with everyone else. We became a collective organism of sorts, cycling through escalating rounds of movement and song together.

All four corners of the palais were lit with candles, and calabashes containing ritual substances, such as water or olive oil, marked the cardinal directions. Three drummers sat on wooden benches attached to the inside of the waist-high walls of the palais. A circular area around the central pole was filled with candles, calabashes, red hibiscus, green leaves and branches, and cloths and implements associated with the gods. Ceremonial paraphernalia also adorned the central pole. People gathered shoulder to shoulder in concentric circles around the inside perimeter of the space; the circles stabilized around three or four persons deep, though people came and went throughout the entire proceeding. Between the undulating congregation and the area around the central pole was a distance of another several feet where the most theatrical action took place, especially individual mediums manifesting specific powers (orishas, saints, or other spirits) as well as devotees shaking and vibrating with a more diffuse and generalized form of *ashé* (mystical energy—a Yoruba-based term).

That night two orishas dominated the feast. The first of these was Erile, the "man of the sea"—as he is often called—who is also connected for many with St. Jonah, the Hebrew prophet swallowed by a great fish in the ocean in order to carry out his divine mission. Erile materialized within the body of a large black woman and carried out his work for well over two hours. In fact, I had seen Erile earlier as he interacted with folks assembled out on the road, either blessing them or chastising them for loitering before moving down the road alone, where he held a long *roseau*—the bamboo rod that is one of Erile's primary ritual tools—and blew olive oil into the air after taking swigs from a bottle in hand. Misty oil spray glistened in the air above the medium, refracting the streetlight above. Erile's performance was the most prominent one in the first half of the night, the only constant throughout this phase of the proceedings.

At times he was joined briefly by other manifestations as well as by a changing cast of more generalized trance dancers. He stomped around the palais, alternately spinning and dancing, interacting with almost everyone present. Devotees intermittently joined the arena with him, either shaking with ashé themselves or simply dancing alongside. By contrast with Erile, those experiencing more diffuse ecstatic vibrations lunged erratically to and fro, shaking, trembling, or spinning about without any obvious agenda, all the while with their eyes closed. Erile's gaze, on the other hand, was piercing. He ruled the scene, uttering hardly a word.

At one point both Erile and another, more briefly manifesting, orisha who had mounted a male practitioner made their way ecstatically around the palais in tag-team fashion, pouring olive oil into the mouths of their "children," a blessing for everyone who partook. Erile initially skipped me. Feeling awkward for being left out, I wondered if the manifesting medium was unsure how to interact with the stranger in a strange land. Eventually, his medium made her way back and, after tending to the woman next to me for a second time, turned and looked at me with an extrahuman look in her eyes, motioning me forward. I bent down and opened my mouth to receive the blessed libation. I braced myself for the slug of oil and managed to swallow most of it, a few drops escaping from the corners of my mouth.

Erile leaned in closer and asked: "Do you believe?" His eyes bore searchingly into mine. A voluminous head of hair—having been released from his medium's head wrap as soon as the manifestation materialized—splayed out in all directions.

I searched for the appropriate answer. How could I express what I really thought, that I was more interested in sociological dimensions of religious behavior and that my research required bracketing the question of the ultimate truth content of belief? This was no time for anthropological platitudes. "I think so," I blurted out finally, wanting to affirm the cultural reality of what was transpiring around me. Erile seemed pleased, because he immediately grabbed and pulled me into the main performance area. His medium held my arm and crouched down, doing a tight rhythmic step. Trying not to be distracted by the blur of faces around me, I concentrated on following the orisha's footsteps. We went round and round the pole. I'm sure I blushed under the congregation's gaze.

Finally, Erile stopped in front of the drummers, did a few more steps, and then spun me around in quick, tight circles. The blur accelerated. He spun me around backwards several times. Before sending me back to my original perch along the inside of the palais walls, Erile put his forehead against mine, staring directly into my eyes once more. Sweat and olive oil from the medium's head lathered mine, and she rubbed the residue all over my face and neck. When she let me go, I did a nondescript little jig back to the sidelines, feeling a little dazed.

Just before the break at about 3:30 a.m., the young woman next to me collapsed. She had been trance dancing for an extended period of time, bumping into me repeatedly. I had kept her from falling into the fence just outside the palais at one point, but this time she slumped down to the earthen floor. She recovered soon after Erile vacated the space, however, and afterwards was outside having her meal of stewed rice, goat, and potato salad with the rest of us. One wouldn't have guessed she had just danced herself into a state of unconsciousness only minutes before.

After the break, a different priestess—this time manifesting Shango, the Yoruba god of thunder and justice—made her way into the center. Though Shango danced around the palais for some time, I spent the next part of the evening conversing with one of the drummers I recognized from James Houk's monograph, *Spirits, Blood, and Drums* (1995), whom I met over refreshments. James and I had become acquainted once I decided to visit TT in 1997 as part of my pilot graduate research, and in addition to giving me advice on navigating the country and feedback on my ideas, he sent me copies of his book to distribute to friends and informants whom he had not seen since its publication.

Soon the focus of activity shifted from the palais to the *chapelle* (from the French patois word for "chapel") located in another area of the shrine's yard. The chapelle is a more private structure within orisha yards, containing an altar where various implements and paraphernalia associated with the deities and their ritual practices are kept. Sometimes the chapelle and palais are directly connected; other times, they are separated physically and connected only through ritual action. Shango, the main ritual priest (called *mombwah*), his assistants, the slayer, and several others made their way into the chapelle while the rest of us found places in front of it. The drummers repositioned themselves just outside the chapelle's door, and their percussive efforts intensified again. Several devotees shook or heaved as waves of ashé coursed through their bodies. Three goats and about six to eight chickens were lined up as offerings to the deities of the chapelle.

Through the doorway of the structure, I could see burning candles on an altar decorated in red cloth, Shango's primary color. His ecstatic medium was inside along with the priestess who had earlier manifested Erile and other chief personnel. Accompanied by the drumming, the animals were each led into the chapelle to meet their fate; their heads would remain inside at the stools of the powers to whom they were dedicated. When the sacrifices were complete, Shango exited the chapelle, reveling in the postsacrificial glow.

Then—to my surprise—everything came to what seemed like a screeching halt. Shango's horse, which quickly became quiescent after the sacrifices, was hauled into the house after several minutes of lying motionless on the ground. Drumming ceased for the first time, other than the one standard break midstream. It was six o'clock in the morning and light had begun to permeate the sky.

Because of the troubles with their car, the McFarlanes had left several hours before, after introducing me to a middle-aged fellow named Sevray who was going back to "town" (Port-of-Spain) by bus. He promised to make sure I found my way back to the little apartment where I was staying that summer, in a housing project in the East Dry River area between Belmont and Laventille. At the time I did not know that East Dry River was in fact known as "Yarriba Village" or "Yaraba Town" (Yoruba) in the nineteenth century (Brereton 1979:135). Despite the hour, however, Sevray was in no hurry to depart. He and a handful of other men settled in for some early morning "liming" (hanging out) and were slamming shots of puncheon rum, the cheapest, strongest rum available. They were friendly, insisting that I take at least one shot myself; I complied even though I was exhausted, relishing sleep much more than alcohol.

We finally left, first hitching a ride with someone to San Fernando, a half hour away. There, we waited in line at the bus station to purchase tickets, and then waited another half hour until the bus for Port-of-Spain made its departure. Next came the hour-long ride northward to Port-of-Spain, in Friday morning rush-hour traffic. Sevray was exhausted too, sitting with his eyes closed and head resting on the seat back. We rode silently. Talking seemed impossible, though my mind was racing with questions about what had just transpired.

Upon arrival in Port-of-Spain, my chaperone first wanted to stop and inform his boss at a warehouse downtown that he would not be in that day. Plus there were intermittent showers that morning, and Sevray—like so many West Indians—was adamant about not getting wet, insisting that we wait out each burst of rain under roadside cover. Thus it was not until noon, after thanking him with as much energy as I could muster, that I stumbled into bed and slept until evening. It had been a long but fascinating night. Upon waking, I realized I had left my umbrella with Sevray, which seemed fitting as a small token of my gratitude.

Ecstasy in Exile

This book is a comparative historical ethnography of African and Hindu popular religions in the twin-island Republic of Trinidad and Tobago. It analyzes the Old World backgrounds as well as the New World cultural histories of two subaltern traditions of trance performance and spirit mediumship—linked, respectively, with African and Indian ethnicity in complex ways—from the mid-nineteenth century through the turn of the twenty-first century. Comparing and contrasting the trajectories of these traditions allows for a deeper understanding of globalization and religious transculturation in relation to racial and class stratification in a precociously modern context.[3]

I consider not only convergent similarities of these diasporic traditions, but also their very different political fates in the wake of decolonization and the development of postcolonial multiculturalism. I illustrate how contrasting colonial ideologies of racial subordination continue to cast a spell upon the postcolonial politics of religion and diaspora. By considering Caribbean Hinduism along with an African tradition, *Trance and Modernity in the Southern Caribbean: African and Hindu Popular Religions in Trinidad and Tobago* expands upon understandings of transculturation and seeks to recast the study of religion and modernity more generally.

Western secularization theory has oversimplified not only "Modernity" and the fate of religion in the West, but also modernity's ostensibly nonmodern "Other(s)." Grappling with the inadequacies of theory based on an idealized model of the West requires engagement with those Others—the traditional charge of anthropology—as well as empirical *de*-idealization of the West, for which the experience of liberalized subaltern spiritisms in the southern Caribbean is so instructive. This study demonstrates that Orisha Worship and Shakti Puja in Trinidad and Tobago have been as globalized and modernized as the so-called world religions. Charting the genealogies of each in the southern Caribbean, I examine patterns of structural convergence and subaltern liberalization experienced as a result of lateral adaptation to a shared colonial environment. The fact that seemingly "primitive" religious practices involving trance and ecstasy have neither declined nor disappeared under the shadow of modernity drives another nail into the coffin of conventional secularization theory.

It is instructive to ask how and why this is the case. In so doing, I extend the Atlantic school of historical anthropology's critical perspective on the "precocious modernity" of the Caribbean deeply into the realm of religion. The multiplex condition of ecstasy in exile is shown to embody local and translocal meanings, both equally portentous regarding the disenchantments of modernity and its multifarious reenchantments in the global ecumene.

Catching Power, Playing Deep

When the manifestation are on you, you really doesn't know anything, yuh
know—you really doesn't know anything. Because the powers, now, they use
your body to do what they have to.

Mother Joan, July 2000

Conceptualizing "Power" and the "Powers"

As the round of invocations and offerings progressed in the Shakti Puja, devotees "vibrated" with diffuse forms of shakti and "played" throughout the temple.
They were attended by assistants but never approached as divinities in and of
themselves. This general "shakti play" is no simple matter, involving as it does
variable forms of trance dancing that may be highly cathartic or revitalizing.
Practitioners gyrate and spin and tremble and oscillate, entering a temporarily
buffered cocoon of ecstatic praxis, dancing with their eyes closed, and careen-
ing throughout the temple while attended and corralled by others. They emit
high-pitched shrieks, repeat the names of chosen deities in guttural voices,
moan and groan, or simply dance silently, oscillating like gyroscopes. *Lotas*
(brass ritual vessels) of holy water soaked with turmeric—a concoction known
as *manjatani*—is intermittently poured over the heads and down the bodies
of these shakti players in order to purify and embellish their vibrations. The
long, wet hair of female devotees may flail around, intensifying the action's
theatricality.

This form of catching power is related to but nonetheless distinct from the structure of the Guru's Kali manifestation. He initially conjured his trance that day in ways that recapitulated the more generalized forms of shakti play. However, this phase was brief, involving initially spasmodic gyrations of the head, torso, and arms and some dynamic trance dancing around the temple's large statue of Kali. Having completed these preliminaries, however, the Guru's vibration transmuted into a specific routine based primarily on an ever-shaking head, from side to side, riding the crest of the driving percussion. Every once in a while he would break into a more flamboyant and less focused trance dance, but these flourishes served to punctuate his more controlled impersonation of Mother Kali.

As Kali, the Guru was planted just in front of the Mother's murti. His eyes were closed, but hers were open and thereby amplified by her servant's enactment. She spoke and acted through him in order to heal supplicants and deliver sermons, as if becoming a radio transmitter for a divine signal emanating from the deity's iconic station.

Indeed, each murti is sacred and potent. When ritually installed, the icon's eyes are the last to be "opened," after which point the god is held to be present in the murti and therefore permanently situated within the sanctum of the temple. This procedure is connected with South Asian cognates.

I refer to the pattern of ecstatic practice exemplified by the Guru's Kali manifestation as "individuated mediumship" or as "manifesting divinity," in contrast with "generalized ecstasy" or "catching power" as embodied by the other, less specific, shakti players in the temple. Equivalently structured levels of ritual praxis are together encompassed within each overall framework of Orisha and Shakti Worship alike. They are recursive and complex in practice. The boundary between them is contingent and not always distinct. Indeed, the individuated form of mediumship is built upon and grows out of the more prevalent form of baseline ecstasy, which involves no channeling of specific divinities such as Kali, Dee Baba, or Mother Katerie—as individuated mediumship in heterodox Hindu Shakti Puja does. Nonetheless, it involves the manifestation of shakti understood in the most generalized sense: as mystical energy tapped for spiritual purposes.

In other words, both of these forms of ecstasy involve the manifestation of power. In generalized ecstasy, this power is activated, or "elevated," in practitioners as they attain a temporarily special ceremonial status and engage in chiefly inner-directed practices of spiritual exploration. This form of ecstasy does not constitute a conduit for the worldly action of specific deities, nor do practitioners operating within this modality become sublime objects of devotion.

Individuated mediums, on the other hand, transform the envelope of generalized ecstasy in crucial ways. They cultivate it within their bodies, channeling this "energy" into full-fledged spirit mediumship, becoming a locus for the divine in human form that can interact with devotees and seekers of healing efficacy. These spirit mediums synergize with the iconography of the gods they embody. They speak with the sacralized voices of the "powers" they "raise," channeling the authority of the gods for whom they serve as vessels. Baseline players catch power in a theologically generic sense; individuated mediums manifest divinities with distinct identities, capacities, and mythistories—the shakti of specific gods and goddesses.

This differentiated conceptualization of ceremonial ecstasy in the manifestation of power is analogous to primary structures of practice within Orisha Worship as well. Thus the manifestations of Erile and Shango discussed in the prologue represent corresponding examples of what I am here calling individuated mediumship within this African tradition.

Each of the orishas manifested upon his priestess, dancing and doing work throughout the night, enveloped by drumming, singing, and other forms of operational support. When Erile's medium "fell" under his sway, she first started hopping up and down on one foot while backing up into folks behind her. She shook her head erratically while pumping her torso up and down like a marionette on invisible strings. During this phase her eyes were closed as ecstasy pulsated throughout her body. Yet Erile soon "settled" and was recognized with libations of olive oil rubbed upon his feet and head, a greeting with clasped hands and alternately touching elbows from the mombwah. His arrival prompted a corollary shift toward Erile's liturgical song-chants, which Michel Laguerre (1980) characterizes as the "mystical geography" of ecstatic Afro-creole deities. Once fully present, Erile opened his medium's eyes and commanded a penetrating gaze throughout the entire performance. Shango's ecstatic script is comparable, though organized by the local persona of the thunder god.

However, these divine impersonations were accompanied by trance dancers who emerged intermittently throughout the night's proceedings. Congruent with the Hindu case, these more generalized players within orisha praxis are neither understood nor approached as vehicles of specific powers, per se, though they attain a quasi-sacred status within the ceremony and represent the more diffuse form of cosmic power known by the Yoruba-creole term *ashé*. There are usually more baseline trancers than individuated mediums active throughout the feast, since manifesting a particular orisha or saint or other power is more difficult than the baseline play of loose, yet self-absorbed, ashé.

Individuated mediumship therefore represents a more rarefied and accomplished form of ceremonial ecstasy. Only a smaller subset of practitioners has the experience and competence enabling them to manifest the full-fledged deities. Impersonating the orishas is especially challenging within this Afrocreole tradition, as the iconography of the gods must be embodied by the individual medium, by contrast with the proxemic relationship between the icon and the deity's individuated medium in Shakti Puja. Each tradition exploits affordances of the "mindful body" (Scheper-Hughes and Lock 1987, 1991) in order to cultivate alter-cultural experiences at the level of baseline ecstasy that, in turn, may be differentially modulated by variant conventions of iconopraxis at the higher level of individuated mediumship (see McNeal Forthcoming a on embodied symbolism and visual culture in trance and mediumship).

"Manifestation" versus "Possession"

Let us further consider the most salient metapragmatic constructs in both domains of ecstatic praxis: "power," "manifestation," "work," and "play." These conceptual discourses are central within Orisha Worship and Shakti Puja alike, but they are also found within Spiritual Baptism, for example, and to some extent within the "play" of Carnival masquerade as well.

The action of an adept becoming "activated" and manifesting a power is understood in terms of an external locus of control or agency, as in "de power come on she," "de power come an' throw meh down," "de power take he," "power does come on meh." As we have already seen, "power" may be used generically, as well as more specifically, to refer to individual divinities that use the bodies of their devotees as vessels for action. Practitioners may use "power"—as a category of spiritual force—grammatically either as subject (exemplified above) or object (as in "he catch power"). That "power" may be understood in the latter sense reflects tacit recognition of human agency on the part of practitioners despite the prevailing ideology of a self temporarily displaced by a deity. This accords with their understanding of trance praxis as "play," discussed below. It means that "power" is a polytrope (see Friedrich 1991 and Ohnuki-Tierney 1991 on polytropy).

The West Indian discourse of "manifestation" resonates with that of "power" and "the powers." "Shakpana go manifes' tonight" would mean that the local Yoruba god of medicine and disease—syncretically identified with St. Jerome for many—will use someone as his medium while feasting. This pertains as well to Catholic saints, Hindu deotas, ancestors, other categories of powers or "entities" associated with Afro-Trinbagonian Spiritual Baptism or Kabba, and the Holy Spirit as inflected by various local forms of Christianity such as

Pentecostalism. With regard to "manifestation," one hears things like: "I does manifes' de Master" (Bhairo Baba) or "Shango go manifes' on him" as well as "I's a child of Ogun," the latter implying one's being an ecstatic vessel for Ogun's earthly manifestations.

The emic category of "possession"—by contrast—is attributed to intrusion by demons, malevolent spirits, irascible ghosts, and the like. This lexical differentiation between *positive* manifestation and *negative* possession in creole Anglophone terms seems most likely rooted in the complex and ongoing legacy of the interface—originally colonial, now postcolonial—between multiple non-Christian (African and Indian) religious streams and dominant forms of Christianity. "Manifestation," then, refers to vitalizing experiences of ecstasy cultivated through trance, whereas "possession" is used regarding undesirable experiences of affliction. Such misfortunes typically arise *outside* of the ritual arena and are not chiefly characterized by entranced behavior per se. This point cannot be overstated: *manifestation is to ecstasy as possession is to agony.*

As submodalities of manifestation, both baseline ecstasy and individuated forms of mediumship involve the cultivation of mystical states arising from the ritualized alteration of consciousness scholars often refer to as trance or dissociation. "Possession" as locally conceived, on the other hand, largely speaks in the language of the symptomatic body, riven with conflict or anxiety and expressed in the idiom of mystical attack or affliction: it is not typically expressed through entrancement. If these illnesses or disorderly states are to be understood in terms of "dissociation," then, we must be careful not to confuse positively cultivated ecstatic trance forms with the very different sort of dissociation experienced by the afflicted self or hysterogenic body. Anthropologists have too often employed the terminology of "possession" to encompass both "manifestation" and "possession," which obscures important aspects of both.[1]

When the powers manifest within the ceremonial sphere, they do positively *non*-pathological spiritual work, that is, bless, transform, heal, sustain, affirm, reprimand, perform, as in "doin' de Mudda wuk" (Mother Kali), "she wuk wid de Indian man" (Osain), "sometime Shango wuk with de *pessie*" (a whip made from dried jungle vine), and so on. Work here centers primarily upon human problems. The phrase "spiritual work" is a generalized designation meaning that one spends considerable time and perhaps even derives at least part of one's livelihood from keeping, supporting, supplicating, channeling, and nurturing relations with the divinities in order to provide for popular, lay contact with the subaltern spirit world.

Like the others, "play" terminology operates as a complex metapragmatic discourse within both traditions, yet it also circulates expansively throughout varied contexts of local performance culture more broadly, such as Carnival, as in "playing mas"—*mas* being the colloquial word for Shrovetide masquerade. In Kali temples one speaks of "shakti players," those through whom shakti energy manifests and who may in turn come to wield the authority and implements of healing power associated with the gods at the higher level of divine manifestation. A shakti priestess once quipped, "I go an' play de Mudda in Mat'nique!" meaning that her talent and skills in mediumship find reception beyond national borders in the French West Indian island of Martinique. "He play Oshun" is a way for someone to specify which person may likely manifest the goddess Oshun and dance for her, or at least commonly does so.

I want to emphasize that dancing, healing, and the like under the auspices of divinities who temporarily take human form through sacred play are ways powers do their varying kinds of work. Humans play while divinities work, in other words. It is important to appreciate not only these resonant conceptualizations and patterns of performance, but also the fact that they operate simultaneously in the same Anglophone tongue.

The Ritual Arts of Trance as Alter-Cultural Praxis

The cultivation of ecstasy and practice of trance are sacred ritual arts utilizing ceremonial paraphernalia and other material objects in spectacular performances. Yet the vitality and character of ecstatic performance arise primarily from intensified use of the mind and body. The ecstatically cultivated body is central in the shrine and temple arts of trance, involving complex and theatrical "somatic modes of attention," defined by Thomas Csordas (1993:138) as culturally elaborated ways of attending to and with one's body in surroundings that include the embodied presence of others. Affordances of the body-mind are therefore tapped into and marshaled for both instrumental and expressive purposes experienced as outside of, or other than, self.[2]

Anthropologist Alfred Gell (1978) viewed ecstatic practices among the Muria of central India as forms of "vertiginous play" that subvert quotidian structures of intentionality and experience, producing a sense of exhilaration and transcendence derived from the ritualized "maintenance of endangered equilibrium" (226). Gell was inspired by French philosopher Roger Caillois's (1961) reflections upon the significance of vertigo and equilibratory play in human cultural forms. Scaffolded by their praxis, ecstatics attune themselves to what Gell termed "rhythmicities" that may be experienced as originating in something other than their own conscious agency. The body becomes hyperobjectified through controlled cultivation of a gap between intention and experience, transforming the ecstatic body into a vehicle of alterity and culturally apperceived as divine. These practices model numinous cognition, evoking sensations of powers outside of and greater than ourselves (Tuzin 2002).

Trance performance and spirit mediumship are thus psychological as well as ritual arts. Ecstatic praxis traffics in the sacralizing arts of virtualization, incorporating dramaturgy and theatricality along with cathartic and therapeutic engagements. Ceremonial impersonation involves performative simulation, mobilizing mind and body in complex patterns of expressive as well as instrumental social action.[3]

Caillois emphasized differentiation between more spontaneous and more rigidly organized patterns of expression in human playfulness. He suggested that all forms of play, game, and ritual could be placed upon a continuum spanning from *paidia*—tumultuous, exuberant, spontaneous, and active—to *ludus*—involving artifice, convention, calculation, and subordination to rules. Baseline ecstasy might be considered closer to paidia, whereas individuated mediumship graduates nearer the ludic pole. Caillois offered a four-part working typology for classifying the varieties of play, game, and ritual, namely, *agôn* (competition), *alea* (chance), *mimesis* (simulation), and *ilinx* (vertigo), which coexist and comingle as ideal-types in reality. He explored masking and trance practices from Australian, Amerindian, and African traditions in order to illustrate the complex interface between mimesis and ilinx, which so inspired Gell.

Erika Bourguignon (1973, 1976) examined a worldwide sample of 488 societies and found that 90 percent of them have some ritualized form of trance or dissociation: "Most societies have found it adaptive to institutionalize one or more forms of the universal capacity for altered states, to utilize it, or at least, to bring this potentially dangerous force under social control" (1978:502). In this regard, societies *without* such institutions represent an exception to the rule and should bear the burden of explanation rather than being taken as the standard. In fact, Bourguignon speculates that better reporting and further analysis of the ethnographic record may well reduce the percentage of nontrance cultures overall. The view that emerges is one of a species-wide psychobiocultural capacity institutionalized and socially elaborated in variable ways across space and time (see also Ludwig 1972; Walker 1972; Lex 1979; Wedenoja 1990; Bourguignon 1991, 1994a, 1994b; Ingham 1996).

Indian psychoanalyst Sudhir Kakar (1991) views ecstatic mysticism as a spiritual path involving the "radical enhancement of the capacity for creative experiencing" (x). Mystics cultivate the "controlled illusion that heals" (30). Thus ecstatic states must be seen as the most creative of the psychodynamic defenses, even more than sublimation (22). As a secular rationalist, Sigmund

Freud recognized creative and progressive sublimation in art (1910) but was less ready to do so with religion. In Kakar's view, a psychoanalytic approach to religious experience and forms of mysticism must involve a less narrowly defined emphasis on regression, drives, and defenses as well as an expanded view of religious experience in terms of creative and restorative sublimation and transformation. "The point is not the chaotic nature of the mystical experience, if it is indeed chaotic," he writes, "but the mystic's ability to create supreme *order* out of the apparent chaos" (1991:4).

Indeed, confusion in the literature on "possession" has been abetted by the frequently "pathomorphic" (Jilek 1971, 1974, 1982) or "pathomimetic" (T. Schwartz 1976), yet largely *non*-pathological, character of trance performance. Csordas (1985) makes a similar point. He notes a study by Levy et al. (1979) in which epileptic Navajo hand tremblers were found to be neither as competent nor as successful as practitioners free from epilepsy. I suggest that ritualized trance forms be understood as alter-cultural practices of creative psychodynamic homeopathy, variously mobilized and stylized in ritual form for the benefit of self and other, reflecting a deeply playful relationship to experience and existence (see McNeal Forthcoming b).[4]

The ideological nexus of pathology and possession in English is critical here. Indeed, Bourguignon and Pettay (1964) warned against the misleading connotations of the word *possession* many years ago. Scholars who labor in this area are only too aware of pejorative connotations of the term in English, with its heavy Judeo-Christian and modernist symbolic loading (see Oesterreich 1930 for an early discussion, Bourguignon 1976 for an overview). Csordas (1987) observes a medicalizing trend in Anglo-American scholarship in particular. The French, by contrast, have adopted a less pathocentric frame of interpretation related to their affinity for a dramaturgical approach. I find it therefore telling that the closer Anglophone scholars get to Anglophone practitioners of ecstatic spiritism, the more we grumble about the discourse of possession (see, e.g., D. Stewart 2005).

Symptomatologies of possession in the emic sense vary considerably, but they are *not* usually accompanied by or expressed as forms of trance or states of dissociation per se. There may be some usefulness in thinking of illnesses and pathologies as dissociative, or possibly even trancelike, in that they are experienced by their victims as ego-alien and other-than-self: suffering that intrudes upon and subverts—perhaps even shatters—the world they know. However, when understood in relation to positive local expressions of ecstasy as well as the cross-cultural scene more broadly, the bodily based spiritual afflictions of possession in people with whom I am most familiar seem more like somatoform symptoms and idioms of distress. One might want to call these dissociative in that they take on lives of their own, but in the West Indies I have found them more akin to the cases of "hysteria" treated and discussed by Josef Breuer and Sigmund Freud (1895) than the florid, dramatic specters so often associated with exorcism or multiple-personality disorder (on "idioms of distress," see Kleinman 1980, 1986, 1988).

Anthropologists have used the term "possession" to talk about such afflictions with good reason. John Ingham (1996:115–43) considers a range of specifically negative cases—afflictual and conflictual—of spiritual possession from the ethnographic literature in his discussion of the anguished and oblique language of the hysterogenic body in culture. His synthetic sleuthing leads him to a phylogenetic link between pain or trauma and role-playing or theatricality across the spectrum of somatoform and dissociative disorders. This connection reflects a human propensity for "as-if" simulation to deal with traumatic memories and experiences of anxiety or pain. In Ingham's view, spirit affliction signals an attempt to re-create lost relationships with self or other (125). There seems to be an inverse relationship between playfulness and madness here, though the line between the two is hardly static or straightforward.

Psychological illnesses and idioms of distress often speak in the muzzled, esoteric language of the afflicted body. Michael Franz Basch (1988:28–48) observes that psychological illnesses are paradoxical metacommunications serving hidden purposes and disclosing attempts at problem solving (see also Ruesch and Bateson 1968; Schwartzman 1982). Conceptualizing them as spiritual or extrahuman recognizes their underlying significance, however oblique or discordant. Thus symptoms are also "signs of self-alienation" (Habermas 1971:228). Nancy Scheper-Hughes and Margaret Lock (1991) refer to this as the "message in the bottle," disclosing hidden meanings in the "secret language of the body," at least for those who care to disentangle and reinterpret them. Translated into the phenomenology of Drew Leder (1990), the anxious, painful, or afflicted body "dys-appears" in consciousness, exerting hermeneutic and instrumental demands alike. This accords with the cultural phenomenology of possession in West Indian spiritisms, both African and Hindu.

Although anthropologists have referred to it as "possession," West Indians see ecstatic mysticism as diametrically *opposed* to what they call "possession." Ecstasy is the movement of spiritual power and the worldly actualization of divinity; calling it "possession" would be misleading in light of their own nuanced formulation. The matter is tricky, however, as the lexical contrast between "manifestation" and "possession" refers to essential but related distinctions. We might think of these poles of experience as inversely related to one another in ideal-typical terms, and therefore infelicitously referred to collectively as "possession."

Richard Handler and Daniel Segal (1990:80–89) propose the concept of "alter-cultural" practice to speak of cultural action or ritual institutions that introduce reflexivity and creativity into social life. Alter-cultural praxis is "serious play" (15, 100). Here I extend their concept of alter-cultural praxis to the study of trance performance and spirit mediumship. I argue that the ritual arts of trance—what Anglophone West Indian spiritists talk about as "manifestation," *not* "possession"—be understood as compelling and spectacular forms of alter-cultural practice.

Melville Herskovits was a powerful early voice in American anthropology contesting the pathocentric Anglophone view of possession. It is not coincidental that he developed this view in relation to Afro-Atlantic materials ranging from Suriname, Haiti, Trinidad, and Brazil in the Americas to Fon-speaking Dahomey (now Benin) in West Africa. He was deeply impressed by transatlantic connections and cultural continuities in domains such as kinship, economic organization, religion, and what he called "motor behavior." Herskovits took the behavior of ecstatics seriously (1937a, 1941, 1952; Herskovits and Herskovits 1947), noting the psychological benefits of cathartic expression and self-restoration in entranced performativity. He appreciated the significance of specific dances for separate deities, as well as the musical and polyrhythmic significance of iron, rattles, and, especially, drumming (Herskovits 1944). He viewed singing as an accompaniment in Afro-Atlantic musical traditions, rather than the reverse (Herskovits and Herskovits 1947) and emphasized that trance performance is culturally patterned and cannot be equated with psychopathology (1948). He noted variability in depth and experience of dissociation in trance performance.

Frances Mischel, a Herskovitsean, along with personality psychologist Walter Mischel (1958), expanded upon this perspective based upon field research on Trinidadian Shango in the mid-1950s. They observed a range of psychological aspects in ecstatic orisha performance: an enlarged arena of personal agency and empowerment, including assertion of control over others; the acting out of repressed or culturally proscribed erotic or aggressive behavior in sublimated form; the reversal of sex roles; and temporary freedom from ordinary expectations and constraints—all facilitated under the guise of spirit alters.

The work of Mischel and Mischel anticipated that of Bourguignon, another Herskovits protégée who conducted fieldwork in the Caribbean. Herskovits viewed Haitian society as the result of "acculturation," a partial amalgam of

European and African elements (1937a) and indexed, for example, by cross-identifications between African gods and Catholic saints in Vodou (1937b). Haitian culture was neither homogeneous nor harmonious, but conditioned by the interaction of hierarchical polarities—the European and the African—and therefore characterized by differential forms of "socialized ambivalence" across the whole. Bourguignon saw Haitian social stratification as obliquely mirrored within the popular world of Vodou (1965). She found evidence for what Herskovits termed "retentions" and "syncretisms" of African culture in Haitian society, especially the "continued capacity" for ecstatic mediumship with regard to Herskovitsean "Africanisms" (1978).

Bourguignon's study points to continuities of self and motivation in spite of breaks in consciousness and discontinuities of self-representation and experience. Ceremonial trance is "self-serving and self-enhancing" (1978:487), suggesting that alter-cultural experiences may be valuable for individuals dealing with the challenges and discontents of life. She came to view trance performance as "dissociation in the service of the self" (see also 1989, 1991, 1994a, 1994b, 2004). Moreover, her approach to the analysis of altered states of consciousness arises in relation not only to the seminal work of Herskovits, but also to that of A. I. Hallowell (1942, 1955, 1966, 1972), who understood imagination as necessary for the construction of reality. He viewed dreams, fantasies, myths, religion, art, and cosmology as resources for both personal adjustment and cultural adaptation.

The Hallowellian line also stems from the work of Gananath Obeyesekere (1970, 1977, 1981, 1990) on popular Hindu-Buddhist ecstatics in Sri Lanka. Obeyesekere channeled Hallowell through engagement with the work of Melford Spiro (1961, 1965, 1967, 1970, 1982) on the psychoanalytic anthropology of religion. Obeyesekere's case studies demonstrate the flexibility and generative ambiguity of the spirit idiom, its capacity to facilitate growth and change, and the creative personal use of cultural symbolism. Drawing from the well of public culture, effective ecstatic ritualists may sublimate desire or fantasy, as well as recontextualize and transform conflicts or concerns that might otherwise get the best of them. Mythology and ritual praxis serve as linking conduits between self and society. He highlights the capacity of cultural symbolism to operate on intrapsychic, interpersonal, and sociological levels simultaneously and, taking inspiration from Freud's concept of "dreamwork" (1900), speaks of the "work of culture" in personal and public life.

Douglas Hollan (2000a) draws upon work among the highland Toraja of Indonesia to extend this view. He highlights trance ceremonialism as animated by the paradoxical notion that order and well-being can be accessed or reconstituted through periodic encounter with the experience of chaos and disorder. No Toraja cases evinced pathological etiology, and Hollan emphasizes the difference between affliction outside the ritual arena and cultivated dissociation within performance. As idioms of communication, cultural trance forms are multivocal and evolve in contexts over time, facilitating dynamic as well as creative use by individuals. Toraja culture not only warns against too much disorder and disintegration in everyday life, but also suggests that splits in self-experience are inevitable and even sometimes adaptive.

Hollan draws insight from the interpersonal psychoanalysis of Harry Stack Sullivan (1953) in order to develop the view that all cultures produce shadowy, potentially "not-me" selves that relate intimately to the larger cultural matrix of meaning and value (also see Hollan 2000b). The alternative voices of ecstatic performance may serve as "a source of gnosis—revealed knowledge immediately recognizable to everyone as being intuitively true, but coming from beyond the overtly tolerable, discussible, and often, thinkable knowledge of family and culture" (R. Levy et al. 1996:19).

A resonant view of spiritism as alter-cultural praxis comes from Vincent Crapanzano's (1973, 1975, 1977a, 1977b, 1987, 1994) analysis of Moroccan ethnopsychiatry and the trance cult of Hamadsha. He emphasizes polysemy of the spirit idiom, observing that it must speak multivocally in order to operate compellingly within a community or culture. Spirit idiomata obliquely reflect and refract experience. Their meanings are dialectically constituted through interaction. Crapanzano highlights rhetorical and pragmatic dimensions of ecstasy and possession in the dramaturgy of life. He discloses paradoxical gestures in therapeutic spiritism and criticizes an older anthropological position on the "circle of exploitation" in African spirit cults of affliction.

Other important work in the Africanist anthropology of religion corroborates this line of interpretation. Janice Boddy (1988, 1989) has shown how acceptance of possession diagnosis and ensuing participation in therapeutic trance rites offer rural Sudanese women the scope to expand and regenerate their senses of self and to recontextualize their experiences in the face of a highly constraining sociocultural order. Elsewhere (1993), she highlights the role of *zar* performance as a forum for the negotiation and reworking of women's social networks in northern Sudan, especially in the articulation of covert matrilineal ties. In so doing, zar may be seen as a recessive repertoire of pre-Islamic values and practices stemming from before the advent of Arab patrilineality. Thus Boddy shows how zar spirits constitute alter-cultural exemplars of rural Sudanese female selfhood: the process of spiritual affliction followed by its domestication within ceremonial communities provides an idiom which not only defends the self through culturally constituted dissociation, but also paves the way for transformation in the future. Echoing Bourguignon, Boddy writes that trance represents "at once a self-enhancing and self-maintaining condition" (1988:19).

Anthropologist Michael Lambek reaches similar theoretical ground in his analysis of spiritism on the island of Mayotte in the east African Comorro Archipelago. He observes that trance praxis must be understood culturally as a form of communication, and not just for those who may be troubled or unwell (see 1981, 1989, 1996). He finds personal style in trance performance to be characterized by an increasingly mediated "dialectic of self-concealment and self-revelation" (1988:67). Multivocality of the spirit idiom operates as a cultural resource from which individual interpretations and experiences can be constructed. Ecstatic mysticism in Mayotte is "broad enough and esoteric enough to allow for numerous personal significations to be constructed from it, above and beyond those that are central to its own construction" (1981:148). Thus Lambek advocates a performative approach to trance and possession: situated within interpretive communities, subject to grammars or production and coordination as well as genres of expression, and characterized by multiple avenues of innovation and creativity.

More recently, Lambek (2002) has proposed a view of trance and mediumship as vehicles of collective sublimation. The idiom of ecstatic spiritism enables the working-through of psychodynamic issues for its practitioners and patrons, facilitating the articulation and assimilation of experience, in an ongoing interplay of projective and introjective processes. Ecstatic mysticism carves out alter-cultural space for playfulness and growth (208). Religious and ancestral figures are not projective illusions to be dissolved in the light of rationality, but culturally constituted self-objects available for transmuting patterns of internalization. Thus spiritism provides a "relatively durable resource for interpreting the human situation in all of its personal and historical specificity" (209). Shifting between alternative characters within the sociocultural frame of trance ritual may open up space for intrapsychic and interpersonal change as well as for playing with reality and imagining alternatives.

Alter-cultural practices vary through time and space, and the point is not to be reductive. However, ecstatic mysticisms cast in the idiom of spirits seem to overlap and resonate with one another in a range of compelling ways. I approach trance, ecstasy, and related forms of ritualized dissociation as culturally mediated articulations of a panhuman capacity and argue that this behavioral repertoire may be understood as an expression of the deeper metapsychological ability of humans to play with reality in order to explore, simulate, model, experiment with, and master it (see McNeal Forthcoming b). By "deeper," I do not mean acultural, yet no simple culturology suffices, either.

Psychoanalyst D. W. Winnicott emphasized the ways people are always in the process of growing, changing, adjusting, and exploring through interdependence with others. Consciousness emerges in an increasingly complex and mediated dialectic between subjective and objective realities. He brought to light an "intermediate zone of experience" in the borderland between external and internal life, "a resting-place for the individual engaged in the perpetual human task of keeping inner and outer reality separate yet interrelated" (1971:2). Because of the paradoxical interface between inner and outer, we do not usually question whether the "transitional" objects and phenomena of this zone are real or not: they are *both* real and not real, me and not me.

Though he developed this view in the course of clinical work, Winnicott extrapolated the concept of transitionality into a broader vision of mental health and human creativity. Transitional objects and experiences are neither fully subjective nor fully objective. Yet their ambiguity and paradoxical character are what make them so valuable for living: we must adapt to the overlapping realities of subjective and objective life, navigating the overdetermined field of tension within which those worlds interrelate and collide.

Human playfulness thrives within this intermediate space. Winnicott believed that in playing—and perhaps only in playing—the self is free to be creative. "It is assumed here that the task of reality-acceptance is never completed, that no human being is free from the strain of relating inner and outer reality, and that relief from this strain is provided by an intermediate area of experience which is not challenged (arts, religion, etc.). This intermediate area is in direct continuity with the play area of the child who is 'lost' in play" (1971:13). In an important sense, playing provides the foundation for cultural experience altogether. Hence Winnicott writes that "on the basis of playing is built the whole of humanity's experiential existence" (64).

A view of playfulness as arising within fertile intermediate space and in relation to transitional experience not only plugs directly and productively into a view of the ritual arts of trance as alter-cultural praxis, but also connects, in turn, with an examination of the resilient dynamism of ecstatic mysticism across oceans and through time in the West Indies. As Sidney Mintz writes, "Because of its lengthy colonial past and the role of coercion in regional labor history, the Caribbean has much to tell us, both of the ways oppression can be practiced, and of those ways, both explicit and subversive, in which it can be resisted" (1974a:xv). Indeed, surviving and adapting to the perverse vicissitudes of slavery, indentureship, and colonial domination must be seen as intensely "transitional," summoning resilience and creativity out of the depths of the human spirit. We cannot fully understand the multiplex play encountered in changing traditions of trance performance and spirit mediumship without considering both the nature and the culture of play in the contexts in which they unfold.

Playing Deep

In *Afro-Creole: Power, Opposition, and Play in the Caribbean* (1997), the late Richard D. E. Burton makes a bold argument about the evolution of Afro-Caribbean cultures through case studies of popular religion and politics in Jamaica, Carnival masquerade in Trinidad, and the cultural politics of Vodou in Haiti. Burton discloses the ambiguity and ambivalence of "oppositional culture" manifest in an extraordinarily wide range of forms: "West Indian popular culture appears to combine a perpetual rebelliousness with an inability to effect lasting changes in the structures of power it rebels against: a culture of opposition and inversion, it depends on the existence of those structures in order to exist at all" (264).

Burton employs Michel de Certeau's (1980) distinction between "resistance" and "opposition" in order to illuminate the kaleidoscopically shifting sets of ritual, game, and performance that have emerged through time and space as vehicles of Afro-creole expressive culture. By "resistance," de Certeau denotes those relatively rare, fully materialized acts of revolt or revolution that become possible by attacking from a position located outside the system in some way. "Opposition," by contrast, deals with those more common, indirect, and ultimately less radical modes of contestation that are unable to transcend their positionality from within by using weapons and concepts derived from and ultimately redomesticated by the system in question.[5] By these standards, full-fledged resistance has been less frequent than usually supposed in Caribbean history. Burton identifies Tacky's uprising of 1760 in Jamaica as well as that of Cuffee in 1763 in British Guiana (both African-led slave rebellions); the Saint Domingue Revolution between 1791 and 1804, which produced the world's first black republic in Haiti; almost, but not quite, the great Jamaican slave uprising of 1831–32 known as the Baptist War; and the Cuban Revolution of the late 1950s. Otherwise, opposition has more commonly characterized the regional landscape. He argues that this distinction "enables us to retain and refine the distinction between 'physical' and 'psychological' forms of resistance—all slaves, we might say, *opposed* slavery at all times, but only some slaves *resisted* it some of the time—and also to clarify the conditions that made it possible to move from opposition within the system to resistance to the system as such. . . . Opposition takes place when the strong are strong and the weak know it; resistance becomes possible when the weak sense both their own strength and the weakness of the strong" (1997:50–51).

Burton's analysis turns especially upon the element of *playfulness* at the heart of Afro-Caribbean expressive cultures. He draws upon the notion of slave "plays," a term used for weekend celebrations or ceremonial activities involving dance, music, dress, food, and drink, which came to dominate the cultural heart of slave societies. Slaves dubbed any day away from the cane field or mill, including wakes, a "play-day" (Abrahams and Szwed 1983:34). As a counterpoint to their dehumanization as plantation-laboring chattel, slaves turned their weekend dances and festival times into extravagant affairs of costume and reverie, performing reversals of the hegemonic structures governing their lives. Each Saturday night, play became "a carnival in miniature" (Burton 1997:41), offering slaves a communal focus and embodied freedom. In the Caribbean, Burton argues, "all play is oppositional and all oppositionality is 'playful' or contains a 'play element.' At the same time, it is still intensely serious" (Burton 1997:8–9).

To be sure, slave plays and related rituals became catalytic sites of resistance to domination in de Certeau's sense when resistance did manage to fully coalesce. For example, the great Antiguan slave conspiracy of 1736 was staged through masquerade festivity under the noses of planters. Yet such are exceptions that prove the more common rule for Burton. Ritual and performative play has much more often condensed and crystallized the ambivalent dialectics of power in the Caribbean in far less radical—indeed, sometimes downright conservative—ways. Roger Abrahams and John Szwed (1983:34) observed that designating Afro-creole ritual and performance activities as plays was but one of several black uses of the term, but that Europeans fastened onto it in their colonial memoirs and travelogues since it departed so distinctly and subversively from their own notions of "work" and "play." The plantocracy not only encouraged such festivities, it also occasionally even participated as well.

Drawing on Victor Turner's (1987) late work on the subjunctive mood of culture, Burton shows how trance mediumship and popular masquerade resonate as analogous expressive arenas: "Cult and carnival interpenetrate as ways of transcending, expanding, or multiplying the self, the first through trance and vertigo and the simulation of spirits, the second as mimicry, theater, and disguise, to create a condition in which antistructure or communitas reigns supreme before society finally returns to its indicative mood at the end of the ritual or on Ash Wednesday morning" (1997:222). Burton sees ecstasy as a "magical mirror" of power relations at large: "Whether it is the power of the slavemaster, the colonial apparatus, or the charismatic political leader in the 'independent' Caribbean," he writes, "power always *descends*, like the spirits, onto the powerless below. It may empower them—for a time—but it does so only by dispossessing them of themselves and filling them with a power that, since it is other and originates elsewhere, can be taken away as quickly and as easily as it was bestowed" (223).

Burton observes that the most important objects of power within the subaltern spheres of Afro-Caribbean spiritism typically belong to the innermost sanctum of the cult area, brought out in the form of flags, tools, and other paraphernalia in the midst of performance. For him, this represents a subaltern analogue with power in its most hegemonic West Indian sense as always Other: coming from above or elsewhere, operated *for* the people rather than *by* the people. Thus Burton views Afro-creole cultism as an intermediate zone or intercalary space mediating some of the deepest contradictions and most enduring dilemmas of culture and power in the region. Spiritism exorcises the slave master or his postemancipation and postcolonial counterparts from power over folk by replacing them with mystical surrogates, making the ecstatic priest a peripheral power broker between the state and the spirits.

The play of power in trance and mediumship, then, is paradoxical. The reversals accompanying them are bounded. Burton argues that Afro-Caribbean performance cultures are simultaneously subversive of social structures as well as *subversions of that subversion*. Yet recuperation by the status quo in no way diminishes the dynamism, creativity, and competitiveness of ritualized reversals, however, ranging from masquerade and trance performance to word games, storytelling practices, numbers and gambling games, rum shop games, cockfighting, kite flying, mock auctions, and beauty or other contests associated with Carnival to international sports such as boxing, soccer, basketball, netball, and, especially, cricket, which seems to have inherited the legacy of stick fighting from colonial times. Burton is wary of romanticism in the discourse on "rituals of reversal," so he draws on Scheper-Hughes's (1992) analysis of Carnival in northeastern Brazil to suggest that Afro-Caribbean play forms may be more appropriately characterized as *rituals of intensification* "in which the forces that govern 'ordinary' life are expressed with a particular salience, clarity, and eloquence" (Burton 1997:157). Thus festivity and ecstasy both challenge and reinforce the status quo, serving as vehicles for social protest as well as methods for disciplining that protest. Their ludic dimension helps account for the ambiguities and paradoxes of subversion and countersubversion on the ground.

Here, it is worth revisiting the concept of "deep play." Jeremy Bentham (1748–1832) introduced the notion to explore seemingly irrational human behavior, such as gambling or dangerous sport. Deep play is playing with fire—going deep in an alter-cultural sense by putting more than one's immediate stakes on the line—and Bentham, reformist that he was, thought it should be outlawed. Clifford Geertz expanded the concept of deep play anthropologically through an analysis of Balinese cockfighting, arguing that because "men *do* engage in such play, both passionately and often, and even in the face of law's revenge" (1973:433), we must peel back the layers of meaning shrouding such events. Cockfighting is hardly a simple matter of gambling; it is a ritualized drama of status, gender, and power, with elements of subversion and its domestication thrown equally into the mix.

Seen in this light, what makes the play *deep* in subaltern African and Hindu spiritisms in the Caribbean becomes evident: West Indian trance performance and spirit mediumship traffic in the most poignant of human passions and energies, scaffolding a wide gamut of alter-cultural experiences and relations in the face of stigma from the society at large and, all too frequently, under conditions of state control and suppression.

But what about the *playfulness* itself? Can it be understood as readily as its depth? Has Burton exhausted the story of ludic West Indian subcultures in relation to their political contexts and sociological dynamics? Is it coincidental that West Indian slaves and their descendants described their oppositional ritual forms and enthusiasm for dramatic, participatory, competitive performance practices as "play"? Indeed, should we understand these forms as playful primarily because of their oppositionality, as Burton suggests? Or is there something about play that supersedes and therefore cannot be reduced to its oppositional manifestations? Drawing upon the comparative analysis pursued here, we may push his line of inquiry further in cultural, historical, and psychological terms.

More or less implicit throughout Burton's discussion is the African background of the similarities of Caribbean expressive cultures. Yet, as ludic themes crop up throughout the Afro-Americas, it is crucial to consider African prototypes and influences in light of these profound resonances in Afro-creole culture throughout the Black Atlantic.[6]

In West Africa, mediumship and masquerade have been highly prominent and dynamic ceremonial institutions in the social and religious lives of most peoples past and present. Yorubas, in particular, have a highly refined cultural understanding of play in relation to other categories of performance such as ritual, spectacle, and festival (M. Drewal 1992). Yoruba speakers consider what they call "play" and "spectacle" to be superordinate categories of human performativity. The Yoruba word *iran*—"spectacle"—refers to performances making the unseen seen, as in mediumship, masquerade, and so forth. Performers are responsible for manifesting the otherworldly or "spectacular" periodically into this-worldly being. There are no fixed, bicameral roles for actors and audience in Yoruba spectacle; relations between spectators and spectacle are characterized by fluidity of subject and object positions mixing autotelic and reflexive forms of experience (M. Drewal 1992:13–15). Yoruba "play"—*ere* (noun), *sere* (verb)—however, is a broader and more generic concept than "spectacle." Play for Yorubas subsumes the spectacular in an engaging, transformative process that may be competitive but is always exploratory, improvisational, and deep (15–23). Yoruba cosmology conceives of an intertwined proximity between the phenomenal world of humans, animals, plants, and things and the noumenal otherworld of the orishas, ancestors, and other spiritual forces, with spectacle and play mediating relations between the two metaphysical spheres. In this context, specialists communicate with the otherworldly domain—*orun*—through ritualized interactions such as divination, masquerade, and trance.

This perspective enables us to better understand the Yoruba concept of ashé, an indigenous notion referring to the power of transformation and to performative efficacy: the power to make things happen (R. Thompson 1983). Margaret Drewal observes that ashé is what the work of ritual is all about; the very efficacy of Yoruba performance resides in its deeply serious playfulness (1992:27–28). The Yoruba religious system is characterized by what Drewal calls "structural pluralism," a reflexive malleability of ritual praxis that has enabled it to survive and adapt to forms of Islam and Christianity, and to survive, adapt to, even sometimes subvert forces of colonial domination on both sides of the Atlantic.

Yet what are we to make of ludic resonances not just within the kaleidoscopic matrix of black performance cultures but across the more broadly conceived terrain of Afro- *and* Indo-Caribbean ritual genres? We have already seen how conceptualization of trance as play is as fundamental within Hindu ecstatic spheres as it is among African ones in Trinidad and Tobago. Burton opted not to consider the local Indian saga in his Caribbeanist study, on the premise that it would open an unmanageable Pandora's box of conceptual problems. Yet I believe that dealing comparatively with African and Hindu ritual forms affords fresh inquiry into the globalization of trance performance and the modern history of human playfulness.

Consider the West Indian Hindu case and the centrality of play within ecstatic forms of Shakti Puja. What are the cultural and historical origins of play in Indo-creole trance performance and spirit mediumship? Even allowing for whatever complex, partial, or recursive influences that deserve analytical attention between different arenas of African and Hindu traditions, an adequate account of Hindu ecstatic ceremonialism *cannot* consist solely in attributing this play to the influences of black ritual culture. Certainly, there are many possible, probable, even definite avenues of influence between the spheres of Afro- and Indo-creole performance in Trinidad to be explored. However, Hinduism in its South Asian and diasporically rhizomatic forms is also informed by a complex cosmological conceptualization of "play" embodied in the notion of *lila*. Interconnected with the notion of *maya*, or "cosmic illusion," lila is fundamental in Indian metaphysics, referring to the divine sport, drama, or play of the gods amidst the world of human experience (see T. Hopkins 1971; Biardeau 1981; Knipe 1991; Fuller 1992), and to the inevitable paradoxes of finite consciousness grasping for the cosmic logic of the infinite.

Lila and its derivatives have animated the highest levels of philosophical speculation as well as the most vibrant aspects of popular culture and religious devotion (Hawley 1981; O'Flaherty 1984). David Kinsley (1975:73–78) notes that lila is descriptive of divine activity in Hinduism in at least two ways. First, "it underlines the completeness of the gods. The gods need and desire nothing, yet they continue to act. . . . Because the gods are complete and therefore do not act according to pragmatic laws of cause and effect to fulfill this or that desire, their actions are called play" (73). Moreover, "The gods as players are revealed to act spontaneously, unpredictably, and sometimes tumultuously. To play is to be unfettered and unconditioned, to perform actions that are intrinsically satisfying: to sing, dance, and laugh. To play is to step out of the ordinary world of the humdrum, to enter a special, magical world where one can revel in the superfluous. To play is to display oneself aimlessly and gracefully" (74).

Yet lila refers not just to God's play, but also to human ritual "plays" commemorating the play of divinity in performance. As William Sax puts it: "The idea that gods should temporarily incarnate themselves in the bodies of human devotees is not at all unusual in Hinduism, which, unlike the religions of the West, does not posit a sharp ontological rift between humans and gods. In other words, gods are people, too, and people sometimes become gods" (1995:8). For example, an important Hindu religious practice is represented by the array of sacred performances known explicitly as "lilas." In Ram-lila, for example, the mythic pursuits and tales associated with Rama—Lord Vishnu's seventh avatar—are enacted in performance grounds over periods of up to a month, drawing crowds of spectating devotees. The young boys honored with the opportunity of playing roles in Ram-lila, Ras-lila, or Krishna-lila are considered *svarups*, embodied forms of the gods, within the ceremonial frame. Like spirit mediums and akin to temple murtis, they do not simply represent the divinities but are indeed vessels for them. And vernacular traditions of lila in South Asia often foster symbolic reversals and transgressive behavior (see studies in Sax 1995).

Turning back to the Caribbean, practices of Ram-lila and Krishna-lila performances were brought across the Kala Pani (Dark Waters) and reproduced for some time before beginning to wane in the latter twentieth century (see Niehoff and Niehoff 1960; Klass 1961; Gibbons 1979). Akin to their African counterparts, Indian labor migrants brought a culturally significant notion of play to the Americas, the strongest candidate for the cultural origins of play in ecstatic Caribbean Shakti Puja. Odaipaul Singh (1993:83–94) argues this exact point, that the emic discourse of play in Guyanese Shakti Worship derives from the South Asian cultural hermeneutics of lila, with which I concur for the Trinidadian case.

Thus it turns out that West African and South Asian cosmologies are both characterized by sophisticated conceptualizations of play in relation to the interface of divinity and humanity. And, as we have seen, these resonances find a particularly suggestive parallel in the analogous discourses of play in Indo- and Afro-Trinbagonian forms of trance performance and spirit mediumship. Is this a case of the creolizing convergence of ritual streams that just so happen to share an analogous set of metaphysical notions subsequently embodied in lateral, subaltern forms in the southern Caribbean? How is it that practitioners of these traditions have perceived something similar enough in what they do to have found the term "play" germane as their respective mother tongues shifted over the generations toward a shared Anglophone Creole?

The fullest anthropological account of these ritual traditions must be pursued not only through a more deeply comparative triangulation of the historically oriented cultural analysis, but also in light of what we know about the psychoanalytic anthropology of ecstatic mysticism and popular spiritisms. Burton has not exhausted the story of West Indian play cultures, nor do I think it incidental that African slaves and their Afro-creole descendants employed the English word *play* in reference to their oppositional forms of subalter-cultural praxis. Burton's analysis leads unquestionably toward a more nuanced understanding of Caribbean ritual life as a complex synthesis of generative African cultural forms recontextualized and reformulated within the cauldron of New World experience as Afro-creole. Yet we are obligated to consider the implications of Indian resonances in cultural performance to extend the study of popular religious cultures in the Caribbean in new directions and establish a comparative context for reflecting upon the fate of play—through the lens of religion—in modernity.

Orientation, Overview, and Methodology

The Anthropological Ethic and the Spirit of Comparison

The religious landscape of the Americas has been hotly contested since the sixteenth century, driven by local contingencies in relation to changing patterns of globalization. As the oldest sphere of European colonialism, the Caribbean is a precociously modern region from which most original inhabitants were expelled or exterminated and replaced by peoples from Sub-Saharan Africa, Asia, Europe, and beyond, leading Antonio Benítez-Rojo (1992) to dub the area a "Repeating Island" manufactured by the "Columbus Machine." Predicated upon slavery and indenture, the enforced proximity of diverse sociocultural streams in the midst of the most massive demographic transformation in human history precipitated the emergence of a range of overlapping island and coastal mainland societies exhibiting core similarities as well as seemingly endless differences.

This book is a comparative historical ethnography of two heterodox religious subcultures in the "New World" brought into being by colonialism and capitalism in the modern era. Neither the Hindu nor African traditions simply replicated those of their respective homelands. Indeed, what was brought to the colonial West Indies in the hearts and minds of slaves and indentured laborers were not "religions" per se, but a variety of ancestral religious ideas and ritual practices necessarily reconstituted under the radically different conditions of displacement and domination within colonial plantation economies.

Thus this story is not simply about the adaptive reconstitution of religion under conditions of radical change and social domination. The traditions considered here evolved into innovative formations comprising diverse ritual and symbolic materials both remembered and redeployed from highly varied regions and communities of India and Africa. Complex processes of amalgamation and synthesis took place within—and were driven by considerations stemming from—the peculiar environment of the colonial Americas. It is more accurate to characterize these traditions as New World constellations, inherently translocal and transcultural even though they draw upon ancestral patterns. Continuity and change may be properly understood only in relation to one another as well as in terms of the "glocal" (Robertson 1995) contingencies of culture, power, and history that define the region.

The traditions examined here have exhibited remarkable dynamism over the long run. The development of each must be apprehended in relation to the larger socioreligious field in which they have taken shape. This requires a consideration of the vicissitudes of Christianity and Hinduism in relation to hierarchies of race and class since the end of the eighteenth century in the southern Caribbean. The relationship between each tradition and the larger playing field is one of figure and ground—really, two figures and a ground—and my lens constantly shifts between them. This exercise gains traction by considering the "glocalizing modernization" of traditions hardly ever seen as such. This is largely because each is centered on the subaltern ritual arts of trance too often seen as a "primitive" reflex or survival. Exploring how the displacement and fragmentation of diverse African and South Asian ritual streams took place in relation to the colonial peopling of the West Indies—and understanding how these peoples drew upon remembered as well as invented resources as they adapted to the changing conditions of their New World home—facilitates reflection upon the ways globalization and the development of capitalism shape popular ritual and religious culture and upon how religion remains an operative force within modern conditions as well.

By looking bifocally at the evolution of African and Hindu traditions, this study is akin to what Fred Eggan (1954) once called the "method of controlled comparison." He emphasized that problems of generalization are always connected with matters of comparison. Although he believed we should indeed aspire to comparativism, he also thought anthropologists should pursue it on a smaller scale than was common among his British colleagues, "with as much control over the frame of comparison as it is possible to secure" (747).

Although Franz Boas (1940) thought histories should be compared in order to formulate general principles of culture, which he saw as essentially psychological in character, he also critiqued the comparativism of his day, ultimately favoring the "historical" over the "comparative" method, thus giving rise to particularism in North American anthropology—what Alfred Kroeber (1935) once dubbed anthropology-as-history as compared with anthropology-as-science. Boas not only thought uniformity of process was essential for comparability, he also believed only phenomena deriving historically or psychologically from common causes could be adequately compared. As Eggan noted, these stipulations predisposed many who followed against comparativism. Boas's complementary ideal of formulating "general laws" of cultural process through comparison—which he even saw as more important at times—became increasingly

recessive within the discipline. While I would certainly not claim to be formulating "laws" of culture in this study, I do document and analyze cultural
processes as well as the complex forces that drive and give them shape through
comparative analysis.[7]

Eggan focused upon comparing relatively homogeneous cultural areas or
working with specific sociocultural types as tactics for controlling the frame of
comparison. Interestingly, in his work on Amerindian kinship systems (1937),
he employed the comparative method to demonstrate that tribal groups with
dramatically different social structures who converged upon the Plains area
from surrounding regions nonetheless developed resonant cultural configurations not simply because of diffusion. It is clear that he did not have contexts so
anomalous to the traditional anthropological imagination as the Caribbean in
mind.

Yet by examining African and Hindu traditions in the southern Caribbean, I have "controlled" for social ecology and historical factors in a sense. It
is through comparing and contrasting these two religious subcultures—stemming from radically different ancestral sources—that we may more fully grasp
their complexity as well as the sociocultural processes and histories that have
produced them. As Aram Yengoyan writes, "the most critical aims of comparison are to make discoveries through different ways of seeing things—by drawing forth new, unique, and possibly odd implications that bear on what is being
compared—and to direct our attention to other contexts which on their surface
might appear to have no connection" (2006:4).

It important to note that Eggan also viewed temporality as equally critical for
the comparative method. In fact, he believed "our best insights into the nature
of society and culture come from seeing social structures and cultural patterns
over time. Here is where we can distinguish the accidental from the general,
evaluate more clearly the factors and forces operating in a given situation, and
describe the processes involved in general terms. Not to take advantage of the
possibilities of studying social and cultural change under such relatively controlled conditions is to do only half the job that needs to be done" (1954:755–56).
Here Eggan is preaching to the choir when it comes to the anthropology of
the Caribbean, since historical anthropology has been at the forefront of disciplinary inquiry in the region. I argue for an understanding of "transculturation" based on temporality as much as on hybridity, as it is more commonly
understood.

Although the virtues of comparativism are compelling and evident, the reality of conducting comparative research may be another story altogether. Indeed, this project has continually tested my fortitude and called for enormous

patience and care. There were occasions when I considered giving up alto-gether. However, a fateful meeting with Bridget Brereton—one of Trinidad and Tobago's preeminent historians—convinced me otherwise. While any research is valuable, she opined, a comparative analysis of this kind would be fresh and innovative, with the potential to reframe scholarship and debate.[8] The inimitable challenge of such a project, however, required more research, analysis, and follow-up than was evident at the time. It has also made for a longer period of gestation in the writing of this book, whose fruits—I hope—will prove to have been worth all of the blood, sweat, and tears.

Overview

A historical anthropology of religion in colonial Trinidad and Tobago is pur-sued in chapter 2 in order to contextualize the traditions in question and bring macrostructural vicissitudes into focus. Shango (or, more recently, Orisha Wor-ship) and Shakti Puja are neither fully documented nor adequately analyzed in the regional literature. Both are popular traditions that have undergone forms of postcolonial resurgence in the wake of TT's first decade after political inde-pendence in 1962 and the experience of an economic oil boom during the 1975–83 period. They are dispersed throughout the entirety of this twin-island nation and are based upon subaltern ceremonial circuits of trance performance and spirit mediumship neither easily accessed nor tracked by outsiders, whether those be locals or foreigners. Considering patterns of colonial transculturation is crucial for comparative analysis and for making sense of transformations in the postcolonial era.

Chapter 3 examines Shango, one of three semi-independent ecstatic Afro-Trinbagonian ritual systems. This tradition evolved and consolidated through the colonial period as a dynamic synthesis of precursors brought principally by indentured Yoruba and Fon laborers in the postemancipation period of the nineteenth century, along with a host of other traditions and influences, through complex processes of adaptation and innovation. Most often described as an Afro-Catholic syncretism due to a system of cross-identifications made between West African orisha deities and Roman Catholic saints, Shango's cul-tural history is characterized by far more hybridity than is captured by the more common "Afro-Catholic" gloss alone. Indeed, despite the genuine significance of Afro-Catholic bricolage in Shango belief and praxis, the spectrum of Afro-Christian as well as inter-African syncretism is much more complex and con-voluted than most analytical models have heretofore surmised. Indeed, Shango reflects the appropriation of symbolism and practice from Indians, Chinese, and sundry other sources in the southern Caribbean. Yet I also argue that these dynamic and multilayered forms of transculturation nevertheless reflect the tradition's resilient Africanity.[9]

If locals as well as scholars have tended to take Afro-Trinbagonian religion to be quintessentially "syncretic," Hinduism, by contrast, has been overlooked in considerations of creolization and syncretism until recently. Chapter 4, then, focuses on Shakti Puja and examines the development of Hinduism throughout the colonial period of Indian labor indentureship, and accounts for the marginalization and reconsolidation of syncretic religious practices in relation to the twentieth-century construction of a class-stratified, "orthodox" form of West Indian Hinduism. "Creolization" refers to processes of localizing mixture and the genesis of new sociocultural forms (see Appendix on the intellectual histories and pros and cons of "creolization" and "syncretism" as analytical concepts). It was not until the postcolonial period that varied streams of ritual praxis, including formerly north and south Indian Hindu forms, appropriations from Islam, and religious and psychiatric influences from Guyana, came fully together and were amalgamated in heterodox temples established under the aegis of Mother Kali. An analysis of the creolizing dynamics and syncretic processes involved in the development of this ritual tradition is therefore paramount.

Chapter 5 presents a comparative investigation of the ways these two traditions have undergone processes of evolution specific to the southern Caribbean, such as the parallel convergence of structural form, especially with the privatization and subaltern liberalization of trance performance and devotional practice; comparable dynamics of pantheonization and syncretic amalgamation; resonant heterodox marginalization and sociocultural stratification; congruent patterns of transracial recruitment; and progressively therapeutic reorientation.

My original intent was to investigate the significance of "crossover" recruitment, in which Africans become involved in Kali Worship and Indians in Orisha Worship, and the degree to which transracial activity catalyzes reracialization of consciousness through the reworking of natal by spiritual kinship idioms. Tentative evidence suggested approximately 10 percent racial crossover participation in both cases (Houk 1995; N. Mahabir, pers. comm., 1997). Yet, while I found such participation to be evident in the on-the-ground operation of these traditions, other empirical and conceptual problems began to multiply. The more I learned, the more I reconsidered the project's initial, more limited, rationale.

It was not that crossover participation is insignificant. The transracial recruitment and participation of Indians in Shango and Africans in Shakti Puja is clearly evident in both. Moreover, crossover on both sides seemed to me to be relatively stable and—perhaps most importantly—took place without much fanfare. This was hardly the transgressive specter I painted in my research proposals. Thus the question became how to understand the significance of this crossover in relation to broader ceremonial patterns and sociocultural processes within which each is embedded.[10]

Indeed, significant though this transracialization of experience may be, there is another level of crossover that must be distinguished in analysis: the transculturation of racially inflected sociosymbolic constructs including gods and goddesses as well as ritual paraphernalia and liturgical practices. Again, one encounters noteworthy convergences and divergences when considering the two traditions through comparison.

On the one hand, Shango has not just exhibited remarkable forms of inter-African and Afro-Christian hybridity but significant Afro-Indo creolization as well. These patterns index the tradition's amalgamating capacity and creativity at the grassroots level and pose a complicating foil for cultural politics in an era of postcolonial multiculturalism. Kali Worship, on the other hand, may be marginalized from the perspective of the mainstream, but as a form of Hinduism it has rarely been understood in terms of creolization or syncretism. As alluded to above, ecstatic Shakti Puja represents a dynamic and vibrant stream of popular transculturation. This tradition is less evidently hybrid across an Afro-Indo axis but evinces considerable creolizing patterns of inter-Indian syncretism. Here, Shakti Puja is treated as every bit as "syncretic" as Shango—to use an unsatisfactory concept when invoked simplistically or without appropriate empirical grounding (see Appendix)—prompting revision of the cultural history of Caribbean Hinduism. I additionally consider the problem of creolization in Shango, arguing against the influential "camouflage theory" of syncretism and examining forms of hybridity that extend far beyond the Afro-Catholic framework, consider how each ritual tradition forms a coherently flexible system of popular ritual praxis, and address the degree to which practitioners of each perceive their tradition as syncretic.

Chapter 6 examines the highly contrasting political trajectories of Shango and Shakti Puja in the postcolonial era. The Afrocentric amplification of racial identity in relation to Shango becomes less and less consequential among practitioners within the lower strata of local class relations. The role of Shango as a vehicle for the racialization—or reracialization—of consciousness turns out to be most significant not among my so-called crossover participants, but, on the contrary, among *non*-crossovers, especially upwardly mobile and middle-class *Afro*-Trinbagonian practitioners of Orisha Worship who came of age in the postcolonial era.

On the Hindu side, by contrast, ecstatic religiosity has not been politicized, or, to put it more precisely, has been politically castigated. Indeed, only "respectable" forms of Hinduism have become vehicles for the expression of Indocentric politics and sentiment in the late colonial and postcolonial periods. Though Shango has become highly politicized by a vocal vanguard of Afrocentrists as a vehicle for reclaiming and rehabilitating "blackness" in response to the 1970s Black Power critique of the legacy of colonial racism and hegemony of Christianity within the sociohistorical experience of Afro-Trinbagonians, Kali Worship has *not* been similarly politicized, even though Indian nationalists have nevertheless also turned to religion—in their case, mainstream Hinduism—for the assertion of Indian ethnicity and articulation of Indocentric politics.

The central question addressed in chapter 6 therefore concerns why each of these traditions—Afrocentric embracing of Shango versus an Indocentric blind eye toward Shakti Puja—has experienced such different political fates in the postcolonial era. If these traditions are convergent in so many respects at the grassroots level, then why have they become so divergently politicized in the postcolonial era? I account for this divergence in terms of differing colonial ideologies of racial subordination regarding Africans versus Indians in the articulation of hierarchy and religion in the West Indies and their reiterative effects within the field of multicultural politics that emerged in the time-released wake of decolonization. Indeed, colonial ideologies of racial subordination continue to cast their spell across the terrain of religious and cultural politics in Trinidad and Tobago, despite the aims of activists on both sides to contest colonial ideology and overturn the colonization of spiritual consciousness inherited from the past. My analysis considers the changing politics of religion in an era of postcolonial multiculturalism and proceeds with an understanding of diasporas as alternative counternationalisms, as resources for emergent postcolonialisms.

Despite these contrasting political fates, however, social class and bourgeois attitudes nonetheless influence the politics of Indocentrists and Afrocentrists across the ethnoracial spectrum. Indocentrists have generally embraced a gentrified form of "mainstream" Hinduism that looks down upon ecstatic religious practices such as spirit mediumship, fire walking, or animal sacrifice as "backward" or "premodern." Afrocentrists, by contrast, and despite their political embrace of a subaltern tradition centered on trance ceremonialism, nonetheless tend to be less involved in the everyday activities of grassroots shrines and shy away from the theatrical dramaturgy of trance performance in favor of more middle class–inflected forms of devotion, including in their politics. In this regard, my analysis substantiates the theory that religious charisma in the context of modernity may be understood as a dialectical counterpoint to the liberal bourgeois ethic of possessive individualism, addressed in the Epilogue.

Contrasting ideologies of racial subordination vis-à-vis Africans and Indians have differentially influenced the cultural politics of religion in colonial and postcolonial Trinidad and Tobago. I track transculturation operative in differing cultural registers—especially in relation to race and religion—and how they may influence one another recursively through time (also see Khan 2004). The concept of "transculturation" stems from the late Cuban ethnologist Fernando Ortiz (1947), who intended it to supersede received wisdom concerning "acculturation" through an emphasis on New World cultural processes of interpenetration and mixture as complex, reciprocal, and multidirectional. I build on Ortiz's notion of transculturation in light of its shortcomings as well as through recourse to Indo-Caribbean materials beyond his frame of consideration. Focusing on the dynamic affordances of "spirits" as popular vehicles of transculturation inflects the concept with new meaning, highlighting the "trans" in trance and vice-versa.

"Transculturation" is thus deployed as a multiplex concept requiring coordinated theorization of both the psychology and the history of culture. By focusing upon processes of sociocultural interaction as well as emphasizing the dynamism of cultural knowledge and action through time, I seek to recuperate the anthropological concept of "culture." I believe we should not abandon the culture concept now that it is loose in academia and on the streets, as well as politicized in debates concerning inequality and identity. The notion of transculturation also connects provocatively with the experience and significance of trance conceptualized as the play of spirits in the globalizing traditions of ecstasy and mediumship considered here. Innovation and change have been driven in each tradition as a result of synergy between processes of subaltern liberalization and popular contact with a populist notion of the sacred. Relatedly, we may better understand suppression of the ritual arts of trance down the social ladder of local class relations in relation to the legacy of liberal bourgeois culture inherited from imperial Britain throughout the colonial period; doing so requires a brief return in the Epilogue to utilitarianism and Bentham's critique of deep play as antithetical to economic rationality and liberal bourgeois materialism.

Methodology

Research in Trinidad and Tobago involved a summer of pilot fieldwork in 1997, two full years of field research in 1999 and 2000, and approximately one month of follow-up fieldwork in the summers of 2002 through 2005. I also spent a month in 2001 conducting archival research at the British Museum Library in London. Fieldwork has involved participant observation, informal interviewing, audiotaped semistructured interviewing, videographic filming of key ceremonies and ritual events, and intermittent archival investigation. Archival data collected in the Caribbean and London have enabled me to deepen the analysis by providing historiographical data to reconstruct the social histories and cultural dynamics of the project's two focal traditions in conjunction with ethnohistorical information collected on the ground among practitioners.

My research was slow-going in early 1999, leading me to get swept up in the sociocultural tidal wave that is Carnival, which took place relatively early that year. Given the dominance of this Shrovetide festival in many studies of Trinidad and Tobago, I had entered the field intending to steer clear of it, wanting to not get distracted from the arenas of performance with which I was chiefly concerned. However, moving slowly but deliberately expanded my understanding of the national festival cycle and of the complex and recursive interrelations among performance practices at large. I participated in the many events and activities associated with Carnival, including playing mas in Peter Minshall's band that year, the Lost Tribe. Although the band's symbolism and ten internal sections were based upon Minshall's interpretation of Jewish Kabbalah esoterica, we were dressed in gauzy, loosely flowing, Saharan nomad–style costumes. This experience not only brought home to me the deep cultural and historical significance of Carnival, but also oriented me to the generative meanings of "play" in local performance culture more broadly.

My research activities took me all over Trinidad and increasingly to Tobago, as I followed the ever-shifting flows of ceremonial activity and personnel. Indeed, the geographically dispersed nature of African and Hindu forms of ecstatic religion necessitated my continual movement at all times of day and night. As I got to know the twin-island society in more depth, and through learning about experiences of colleagues—both male and female—who have worked in Trinidad and Tobago, I became increasingly aware of how my being a white, foreign male afforded me considerable leeway in terms of mobility and access.

A good deal of my time was spent at temples and shrines during explicit ceremonial periods, but I also spent increasing amounts of time with people outside of formal ritual activity. Most of my interaction and conversation with practitioners took place while hanging out and engaging in a sort of informal interviewing. I kept running field notes—often vocally recorded while driving around the island—about what I observed, what people said, and so on. More formal audiotape-recorded interviews with specific practitioners were arranged at times and places convenient or comfortable for them. Thus, whereas my informal interviewing throughout almost two and a half years of ethnographic fieldwork cannot be quantified in any meaningful manner, I have several hours of life history–oriented interviews recorded with seventeen shakti and fourteen orisha practitioners and leaders with whom I interacted in increasingly broad-ranging ways, including phone contact (when possible) if our paths had not recently crossed. In the United States, I have maintained contact with a few people by telephone and e-mail and on shorter trips back to TT during summers.

Toward the end of 1999, I began videotaping various ritual performances with the consent of and some encouragement from shrine and temple leaders. Sometimes they were interested in obtaining copies of the footage for themselves or their community, which I was happy to provide. I have approximately sixty hours of digital footage from which I draw my documentation and analysis. Copies of all footage were donated to the archives of Banyan, Ltd., in Port-of-Spain, the leading independent filmmaking house in the southern Caribbean. Video data has not only expanded and enriched the scope of my work, but acting as the local videographer has also involved me with people in ways I could not have foreseen.

A final reflection pertinent to contextualizing the project: my having been in India for an academic year as an undergraduate in South Asian religious studies proved important to many Hindus. I was constantly asked about what I knew about practices and beliefs in India, and my experience gave me a certain clout and prestige. My background in Hindu and Buddhist studies also meant that I was able to assimilate the materials I was learning more rapidly in relation to the domain of Shakti Puja. Not having been to Africa, and having little previous background in African or Black Atlantic studies, made my progress on the Afro-Trinbagonian side of the ecstatic religious spectrum slower and more challenging. This was exacerbated by the fact that the field of Orisha Worship is much larger and vaster than that of Kali Puja. Tracking the orisha circuit took me to Tobago as well, where there are a few Indians, but no Shakti Puja to speak of. Hence I intentionally use the term "Trinbagonian" when speaking about both islands, with "Trinidadian" in relation to Trinidad alone.

Hierarchy and Heterodoxy in a Maze of Color

Slavery has gone. But capitalism remains.

Gordon K. Lewis, The Growth of the Modern West Indies

Precocious Modernity and the Caribbean as Alter-Native

The Caribbean is a region of great and deeply poignant cultural and historical dynamism from which most of the original inhabitants were expelled or exterminated, to be replaced by peoples from what are today Sub-Saharan Africa, India, China, Indonesia, the Near East, and Europe. Compacted into social forms established by the economic enterprises of an expanding European capitalist system based on commerce, these peoples multiplied their social and cultural resources through complex, interactive, polyethnic processes of adaptation, accommodation, and resistance. The region has therefore stood in an awkward relation to anthropology because it has no classically indigenous peoples to study (Horowitz 1971)—ruling out engagement with "native" or "pure" cultures—and because it has been considered neither center nor periphery. Based on "nothing but contact" (Mintz 1974a:ix–xxi), Caribbean societies are inescapably heterogeneous and colonial or postcolonial to their core.[1]

The first colonies were established three centuries before Europeans conquered Africa. Sidney Mintz argues that the "precocious modernity" of the region, as the oldest sphere of European colonialism, must be seen as the most Westernized part of the so-called First World: the First World's first world (1971a,

1974a, 1977, 1987, 1996a, 1996b, 1998), a line of argumentation inaugurated by the late Trinidadian Marxist C.L.R. James (1963). The growth of colonial economies based on African slavery, the plantation system, and sugarcane was integral to the rise of European capitalism, introduced into the region within twenty years of its "discovery" in 1492. Mintz observes: "The peoples of the Caribbean are the descendants of those ancestors dragged into European experiments, and of the Europeans who dragged them, at an early point in Western history. Indeed, those peoples and this region mark the moment when the 'West' became a conceptual entity—for these were the West's first genuine overseas colonies" (1974a:xxi). As Édouard Glissant puts it, "the West is not in the West; it is a project, not a place" (1989:2). Trouillot (2003) argues that the place projected as the West is better understood as the North Atlantic, not only because it is more precise but also because it encourages us to remember that the "West" is always a fiction.

Several points regarding the history and development of regional patterns of social organization in relation to political economy are important for my analysis. The swift extirpation of native populations and the early definition of the islands, and bits of the mainland, as a sphere of overseas agricultural capitalism based primarily on sugarcane, African slaves, and the plantation system spurred—and then continued to frame—the development of insular social structures in which local community organization was slight in relative terms, as well as managed by the state. Class stratification was paramount from the beginning. Overseas domination, sharply differentiated access to land, wealth, and political power, and the use of racial differences as status markers and mechanisms of social control sustained these structural arrangements. Massive new foreign populations of diverse origins were successively introduced into the lower sectors of these insular societies under conditions of restricted opportunities for upward mobility. Moreover, the region has generally been characterized by the persistence of colonialism, and of the colonial ambiance, longer than any other area outside Western Europe, and by the relative absence of compelling ideologies of nationalism mediating mass acculturation.

Mintz (1974a:xix) emphasizes that this shared conglomeration of experience did *not* generate cultural homogeneity: "Because Europe itself was not a monolith, consisting instead of contending states, contending churches, contending cultures, contending peoples and classes, the resulting uniformity in the colonial societies of the Caribbean was of a sort that arose more out of the intentions of the conquerors, than out of the content of their cultures" (also see Mintz and Price 1992). By striving to fulfill those intentions, the colonists achieved a uniformity that was more sociological and technological than cultural. Forms of governance, political and legal order, and commerce resembled one another from society to society because those in power had similar objectives.

The development of plantations to produce commodities for European markets was a vital first step in the history of overseas capitalism. Indeed, the growth of slave-based economies in the New World not only was an integral part of the rise of European commerce and industry, but also was connected with the evolving political economy of labor in Europe (Mintz 1971a, 1974a, 1985b, 1987, 1992, 1996, 1998; Segal 1988, 1989; Solow 1991; Segal and Handler 1992; Handler and Segal 1993). Joseph Inikori (1998) highlights the critical contribution of slavery to the growth of large-scale industrial production in England through the growth of Atlantic commerce. The role of slavery in fueling the development of capitalism itself cannot be underappreciated: unfathomable "surplus value" was violently conjured into being and put magically into circulation.

Slaves demographically dominated the populations of all export-producing regions of tropical America. African slaves and their descendants produced about 75 percent of the total value of American products traded in the seventeenth- and eighteenth-century Atlantic world, all under the sign of Europe's Age of Enlightenment. In turn, the growth of England's reexport trade from 1650 to 1750 laid the foundation for the growth of industrial production in the metropole from the mid-eighteenth century onward. Indeed, the rapidly growing export of local manufactures to the slave-based societies of the Americas was central for accelerating manufacturing in late-eighteenth- and early-nineteenth-century England. These processes accompanied the proletarianization of remaining peasant institutions at "home" in the metropole, sustaining considerable population expansion and thus building a domestic market for the products of English industry. Today, countries and territories throughout the region continue to forge a precarious survival dependent upon the export of commodities—sugar, coffee, bauxite, oil—and services—tourism, sex, and tax-free banking. The region is also known for its part in the transshipment of illicit substances (Hagelberg 1985; Stone 1985; Richardson 1992; Fernández 1994; Pattullo 1996; Levitt and Witter 1996; Maurer 1997; Maingot 1998; Sheller 2003; Padilla 2007).

Approximately 12 million Africans were forcibly brought to the New World as chattel slaves (Eltis 1998). The British alone transferred at least 3.1 million slaves across the Atlantic to labor on tropical American plantations (Inikori 1992; Eltis 1995; Richardson and Behrendt 1995; Eltis and Richardson 1997). Based on techniques pioneered by the Dutch in northeastern Brazil, the British West Indian sugar venture began in Barbados in the 1640s and quickly spread throughout the region, especially in competition with French colonial expansion (Dunn 1972; Sheridan 1974; Higman 2000). Overall, "King Sugar" absorbed 90 percent of all African slaves from the seventeenth century to the 1820s (Eltis and Richardson 1997).

Mintz, viewing slaves as proletarians in disguise, frames the plantation experience as agro-*industrial* in character, which compels us not to be fooled by any misleading rural-urban or temporal distinctions (1953, 1974a, 1974b, 1977, 1985, 1996a, 1996b, 1998). The features of this plantation system—which include monocrop production for export, strong monopolistic tendencies, a rigid and oppressive system of social stratification characterized by a correlation between racial and class hierarchies, and relatively weak community structure—contributed to the shared contours of Caribbean societies and cultures (also see Knight and Palmer 1989; Bolland 1992a; Trouillot 1992a, 1992b; Brereton 1993; Levitt and Witter 1996; R. T. Smith 1996). This system also gave rise to a range of reconstituted peasantries situated on and across the margins of the system, a mode of socioeconomic organization that has existed—even thrived—in tension with plantation domination (see Besson 1992, 1995). Mintz observed, "The relatively highly developed industrial character of the plantation system meant a curious sort of 'Modernization' or 'Westernization' for the slaves—an aspect of their acculturation in the New World that has too often been missed because of the deceptively rural, agrarian, and pseudo-manorial quality of slave-based plantation production" (1974a:9). That Caribbean peoples have developed the habits and skills required of labor and capital in industrial and postindustrial societies has made them desirable as immigrant workers, undergirding a long tradition of transnational migration and return. They have always been modern, a "modernity that predated the modern" (Mintz 1985b, 1996b, 1998; Richardson 1983, 1989, 1992; Mintz and S. Price 1985; Miller 1994, 1996; R. Smith 1996; Maingot 1998; Trouillot 2003; Scott 2004).

Just as Caribbean peoples experienced slavery from a range of positions, so too did they experience the transition to emancipation and freedom. Though emancipation brought legal freedom to the great majority of Caribbean peoples, it did *not* fundamentally change the grossly unequal distribution of socioeconomic resources and political power (Brereton 1989; Scarano 1989; R. Smith 1992, 1996; Olwig 1995). No longer "protected" as chattel in a paternalistic slave system offering limited customary rights to subsistence and medical care, the newly emancipated were "left to fend for themselves" (Olwig 1995:4) and, therefore, left to be blamed for their "own" future failures. As Olwig observes, "The ability to absorb the contradictions of freedom may well be one of the most important legacies of emancipation for Caribbean societies" (1995:7). Ideologies of liberalism in the postemancipation Caribbean incorporated racist elements, enabling elites and the socially mobile to maintain recontextualized positions in the postemancipation hierarchy through Anglicization of concepts of achievement, for example (R. Smith 1982).

Antillean society in the postslavery era was dominated by poverty and underdevelopment. Elites dominated the good agricultural land, controlled business enterprise and financial institutions, and populated the professions and top ranks of colonial administration (Williams 1970; Mintz 1974a; Brereton 1989; Turner 1995). Many former slaves continued working on plantations as wage laborers, as full-time resident workers or temporary laborers during busy seasons, supplementing meager earnings from autonomous cultivation (Hall 1978). Some were able to become independent farmers, though underemployment was the norm for the majority. Some former slaves migrated to towns in order to escape low wages and seasonal employment on the plantations and impoverished existence on small peasant plots (Hall 1978; G. Lewis 1985; Stone 1985; Brereton 1989; Knight and Palmer 1989; Scarano 1989). This urbanization became increasingly significant, creating serious problems by the 1930s: towns had fewer jobs than arrivants, and health and housing conditions frequently deteriorated as people crowded into slums and other poor areas.

To mitigate and manipulate difficulties precipitated by emancipation of the slaves, the region's planters and the colonial government resorted to the importation of nominally free laborers from India, China, Indonesia, and Africa under contracts of indenture. Apart from the condition that they had a legally defined term of service and were guaranteed a set wage, indentured servants often were treated similarly to the former slaves they replaced (Brereton 1974, 1989; Knight and Palmer 1989; Look Lai 1993; Khan 1996; Galenson 1998). Between 1838 and 1917, over half a million "East" Indians—from South Asia, that is—came to work on the British West Indian sugar plantations, the majority going to the new sugar producers with fertile lands such as Trinidad, which received about 144,000 indentured migrants. Between 1853 and 1879, more than 14,000 Chinese workers reached the shores of some of the very same territories; Cuba also imported more than 100,000 Chinese between 1847 and 1873 in order to facilitate the transition to free labor. South Asians also went to work on plantations in French Martinique and Guadeloupe as well as Dutch Suriname, with an equivalent number of Javanese joining them in the latter. And between 1841 and 1867, some 32,000 indentured or newly freed Africans also arrived throughout the British West Indies, the greatest number going to Jamaica, British Guiana, and Trinidad.[2]

Indentured labor servitude did not resolve intractable problems of economy and governance, but it did enable plantations to weather the transition from slave labor. Successive migrant streams continued to contribute to regional dynamism in social, economic, cultural, and ethnic terms in ways partly dependent on the relative numbers and configurations that ended up in each colony and partly on the sociohistorical idiosyncrasies of the local geocultural environment (Elder 1970; Brereton 1974; Trotman 1976, 1986; Brereton and Dookeran 1982; Birbalsingh 1989; Look Lai 1993; Dabydeen and Samaroo 1996).

This labyrinthine dialectic of power and differentiation manifests in relation to the challenges and contradictions of postcolonialism throughout the region as well. Anthony Maingot (1998) characterizes Caribbean societies as "modern-conservative" ones because of their peculiar mixture of political conservatism and radical individualism and skepticism. The Caribbean modern-conservative society is not only capable of social change, but it is also prone to calls or movements for it. Racial ideologies and other legacies of colonialism inhibit universalist approaches to politics in the region, simultaneously producing intense processes of continuity and change (Maingot 1998:443–44). The region is home to the largest global concentration of territories that have voluntarily retained colonial status, reaping the benefits of imperial paternalism while postponing the burdens and responsibilities of independence. As Jamaican political scientist Carl Stone observes, "This compromise between the impulse for sovereignty and a pragmatic sense of economic realism represents an interesting aspect of the complex patterns of ambivalence that underlie the colonial connections in the Caribbean" (1985:14).

The Caribbean, then, is a region in which "tradition" grew directly out of the colonial order (Olwig 1993; Miller 1994) and "modernity predated the modern" (Mintz 1985b, 1996b, 1998; Mintz and S. Price 1985; Scott 2004). Scholars have paid insufficient attention to the Caribbean as "alter-native," the West's hidden underbelly and, perhaps, even a crystal ball for the global future (Glissant 1989; Mintz 1996b, 1998; R. Smith 1996; Trouillot 2003).

From Colonial Backwater to Slave Society in the Southern Caribbean

Trinidad and Tobago did not become an official, twin-island, political entity within the colonial British Empire until 1889, when Tobago first became a ward of Trinidad. This development accelerated the eclipse of Franco-creole power and language, which was more or less complete by World War I. Though Trinidad was never officially French, French West Indian planters, free Coloreds, and patois-speaking Africans and Afro-creoles were central agents in the development of nineteenth-century society in the southern Caribbean, in spite of the fact that Britain had taken the island from Spain without a fight between 1797 and 1802.

Trinidad was a colonial Spanish backwater before the end of the eighteenth century. Spain's imperial vision focused on the rush for precious metals in the Andes and Mesoamerica, with the Caribbean valuable primarily as a way station to and from the mainland jackpots (Brereton 1981; Millette 1985). Christopher Columbus dubbed the island La Trinidad in commemoration of the Holy Trinity in 1498, on his third voyage to the New World, after spotting three small mountaintops on the southern coast from his ship (Carmichael 1961; Newson 1976). But Columbus did not, of course, discover Trinidad. That honor belongs more properly to Amerindian Arawak peoples who had lived there for centuries, and to the Island Caribs, who began to raid the island long before 1498 and had established settlements on the north coast almost certainly before the end of the sixteenth century.

African slave labor was negligible until the 1780s, since, up to that time, indigenous Amerindians supplied the labor for colonial estates and grew much of the island's food. Spanish colonists made requests for the importation of enslaved Africans early in the seventeenth century, but these went unheeded by the Crown, so they turned to smuggling instead (Newson 1976).

Meanwhile, two primary institutions developed with preferential access to Amerindian labor—the imperial *encomienda* land grant and the Capuchin missionary station—but these never became extensive, and the number of Amerindians declined rapidly under Iberian rule along with their prospects for livelihood. With a population of approximately 30,000 to 40,000 at the time of Columbus, their numbers had declined precipitously by the end of the sixteenth century to probably no more than 20,000. Smallpox further depleted both the Spanish and the Amerindian communities in 1739.

Although Trinidad was ceded by Spain to Britain in 1802, the real story begins in the 1780s with the influx of French Catholic planters and their slaves under the Spanish imperial *cédulas de población* of 1776 and 1783. Despite the island's being a colonial outpost, Spain did not want to abandon it because of its strategic location near the South American continent. Trinidad's small eighteenth-century economy had stagnated until the accession of Carlos III to the Spanish throne and the advent of an era of imperial reform and revitalization under the Bourbon kings, beginning in the 1770s and characterized by a new spirit of enterprise and the liberalization of trade. Spain's rulers came to understand that its tropical islands would have to be developed along lines carved out in the British and French West Indian colonies, driven by the technical rationality of plantation agriculture and capitalist adventurism. Trinidad would be transformed into a full-on slave colony (Wood 1968; Millette 1985; John 1988).

France and Spain had been closely allied since 1761, and, by 1776, the Spanish government had accepted the reality of foreign immigration as essential for developing the island's economy. French planters from islands granted to Britain in 1763, after the Seven Years' War, were encouraged, with various tax incentives, land grants, and the promise of protection under a Catholic power, to immigrate to the island. The more slaves one brought, the more land one received, and, given the Spanish Crown's desire to prevent the spread of Protestantism, immigrants had to be Catholic subjects of a nation friendly to Spain.

Migration was attractive to planters plagued by agricultural problems or, eventually, by fallout from the Napoleonic Wars in the French West Indian territories or by revolution in Haiti, as well as by political problems for those in the group of British isles recently ceded by France, such as Dominica, St. Vincent, Grenada, and Tobago. After the turn of the nineteenth century, refugees escaping revolutionary warfare on the Spanish Main also made their way to the island. What began as an experimental trickle of foreign migration to Trinidad in 1777 soon became a flood engulfing the entire colony once the policies were fully accepted and formalized with the cédula of 1783. Thus, although Spain ruled in theory, it was the French who dominated the island in practice. Even after British succession, their influence was profound.

The early Bourbon reform period was pivotal for the southern Caribbean, since the effects of the cédulas radically transformed the size, composition, and nature of Trinidad's colonial population by kick-starting its economy. Dominated by the plantocracy, Trinidad virtually became a French colony as early as 1784, after the first wave of emigration from Grenada, Guadeloupe, Martinique, St. Lucia, and Cayenne (French Guiana). French planters were slave owners whose wealth was based on the land. Afro-Franco-creole forms of language and culture came rapidly into ascendance, with a patois the lingua franca and Catholicism a broadly cast sacred net, and with Carnival alive and well initially among the elites, only to be appropriated by Blacks as part of their own festival tradition after emancipation in 1838.

Yet free Coloreds who came and adopted the island as home outnumbered the French planters. "Colored" (British and West Indian spelling, Coloured) is an important and complex racial category regarding people of mixed Afro-Euro descent and cast in a variable idiom of "shade," discussed further below. The cédula gave legal sanction to a colored property-owning class—although they received only half as much incentive land as their white counterparts—and made no distinction between white and colored immigrants in the article granting citizenship rights to settlers after five years' residence. Thus free Coloreds from the French colonies and the formerly French isles enthusiastically flocked to Trinidad in sizable numbers. Some free black immigrants also came, becoming petty rural smallholders or artisans and domestic servants in towns or villages.

Even so, it was black slave labor that became the basis of the new society created in late-eighteenth-century Trinidad. The majority of slaves came with their owners, were patois speakers, and—like many of their owners—were creole-born (that is, in the Americas) and thus were at least nominally Roman Catholic. British merchants quickly entrenched themselves as purveyors of slaves for this late-blooming colony. In 1786, the exemption of the slave trade from import duties was made permanent (Carmichael 1961:393–99).

Between 1777 and 1783, Trinidad's population exploded from an initial 3,432 inhabitants to almost 19,000, with the French far outnumbering the Spanish among Europeans, who together were nonetheless in the minority (John 1988). French planters brought their capital along with slave labor in order to exploit the island's rich resources. Plantation-based sugar production accelerated rapidly and lucratively. Yet instability roiled throughout the region in that volatile, turn-of-the-nineteenth-century era of the North American, French, and Haitian revolutions. Liberal democratic ideologies threatened the legitimacy of colonialism and slavery, at least in theory, and elites feared political subversion. British West Indian planters, for example, had little to gain and much to lose from supporting the North American War for Independence (O'Shaughnessy 2000).

Spain offered only minimal resistance and easily capitulated to the British in 1797. The new colony had a novel population in British imperial experience: Spanish and French Catholics composed the majority of Trinidad's European inhabitants, with twice as many free Coloreds—many of whom owned both land and slaves—as Whites. Nonetheless, two-thirds of the colony were slaves. Those ideologically aligned with the new French Republic were deported upon the arrival of the British. In 1800, the first British governor—Thomas Picton, a tyrannical ruler—put out a new slave code that turned back legal advances made in 1789 as a result of the Bourbon reforms. The island was formally ceded in 1802 through the Treaty of Amiens.

Plantation agro-business nonetheless continued to expand, though the official British slave trade subsequently came to a halt in 1807, leading to deceleration in the growth of the island's slave population. Sugar production had become closely tied to British capitalism, and planters were only just beginning to experience the economic advantages of slave labor at the time of emancipation. In 1813, the majority of slaves in Trinidad, about 14,000, were African-born, compared with just under 12,000 locally born "creole" slaves (Brereton 1981:55). Slave mortality rates were high, and not a few planters turned to illegal trading in order to replenish their pools of enslaved labor.

Creole Society and the Advent of Freedom

Emancipation in the British colonies came about through the complex interplay of metropolitan and local forces. An antislavery lobby emerged in London by the end of the eighteenth century, steadily gaining influence in governmental circles. This movement was driven by changing attitudes due to the spread of Enlightenment ideas concerning natural rights, political liberty, and emergent evangelical and nonconformist Christian convictions pitting enslavement as contrary to the Gospel. Christianity had inherited the Roman position condoning slavery and more or less held that view until the late eighteenth century (Davis 1970). Abolitionism gained ground from the mid-1780s, and British participation in the Atlantic slave trade was comprehensively abolished by 1807 (Temperley 1998).

Thereafter, West Indian planters suffered from a shortage of field labor and falling sugar prices, even though production continued to increase. Yet the sugar trade became less important to the overall economy by the early 1830s (Brereton and Yelvington 1999:4–5). Moreover, sugar interests in the East Indies had emerged by the early 1820s, making common cause with the abolitionists. Back in the Americas, the West India interests lost political clout as a result of their slave smuggling and recalcitrance in the face of amelioration ordinances imposed by London. Furthermore, local free Coloreds launched their own campaign for civil rights in 1823, gaining a sympathetic ear from the British government.

The antislavery movement gathered intensifying momentum in the 1820s and was able to sway Parliament in 1833 toward the Act of Emancipation, which legislated the formal end of slavery in the British Empire on 1 August 1834. A time of great liberal fervor, the final stages of the campaign against slavery coincided with excitement over the Great Reform Bill of 1832. The latter not only reapportioned political representation more equitably in Parliament, but it also extended suffrage further down the national socioeconomic scale.

Yet, although the reformed House of Commons was prepared to end slavery, there was no hope of getting such a bill through the Lords without compensation for the slaveholders and a period of "apprenticeship" designed to allow for transitional adjustment. In exchange for their freedom, former slaves were required to devote three-quarters of their labor in service of their former owners. Planters received compensation of twenty million pounds altogether: an enormous sum equivalent to half the nation's annual budget (Temperley 1998:13). Indeed, the cost of emancipation was considerable, given that it was ultimately paid by taxpayers, in addition to the fact that sugar prices increased sharply following the shift to free labor. Brereton writes: "The Act represented a compromise between the anti-slavery party and the West Indian interests; if anything it gave the West Indians more than the abolitionists" (1981:63).

Antislavery sentiment therefore was restrained by respect for wealth and property. Only a small minority of the former slaves actually received the full rights to life, land, and mobility promised to them (Blackburn 1998). While emancipation may have undermined legal property rights to humans, it granted only nominal freedom. Dominance did not substantially change. In many ways, elites actually managed to tighten the reins of social control after emancipation. The unequal struggle over labor and land fundamentally shaped postemancipation society. Without recourse to the whip or on-the-spot punishment, those in power quickly turned to the punitive and rehabilitative possibilities of law, policing, courts, and prison. Elites were slow to embrace education as a mechanism for manufacturing consent (Trotman 1986).

The Emancipation Act of 1833 outlined six years of "apprenticeship" during which former slaves remained bound to plantations in order to "ease" the transition to freedom. But this period came to an end earlier than planned, in 1838. Emancipation met West Indian planters in "different postures and attitudes on the road to riches" (Munasinghe 2001a:50), precipitating widespread redefinition of labor relations throughout the region. Planters inherited the problem of compelling free individuals to labor steadily and cheaply on their estates. They sought simultaneously to constrain the economic alternatives of former slaves as well as increase the overall labor supply through immigration, thereby fostering competition among the laboring classes. At emancipation, the colonial state recorded a population of just under 21,000 slaves, 16,300 Coloreds, 3,200 Whites, and only 750 Caribs. Trinidad's potential for further economic expansion was tremendous and the field labor force still relatively small.

The colonial government experimented with various schemes of labor importation, including from Madeira and the Azores, China, North America, and even West Africa in the form of newly freed Africans from foreign slave ships. Yet none of these strategies proved especially successful. Many migrants abandoned agriculture and joined the expanding service sector. Thus, in order to mitigate and manipulate the labor problems prompted by emancipation, those in power resorted to the importation of nominally free laborers from then British India under contracts of indenture. Apart from a legally defined term of service and a set wage, with the promise—neither always kept by the authorities nor necessarily requested by the migrants—of return passage to their homeland, these indentured servants were not always treated so differently from those they replaced in the fields and factories (Brereton 1989; Galenson 1989; Knight and Palmer 1989; Scarano 1989; Look Lai 1993; Khan 1996, 2004;

Munasinghe 2001a). Between 1838 and 1917, Trinidad received almost 144,000 indentured emigrants from South Asia, the majority of whom never opted to return to their homeland.

Before continuing with the East Indians who came and forged lives for themselves in the West Indies, however, we must consider the complex "creole" social system whose development had already been set in motion, and whose structure set the terms and constraints of—even as it accommodated to—successive waves of newcomers. This system was one in which all constituent groups were integrated into a coercive and hegemonic social order ranked by race and ostensible approximation to the "civilized" customs of the dominant European stratum—in Trinidad's case, a complex and contested mix of British and French that superseded an initial layering of Spanish.

The Anglophone word *creole* bears an Iberian etymology—*criollo* in Spanish, *crioulo* in Portuguese (from the Latin root meaning "to raise" or "to bring up")—originally referring to persons of foreign descent born in the New World, as distinct from the European- or African-born. It referred to anyone—black or white—born in the West Indies and was extended to plants, goods, habits, and ideas arising from localization in the Americas (see Crowley 1957; Hoetink 1985; Cashmore 1996; Mintz 1996b; Balutansky 1997; Allen 2002; Palmié 2006, 2007a; C. Stewart 2007a, 2007b). "Creole" did *not* originally refer to any sort of mixture; this definition came much later, though the extension in meaning makes semantic sense, referring as it does to forms of mixture resulting specifically from New World conditions. Thus "creole" connotes locality and rootedness independent of autochthony and has therefore been subject to a dizzying range of meanings and politics (see Appendix for more on the genealogies of "creolization" and "syncretism" and their pros and cons in scholarship).

Focusing upon kinship as a dynamic nexus of both racial and class differentiation, Raymond T. Smith (1988, 1996) has shown how the logic of the emerging "dual marriage system" emerged at an early point in the development of West Indian colonies, binding everyone together: black and white, slave and free, mixed and pure (also see Mintz and Price 1992). This hierarchical creole social system was redundantly organized and finely regulated, animated by the contrastive meanings of different types of union—legitimate and Christian or variously otherwise—that were widely recognized and differentially valued. These hierarchical principles of color and class have remained operative despite changes in the legal and overt bases of differentiation within the system over time.

For the upper class, marriage meant alliance between status equals, and its values included permanence, religious sanction, and the reproduction of social position. The lower classes—originally enslaved Africans but over time their emancipated descendants—practiced forms of conjugal relations and household organization that placed less emphasis upon official marital union. Thus the free colored population came to represent an intermediate level in this stratified cultural system, paradoxically embodying the structural opposition between legal and nonlegal unions as well as white and black. Though the number of unions among Whites, Coloreds, and Blacks—as well as the number of offspring or families resulting from these unions—may have initially been small, their numbers grew and their significance was always important symbolically. Abolition of the slave trade led to an increase in the proportion of mixed-race people and, subsequently, the gradual emergence of a colored middle class.

Raymond T. Smith (1996:72) observes that the convergence of an upwardly mobile colored population with the downwardly mobile remains of the white planter class resulted in the formation of the nineteenth-century Afro-West Indian middle classes, for whom Christian marriage was the quintessential index of "respectable" status. Thus the dual marriage system—fueled by a driving concern with hierarchy cast in terms of race and class—neither disappeared nor radically changed with the demise of slavery. Rather, there was a dialectically evolving reallocation of positions within it over time in the face of changing socioeconomic stresses and strains. Indeed, these processes eventually led to the time-released growth of a black middle class as well.

The most important division within the white upper class in Trinidad's postemancipation decades was between the French-Catholic and English-Protestant sectors. This tension was quite turbulent at the top of the social pyramid, filtering down among the masses in complex ways. It was fought out within the spheres of language, law, education, and church-state as well as interdenominational relations. This unique Anglo-French dynamism within the colony generated pervasive effects—even where indirect—on the history of religion more broadly and on the prism of Afro-creole religious differentiation in particular. In fact, the Anglican and Catholic churches in mid-nineteenth-century Trinidad shared the rare experience of having been dually established for several generations. Ironically, the first Catholic bishop of Trinidad was confirmed in 1820 by the head of the Anglican Church, George III. But by 1870, the Church of England was disestablished throughout the British West Indies except for Barbados, thereby bringing the same fate to the Catholic Church in Trinidad (Dayfoot 1999:143).

Relations between the English and French heated up especially after 1838, when London mounted a more systematic policy of Anglicization. Matters of power and privilege among Whites were played out within the sphere of religion and, by extension, education and language. This was because Christians agreed that school-based education was the best means for increasing their flocks and bettering their own position vis-à-vis rivals. Christianization continued apace throughout the nineteenth century yet was anything but smooth, consistent, or unidirectional.

After emancipation, the majority of Trinidad's population was Catholic, but the Anglican Church was nevertheless very influential. The island initially fell under the auspices of the Anglican diocese headquartered in Barbados but, with the Ecclesiastical Ordinance of 1844, the Anglican Church became fully established with a formal base in Port-of-Spain, under a government with ready hostility toward Catholicism. For its part, and despite persistent turbulence over issues such as foreign appointments and marriage ordinances, the Catholic Church managed not only to weather the mid-century storm, but also even to gain ground, securing its own local archbishopric by papal announcement in 1850 (Harricharan 1981b, 1993). The Catholic Church maintained its tight interconnection with the French planter class, and together they were able to project their values and influence.

These church-state problems and interdenominational tensions were resolved with the passage of time as the communities coadapted to local idiosyncrasies of colonial power. The last three decades of the nineteenth century brought diminution of Anglo-French tensions, characterized on the one hand by relatively untrammeled Catholic expansion and evangelization in the society at large, culminating in Trinidad's first Catholic governor in 1897. On the other hand, an increasingly systematic and effective policy of Anglicization in the civil spheres of education, law, and governance gradually gained traction more broadly. English and French Creoles formed a single power bloc by the turn of the twentieth century, yet their position as the colony's ruling class was also slowly undermined, in turn, by the rise of educated colored and black middle classes, which became increasingly assertive in their own claims to power. Nonetheless, the stratified sociology of Christianity and related patterns of denominational affiliation had been firmly established.

Though Caribbean colonies were extensions of European Christian society, before the late eighteenth century there were too few clergy to proselytize an overworked and ever-changing slave population. Many in the plantocracy initially opposed Christianization of the slaves. The church line emphasized separation between earthly fate and heavenly reward as well as those aspects of Christian teaching upholding virtues of obedience, humility, and submission. With the turn of the nineteenth century, however, the abolitionist doctrines of nonconformist Christianity benefited from "the ripening of the contradictions within the system of plantation slavery and mercantile capitalism which supported it" (R. Smith 1976:314). Smith (1976) delineates the embrace of Christianity by former slaves in the emancipation era as having had less to do with any essential spirituality of Blacks in the Americas—though religious many of them no doubt were—than it did with earthly expectations in actual historical circumstances. The main attraction of Christianity was the promise of a better social order, since becoming Christian meant affiliation with the local representative of the abolition movement and the promise of social, as well as spiritual, transformation (also see Russell 1983; Austin-Broos 1992). Slaves displayed "little interest in Christianity" (which was, after all, even less related to their social condition than were African beliefs) until it came to symbolize an improvement in the conditions of daily life by expressing their situations and providing "a message of hope for the future" (R. Smith 1976:319). Thus, despite sporadic missionizing in the West Indies, it was not until after abolition of the slave trade that a real movement began to build, intimately linked with the development of evangelism in England itself. Imperial policy turned increasingly toward conversion of slaves owned by Anglican planters to the Anglican Church after the turn of the nineteenth century in an effort to counterbalance the "radical" activities of nonconformists.[3]

Christianity therefore played a key role in the transition to a new social order after emancipation, signifying the integration of society around core elements of the colonial order. Thus, even though Christianity functioned for a short while as a vehicle of radical expectations and change, it soon became a major ideological support for colonialism. Churches operated as a pivotal locus of affiliation and mobility for the incipient middle and proletarian classes. "Christianity and church membership had come to symbolize progress and, in the West Indian vernacular, 'upliftment,' and it created avenues of social mobility for the former slaves—avenues which tied them in directly with the highest status levels of the total society" (R. Smith 1976:327).

Yet the emancipation upsurge of interest in Christianity was neither uniform nor totalizing. Not all former slaves were baptized, and not all of the baptized became full-fledged church members, although it is true that at least nominal Christian adherence became widespread. Christian symbolism would prove to be a polysemically rich resource marshaled variously in political and cultural struggle.

Demographic factors such as a high ratio of Afros to Euros, work patterns minimizing interracial interaction, and constant pre- and postemancipation infusions of native-born Africans were all at work in the transoceanic transfer and reproduction of recontextualized religious beliefs and practices from

Africa. Africans and Afro-creoles were active interpreters not only of Christianity, but also of their own creolizing religious traditions, cunningly reconstituted under subaltern conditions. Many among the grassroots and proletarian classes anchored their spiritual lives in resilient ceremonial communities offering spiritual kinship as well as alternative sources of sustenance and healing power.

To the extent that religious concepts and ritual practices were transported and reconstituted through the ordeal of the Middle Passage, Africans drew upon what they knew and had access to in the context of life in the New World, a world as new to them as it was to Europeans. "Traditions" were reproduced and reinvented insofar as beliefs and practices dealt with problems of being and becoming rooted in new ground. The enduring significance of drumming and dancing in Afro-creole religious and aesthetic forms, for example, stems from reiterating shifts in the meaning of those practices over time in keeping with contexts of use and experience. A kaleidoscopic multitude of Afro-creole subaltern forms and hybrid reconfigurations proliferated in the colonial West Indies, albeit in idiosyncratically local ways ranging from ancestralism to Afrocentric cultism and Afro-Baptist traditions to herbalism and client-based sorcery.

Trinidad's black and colored population was heterogeneous and dynamic in the nineteenth century. Between 1841 and 1877, immigrants averaged about 42 percent of the total island population (Trotman 1976:11). Seven percent of the black populace was African-born in 1861, compared with only one percent in 1891 (Brereton 1979:152–53). This population included former slaves and their descendants, who were largely Roman Catholic and French patois speakers; the descendants of free colored and free black peasants and laborers, many of whom were also Catholic; large numbers of mainly English-speaking, Protestant labor migrants from throughout the eastern Caribbean; former slaves from North America who had fought for Britain in the War of 1812 and were settled in a number of "Company Villages" throughout the southern part of the island, bringing their own form of Afro-American baptism; black former soldiers of the British West India Regiment disbanded in 1815 and settled in various parts of the island; "peons" of Spanish-African-Amerindian background who came from Venezuela throughout the century to work in cacao agriculture and as backwoodsmen; and a number of "liberated Africans" of many different tribal and ethnic West African backgrounds who had been freed from foreign slave ships by the British Royal Navy and sent to colonies such as Jamaica, British Guiana, and Trinidad. Brereton observes: "It would be difficult to establish that all these groups shared a common creole culture, for there were wide cultural, linguistic, and religious differences between them. All one can safely state is that they were rigorously excluded from political or civic life, their most characteristic cultural forms tended to be despised by the upper and middle classes, and they were in a low economic position: they were plantation laborers, smallholders, squatters, hunters, lumbermen, fishermen, artisans, longshoremen, domestic servants, vagrants, unemployed, and criminals" (1979:110).

Of particular significance here for the evolution of black religious forms in postemancipation Trinidad was the infusion of Yoruba-speaking West Africans who came not as slaves but as indentured laborers between 1838 and 1870, carrying elements of continental Orisha Worship with them in their hearts and minds.[4] These were migrants who had been liberated by the Royal Navy from slave ships bound for Cuba, Brazil, and the United States, settled temporarily in Sierra Leone or Saint Helena, and then compelled to immigrate anyway as plantation laborers under contracts of indenture (Warner-Lewis 1994:5–7). Indeed, it was to such "liberated" Africans that the British government and plantocracy first looked to secure indentureds for work on the plantations after emancipation (Warner-Lewis 1996:29).

The system was increasingly corrupted by the sway of economic interests. For example, the period of time required for newly liberated persons to be given to decide whether to indenture themselves while in port at Freetown, Sierra Leone, was progressively decreased at the same time that the length of indentureship crept up from one year in 1842 to five years in 1863 (Warner-Lewis 1991:12–13). Overall, various factors militated against development of black indentureship on a truly large scale, and very few of these Africans were repatriated to Africa. Still, this thirty-year labor experiment had considerable implications for the development of local culture and popular ritual traditions.

By the turn of the nineteenth century, increasing numbers of such displaced Africans were from Yorubaland due to collapse of the Oyo Empire and endemic civil war and political conflict in the area, which facilitated the increased exportation of Yoruba, Dahomean, and related groups first as slaves then, later, as "liberated" indentured migrants (Childs and Falola 2004). Yoruba refugees and war captives were channeled by the thousands through several ports on the Slave Coast, a two-hundred–mile stretch along the Bight of Benin between the mouth of the River Volta in today's Ghana and the island of Lagos in Nigeria. While significant numbers of Yorubas landed in Cuba and Brazil, where slavery was still active, a large number of them also found their way to the newly emancipated British colonies of the southern Caribbean. Approximately 14,000 indentured Africans went to British Guiana and about 9,000 arrived in Trinidad, large proportions of which were Yoruba (Trotman 1976). In Trinidad, they were able to cluster in ethnolinguistic enclaves for a time, ensuring some degree of group solidarity, economic independence, coordinated family life, and symbolic reproduction (Elder 1970; Warner-Lewis 1991, 1994, 1996; Trotman 2007).

With regard to religion, several factors seem to have facilitated the reproduction of orisha-based forms of ecstatic worship in this context. First, there are polytheistic resonances between the orisha pantheon and the array of saints within Catholicism. Indeed, historically, many so-called Shango practitioners have not seen their religiosity as mutually exclusive from, or necessarily contradictory to, Catholicism. While the nature of this syncretic dynamism has become a source of contention among scholars and practitioners, it is incontrovertible that some kind of creolizing process unfolded, incorporating elements of both the Yoruba and the Catholic religions.

Second, long-standing intraclass conflict between the French plantocracy and English bureaucracy for control of colonial society in nineteenth-century Trinidad made convenient allies of Francophone planters and grassroots Blacks, benefiting Yoruba religious practices in various ways. In 1883, for example, Franco-creoles supported the fight against a colonial ordinance banning drumming and related activities central to African ritual life (Trotman 1976:11).

Moreover, the demographic significance of free colored Catholics who came to Trinidad in response to the cédulas—many with slaves—may well have facilitated the "retention" of Africanisms more than their European counterparts.

Fourth, the relative recency of Yoruba immigration into the colony bolstered the infusion of orisha ritualism in its diasporic home (R. Thompson 1983; H. Drewal et al. 1989; Mintz and Price 1992).

Finally, Yoruba religious practices must have been buttressed and reinforced through resonance and cross-fertilization with Dahomeans, whose belief system was quite similar to the Yoruba and who were strongly represented among Afro-Franco-Catholic slave transfers to the island several generations before (Trotman 1976, 2007; Warner-Lewis 1991, 1994, 1996).[5] Yoruba religious concepts and practices have exhibited an expansively adaptive element of flexibility across varying inter-African and Afro-Christian spaces of interface in local history, as we shall see. Yoruba religious culture, therefore, has not only had a profound influence well beyond its original, nineteenth-century parameters, but for many more recently, it has become the privileged paradigm for conceptualizing the African legacy in Trinidad and Tobago altogether.

Overall, the field of religion evolved into a complex and contested local continuum characterized by stratification rooted in race and class, with status and mobility measured vis-à-vis degrees of approximation to an idealized Euro-standard. African and Afro-creole religious forms—castigated as primitive and backward—were glossed as "obeah" and rebuked as demonology, witchcraft, or superstition by the plantocracy and colonial government. The etymology of *obeah* seems to derive from Akan (Ghanaian) concepts concerning magical or mystical power (Patterson 1967; Barrett 1974). Yet, as Dianne Stewart notes, "while the etymological origin of the term *obeah* situates it within the cultural context of the Asante and Fante Twi–speaking populations of Ghana, it is probable that obeah has evolved to include beliefs and practices from other West African ethnic groups." Even so, there is also a substantial gap between "obeah" understood as a complex of black practices on the ground and as a derogatory imperial discourse (see A. Richardson 1997 on the latter).

Anti-obeah sentiments emerged most forcefully and punitively *after* emancipation, reflecting the ever-deepening differentiation of Christianity as a hegemonizing sociocultural force in the wake of legal freedom. After all, sectarian evangelicals and nonconformists may have been abolitionists, but they were hardly anticolonialists. Postemancipation Christianization as a "civilizing" mission was intensified not only by competition between Catholicism and Anglicanism in Trinidad, but also by other competing groups as the century progressed, such as Wesleyans, Presbyterians, Baptists, and Moravians, who trailed in numbers and complained about the moral laxity of the Catholic clergy and the unequal distribution of state funds for religious work.

Yet despite this missionary work and what appears to be somewhat rapid black conversion to Christianity in the emancipation period, complaints about the prevalence of African religious rites nonetheless mounted throughout the nineteenth century. Elites were uninterested in nuanced distinctions, viewing black religiosity with fear and suspicion. *Obeah* was legally defined in Ordinance 6 of 1868 as "every pretended assumption of supernatural power of knowledge whatever, for fraudulent or illicit purposes or for gain or for the injury of any person" (Trotman 1986:223). Though the legal code emphasized use of magic for the purpose of making money, in practice the law was used and abused much more broadly in reference to any religious or ritual practices considered "African." Those convicted of the crime of practicing obeah were sentenced for up to six months in prison and/or subject to as many as thirty-six lashes with a whip. However, witnesses were difficult to solicit, and the authorities relied on police entrapment or the possession of certain paraphernalia as proof of involvement in obeah, leading to harassment and numerous miscarriages of justice (Trotman 1986:224–26). As Trotman observes, "describing all obeah as fraudulent and defining it so broadly that obeah included all rites of African origin criminalized African religion, made participation in the rites dangerous, undermined its authority and respect, and effectively reduced its potential as the organizing base for an attack on the hegemony of the planters" (228).

Colonial authorities also denigrated other aspects of black expressive culture. Wakes were often boisterous affairs and considered evidence of primitivism by the middle and upper classes. Similar sentiments prevailed in relation to "drum dances" as well as black celebration of Christian holidays such as Christmas and All Saints' Day, and black musical practices became subject to legal restrictions throughout the nineteenth century. Laws passed in the 1870s made the playing of drums, gongs, tambours (bamboo percussive sticks), *chac-chacs* (gourd rattles), and several other instruments illegal between 10 p.m. and 6 a.m. without obtaining prior police permission. "Bongo" or "drum" dances were deemed illegal at any time without police license (Brereton 1979:160).

Though aimed especially at repressing unruly lower-class black Carnival activity, Ordinance 11 of 1883 struck a serious blow at Afro-creole religiosity by making it illegal for groups of people to assemble for drumming and singing (Trotman 1976:15). Two subsequent ordinances passed early in 1884 gave the colonial governor power to prohibit by proclamation public processions, drum beating, and any "disorderly" assembly of ten or more persons wielding sticks or other paraphernalia that could ostensibly be construed as a weapon (Brereton 1979:173).

Much of this anti-obeah legislation was consolidated in the Summary Offenses Act of 1921. This law exerted dominating effects and became the basis of serious political contention in the postcolonial era. It was only somewhat recently—in the Miscellaneous Laws Act of 2000—that obeah infractions were removed from Trinidad and Tobago's national legal code, but this was hedged by substituting an offense of obtaining money "by any fraudulent means" (Paton 2009:16).

I approach the complex and evolving spectrum of Afro-creole religiosity with an understanding of "Christian" and "African" as explicit—or visible—interlocutors in cultural history, however unjustly the cards were stacked in the Euro-Christian direction. African symbolism and ritual praxis have been historically subordinated and pushed to the ideological margins of social life, yet this seems to have been repression destined to return. Relatively independent cult activity such as Myalism, Kumina, and Revival Zion in Jamaica or Comfa in Guyana or Shango and Spiritual Baptism throughout the eastern Caribbean have flourished among the rural and urban proletariat and the lower classes, while the more established churches became the province of smallholders and the petite bourgeoisie.

Yet whereas African cultural forms came to represent the negative ideal, the "lowest" in colonial societies such as Jamaica, St. John, or Barbados, the playing field was given a complexifying twist in places like Guyana and Trinidad with the introduction of relatively massive numbers of South Asian indentured laborers for three-quarters of a century after emancipation. Their "Oriental" culture and "heathen" religions symbolized the lowest-of-the-low, including for Christian Blacks, for whom Indian religion became a convenient scapegoat for their own conflicted ambivalences. Indeed, it was only with time and much effort that Hinduism and Islam came to garner any respectable status in the southern Caribbean.

Enter the East/West Indians

Thus we return to postemancipation labor schemes and the successive introduction of almost 144,000 East Indian migrants from South Asia to Trinidad between 1845 and 1917. Although many fell prey to unscrupulous and misleading recruiting tactics, most Indians willingly indentured themselves for a variety of reasons. The voyage by sea from South Asia took three months, and the overall system was characterized by faults, abuses, and hypocrisies (see Brereton 1974b, 1981; La Guerre 1974; Tinker 1974; Dabydeen and Samaroo 1987, 1996; Vertovec 1992; Munasinghe 2001a; Khan 2004).

The great majority of indentured laborers—roughly 90 percent—came from the Gangetic plains of northeastern India, having sailed through the Bengali port of Kolkata en route to the Americas. Bhojpuri Hindi became the predominant language among East Indian migrants, so much so that nonspeakers learned it. A complex mix of people from varying caste backgrounds arrived, yet there is no clear consensus as to the exact nature of their demographics vis-à-vis caste distribution. Though a majority were Hindu, with a smaller but significant minority of Muslims among them, the most important early distinction made by and about the indentured Indians concerned whether they were northerners who had sailed through Kolkata versus southerners via the port of Madras on the coast of Tamil Nadu: Kolkatiya versus Madrassi.

By 1854, the indentureship system was characterized by a long contract and maintained by legal sanctions that made breaking a contract a criminal offense. Recruits were legally unfree during the period of indenture, and—after 1895—a portion of the return passage to India had to be paid by the indentured servant should he or she decide to quit the Caribbean at the termination of the contract. This system of indentureship finally came to an end only at the behest of the Indian government (G. Lewis 1968:200), just before the outbreak of World War I.[6]

Colonial discipline, accompanied by frequent prosecution by employers and wretched living conditions, saturated the lives of indentured migrants. These factors presented considerable challenges to establishing a stable family life, initially exacerbated by a high male-to-female demographic ratio disparity, problems originally faced by Africans as well. The majority of immigrants ended up settling permanently and, as early as 1860, both indentured and, increasingly, free Indians became the backbone of Trinidad's plantation labor force. Indeed, economic survival of sugar in the nineteenth century was largely due to Indian labor. Thus, while they also eventually enriched the economy through nonagricultural means, the "special contribution" of Indians was to agriculture, with many leaving the plantations to become independent peasant farmers (Brereton 1974b:27). Many also took up work in cacao after 1880.

Thus an important overall dimension of Indian experience in late-nineteenth and early-twentieth-century Trinidadian society was the formation of a vibrant peasant class. They formed villages and have been characterized as pioneers in cultivation, although they were marginalized from important sectors of public culture and the emergent civil society. In spite of segregation and the lowly status of the Indian population, profound sociocultural changes nonetheless unfolded—including the loss of effective distinctions and patterns of social organization based on caste—as the population was brought within the framework of colonial social relations (B. Schwartz 1964; R. Smith and Jayawardena 1967; Jayawardena 1968; Ramesar 1994; Khan 1995, 2004; Munasinghe 2001a; Seesaran 2002). Raymond Smith (1959, 1996) observes that plantation labor proved itself compatible with markedly different patterns of domestic and familial organization, which is relevant for understanding the local history of religion as well.[7]

The structural position Indians occupied in colonial society was an inherently antagonistic one vis-à-vis that of the black populace. The goal of fostering "racially" segmented labor competition was explicit in the intentions of planters and the metropolitan Parliament members, who legalized indentureship. Indeed, the massive infusion of Indian labor crushed whatever hopes and moderate privileges former slaves might have garnered with the end of apprenticeship. Colonial planters rationalized their legitimation of contract labor through an assault on the ills of "Negro" character.

Thus the entry of Indians into nineteenth-century Trinidad not only deflated wages, but also diminished job opportunities for, and exacerbated negative stereotypes about, black laborers. Expansion of sugar cultivation supported by the indentured labor boost led to Blacks being evicted from the land on which they squatted. Moreover, the problem of financing the indenture system was another serious bone of contention, since local taxes were levied in order to subsidize the scheme. Afro-creole laborers saw Indians as "scavengers" who compromised their own leverage. Black frustration found a scapegoat in "coolies," with their inferior culture and religion (Samaroo 1974; Look Lai 1993). For its part, the new migrant labor force was more easily manipulated and controlled by colonial elites than was the local labor force.

These structural dynamics were digested by the social system in the form of ideological prototypes. Munasinghe (2001a:64) writes: "Many of the stereotypes of Creoles [Africans] and East Indians that were propagated primarily by the plantocracy in the immediate aftermath of slavery were selectively internalized and used later by both Creoles and East Indians for their own purposes" (see also Brereton 1974a, 1979). Such stereotypes were exacerbated by the legal differentiation and spatial isolation of Indians in relation to the wider society, a judicial system heavily weighted in favor of elites, occupational segregation and prejudice, and the ideological representation of Indians as outsiders, that is, as "East" rather than "West" Indians. Africans and Indians were subjected—and coadapted—to differing ideologies of racial subordination in colonial society, both of which have had long-term implications for the development of nationalism and the politics of colonial and postcolonial state power in the twentieth century, as Daniel Segal (1989, 1993, 1994) has shown.

Trinidad's Indian community underwent fundamental growth and development during the final few decades of the nineteenth century. Whereas Indo-creoles made up only 16.5 percent of the total Indo-population in 1871, by 1901, they constituted 44.8 percent—nearly equivalent to the India-born. By the early years of the twentieth century, most Indians were off of estates, living in villages and scattered settlements as small cultivators. The center of cultural gravity within the Indian population gradually shifted from indentured labor in sugar to peasant proprietorship, and a settled community emerged that was recognized as such by the rest of society. "East Indians" therefore established themselves as permanent even though they continued to be seen as outsiders by everyone else (Brereton 1981:chap. 6).

The official colonial posture toward Hinduism and Islam was one of bias and condescension: Indians were seen by elites as the heathen part of the population. Hence government subsidies were made exclusively to Christian denominations. Neither Muslim nor Hindu marriages were fully legalized until the 1930s and 1940s, respectively, which meant the vast majority of Indian children during the colonial era were technically illegitimate. Very few Indian children received any form of schooling before 1870, attributable not simply to their exclusion from the schools but also to parental reluctance to have their children converted to Christianity (Brereton 1974b:28). This changed with the coming of the Canadian Presbyterian Mission to the island in 1868. The Presbyterian school system became a conduit for upwardly mobile socialization and partial

integration into the rest of society. Indeed, most of the island's first Indian no-
tables were affiliated with Presbyterianism (see Ramesar 1994; Seesaran 2002).

It is only with this context in mind that we may appreciate the fact that most
Indians in the late nineteenth and early twentieth centuries actively resisted
Christianization in the face of persistent prejudice against "inferior" Islam
and—even more so—"idolatrous" Hinduism. Despite the best efforts of missionaries, only about 12 percent of the local Indian population had converted
to Christianity by 1921. "For the Indians, religion provided psychological protection, a sense of self-worth with which to arm themselves against the contempt of the society. The pundits and the imams became influential leaders of
the Indian community because they could offer this kind of psychological aid"
(Brereton 1981:112). The language of becoming here is crucial not only because
the colonial environment did not facilitate non-Christian forms of religiosity or
affiliation, but also because the communal roles of Hindu pandit and Muslim
imam did not come fully into their own until well into the twentieth century.

Indian community development underwent two broad phases in the first
half of the twentieth century: a first, more straightforwardly political phase lasting until around 1930, followed by a second phase based more fundamentally
upon religious identities (Campbell 1974). Thus, although Hindu and Muslim
religious figures were operative on the ground throughout the indentureship
period, the explicitly East Indian organizations that emerged among the incipiently mobile after the turn of the twentieth century were primarily political in nature and backgrounded the distinction between Hindu and Muslim,
just as early migrants had also done in their privileging of Kolkatiya-Madrassi
distinctions.

Yet after 1930, the majority of Indocentric associations became more religious and differentiated by a mutually exclusive distinction between Hindu and
Muslim (Khan 1995, 2004). Kusha Haraksingh (1985) emphasizes the influence
of labor activism and trade unionist politics on the post-1930s efflorescence of
Indian religious associations.

The complexity of such long-term processes of change and differentiation are
exemplified by the transoceanic transfer and recontextualizing development of
Hindu ritual traditions from both north and south India. From a society-wide
historical perspective, ecstatic Shakti Puja has been transformed from an assortment of openly practiced ritual performances observed on behalf of communities to a marginalized, somewhat clandestine therapeutic ritual carried
out weekly on behalf of individuals and families in peripheral contemporary
temples dedicated primarily to Mother Kali and her most important spiritual
associates. During the period of indentureship (1845–1917), ritual supplications

in honor of "de Mudda"—the Mother, as she is often called—were an important aspect of village-based pujas within the sacred calendars of many local communities. But these forms of practice became progressively marginalized within the Indo-creole community throughout the twentieth century and have come to be looked upon with mixed degrees of ambivalence, contempt, and fear by the society at large, Hindus and non-Hindus alike. Despite the fact that Shakti Worship has undergone revitalization since the 1970s in a new form of temple devoted specifically to ecstatic puja, these are subaltern practices enacted on the margins of an ostensibly mainstream Caribbean Hinduism.

Contemporary temple-based Shakti Worship has many syncretic influences, including older, community-based, sacrificial Kali Puja brought by indentured migrants and the vintage Madrassi fire-walking ceremony, among others. Specifying the heterogeneous and hybridized origins of contemporary temple-based Shakti Puja is important because it has most often been attributed to the low-caste, dark-skinned Madrassi emigrants from south India alone. This local-origin ideology seems to reflect a scapegoating impulse in relation to the vested interests of an emergent twentieth-century, respectable Hindu orthodoxy. To be sure, there is no question of an important Madrassi influence upon contemporary Shakti Puja on the island, but the complexities and partialness of this influence have been elided within the mystifying reductionism of the Madrassi origin ideology, as we will see.[8]

This ideology of Kali Puja's origin derives some of its biased historical force from anti-Madrassi prejudice prevalent among nineteenth-century planters. Yet more importantly, it was a product of the larger Hindu community's project of forging an orthodox or official Hinduism in response to critical Christian currents within colonial society that saw Indian religion as heathen idolatry. The disempowered diasporic situation of being a criticized minority religion within a heterogeneous, stratified, colonial island society seems to have precipitated a sense of insecurity and self-consciousness about beliefs and practices among Hindus in Trinidad, and this would have made them more inclined to dissociate themselves from ritual practices such as fire walking, animal sacrifice, or spirit mediumship—deemed primitive or pagan and therefore despicable within a purportedly respectable frame of reference.

Steven Vertovec (1992, 1996) observes that the growth of an "orthodox" Hinduism was facilitated by attenuation of the caste system in the Caribbean, where caste could never be transplanted as a *system* of social structure, economic relations, and ritual hierarchy. What happened from the late nineteenth century onward was the gradual reorganization and consolidation of diverse beliefs and practices brought from various parts of India into a sort of generalized, more standardized type of Hindu sociocultural system in the New World. As Haraksingh (1986, 1988) emphasizes, the immigrant Indian population was more diverse than has usually been supposed, but in the "collapsed" space of Trinidad, people who would not normally have met each other in the ancestral land engaged in a highly compacted jostling for status and dominance. Instead of leveling, the result was a "leavening" process in which beliefs and practices from varying localities and communities in India were submerged and reformulated in relation to one another in their New World context.

But attenuation of the caste system in the West Indies did not produce the demise of "caste" altogether. Hinduism and caste ideology have been simplified under the rough, oppositional principles of "high"/"low," "pure"/"impure," and "Brahmin"/"Chamar" (Vertovec 1992, 1996; Khan 1995, 2004; Samaroo 1996; Munasinghe 2001a): protean categories constrained and mediated by the contingencies of local power relations. "Chamar" originally referred to a demographically large, low-caste group in India who worked traditionally as cobblers in the leather-working trades and were therefore considered ritually unclean. However, the term has been broadened throughout much of the Indian diaspora to refer derogatorily to low-caste persons more generally. Structural transformations reflected by these categorical modifications enabled aspiring Indians to take advantage of the overseas experience by shedding previous caste connections and elevating themselves as New World higher castes of a sort.

The overwhelming majority of indentured immigrants came from north rather than south India, and the evolution of Indo-creole culture is deeply conditioned by this fact. For example, earlier binarisms of high-low, Brahmin-Chamar, and Kolkatiya-Madrassi have been further condensed, as reflected in the contemporary discursive practice among Indians positing Hindu versus Madrassi. When invoked, "Hindu" connotes high-caste, Brahmin, north Indian, and respectable, whereas "Madrassi" is associated with low-caste, Chamar, and darker, south Indian primitivity.

The development of a standardized Hinduism accelerated in the 1920s in response to reformist Arya Samaj missionaries from India and consolidated much of its support among conservative rural Hindus. By mid-century, the Sanatan Dharma Maha Sabha (SDMS) was formed out of two rival Sanatanist organizations, and this body has exerted enormous sociopolitical influence through the course of the twentieth century via temple-based and school-building efforts. A Sanatanist is a follower of Sanatan Dharma, usually translated as "eternal duty," "order," or "religion" and used in reference to a neo-Hindu paradigm that evolved through complex engagement with colonialism and globalization in South Asia and its diaspora (see Forbes 1987; Vertovec 1992; Khan 1995, 2004).

In their search for legitimacy and the gradual forging of a respectable ortho-dox Hinduism, the larger Caribbean Hindu community—or at least a signifi-cantly influential group among them—internalized values espoused by colonial elites and adopted them as their own moral terms of reference. Significantly, this orthodoxy has sought to dissociate itself from religious modalities that smack of morally suspect, primitive practices such as blood sacrifice and trance performance, or that fall under the aegis of a seemingly undomesticated, inde-pendent, female goddess. Where the elimination of these has not been feasible, the strategy seems to have been to marginalize them as low practices connected with the darker-skinned Madrassi legacy.

Religion thus became an important, if variable, idiom for refashioning com-munity and culture within the wider contexts of class stratification and racial segmentation as well as in the intracommunity forms of conflict and differen-tiation that emerged among Indo-creoles in Trinidad. These "fissiparous ten-dencies," as Khan (1995:131) describes them, exacerbated by factionalism and the emphasis community leaders came to place on religion, partly weakened the Indian population. Paradoxically, then, the mobility and resourcefulness that facilitated the cultivation of a broader Indian form of ethnic consciousness also facilitated further differentiation and conflict as well (Khan 2004).

All of this is complicated by the fact that Christianity retained hegemony as the dominating cultural barometer of legitimacy and social status throughout the colony. For example, an influential leader of one of the Maha Sabha's two institutional precursors—the Couva-based Sanatan Dharma Association, of-ficially incorporated in 1932 but with roots stretching back to 1881—was an An-glican, the Hon. Michael Sarran Teelucksingh (Samaroo 1987). In addition, the secretary-general for the Maha Sabha, Satnarayan Maharaj, informed me that the organization's mid-century founders used the Catholic Church as an insti-tutional role model. Presbyterianism, the most dramatic early vehicle of Indian ascendance within the colonial social hierarchy, is one of the least ambivalently embraced elements of local Indian history.

Thus there was deep, incipient class bias within the emergent conscious-ness of the colonial Indian community, based on a complex constellation of racial, religious, and political factors and which entailed a failure on the part of Christian Indians to forge links with village imams and pandits as grassroots leaders. Christianity has therefore exerted a centrifugal force vis-à-vis Indo-creoles, pulling ethnic traditions away from the early core of Indian experi-ence in complex and recursive ways. It has operated historically more as "invis-ible interlocutor" (Khan 1995:141–42) in the constitution and reconstitution of Indo-Trinidadian culture and consciousness.

Colony into Nation

In order to fully appreciate twentieth-century developments, especially the cultural politics of nationalism and decolonization after World War II, we must return to the political economy of the postemancipation era. Because Trinidad developed so late compared with other British West Indian tropical plantation colonies, it was relatively immature as a slave society on the eve of emancipation and its demographics unique (Higman 1978).

Whereas the slave proportion of the population topped 90 percent in other West Indian societies by 1810, it was 67 percent in Trinidad (Brereton 1981:77). An astonishing number of Coloreds and even some Blacks owned slaves. Moreover, whereas the ratio of free colored to slave in Barbados in 1786 was 1:74, and 1:63 in Jamaica in 1787, in Trinidad that figure was 1:2 by 1797 (Dhanda 2002:234). Additionally, slaves lived and worked in relatively small holdings. In 1834, the average owner held just 7 slaves, with only 1 percent of the plantocracy holding over 100. An unusually high proportion of slaves lived and operated in urbanizing areas of the island. Fewer than 21,000 slaves were emancipated overall. Many of them were domestics, women, and children. This meant that a small force of field laborers contrasted with a vast abundance of uncultivated land at emancipation.

Legal freedom was largely nominal. Former slaves occupied a position of "virtual serfdom" (Brereton paraphrasing American journalist William Sewell) in their postemancipation world. They experienced little economic security or political autonomy. This new dispensation encouraged departure from the estates in order to seek smallholding, yet also presented incentive for maintaining plantation connections via seasonal wage labor. By 1846, only 40 percent of the former slave group continued to reside on estates. Regardless of trajectory, however, the majority of former slaves maintained their livelihood in agriculture, acquiring or squatting on land as well as engaging in part-time wage labor. Many lived in emergent circumplantation villages throughout the agriculturally developed areas. Some left agriculture, and a few became traders or petty shopkeepers, spurring further townification throughout the island.

Problems of land and squatting intensified in the decades after emancipation and came to a head in the late 1860s. Gov. A. H. Gordon, adopting a policy of offering the sale of land to squatters residing on it, intervened by making the sale of Crown lands easier and much cheaper. This development was inaugurated by a successful experiment in the central ward of Montserrat, where Afro-creoles; black West Indian migrants from Grenada and Barbados; indentured Yoruba, Ashanti, Mandingo, and Kongo African migrants; and Spanish-creole *peones* from Venezuela either bought their holdings or were resettled on comparable land made available for purchase. Additionally, by 1869, Crown lands began to be offered to time-expired Indians in lieu of return passage back to India. A vibrant black peasantry had been established by the mid-nineteenth century, with an Indian analogue not far behind. As lands were sold, cultivation spread, progressively transforming Trinidad's untamed wilderness into increasingly wide swaths of agricultural lands and, in turn, prompting further development of the island's infrastructure.

The changing political and economic winds in nineteenth-century Trinidad produced demographic patterns in which an urban-based, female-biased population became more Afro-creole whereas the rural, circumplantation population was more Indo-creole and male-biased (Trotman 1986). Lower-class urban conditions were hardly better than their rural counterparts. Both spawned disease and violence. Urbanization and slumification developed with rural-to-urban as well as immigrant-from-outside migration. The urban proletariat must therefore be seen as a corollary to the reconstituted peasantry of the countryside (Brereton and Yelvington 1999:10–13).

Thus social life through the nineteenth century became increasingly more complex, precipitating institutional and occupational differentiation in the civil service, professions, lower-level management, commerce, and the like. Continuity and change were both increasingly mediated by the development of education. Indeed, Trinidad's educational system grew and expanded, but only gradually and with conflicts as well as contradictions.

Education from the 1870s until the 1920s was characterized by institutional expansion and curriculum development. The century after emancipation saw considerable social mobility achieved through education, with public culture and political discourse increasingly animated by the changing social consciousness and confidence of those entitled by learning and literacy. This upward mobility of Coloreds, Blacks, and, eventually, Indians via schooling, along with the ability of the expanding educational system to simultaneously transform and reproduce class relations over time, meant that society remained stratified but never static.

Elementary education in the nineteenth century was valued for spreading Christianity and social control at large, whereas secondary education was restricted to two elite schools in Port-of-Spain (Campbell 1992:54–55). St. Mary's College initially outran Queen's Royal College in enrollment, since the Franco-creole Catholic community was more numerous than the Anglo-creole Protestant one early on. Indo-creoles were not brought fully into the mainstream of education and civil society until well after World War II. It is with this context in mind that we may understand the rise of Indian leaders from the late 1920s and 1930s determined to establish separate Hindu and Muslim schools and halt the slow advance of Christianity.

Some of the earliest twentieth-century proponents of self-government connected nationalistic strivings with educational reform and development—including a less imperial curriculum. What distinguishes the developmental path of education in Trinidad and Tobago vis-à-vis the wider Commonwealth Caribbean since the mid-nineteenth century has been the view that education should be intentionally used as an integrative force in society. Indeed, it is in Trinidad more than anywhere else in the nineteenth-century British West Indies that government action in education was used specifically in pursuit of social integration (Campbell 1992:96).

The emergence of nationalism in the mid-twentieth century must therefore be seen in light of longer-term processes of class differentiation and social mobility facilitated by access to formal education. The gradual rise of, first, colored and, then, black middle classes increasingly challenged and eventually overtook the Euro-creole monopoly on political power and intellectual leadership in the colony. The colonial governor appointed Trinidad and Tobago's first black member of the Legislative Council—C. P. David—in 1904.[9] Indeed, those with an incipiently new kind of black consciousness, whose outlook contrasted with that of preceding generations, began to coalesce by the turn of the twentieth century.

Alvin Magid (1988) examines developments in the immediate pre–World War I period as a staging ground for the evolution of a decolonizing nationalism after the war. A provisional sort of anticolonial political culture grew out of the parochial issue of municipal governance in Port-of-Spain. Crown Colony rule—in which the Legislative Council had no locally elected seats—had stimulated resentment and provoked increasingly confrontational political strategies. The economy was mostly extractive and foreign-dominated, characterized by chronically high levels of under- and unemployment and high food prices. These conditions made for popular discontent concerning public welfare, health, sanitation, and education and triggered strikes and disturbances. Social mobility had begun to produce a revolution of rising expectations while ethnic tensions simmered below the surface.

Until World War I, opposition politics revolved around the more conservative reformism promulgated by Whites and Coloreds from a privileged economic and professional base. Ironically, however, the deficiencies of their efforts only served to advance the radicalizing push for constitutional change (Magid 1988:217). Thus Whites dominated political struggle less and less after

World War I. As Gordon Lewis observes, "It was symptomatic of the absence of any deeply felt all-Trinidadian sense that it was not the plantocracy nor the mercantile-professional groups, but the colonial working class that became after 1918 the chief element leading the self-government movement" (1968:201). This evolving "urban nationalism"—to invoke Magid—fed into the decolonizing nationalism of the post–World War I era.

Seen in retrospect, Trinidad and Tobago's experience during the first half of the twentieth century, leading to independence from Britain in 1962, was characterized, first, by the rise and fall of politics centered on trade unionism and the labor movement, and, second, by the emergence of party-based mass electoral politics based on universal adult suffrage. These roller coasterish years were punctuated by serious labor riots in 1937—one giant wave in a larger sea of labor unrest throughout the region during the Great Depression—and then amplified by Trinidad's direct involvement in World War II.

Mixed as they were, dynamics unleashed by the U.S. presence after 1940 helped usher the twin-island society into a new era of mass electoral politics. Indeed, the postwar period was a challenging transitional one in Trinidad and Tobago's sociopolitical evolution. The end of war in 1945 made way for new developments in the labor movement, as many thousands of workers were displaced by completion of the American bases in 1944. Moreover, the postwar period brought rapid inflation and worker dissatisfaction, generating considerable labor unrest as well as interunion conflict and fragmentation.

Meanwhile, a debate had emerged over extending the franchise as well as eligibility for election to political office. Progress on each of these matters was accomplished by the end of the war, but not without intense debate over English-literacy restrictions on voting (which did not ultimately pass) and property and income restrictions on membership in the Legislative and Executive councils (which, tellingly, did pass). The 1945 order incorporating new constitutional changes extended the vote to all adults over twenty-one years of age without any language qualification, as the proposed English-only restriction had been exposed as a pernicious maneuver designed to marginalize older Indians. Thus TT entered an era of mass electoral politics with the 1946 elections, the first to be held under universal adult suffrage. These elections witnessed debilitating fragmentation of the labor vote, clearing the way for subsequent middle-class domination of the political sphere.

Progressive nationalists began arguing almost immediately for further reform. Through the efforts of a constitutional reform committee set up in 1947 and the workings of those involved in the 1948 Majority Report, a transitional, quasi-ministerial constitution bestowing elected members a clear majority in both councils for the first time was hammered out and became law in 1950. As in 1946, an assortment of politicians and organizations geared up for the 1950 elections, and the new constitution was attacked by an overlapping assortment of labor, radical, and nationalist factions. But again—as in 1946—the elections of 1950 witnessed proliferating political fragmentation. The trade-unionist party of Tubal Uriah Butler—a black, charismatic, deeply religious, nonradical, Anglophile, migrant Grenadian labor leader who emerged onto the political stage during the labor unrest of the 1930s—fared better than any other. Yet no united progressive coalition emerged.

Political maneuvering subsequently allowed the bourgeois establishment to marginalize Butler and his party's influence in politics during the 1950s, the very years in which Eric Williams launched his People's National Movement (PNM) onto center stage. And the contrast is instructive: Butler's was a fiery, grassroots worldview with religious overtones, whereas Williams was an Oxford-trained historian whose intellectual charisma and respectable style signaled the arrival of West Indian "Doctor Politics," a term coined by Lloyd Best in the late 1960s (Best 1985; Sutton 1991). Led by Williams, the PNM became the first party to gain a majority of elected seats in the Legislative Council and formed the first ministerial government. However, though the PNM campaigned on a platform of multiethnic nationalism—its charter claiming that it was "a convention of all for all, a mobilization of all the forces in the community, cutting across race and religion, class and color, with emphasis on united action by all the people in the common cause" (quoted in Brereton 1981:234)—the party's opponents frequently attacked it as the "Pure Negro Movement" (Segal 1989:15).

Relying heavily on the development policy ideas of W. Arthur Lewis (1950), Williams's government launched the first of its Five Year Plans in 1958, emphasizing new industrialization through foreign investment, "modernization" of the national infrastructure by the state, as well as secularization and expansion of the education system. From the 1950s to the 1980s, the political story was almost singularly that of the PNM, first as a government under the modified post–World War II Crown Colony regime and then as the inaugural government of the independent postcolonial state in 1962.

Treating this plotline as Williams's one-man show is understandable: "A brilliant Island Scholar, an outstanding West Indian Oxonian as his autobiographical sketch—*A Colonial at Oxford*—shows, faculty member at Howard University and, later, research secretary of the Caribbean Commission, his academic record as the outstanding authority on Caribbean history fitted him perfectly for his entry into politics; an entry partly the result of choice, partly something forced upon him by the hostility shown toward him, as a West Indian, by the expatriate officials of the imperialist body of the Anglo-American Caribbean Commission, described in his public lecture of 1955, 'My Relations with the Caribbean Commission, 1943–1955'" (G. Lewis 1968:212). The "Doc" was a most compelling public intellectual, giving countless lectures and charismatically weaving critical scholarly insight and political rhetoric. His oratory transformed one of Port-of-Spain's most central plazas into the "University of Woodford Square"—which still operates to this day on a less focal, more organic basis. Indeed, as "Father of the Nation," Williams engineered a remarkable marriage between the colored Afro-creole intellectual and the colonial crowd, for whom he attained the status of demigod.[10]

Though an embryonic national consciousness had long been in the making, the period between 1956 and 1962 catalyzed a fresh new mushrooming of nationalism. Winning first in 1956, the PNM consolidated its earlier victory in the election of 1961, by which time the anti-PNM posture of conservative French and Portuguese creoles, the British colonial enclave, the Chamber of Commerce, and even the Catholic Church had more or less subsided. Williams then turned his attention, David and Goliath–style, toward three main external opponents: the West Indian federal government; the Colonial Office; and the Americans. Ironically, Williams's strong Hamiltonian federalism—as compared with the weak Jeffersonian federalism of Jamaica's Michael Manley—had the paradoxical effect of stirring up strong nationalist sentiment in TT (see G. Lewis 1968:chaps. 14–15, on the failed experiment in West Indian federation after World War II). All three battles only served to fortify Williams.

Yet the end of colonialism resulted as much from accelerating British retreat from empire as it did from the PNM's nationalist offensive. Like emancipation more than a century before, formal independence may have been pivotal, yet it involved no especially radical transformation of life on the ground. In many ways the transition led quite directly from colonialism to neocolonialism. Independence must be seen as having transformed the nationalist struggle with an external metropolitan colonial power into an internal struggle in the midst of a continuing capitalist society dependent upon economic forces outside itself, in which local elites understood the machinations of politics even better than their former British masters did.

Segal (1989) illustrates how nationalism in TT did not so much establish equality and eradicate differentiation based on race and color with the advent of independence as it *reconfigured* hierarchical distinctions inherited from the colonial era. Colonial inequalities became transmuted into problems of "national development." If the most successful nationalisms are constructions that mythologize sovereign power as "self-rule" and establish an "egalitarian" model

of citizenship and state sovereignty, then West Indian nationalisms—and especially that of TT—have been hobbled from the beginning. "Equality" has not
served to objectify the "nation" (see Ryan 1972 on electoral politics during the
1950s and 1960s).

Compounding all of this is the fact that the economies of the region's former British colonies remained squarely tied to absentee-capitalist industrialization and development, and therefore subject to the changing external winds of
global markets, foreign capital, and financial institutions. "The history of the
Caribbean economies as overseas fiefs controlled by expatriate forces is thereby
perpetuated, with the single difference that the forces are now those of the modern multi-national business combines. The capacity of the region to break out of
the traditional system is, as a result, gravely compromised" (G. Lewis 1968:408).
In effect, then, nationalist development schemes have proposed to cure the ills
of economic colonialism by, in effect, perpetuating the very conditions that
produced them.

This trend is quintessentially embodied in Trinidad and Tobago by the long-
term shift from King Sugar to Black Gold. By the time of the 1937 labor disturbances, petroleum had become the colony's most valuable export. In 1932, oil
accounted for 50 percent of export earnings. By the end of World War II, oil
accounted for 80 percent of TT's national exports, whereas traditional forms of
estate agriculture—especially sugar and cacao—had suffered serious setbacks.
"Trinidad became a classic petroleum economy, dangerously dependent on oil
for export earnings and for government revenues" (Brereton 1981:214). In fact,
the impetus for the 1937 agitation first arose among workers in the industrial
oil belt of southern Trinidad, a concentrated proletariat easier to organize than
agricultural laborers (179–80).

The island's oil industry functioned under a system of social organization
defined by class and ethnic segmentation of labor. Administrative and technical
staff were mostly European, drillers tended to be Americans, and the semi- and
unskilled laborers were local or immigrant West Indians. It was not until the
industry's second boom period, during World War II, that significant numbers
of locals began to enter supervisory positions. By that time, oil had come to
dominate the national economy even though it employed far fewer people than
were engaged in the agricultural sector. The postwar, preindependence period
(1946–62) became one of growth, with oil surging ahead of other industries due
to new exploitation of marine fields.

Apart from oil, the most significant postwar economic development was the
emergence of a local manufacturing sector resulting from state intervention,
accompanied by significant growth in local financial institutions. The public

sector played an increasingly central role in promoting growth, so much so that nonpetroleum sectors grew faster than oil after World War II, in fact, even though the latter continued to dominate exports (Brereton 1981:221).

Before the 1950s, most goods were imported, leading the quasi-ministerial government of Albert Gomes (preceding the PNM) to adopt "development" plans for "modernization" based on a strategy of industrialization by invitation. This program was influenced by the work of Sir Arthur Lewis and modeled upon the Puerto Rican "Operation Bootstrap" experiment. Despite the effort to distinguish himself from previous politicians, Williams kept a steady rudder with these industrialization schemes. With the coming of political independence, industrialization-by-invitation policies were modified from an emphasis on production for export to import substitution, in which tariff protection facilitated production for the domestic market by new firms (Yelvington 1995:chap. 2). Import substitution and the protection of local producers were supposed to cut into the power of elites as well as produce nontraditional members of the bourgeoisie. However, rather than undercut its interests, industrialization enabled continued dominance by the commercial elite.

Despite economic growth after World War II, a number of industrialization programs had fallen short by 1962, generating neither expanded employment nor structural transformation of the economy. Indeed, industrialization of this sort placed a heavy burden on government finances and increased dependence on foreign capital. Employment creation and foreign exchange earnings were disappointing and manufacturing stimulated little growth in local sectors, since they created very few backward economic linkages. Underemployment, labor unrest, and income inequality all rose during the country's first decade of independence.

Thus TT exhibited wide disparities across various sectors upon independence from Britain. Under- and unemployment increased as the population grew. Manufacturing created relatively few jobs, and oil and agriculture employed decreasing numbers. Additionally, while the importation of foreign services and capital increased, few interconnections were forged between varying sectors within the local economy. This was the reality facing the PNM, the ascendant nationalist party dominated by bourgeois Afro-creole interests that inherited the first democratic government as an independent nation-state in 1962. Revealingly, Trinidad and Tobago subsequently became a republic fourteen years later, during a spectacular oil boom.

Racial Mythology and the Politics of Postcolonial Multiculturalism

Colonial ideology presupposed the entrance of "pure" races into the evolving society, with "mixing" understood as a local phenomenon. Unlike the notion of hypodescent in North America, the West Indian system of racial classification encoded the mixture of blackness and whiteness within a differentiated lexicon of "color." Specific terms cast in an idiom of "shade"—such as "white," "yellow," "red," "brown," "light black," "black," "black black"—circulated as a way of representing perceived phenotypes in relation to relative proportions of "African" and "European" ancestral heritage. Segal writes: "This vocabulary gave a visible presence to the often unknown 'facts' of genealogy. It kept the elemental races of a person's ancestors from disappearing into a vague and distant genealogical mix: it thus brought ancestral races visibly into the present" (1991:8).

Mixing emplotted whiteness through fragmentation and dilution via interaction with blackness, thereby displacing "local" whiteness at increasing levels of remove from an idealized epicenter abroad. Thus the notion of local or Trinidad Whites marks them as tainted ones who pass only superficially for white: shades of varying Afro-Euro mixture represented within the color spectrum pull whiteness centrifugally away from an essentialized metropolitan core. All of this is captured in the concept of "creole" as simultaneously local to the Caribbean and hybrid in origin, used polysemically in relation to Whites, Coloreds, and Blacks (Segal 1989, 1993, 1994). The lexicon of creole mixture dominated discourse about the local social order; it combined certain "races" but did not ultimately alter or eliminate them. Thus upwardly mobile attainment of respectable sociability—especially in relation to class and religion—became a compensatory source of whiteness for non-Whites. As Segal observes, "'respectability' extended the idiom of 'colour' beyond physiognomy to all aspects of personhood, but at the same time, it placed 'blackness' under symbolic erasure" (1989:112).

Colonial representations continually reshaped reality, reproducing racialized public consciousness about hierarchy and status. The creole symbolism of color memorialized interaction between Africans and Europeans while simultaneously representing Indians as unmixable. Indians were never placed on any sort of color continuum with Whites. No category was used to refer to persons of combined Indian and European descent, and no idiom developed in which Indians and Europeans represented endpoints on a continuum of mixture, as with Africans and Europeans. This meant that Indian and non-Indian mixing remained unlexicalized and therefore culturally forgotten beyond the first generation, as compared with the black-white color continuum.

Segal (1989, 1993, 1994), Munasinghe (1997, 2001a, 2001b), and Khan (1995, 2001, 2004) explicate how the polymorphous symbolism of racial purity and mixture is ultimately rooted in differing colonial principles of subordination. Both Africans and Indians were deemed inferior to Europeans but they were inferior in distinct ways: Africans were seen as mixable and, therefore, partly recuperable, through their intermingling with the master race; Indians were considered unmixable and beholden only unto themselves. These principles entailed differentiation in the contrasting symbolism of nonwhite mobility. Afro-creole achievements contested the inferiority of "Negro" but precluded affirmation of blackness, yet socioeconomic achievements did not make Indo-creoles anything other than East Indians.

Underlying these principles of subordination were contrasting ideological stereotypes of the "culturally naked African," which permitted them to become "Creoles" via New World intermixture with whiteness, versus the "culturally saturated Indian," who possessed an ancient and inferior civilization that made Indians ostensibly unmixable. The latter's inferior civilization turned the re-latedness between East Indians and Europeans into an issue of either-or. Af-ricans—supposedly coming from civilizationlessness—were seen within this construction as having been especially deracinated as a result of the Middle Passage.

Ideological exclusion of Indians from Creole status had considerable im-plications for the politics of the decolonization period, with the rise of a mid-dle-class Afro-creole-dominated nationalist movement that inherited political power and the state apparatus, and that appropriated various forms of black popular culture such as Carnival, calypso, and steel band and promoted them as "national" culture (Stuempfle 1995). Domesticating black lower-class cultural forms to middle-class ethos enabled bourgeois Afro-creoles to figure them-selves as the legitimate representatives of all in staking claims to state power. Their nationalism had roots in varying surges of racialized consciousness and pride among Afro-Trinbagonians at home and abroad, stimulated by pan-Afri-canist response to the failure of Western democracies to support Ethiopia when invaded by fascist Italy in 1935 (Yelvington 1999), for example, as well as by a more general West Indian literary and cultural renaissance efflorescing since the 1930s (Brereton 1981:174–75).

A parallel stream of racial consciousness surged among elite Indians in the 1930s as well. Though this vanguard vacillated at times between sectarian and wider nationalistic concerns throughout the first half of the twentieth century, it generally adopted a more conservative stance, and the majority of Indians did *not* identify with the nationalist movement (Munasinghe 2001b:13). Perceptions of East Indian foreignness were amplified by Indo-creole enthusiasm and sup-port for India's own independence movement as well as by increasingly explicit diasporic identifications mediated by regular visits from a host of South Asian missionaries and performing artists, and later by the rise of Bollywood cinema and Indian popular music.

Positioned oppositionally, then, Creoles and East Indians experienced polarizing political trajectories after the Second World War. Eric Williams and his People's National Movement won the 1956 elections, consolidating the momentum toward Afro-creole nationalist control of state power upon independence. Indeed, from their inception, East Indian political parties have been widely perceived as representing not simply communal interests, but also those of Hindus in particular. The PNM's major opponent in 1956 was the People's Democratic Party (PDP), established in 1953 under Bhadase Sagan Maharaj and essentially the political arm of the Hindu community, since in Maharaj were combined the leaderships of the major sugar union, the PDP, and the Maha Sabha, by that time, the most powerful orthodox Hindu organization on the island (Brereton 1981:236).

An Afro-creole, Williams attacked the PDP and Maha Sabha intensely, sometimes unfairly. He succeeded in winning support from Muslim and Christian Indians as well as some urbanized Hindus. These tactics isolated the PDP in rural Indian districts, intensifying the trend in political culture toward division along racial lines driven by party politics. Opposition groups had to form coalitions to contest PNM ascendance, especially since Williams had sidelined the Indian political elite when forming the PNM's first government in 1956. Thus opposition rallied around the newly formed Trinidad Democratic Labor Party (DLP). But Indian leadership from the PDP faction took over the DLP's reins, making Maharaj party leader in 1958. With this, TT's new era of mass electoral politics became fully incarnate as a racially polarized political party system. Indeed, the following elections in 1961—just on the cusp of independence—have been described as the most racialized in history, constructed as an intensely fought struggle between two nonwhite constituencies for political power (Bahadoorsingh 1968; Malik 1971; Ryan 1972; Oxaal 1982).

The fundamental problem has been that *no* West Indian social grouping has represented an image of the sovereign, national people at large. TT elections produce occupants of political office who attempt to act and speak on behalf of the whole, yet in a context characterized by the absence of any clear and unambiguous democratic objectification of citizens as a national group. Electoral minorities are therefore objectified by elections rather than the "nation" as a whole, making nationality a partisan spoil (Segal 1989:192–94).

Ideologically speaking, redemption of Indian subordination has been prefigured as exclusive to one ancestral kind, whereas redemption of African subordination has, in principle, been open-ended. This helped the PNM recruit many more Indian supporters than the PDP and DLP recruited black voters. Yet, in defining his public and appealing for its support in terms of the creole color

continuum, Williams, as their "Racial Messiah," provided a mode of mass identification and redemption more for Africans than Indians (Oxaal 1982). Thus
the symbolic politics of "creole" permitted local Whites, Coloreds, and Blacks
of respectable status to agitate for political power during the nationalist period
using the notion of their creolized autochthony; this led to the increasing appropriation of white power by Afro-creole groups and interests after World
War II. "Williams's representation of 'the nation' as its Chief Minister had the
effect of making Trinidadian nationality a distinction of the electoral grouping
his campaign had instantiated—'the Negro'—and concomitantly, its party—the
PNM" (Segal 1989:216).

Indeed, Munasinghe (2001a) reports that the idea of an East Indian government or prime minister was unthinkable—even among Indians—as late as
the 1980s. Yet an Indian-dominated coalition—the United National Congress
(UNC)—came to power in 1995 with an Indian, Basdeo Panday, at the helm as
prime minister. A series of economic and political developments in the 1970s
and 1980s facilitated the emergence of an Indo-Trinidadian sociocultural renaissance of sorts, part of which included a shift in rhetoric and critique from
expressing sectarian interests to targeting the formerly uncontested privilege of
Afro-Trinbagonian political and cultural power (Khan 2001, 2004; Munasinghe
2001a, 2001b).

Just as importantly, the 1970s brought monumental developments in the oil
and gas sector, leading to the country's oil boom of 1974–83. Relative to the
size of its population, Trinidad possesses phenomenal petroleum resources,
generating a high gross national product (GNP) and an abundance of capital
for investment when compared with many other postcolonial societies (Segal
1989:314–15). Due to increases in the world price of oil, GNP and government
revenues rose astronomically after 1973, with TT accumulating an enormous
trade surplus held almost entirely in hard currency. Moreover, natural gas was
discovered off the north coast in 1971, and 1975 saw both the establishment
of the Point Lisas industrial estate and the formation of the National Gas
Company. In 2000, revenue from crude oil, natural gas, and petrochemicals
accounted for a quarter of the country's gross domestic product (GDP) and
three-quarters of its exports. Indeed, TT is now one of the world's leading
exporters of ammonia and methanol in addition to natural gas. With state
revenues shooting up in the 1970s and early 1980s, capital accumulated from
the petroleum sector was used to bring virtually the entire financial sector of
the economy under national stewardship (Sutton 1984). By the 1980s, every
bank and insurance company was locally owned and managed along with all
infrastructural utilities.

The oil boom years facilitated diversification in the national opportunity structure, most notably, a steady rise in the average monthly income for both racial groups—with the Indian average surpassing the black for the first time (Munasinghe 2001b:20). Yet many Indians nevertheless perceived Africans to have been the main recipients of petrodollars and understood their own good fortune as having been due to their culture rather than the economy. Before the oil boom, there had been only a small Indian middle-class consisting primarily of Christians and Muslims, with the majority of East Indians still poor, rural, and undereducated. Thus the transformation of the boom years proved to be very considerable indeed, with Indians, relative to other groups, experiencing the most significant degree of overall socioeconomic mobility (Reddock 1991). This drove class differentiation and catalyzed heightened ethnic consciousness among Indo- and Afro-Trinbagonians. Munasinghe (2001b:22) writes: "Indo-Trinidadians' rapid incorporation into mainstream society and the decline of their traditional enclaves, such as agriculture, meant that their destinies would be fundamentally determined by the trajectories of the nation and the state."

The stakes were raised in the mid-1980s with increased competition for state resources resulting from steeply declining world oil prices and the traumatizing end of the boom (see Miller 1994, 1997, on consumption patterns and social change during that time). Dr. Williams died unexpectedly in a diabetic coma in 1981 on the cusp of his sixth consecutive term in office and was succeeded by an Afro-creole deputy leader of the PNM, George Chambers. Nonetheless, Indian confidence had been bolstered. Yet, reticence about Indian political power surfaced in the politics of the National Alliance for Reconstruction (NAR), the coalition that delivered the PNM its first defeat in 1986, after thirty years of continuous rule. Despite its majority Indian support and the tenor of its "One Love" platform, the NAR chose A.N.R. Robinson—an Oxford-trained black Tobagonian lawyer—as leader over Panday, then a leading sugar unionist. Internal power struggles exacerbated by deteriorating economic problems eventually pulled the alliance apart, with the most prominent Indian leaders being expelled from the cabinet in 1988. The NAR's tenure in power under Robinson came to a dramatically conclusive close in 1991, with a clear victory for the resuscitated PNM under Patrick Manning, an Afro-creole Protestant from Trinidad, but not before enduring an insurrectionary attempt by a small, but high-profile, Islamist group.

The experience of fallout with the NAR convinced many Indians that they would have to struggle for state power directly and exclusively in order to preclude their continued marginalization and relegation to second-class status in terms of political power. The United National Congress finally took the reins of government with its carefully orchestrated ascendance in elections at the end of 1995, through a last-minute coalition with the NAR. But this time it was Panday who took the lead as prime minister. As I returned to the United States after my longest period of fieldwork, elections were being held again in December of 2000, but results favoring the UNC were contested by the PNM, leading to political stalemate until October 2002, when a decisive victory brought the PNM back into power under Manning. The PNM was again reelected in the elections of 2007.

Yet, the tables turned again in May of 2010, with the "People's Partnership" government coming into power based on a coalition of the UNC, the recently formed Congress of the People (2006), the Tobago Organization of the People, the National Joint Action Committee (NJAC—on which, see chapter 6), and the Movement for Social Justice. Kamla Persad-Bissessar, political leader of the UNC and TT's first female prime minister, leads this government. The People's Partnership has been characterized as a latter-day resurrection of the NAR and rode to power with an overwhelming electoral mandate. Yet signs of friction from within and discontent from without began to surface after less than a year in power.

Ecstasy, Hierarchy, Heterodoxy

An abiding theme here concerns the significance of capitalism—itself a moving target and turbulent engine of change—in shaping the structures and conflicts of social life from economics and politics to religion and popular culture. The sociocultural field of religion evolved into contested local continua characterized by patterns of differentiation conditioned by interacting relations of race and class, with status based on idealized Eurocentric standards cast in an idiom of respectability. Hierarchical principles have proven resilient despite changes in the overt bases of domination over time. The ability of economic and education systems to simultaneously transform and reproduce class relations has meant that society has remained stratified, but never static. Ecstatic religious forms have survived and even flourished at the popular level, yet have been marginalized because of their association with grassroots proletarian and impoverished classes.

The ensuing analysis draws inspiration from R. T. Smith (1976), who emphasized the significance of context for the evolution of religious forms. He sought to counterweight reigning scholarly emphasis on searching for the origins of particular rituals or beliefs in New World studies, which ran the risk of diverting attention from "the creative use to which these items are put in the ongoing processes of social life" (337–38). Smith identified three major trends in West Indian religious development that include Hinduism and Islam: hierarchical paternalism; ethical and sectarian individualism; and lower-class participatory enthusiasm (338–41). These result from forces shaping social relations and public culture across the board. I bring this to bear on the subaltern African and Hindu spiritisms examined in this study.

In order to synopsize the ground covered here, I offer three diagrams to map key structural and ideological transformations from the colonial plantation slavery period (figure 2.1) to the postemancipation colonial period (figure 2.2) to the postcolonial period of nationalism and postcolonial multiculturalism (figure 2.3). These diagrams are offered as heuristics for readers throughout the rest of my text.

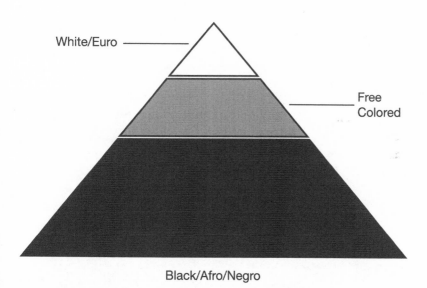

Figure 2.1. Colonial plantation slavery period. Illustration by Erin Dwyer.

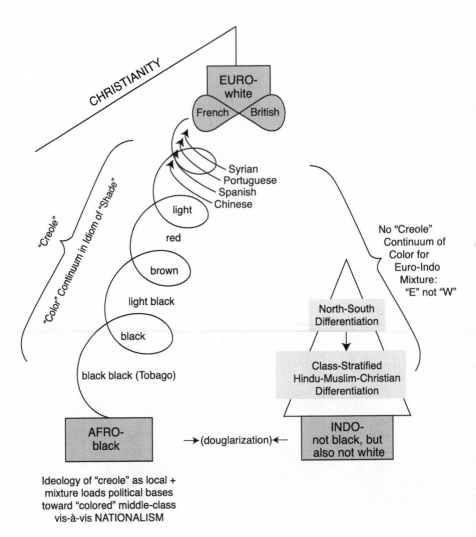

Figure 2.2. Postemancipation into late colonial period. Illustration by Erin Dwyer.

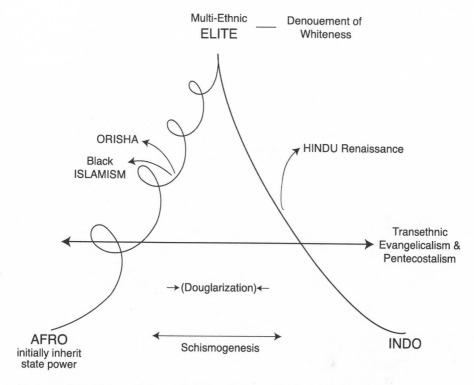

Figure 2.3. Colonial nationalist into postcolonial multiculturalist period. Illustration by Erin Dwyer.

Serving the Orishas

You don't join Shango, it joins you.

Dexter, May 2000, Petit Bourg

I have three of them: Oya, Oshun, Osain. The three of them does affect me.
They are all very passionate.

Juliana, November 2000, Siparia

However far the stream flows, it never forgets its source.

Yoruba proverb

I first met Mother Joan while attending her annual feast in June of 1999. Her
ritual compound sits next to the house where she and her family of children
and grandchildren live, nestled along a dirt trace within an Indian neighborhood just outside the sizable town of Arima. During the ceremonial break, at
about three o'clock in the morning, I chatted with some of Joan's relatives from
Port-of-Spain. They were curious as to who I was and how I had ended up there.
Upon learning of my mission after finishing a tasty meal of curry and roti, they
led me from the yard into the house, which was abuzz with activity.

Mother Joan sat at a large kitchen table. She had removed her hair tie, and
her braids splayed out across her shoulders. After marching me to the table

and announcing who I was, my couriers promptly turned and left me standing there.

"How it is yuh come here?" Joan asked. I briefly explained my interest and how I had learned of her feast. "Is a good t'ing," she observed, "but it a lot 'a work."

Meanwhile, people were coming and going to check in regarding the rest of the night's proceedings. It was Wednesday-into-Thursday: Osain would soon come and walk on hot glowing coals in the midst of the palais, just before a *morocoy* (land turtle) would be sacrificed to him. Much needed to be done and it was not the time for in-depth discussion. Hastening to leave, I commented on the *jhandis* (Hindu ritual flags) planted in her yard alongside the orisha flags. Intrigued by my observation, Joan raised her eyebrows and widened her eyes: "You and I must talk," she said.

Mother Joan's case is fascinating. She was born Anglican yet gravitated toward Catholicism while growing up. She also took to the "Hindu t'ing," as well, as a result of "coming up" in a predominantly Indian area. She is, in her words, "spiritual." She became deeply involved in Spiritual Baptism as an adult, which in turn led to her adoption of "Orisha Work," what she also refers to as "ancestral business." She gave her first feast around 1990, yet this development had been long in the making and "gave the powers their due" for a little over a decade. A year after we met, she suspended her annual feast on account of the exorbitant expense, which required permission from the powers themselves.

Though she resisted their call for some time, Joan repeatedly dreamed of the orishas, albeit sometimes in disguised form, and only became fully responsive to their communications during a period when her children hit an upsurge of problems. Though she initially tried to "fight it off," her first ecstatic manifestation came at the feast of the babalorisha who would become her spiritual father. She did not entirely understand the experience, however, and "stayed away" for quite a while thereafter. Once they were started, she gave her own feasts on the thirteenth of June, the canonical Catholic feast day for St. Anthony, for whom she has an affinity. Indeed, Mother Joan offered thanksgivings for St. Anthony many years before the onset of her most active period giving feasts. Most of her children and some of her grandchildren receive spiritual manifestations at feasts, including one daughter who manifests Lord Shiva.

Joan emphasizes she knew about Shango well before because of deeper experience with Spiritual Baptism. Though some Baptists don't believe or admit it, she observes, they don't fully understand that "whatever we do, we walk Shango road in the Baptist Church." Shango is John the Baptist's "African side." Anything "spiritually African" is Shango. A case in point is *doption*, an ecstatic breathing practice prominent in Spiritual Baptism: "Whenever you hear some-one groan low, that is from Shango—from St. John."

Mother Joan's involvement in Spiritual Baptism is deep and extensive. She is a mother reverend in the church hierarchy, reflected in the fact that her palais doubles as a Baptist church. It has removable windows for use during feasts but which are kept in place during church services. Joan often says she feels stronger on the "Baptist side." "When I pray and call the name of Jesus, I feel stronger." She does what she "has to do for the orishas, but Jesus tells me he is the head, and I believe he is the head. Who don't want to take him as the head . . ." She pauses, then sucks her teeth (known locally as *steups*), indicating disapproval.

Mother Joan continually reiterates that "Hindu Work" has always been one of her "loves." She held an annual puja two days before the beginning of her feast in order to invite the Hindu deotas in advance, which is why Osain—which she pronounces "Hossein"—was so powerfully present at her feasts. It also accounts for why she often refers to orisha flags as jhandis and calls the Af-rican powers by the lovely neologism "deoties," combining the colloquial Hindu word *deota* with the generic term *deity*. Indians attended her feasts and are part of her spiritual family. Many Indians from the area also come for her spiritual guidance. After all, "Africa and India are close," she says.

Mother Joan now devotes more of her time to Spiritual Baptism, as well as to Hindu pursuits, even as she maintains contact with Shango by attending the feasts of associates, offers smaller prayers and offerings to the African powers throughout the year, and tracks the orisha circuit through the activities of her spiritual children. Her case illustrates the variability of Orisha Worship in prac-tice and dramatizes the ways relations with the powers develop and change over the life course.

This chapter focuses upon Shango as a popular tradition, considering its social organization, ritual structure, and complex pantheon as well as its sym-bolism, material culture, and patterns of performance. I emphasize the personal flexibility and on-the-ground dynamism of Orisha Worship as a subaltern reli-gious form and probe its overlapping and complex interrelations with Christi-anity, Spiritual Baptism, Kabba, and Hinduism.[1]

Tracking the Orisha Circuit

Neither the foreign anthropologist nor many locals find their way easily into the heart of an orisha feast in Trinidad or Tobago. A shrine may be located down the road or a feast may be held just around the corner, but this does not mean one will necessarily have contact with it. Indeed, most people steer clear of such activity. A friend of mine reported that he had been asked whether he had a crucifix in the house in order to ward off any wayward diabolical influences I might have "picked up" and brought in with me as a result of my research. The former assured the latter that, indeed, he had "protection." Orisha devotions have been marginalized for more than a century, apprehended with a mixture of fear, scorn, disbelief, ambivalence, and fascination. The stigma of Shango at large ranges from being seen as black magic or pagan sorcery—locally glossed as *obeah*—to being disparaged as hocus-pocus—*simi-dimi*—or even as a money-making scam.

Orisha liturgy traditionally centers on the action of the *feast*, whose annual, island-wide ceremonial cycle now runs from Easter to Christmas (Houk 1995; Aiyejina and Gibbons 1999; Lum 2000). Yet Frances Mischel (1957) reported the cycle as having lasted only from June to the end of September. Thus the feast season expanded in the latter half of the twentieth century. One practitioner highlighted that this period coincides with the wet season, the time when "nature gives," hence an auspicious time for spiritual activity.

Though the word *ebo*—meaning "sacrifice" in Yoruba—has become popular, the more common, traditional terminology of "feast" derives from Catholicism, whose liturgical calendar involves a highly differentiated sequence of devotions for the saints. Many orisha feasts are in fact timed in accordance with canonical saints' days. This Catholic significance does not exhaust the meanings of "feast" in the context of Shango, however, since the orishas are called then supplicated and "fed" with a host of offerings. Animal sacrifices conducted in the early morning hours are not only offered to the gods, but are also used to feed congregants. I was gently reprimanded when I made a move to leave a feast before the climactic round of animal sacrifices. "Don't leave yet," a devotee said, "we goin' to feed de powah an' dem just now and yuh get a special blessing if yuh does stay for it."

Shrine communities spend countless hours in preparation for the multiple-night sequence of the feast. This preparation is a time of fasting and abstinence from sex and alcohol, though there seems to be considerable variation in any individual's commitment to the fast from year to year. A typical feast runs four days and nights, starting on Tuesday evening and running through Saturday morning. Feast holders embellish upon this basic structure based upon personal visions or directives from the powers. One of Trinidad's former elders, for example, held a special annual offering and prayer for Yemanja and Orunmila in the wee hours of Monday morning because of a dream she'd had many years ago instructing her to do so. Another experienced mombwah holds a *re re* table on the Monday night of his feast week, on the eve of its formal commencement on Tuesday night with the planting of Ogun's sword. Re res are a class of spirits historically subordinate to the orishas and known as their children or messengers. They may follow orisha manifestations and frequently behave in cheeky or outlandish ways.[2] Traditionally, an occasion called the "return"—similar in structure to the feast but condensed in format—takes place a week or so after the feast's conclusion. However, the practice of return has become less prominent than has been reported for earlier periods (cf. Lum 2000; F. Henry 2003).

That the island-wide itinerary of feast times has become spread out does not mean there are no conflicts. Indeed, some believe effort is needed to better sequence the cycle of feasts in order to minimize concurrent observance. This is less of a problem in practice, though, since a serious devotee's orientation is typically oriented toward his or her own shrine community, and only secondarily toward the activities of others. If two feasts take place during any particular week, a person or group will attend the ceremonies of the shrine they know best or with which they maintain an affiliation. Those who follow the orisha circuit without formalized ties to any specific yard come and go as they please—feast-hopping, as it were. Overall, the population of orisha practitioners represents a fluid "community" whose ties to one another are generally implicit and based on mutual orientation to a shared ritual tradition.

Each orisha shrine is located within the domestic "yaad" (yard) of its leader, or head. Thus each shrine is maintained on private property. Mombwah—also known as *amambwah* or *mongba* (terminology that originally referred to royal priests for the god Shango in precolonial Oyo-Yoruba state religion)—is the name used for male priests who orchestrate the ritual action of the feast. There are also female ritual specialists—called *iya* ("mother")—who possess the knowledge required for conducting feasts, but they are far fewer than the mombwahs. James Houk (1995:125–28) estimated approximately thirty-five "mongbas" (mombwahs) and iyas in the late 1980s and early 1990s, with fifteen of them responsible for the bulk of feast orchestration throughout the country. Ranking elders within the tradition are known as Babalorisha—"Father of the Orishas"—or Iyalorisha—"Mother of the Orishas," terms also used in Yorubaland and elsewhere in the Black Atlantic such as Brazil. While a shrine head may not necessarily be a mombwah or iya, the latter typically has his or her own shrine. Thus shrine heads who are not feast specialists are dependent upon the ceremonial labor of others for directing their feasts. Mother Joan brought in a mombwah annually to conduct her feast services, for example.

Those who "come up" within the tradition due to their upbringing are seen as traditionalists and have the advantage of knowledge and prestige. They may inherit not only the work of the feast, but also the shrine yard itself. Others commit to building a shrine and maintaining a feast as a result of dreams or visions, often experienced in the course of "mourning" and "building" rituals "on the Baptist side." That is, they come to Shango through Spiritual Baptism, one of whose four spiritual "schools" of astral travel is African—the others being Indian, Chinese, and Syrian.

Mombwahs-in-the-making learn the ropes and cut their teeth out on the circuit. Clout and leadership within this subaltern sphere stem from constant negotiation, making for highly dynamic ritual terrain riven by considerable conflict and contestation. Those who weather repeated challenges to their knowledge and authority gradually emerge as the leaders of highest status. As observed by Houk (1995:132–33) and confirmed by my own experience, the most successful and respected of ritualists are those whose competence includes facility with Spiritual Baptism, Kabbalistic spiritism, Hindu ritualism, and so on.

Participation in a shrine community is characterized by concentric circles ranging from an inner core to the shrine's wider matrix of "spiritual children" to participant-observers with decreasing degrees of affiliation or experience to spectators who find their way to feasts for any number of idiosyncratic reasons. Leadership and role recruitment are fluid and not highly institutionalized; thus social relations and ritual performance within Orisha Worship are subject to flux and change from shrine to shrine and year by year.

Mombwahs and iyas garner the highest status. Following in rank are shrine heads, drummers, *shantwelles* (song leaders), slayers (those who perform animal sacrifices), and various other assistants. Some shantwelles and drummers—usually men—are also mombwahs because of their extensive experience. Drummers may double as song leaders and are crucial, since percussion calls the powers and sustains them during their ecstatic manifestations in the midst of the feast. Slayers perform an equally fundamental role, given their knowledge of proper sacrificial practice, the organization of offerings for the powers, and preparation of sacrificial foods. Assistants for all of these roles function in a less front-stage but no less critical capacity. Unlike mombwahs, drummers, shantwelles, and slayers, both men and women operate in the varied roles of assistant.

Further down the hierarchy lie the majority of practitioners. Frances Henry (1965) described this group as intermediate between the inner circle and outer periphery. Women dominate this level of activity, and it is from this group that the bulk of ecstatic manifestations arise. These devotees tend to position themselves near the ceremonial center of gravity within the primary performance structure—the palais—and facilitate the flow of ritual action with their clapping, chac-chac (gourd rattle) playing, singing, and enthusiasm. They may assist on an ad hoc basis and participate in other feasts on the circuit. However, they do not generally travel as far and wide as those from the higher or lower echelons do.

At the lowest tier, one encounters a demographically smaller grouping of persons positioned on the periphery of ritual action. This transitory population consists of those who are curious for whatever personal reason, as well as friends or relatives of practitioners more deeply involved in orisha ceremonialism that have been brought along to take part, albeit from an intimate distance. Spiritual seekers with some affliction or problem may enter the community at this level, but more or less quickly make their way deeper into the practice based on differential motive and circumstance. All are welcome to a feast as long as they behave respectfully.

Since the 1970s, there has been an influx of artists, intellectuals, university students, and other socially mobile individuals entering the sphere of Orisha Worship, as discussed in chapter 6. There have always been well-off members of society seeking the spiritual instruction and healing intervention of Shango ritualists; however, these forays most often take place on a pragmatic, as-needed basis, under the cover of secrecy. Thus they are exceptions proving a more general rule. Indeed, there has historically been minimal middle- and upper-class participation in grassroots activities or in the shrine communities based in traditional orisha yards.

A shrine leader's authority depends upon a combination of personal charisma, past experience, present competence, and the fluctuating reality of followers and patrons. The matrix of affiliation and attachment within shrine communities is conceptualized in terms of spiritual kinship; therefore the head is "mother" or "father" to the "children" of the shrine, who follow and have often been—or will be—initiated. This parent-child paradigm is paralleled by the way devotional relations are semantically structured between individual devotee and patron orisha(s), with the former as child to the latter. Thus a parent-child trope structures the arena of orisha practice in a series of cross-modal mappings from divinity to devotee and leader to follower. Horizontal relations among practitioners as well as between children of the same divinity are therefore conceptualized as "siblings." The biological and spiritual families of leaders often overlap extensively.

The would-be child of a particular orisha who catches power at a feast will usually be tended to by the mombwah or head of the yard, who helps determine the spirit's identity and interpret the significance of its manifestation. This is often accomplished through divination using *obi* seeds from the kola tree. An individual's head is said to belong to the yard in which she or he fell under the influence of a specific power, and sooner or later, the leader may conduct a more formal initiation. This principally involves "head washing," in which the initiate undergoes a period of fasting and has his or her head esoterically prepared for practice, as well as "head incision," in which sacred ash and other esoterica associated with the spirit are introduced into the head through a small incision in order that the patron orisha may more fully claim its new child.

However, affiliation with particular powers may also develop in a less for-malized way. The period following one's initial ecstatic experience is said to be a delicate, liminal time in which the individual is especially open and vulner-able to cosmic influences and must therefore observe special taboos as well as refrain from entering the space of other shrine yards.

Trinbagonian Orisha Worship has traditionally been practiced and repro-duced within the context of a noncentralized, grassroots-level ceremonial net-work dispersed throughout the entire country, whose subgroupings coalesce around individual shrine heads, mombwahs, and iyas and which is subject to considerable flux and change. These microcommunities are characterized by individualism and concentric levels of participation; their practices are variable and even quite eclectic; and their relations with one another may exhibit the worst of "crab antics" at times—that is, micropolitics based on competition and conflict over small differences (see Wilson 1973; Burton 1997). Because Shango has been largely based upon oral tradition and knowledge transmission, its concepts, beliefs, and practices have displayed the continuous creativity and inventive capacity at work in oral cultural genres.

Shango has accordingly developed complex and overlapping relationships with a number of other religious traditions, including Catholicism, Spiritual Baptism, Hinduism, and Kabba. It also maintains a one-way relationship with biomedicine in that Orisha Worshippers do not necessarily see their practice as mutually exclusive. I became acquainted with an old woman suffering from goiter who sought purification and healing from the orishas at the same time she was receiving treatment at a medical clinic, for example. Indeed, many see "bush medicine" as complementary to the work of medical doctors, and ori-sha healers may refer their patients to them, although the relationship is not reciprocal, given the biomedical bias against obeah. The experiences of many practitioners lead me to conclude that, among many other functions of Shango religious praxis, ranging from caregiving and community to devotional prob-lem-solving and ecstatic mysticism, Orisha Worship compensates for certain weaknesses in—or lack of access to—biomedicine overall.[3]

Of particular significance for charting the sociocultural topography of Shango is the prominent position of women as shrine heads, leaders, and especially spirit mediums. Female practitioners are generally able to garner more status and influence than those in most other religions in the country—except perhaps Spiritual Baptism, which shares much in common with Shango. This seems to reflect so-called matrifocal patterns of Afro-Caribbean mating and kinship characterized by relative male transience and the prominence of female-headed households among lower classes.

Demographic information on Orisha Worshippers is difficult to obtain. As Houk notes: "The multitiered nature of the religion and the varying levels of participation in its activities make estimations of group membership somewhat difficult" (1995:136). Based on survey data, he estimated around 9,000 active orisha practitioners in contemporary Trinidad and Tobago and more than 150 shrines, whereas Frances Henry's (2003) most recent estimate puts the number of shrines at around 60, with approximately 5,000 active practitioners. Two local scholars, Aiyejina and Gibbons (1999), suggest about 80 active shrines, but they do not speculate—perhaps wisely—about numbers of practitioners. The official statistics offered at the Second Convention of the Council of Orisha Elders, which I attended in June of 1999, were approximately 60 shrines and 5,000 practitioners. The constraints of my own comparative work militated against any systematic effort at collecting data that would enable me to enter the debate. Thus, taking it all with a necessary grain of salt, I have generally worked with the assumption that there were at least 80 shrines at the turn of the twenty-first century and at least 5,000 persons, if not more, once we appreciate the proportion of those less deeply involved or otherwise only loosely affiliated with the tradition at large.

What is clear is that, whereas Shango and Spiritual Baptism were both religious expressions of the lower-class black population throughout the colonial period, they have increasingly gained Indian adherents with the dawning of the postcolonial era. I know a considerable number of Indo-Trinidadian drummers and ritualists. Until the 1990s, there was an Indian shrine head widely considered to be among the most popular in the country. Moreover, an Indian sat on the Council of Orisha Elders during my longest period of fieldwork. Houk (1995:137) estimates the demographic presence of Indians within contemporary orisha networks to be around 10 percent, an approximation that rings true to my own experience.

What emerges is an image of a vast subaltern ceremonial circuit dispersed throughout this twin-island nation—predominantly in Trinidad, but also in Tobago—that ebbs and flows just below the surface of public culture. Active microcommunities are not highly institutionalized; they are porous nodal points in a many-tentacled network of subaltern ritual arts. A sizable number of people follow the currents of this circuit, tracking the flow of the feast season as it waxes and wanes each year. The tradition is highly individualistic, as reflected in the diversity of pathways into and out of the religion as well as by the variability and eclecticism of worship patterns and shrine construction.

Habitats of the African Powers

Orisha shrines are diverse. Yet a basic model underlies this differentiation, organizing space into symbolically meaningful form. However differently each may be arranged, the traditional Shango yard consists of a palais, a *chappelle*, and a series of stools. A compound may also house a Spiritual Baptist church, yet church and shrine structures are distinct in ritual terms. This does not rule out interaction or reciprocal influence between the two domains, as a substantial number of devotees operate on both the African and the Baptist sides.

The palais is the structure within and around which people congregate throughout each night of the feast, where drummers play and the powers come on their hosts in sacred rites of divine dramaturgy, all orchestrated by the efforts of the mombwah and his coterie of assistants. The palais is covered—traditionally with a *carrat* roof made from thatched palm fronds, although corrugated iron sheeting has become progressively more common—but its walls are often only half-high (figure 3.1). This configuration enables concentric rings of congregants standing outside the palais to view activity unfolding within its focal space. A palais has benches built on the inside of these walls, where people sit or stand throughout the course of ceremonial action (figure 3.2). Ideally, the floor of the palais is earthen, in order that barefoot practitioners may be more in tune with and responsive to the spiritual energies of the earth and cosmos. Entryways into the palais are marked with a lit candle. Practitioners properly enter and exit by touching the earth at the sanctum's threshold several times in succession.

The palais is decorated "brightly" (emic term) for feasts, which pleases the powers. Colored flags of the orishas are hung from the ceiling crossbeams, as are fruits or ears of corn that have been tied with string. Palm fronds and other organic materials are also used for ornamentation. Some palais have the name of the shrine painted on one of its walls; nowadays, many shrines proudly display an official registration certificate as part of the nationally incorporated Orisha Religion of Trinidad and Tobago.

Each palais reflects the orientation of its owner. Mother Joan's shrine, for

Figure 3.1. View toward the palais of a central Trinidadian shrine from across the yard early on a feast night. Photo by author.

Figure 3.2. Practitioners gather for opening prayers inside another orisha shrine. Photo by author.

example, sports a chromolithograph of the Sacred Heart of Mary prominently over one of the palais doors, as well as a plaque on one wall stating: "Christ is the Head of this House—the Unseen Host at Every Meal—the Silent Listener to Every Conversation." Another prominent palais is more overtly Baptist-oriented. The painted symbols on its walls portray an anchor, a ship's steering wheel, and keys, and during its feast cosmograms are drawn on the floor with chalk, a practice for which Spiritual Baptists are well known. Its walls trumpet "Divine Brotherly Love" and the injunction "Love Ye One Another." Other palais are adorned with the red, yellow, and green of Rastafari-inflected pan-Africanism. I have even been in one palais with a conspicuous image of a crescent moon with a five-pointed star displayed on one wall.

Usually smaller than the palais, the chappelle—"chapel" in patois—is a fully enclosed and far less public structure falling under the purview of the shrine head and mostly open only to his or her spiritual family and the mombwah and "laborers" (assistants) during the feast. This semiprivate room is where much of the shrine's ritual paraphernalia, sacred icons and imagery, spiritual tools and healing implements used by performing mediums, and so on are kept. The chappelle may be physically connected to the palais, but equally often, it is located elsewhere in the yard, detached from the palais structure. There is much movement by shrine heads, mombwahs, their assistants, and spirit mediums back and forth between the palais and the chappelle throughout the course of a feast, linking the two spheres through activity even when they are not physically connected.

It is within chappelles that one encounters perhaps the most significant variability in symbolism and paraphernalia, reflecting the uniqueness and proclivities of each owner. In Tunapuna, there is a palais that looks like many others in layout and decoration, yet its chappelle is uncommonly large and houses a kaleidoscopic array of images and implements: a statue of the Virgin Mary on an altar accompanied by icons of St. Michael and many others; a proliferating assortment of chromolithographs of Catholic as well as Hindu divinities covering almost every inch of wall space; a framed photo of the shrine head decorated with a Hindu flower mala (garland); countless tools of the orishas, from swords and cutlasses to shepherd's rods and a ship's steering wheel; colored cloths for each of the powers; a separate altar containing a profusion of Buddhas; and even a handmade clay statue of Kali standing in one corner. The head of this shrine is not only an avid circle worker (i.e., Kabba priest) who conducts spiritual work via video and teleconference for clients in North America, but also in a common-law marriage with an Indian woman. Their compound has a shrine for Shiva on the roof, complete with a neon-lit sign of the sacred Hindu syllable *om*. Their chappelle therefore reflects a diverse spiritual repertoire.

The southern Trinidadian compound of the late Iyalorisha Melvina Rodney, who passed away in 2008, similarly mirrors her positioning within the traditional system as an "old head" trained by the legendary mid-twentieth-century "Shango king," Samuel Ebenezer Eliot, who laid down the original stools that established her shrine yard. She strongly identified as Catholic, and her practice hewed closely to the system of syncretic interidentifications made between orishas and saints. Iya emphasized fidelity to "tradition"; thus her chappelle contained a mélange of Catholic images and Orisha implements, but no Hindu or Kabbalistic paraphernalia. In the front room of her chappelle, she encouraged me to pray to Orunmila for his blessing on my research. She was eighty-five years old when I first met her in 1999 and was widely respected for knowing more orisha chants than anyone else. She nurtured countless spiritual children.

In addition to their palais and chappelle, orisha shrine compounds also house stools—called "*perogun*" or "tombs"—usually either earthen or concrete mound structures located in the yard outside and inside the chappelle.[4] Stools for Shango and Oya are located chiefly inside chappelles. My offering to Orunmila was made at his stool in the corner of Iya Rodney's chappelle. Each

Figure 3.3. One of the stools in an orisha yard in southern Trinidad. Photo by author.

yard also houses a shrine for Eshu—guardian of thresholds and the trickster-ish right-hand man of high god Olodumare—located just outside or inside the compound's entrance.

Ritual implements, offerings, or other paraphernalia associated with each divinity are lodged or left at a stool, which bears the traces of past activity. The divinity's stool is also where live animal sacrifices are conducted for each of the powers, and fresh blood from the animal is poured over the stool, which is considered sacred. "Your stool stays just so until you die," one expert in southern Trinidad related to me. Stools therefore localize the ashé of each power upon a specific spot in the shrine yard.

A moving example comes from a prominent shrine in central Trinidad, founded around the turn of the twentieth century by an immigrant from Carriacou, yet whose feast ceased after the mid-century passing of its original founder. The founder's granddaughter decided to reactivate the yard. Her head had been washed under Oya as a teen, though she resisted spiritual work well into adulthood when she began manifesting Shakpana and became involved with the United Brotherhood of Time Spiritual School (UBOTSS) in southern

Figure 3.4. A stool located just outside the shrine chappelle in central Trinidad on a feast night. Photo by author.

Trinidad. Ritual experts determined that all of the orishas were still present, locating each of their stools in the yard. The first revitalized feast was held in 1979, and annual observance has been uninterrupted ever since. Members of Kenny Cyrus Alkebu Lan Ile Ijebu Shrine are understandably proud of the yard's vintage as embodied in the seventeen stools of its orishas.

Stools located in the public yard are sites where flags for the powers are hoisted into the air upon tall bamboo poles (see Figs. 3.5 and 3.6). Orisha flags are rectangular and composed of the colors associated with each deity, such as red and white for Ogun–St. Michael. Orisha flags are similar in shape to Spiritual Baptist ones but unlike Hindu jhandis, which are triangular. Due to their conspicuous character, flags signal the subaltern presence of African mystical space to the world outside.

Though stools are considered permanent, an important item on the annual agenda of the feast is the renewal of each stool and its accompanying flag at the beginning of the feast week. The old stool is ritually disposed of while a new flag is hoisted up in its place, accompanied by an esoteric procedure conducted

Figure 3.5. Ceremonial flags rise above the landscape inside the front gate of a southern Trinidadian orisha shrine. Photo by author.

Figure 3.6. Orisha flags mark the entrance to an urban shrine in Port-of-Spain. Photo by author.

in the hole where the flag's bamboo pole is anchored in the earth. This task may be laborious depending upon the number of stools and flags. Candles are then burned at each of the stools during subsequent feast nights.

The layout and composition of a yard's stools vary from shrine to shrine. Each pattern of stools reflects the set of divinities that constitute focal points of spiritual orientation for that shrine head and community. Yet, though the topography of stools from shrine to shrine is varied, one can observe overall patterns, such as the fact that certain deities are found in almost every yard throughout the two islands.[5] Before considering the Afro-creole orisha pantheon in more detail, however, I return to the cultural history of the tradition in order to put Shango's structure and symbolism into deeper perspective.

Shango's Southern Caribbean Genealogy

The indentured Africans who came to Trinidad during the first several decades after emancipation proved to be an influential sector of the evolving black population. As a result of the collapse of the Oyo Empire and civil war throughout

Yorubaland after the turn of the nineteenth century, a significant portion of these indentured transmigrants were Yorubas. Despite the fact that both the northern Oyo and southern Ijebu kingdoms had supplied slaves for the Atlantic trade since the sixteenth century, the number of enslaved Yorubas sent to the Americas in chains was relatively small early on. There was no important slaving port in Yorubaland until the late eighteenth century, when Britain opened a slave market at Lagos to compete with French ports to the west.

Abundant evidence attests that, having completed their terms of indentureship, Africans of similar backgrounds were able to congregate in enclaves, at times, for as many as several generations in some cases. "This desire for ethnic companionship was so noticeable it was believed some Africans would have preferred to work for their countrymen for no wages rather than go on the estates" (Trotman 1976:6). Some broke indenture or refused to renew contracts in order to join their brethren. These were hardly traditional Yoruba communities (also see Trotman 2007), although Yorubas were one of the dominant African groups in Trinidad.

Yoruba prominence did not derive solely from their numbers, but from cultural distinctiveness and social cohesion as well. "Although they were the products of Yoruba imperial collapse, they were inheritors of a long history of territorial expansion and political stability based on a recognition of a hierarchical order among the princes of the realm, and reinforced by a mythico-political rationale" (Warner-Lewis 1996:21). Yoruba "blocks" or "villages" sprung into being throughout the island. Some Yorubas were able to become peasant landholders as a result of landing schemes embarked upon by the colonial government from the late 1860s. The commissioner for the Montserrat district wrote in 1867 that "Yarribas" lived in nice wooden houses with lush, well-tended gardens and were "highly impatient of control." Many also subscribed "towards a fund on which they draw in case of illness or unseen misfortune" (Brereton 1979:135). This form of cooperative saving—known by the Yoruba term *susu*—subsequently became common among all groups in society.

W. H. Gamble—an English Baptist—was sharply critical of Kongos, the other predominant African group during this period, but spoke highly of Yorubas: "The Yarrabas will dwell in clusters, cooperate with one another, becoming small holders of land" (1866:31). They valued "civilization," living in neat, clean houses and rarely appearing in court (30). Gamble noted that Yorubas were not only "apt in learning languages," but in fact also preferred patois French to English (40), reflecting Yoruba acceptance of Catholicism as well as their informal alliance with Franco-creoles over and against the British colonial bureaucracy.

Protestants in Trinidad were aware of these developing links, accusing

Catholics of encouraging "pagan" behavior by using their rituals to endear themselves to the black population. Gamble wrote: "The genius of the Catholic religion is suited to the tastes of the people. The sensuous service, the robes of the priest, the intoned liturgy, the offering up of the host, the frequent processions, the many feast days . . . the confession is, to most illiterate minds, a means of relief to a burdened conscience, while extreme unction holds a very high place in the esteem of the people" (1866:42).

We encounter recurring themes throughout the colonial historiography concerning Yorubas (see also de Verteuil 1858, for example). This literature is imperfect, but nevertheless helps account for why Yoruba subculture became so influential within the evolving Afro-creole sociocultural matrix. Indeed, Yorubas contributed to a plethora of cultural domains, such as religious ritual, calypso and carnival, cooperative banking, and the flamboyance of Afro-Trini character style.

Their ability to establish themselves in microcommunal enclaves did *not* mean that Yorubas were immune to processes of creolization, however. In fact, their very reconstitution as New World "Yorubas" already represented an important sort of creolization in this context. Yet in addition to this intraethnic creolization, Yorubas and other Africans engaged in other levels of creolization as well. They increasingly mixed biologically as well as culturally. This dynamic unfolded in interaction with Afro-creoles, whose deeper local roots and differing subculture placed them at variance with the recently arrived Africans. Indeed, akin with Euro-Christian elites, Afro-creoles commonly looked down upon their black consociates as "outsiders" and "heathens." Africans were therefore disadvantaged not only as a result of colonial racism, but also because they lacked facility with Eurocentric mannerisms and social institutions. Despite their differences, social and sexual relations between African and Afro-creoles were inevitable, probably developing earlier and more pervasively than is generally recognized (Warner-Lewis 1996:47). Furthermore, all of these groups were simultaneously adapting to the dominant configurations and social institutions of colonial society, representing yet another overarching aspect of creolization in this colonial setting.

Over time, indentured Africans and their descendants progressively integrated into the broader black population, contributing to—as well as becoming influenced by—the evolving Afro-creole cultural matrix. Locally evolving orisha tradition involved creolizing developments among Yorubas as well as interactive transculturation with other African religious subcultures. Orisha Worship seems to have been bolstered through resonance and cross-fertilization with Dahomean Vodou praxis, for example (Trotman 2007:220–21). Eastman and Warner-Lewis (2000:409–10) believe the latter was in fact gradually encompassed over the long run by the Yoruba-inspired tradition. Moreover, comparative research on nineteenth-century African life also leads Warner-Lewis (1991:51) to conclude that a similar process took place with regard to aspects of Kongo religious culture over time.

Language exemplifies some of the processes of change Yorubas experienced. Warner-Lewis (1996) conducted historical linguistic research between 1968 and 1972 with more than seventy informants, eight of whom were primary speakers of "Trinidad Yoruba," an increasingly recessive dialect mixture that evolved in Yoruba-creole communities throughout the island in the latter half of the nineteenth century. Warner-Lewis charts its progressive decline into linguistic "obsolescence." Indeed, the function of Yoruba in the daily lives of locals eroded over time, becoming increasingly "hermetic and esoteric" (52). She identifies a tendency among older informants to withdraw into "linguistic individualism and self-idealization" (62) in response to language constriction and the progressive disruption of cross-generational transmission.

Trinidad Yoruba has been retained to a remarkable degree within the sphere of orisha ceremonialism, however, in the form of approximately two hundred liturgical song-chants used in homage to the orishas (see Warner-Lewis 1994 for the complete corpus). These are relatively short and fragmented as compared with antecedent forms and are based on three- or four-line stanzas repeated to the accompaniment of percussion in feasts and related ceremonies (Warner-Lewis 1996:84–85). Given that few practitioners understand the semantics of these songs, their pragmatic function as invocations of and praise for the orishas takes precedence over their referential meaning. The use of xenoglossic songs heightens perception of the ritual language's esoteric power, referred to as "deep Yoruba" by some devotees. The corpus is acquired primarily through imitation, repetition, and practice.

Practitioners describe the non-Christian liturgical language of Orisha Worship as "African," although "Yoruba" is also increasingly salient. The contemporary repertoire of prayers and songs represents a local synthesis of vestigial creole Yoruba combined with patois French and English, mixed with phrases of no obvious provenance or readily understood meaning. According to Frances Henry (pers. comm., 2000), at least half of the chants in the 1950s were sung in patois French, many people sang "nonsense," and it was usually only the leader and a few others who knew the songs well and understood something of their meaning. Aiyejina (2002) views the evidence as pointing to a corpus of diverse and dynamic origins, spanning transfers and retentions from West Africa to New World Yoruba compositions to local creole innovations, and mixed-resource creations to recent importations from Nigeria.

The self-conscious attempt to "Yorubanize" the tradition has accelerated since the 1970s. Aiyejina's estimate (pers. comm., 2000) of 60–70 percent Yoruba materials in contemporary liturgy accordingly reflects changes characteristic of the postcolonial era.

The emergent picture is one in which Yoruba religious subculture in colonial Trinidad not only reconstituted and consolidated in a dynamically compacted form, but also began to expand beyond its initial ethnic moorings through progressive transculturation with aspects of other extant African ritual systems. With time, the tradition took on an independent subaltern life of its own among Afro-creoles, and the term *Yoruba* morphed from an ethnonym into a ritual moniker referring to all Afro-creole practitioners of the tradition operating under the sign of "Yoruba." This religious subculture established webs of alternative spiritual kinship constituted by social ties with shrine or cult leaders and devotional relations with the orishas. Thus, while much has been made of the Yoruba tradition's hybrid interrelations with non-African religious forms such as Christianity, it is important to appreciate its own intraethnic creolization as well as related forms of inter-African transculturation through time. This ability to transform and accommodate itself is one of the tradition's greatest strengths and sources of resilience under transatlantic conditions of domination and colonial marginalization.

Understanding this dynamism in terms of intraethnic creolization and inter-African transculturation sheds new light on the tradition's pattern of Afro-Catholic hybridity. Indeed, Yorubas in nineteenth-century Trinidad attracted the attention of the colonial intelligentsia not only because of their solidarity, organization, enterprise, and independence, but also because of their embrace of Catholicism. Warner-Lewis writes:

A significant reason why the Yoruba created such a formidably good impression with Europeans was their acceptance of Christianity. It is clear from nineteenth-century commentaries that the most heinous offense on the part of non-European peoples was ignorance or rejection of Christianity. De Verteuil's comments on the Yoruba are therefore highly meaningful. He described them as "intelligent, reflective and seeming to appreciate the benefit of civilization and Christianity." This gives the impression that, as a community, the Yoruba sought upward social mobility and from early on perceived and acted on the cultural compromises that were deemed necessary. Oral and documentary evidence suggests that they were overwhelmingly Catholic—the dominant Christian persuasion—and that they were active workers in and financial contributors toward parish projects. (1996:49–50)

Regardless of their relationship to ethnic traditional religion, most Yorubas therefore took their baptism seriously (Warner-Lewis 1991:51–52). They met on their own for Christian worship and engaged in missionary activity among themselves. One of Warner-Lewis's second-generation Yoruba-creole informants reported that his African-born grandfather had been converted to Catholicism on an estate in San Fernando, where "well-reputed" Yorubas would come and preach the Gospel, for example (71).

Conversion to Christianity did not mean Yorubas gave up their own religious heritage. Rather, they seem to have intuited complementarity between cosmological spheres, relating historically unrelated religious spheres with one another and forging dynamic mystical fusions—the local pattern of Afro-Catholic hybridity most often glossed as "syncretism." Relations between Catholicism and Yoruba religion were not altogether harmonious, particularly from the elite side of the equation; yet, given the rise of an antisyncretic program among postcolonial Afrocentrists, it is important to appreciate the authenticity of nineteenth-century Yoruba-creole engagement with Christianity.

The Yoruba penchant for Catholicism was linguistically buttressed by their preference for patois French, the most popular language among the lower classes, especially in the marketplace (Gamble 1866:40). Indeed, Yoruba conversion to Catholicism and the ensuing train of Afro-Christian hybridity it spawned among Afro-creoles is reflected in a multifaceted linguistic legacy. Warner-Lewis (1996:80–84), on the one hand, documented a small but significant repertoire of Christian hymns and prayers in Trinidad Yoruba among her older informants, as well as a belief that the Hail Mary enunciated in French was more powerful than when said in English. Patois French, on the other hand, still surfaces in the ecstatic utterances of orisha mediums in trance performance. It is also embedded in some of the liturgical chants now sung throughout the twin-island nation during orisha feasts. Though these linguistic practices may be receding, the significance of Franco-creole language in orisha ceremonialism is an important cultural legacy.

I deal more explicitly with the problem of syncretism in chapter 5; here I am concerned with grasping the arc of Shango's colonial development in the southern Caribbean. For this we fast-forward from the late nineteenth century to the 1930s, when Melville and Frances Herskovits returned to Trinidad to conduct the study resulting in their landmark book, *Trinidad Village* (originally published in 1947). While spending several days in Port-of-Spain in 1929 en route back to the United States after fieldwork among the African-descended "Bush Negroes," or "Maroons," of Dutch Guiana, they read in a local newspaper "a letter from an aroused citizen expressing indignation at certain practices then being carried on near the capital by Negroes who were worshippers of Shango" (Herskovits and Herskovits 1947:v). Recognizing this as "an important body of direct African cultural retentions," they resolved to return to the island for further research.

They returned to Trinidad ten years later, visiting the remote northeastern village of Toco under the assumption that the intensity of what Herskovits (1941, 1966) had come to call "Africanisms" would be greater in rural areas. Ironically, however, this turned out not to be the case. Tocoans proved to be relatively indifferent to things "African" and—akin with North American Blacks—leaned more toward the Europeanized end of the spectrum. The Herskovitses located African cultural retentions, to be sure, but these were primarily hermeneutic transformations without explicit self-awareness as African. This experience led Melville Herskovits away from a study of Orisha Worship, spurring them to develop the concepts of "cultural focus" and "reinterpretation" in the analysis of acculturation and social change (Herskovits and Herskovits 1947:3–29, 287–317). He contrasted the pattern of Afro-Catholic syncretism with that of Afro-Protestant reinterpretation, viewing the Spiritual Baptist Church—which was popular in Toco—as an intermediate configuration between the Africanist cultism of Shango and the established Euroamerican Christian churches (167–223).

Tocoans harbored no active tradition of Orisha Worship (Herskovits and Herskovits 1947:305). Instead, Shango operated as "a kind of last resort when other modes of appeal to the supernatural fail" (173). Individuals went to the capital for consultations during times of need or in the face of important decisions (228). "In Toco, in answer to inquiries regarding what was known there of this worship, it was asserted that the Shango people form healing and dancing groups, and that those who belong have African spirits" (321).

The Herskovitses encountered only one woman—Margaret Buckley—who self-identified with things African and also happened to call herself "Yarriba" (1964:28–29). She knew a considerable number of Yoruba songs and spoke of other Yoruba-creoles on the island who would come together at New Year's time to "play"—dance and sing—for seven days, during which period a sheep sacrifice was offered for the common weal. Herskovits reported that she understood herself as belonging to a "dying tradition."

In order to investigate orisha ritualism, the Herskovitses spent a short period of time at the tail end of their field trip examining a compound high on a Port-of-Spain hill that is almost certainly Belmont (see their appendix 1, "Notes on Shango Worship"). Structure and practice at this shrine bear close resemblance to the patterns described above as now typical, suggesting that the Afro-creole matrix of Shango had taken shape by the first quarter or so of the twentieth century. A "tent" (palais) and "chappelle" were central, although no mention is made of flags. Head incisions were conducted on those who "fell" to the "powers." Obi seeds from the sacred kola nut were used and animal sacrifices offered. Feasts were given on an annual basis, more often when resources permitted. Chromolithographs of Catholic saints had been incorporated into the practice; indeed, the shrine community was most comfortable with "saint" discourse for the African powers.

Other researchers followed in the footsteps of the Herskovitses. Tobagonian folklorist Jacob Elder began studying black popular culture in the 1950s, focusing his inquiry upon the "Yoruba Ancestor Cult" in the very area of the Montserrat hills where Africans had been able to become landed peasants a century before. He (1976) came to know several "traditionalists" who resisted syncretic hybridization of Orisha Worship with Christianity, yet noted that all Yorubacreoles, including these "stalwarts," were nevertheless Roman Catholics. Elder (1970) saw "Shango" or "Orisha Work" as having accommodated a number of inter-African syncretisms as well as having recruited practitioners from an Afro-creole base well beyond its original Yoruba purview, including Kongos and Hausas in the nineteenth century and Grenadian and Tobagonian migrants in the twentieth. He emphasized the salience of "saint" discourse and observed that the wider pattern of Afro-Catholic hybridity was not necessarily problematical (1970:17) Elder's perspective (1976, 1996) simultaneously acknowledges the sincerity of Afro-Catholic syncretism while attributing subaltern agency and creative resistance to Afro-creoles.

Another important contribution to the ethnographic archive of local orisha studies comes from anthropologist Frances Henry (formerly Mischel). Working in the Herskovitsean tradition, Mischel went to Trinidad in the mid-1950s to study the "Shango Cult," and she too found a deep and sincere pattern of Afro-Catholic interculturation at work within the tradition (see F. Mischel 1957, 1959; Mischel and Mischel 1958; F. Henry 1965). Though the tradition was conceptualized as "African Work," devotees had relatively little explicit knowledge of its African origins and were more comfortable within the Catholicized paradigm privileging the discourse of "saints" for the powers. The general structure and practice of contemporary Orisha Worship is evident, although—like the Herskovitses—Henry does not mention anything about orisha flags. She also makes the first reference in the literature to the appropriation of things Hindu into Shango by noting the significance of Mahabil—"an Indian god who was met by Christ in India and baptized as St. Michael" (Mischel 1957:59)—at one prominent shrine in upper Belmont in Port-of-Spain. This was also the first shrine to bring together Orisha Worship and Spiritual Baptism, to her knowledge (pers. comm., 2007).

Through initial connections with this shrine, Henry was introduced to Samuel Ebenezer Eliot—affectionately known as Pa Neezer—with whom she worked for three months in 1956 (recounted in F. Henry 1981; 2003:202–10). Elliott learned bush medicine and the way of the orishas from his maternal grandmother, a renowned Shango priestess known as Ma Diamond, whose own mother had been born a slave. As Trinidad's undisputed "Shango king," Elliott's authority within the tradition reigned supreme from the 1940s until he passed away in 1969. He was born in 1901 and was raised London Baptist in Fifth Company Village in south Trinidad. He remained a devout Baptist his whole life in addition to practicing his African faith, of which his three main powers were Ogun-Michael, Ajaja-Jonah, and Aba Lofa (Elofa). Henry emphasizes that Pa Neezer was a "devout Christian" and paid a great deal of attention to the Catholic prayers and elements of his feasts. "He fully believed in the dualism between Christianity and the Orisha. For him there was very little difference, as they were one and the same" (2003:206). His therapeutic armamentarium accordingly consisted principally of "bush," obi seeds, and the Bible. Warner-Lewis (1996:67) reports that Elliott acquired a copy of the Yoruba Bible—Bibeli Mimo—in the early 1960s and that it was earmarked on the page with the Lord's Prayer. He was buried in the London Baptist Church cemetery in Fifth Company Village.

After Frances Henry's first investigations, Herskovits student George Simpson visited in 1960 and again in 1962 in order to conduct research at five Shango compounds and five Spiritual Baptist churches. Simpson found—akin to his predecessors—the tradition, spoken about by practitioners variously as "Shango," "African Work," "Yoruba Work," and "Orisha Work," to be characterized by extensive orisha-saint equivalences and related Afro-Catholic interculturations. He observed Catholic symbolism as dominant within the upper spaces of chappelle altars, with African paraphernalia predominating in lower quadrants, and first noted the presence of orisha flags. He encountered the Indian power Mahabil along with another known as Baba. Moreover, he witnessed use of a brass *taria* plate—commonly used in Hindu pujas—in orisha healing ceremonies (1980:67). Additionally, Simpson was the first to note the slight participation of Indo-Trinidadians, including a full-fledged manifestation of Shango upon an Indian man (1980:42). Yet he discovered East Indian involvement to be even greater within Spiritual Baptism (80).

It is in relation to ascendant developments between these two Afro-creole traditions that Simpson's work is most pertinent in historiographical terms. His novel characterization would have been unthinkable earlier: "The Shango cult in Trinidad combines elements of Yoruba traditional religion, Catholicism, and the Baptist faith" (1980:11). Inclusion of Spiritual Baptism in this synoptic description speaks to its significance for the development of Shango at the time. Simpson observed Baptist ritual objects and small altars within the chappelles of shrine compounds and noted a range of paraphernalia as well as common ritual actions shared by each tradition (98–99), including similar healing procedures. Importantly, Simpson documented the phenomenon of Baptist "mourning" and "building" ceremonies among Shango people, as well as orisha-inflected forms of mourning and baptism (56, 90, 97). He knew Shangoists who regularly conducted Baptist prayer services and even some ritual events combining elements of both traditions. Some of these practitioners maintained mixed-use compounds similar to that described above for Mother Joan.

Spiritual Baptists—also sometimes and somewhat pejoratively known as "Shouters"—value the cultivation of altered states of consciousness centered chiefly on glossolalia as a manifestation of the Holy Spirit and initiatory and other related vision-quest activities embodied in the practice of mourning, involving sensory deprivation and retrospectively negotiated group interpretation of individual mystical experience. They consider themselves Christians because they believe in the Holy Trinity and the central authority of the Bible. Stephen Glazier (1983) characterizes Afro-Baptist cosmology as polytheistic, since they conceive of a variety of other spirits, such as African orishas, toward whom a significant number of Baptists maintain devotional practice and whose ceremonial spheres overlap deeply—if not always directly or explicitly. Baptist social structure has exhibited both horizontal and vertical forms of differentiation throughout the twentieth century in relation to changes in mobility and competition among leaders, and in the face of state prohibition during the first half of the twentieth century. Women are prominent as practitioners, though less often as leaders. Increasing wealth among members has enabled Indians to join the faith more recently and to take on a number of leadership positions.

Spiritual Baptism emerged in Trinidad by the turn of the twentieth century and was subsequently transported to Tobago, as well as more recently to New York, Toronto, and beyond. It has been especially strong in the southern part of the island. Though the exact historical origins of the tradition are unclear, there is reason to believe that what was to eventually become Spiritual Baptism developed as a result of deep influences from "Merikin" Baptists—African-American Baptists who arrived in several waves in the mid-1810s, 1841, and 1851 from the southern United States—as well as more proximate probable religious inputs from Grenadian and St. Vincentian labor migrants in the late nineteenth and early twentieth centuries (see J. Stewart 1976; Simpson 1978; Glazier 1983; Houk

1995; Zane 1999; Eastman and Warner-Lewis 2000). Most interesting for this discussion, Warner-Lewis (1991:41–42) reports that "Yorubas in particular seem to have found cultural sympathy among the Americans settled early in the nineteenth century at the Company Villages in south Trinidad."

The faith weathered the ongoing challenge of formal discrimination between 1917 and 1951 under the Shouters Prohibition Ordinance, which outlawed central practices such as bell ringing, the wearing of ceremonial head ties, ecstatic shaking of the body, and the holding of flowers or a lit candle during public services (see Thomas 1987; Houk 1995; Lum 2000; Laitinen 2002a; F. Henry 2003). Even before 1917, the reaction of the upper and middle classes to Afro-Christian sects such as the Spiritual Baptists was quite hostile, and the Shouters often ran into trouble with the police (Brereton 1979:158–59). French missionary R.P.M. Cothonay (1893:157–59) even thought Afro-Baptists were morally and spiritually worse than pagan Africans, who could at least be seen as not having corrupted Christianity.

Thus, despite integral Christian elements in Spiritual Baptist ideology and practice, much of its stigma has derived from dominant prejudice toward any sort of African religiosity. Though an internal continuum exists among Baptists ranging from the more Christianized orthodox to the more Africanized heterodox, there is much in Spiritual Baptism, such as ecstatic trance behavior and vision questing, that is deeply rooted in African mystical forms which cannot be easily exorcised from the tradition. Robert Farris Thompson (1983:111–13) points to the Kongo derivation of mystical chalk drawing in Baptist praxis. It is precisely the religion's Africanity that has been a draw for some in the last quarter of the twentieth century, and the several national Spiritual Baptist associations—along with the newly incorporated Council of Orisha Elders (see chapter 6)—were granted land in Maloney, along the east-west highway, by the former UNC government as part of an "African Spiritual Park" to be used for public celebrations and other miscellanea.

Thus, even though Spiritual Baptism and Orisha Worship are independent ritual systems, they have come to overlap in demographic terms and to exhibit increasing forms of influence on one another. A significant number of practitioners in fact come to Shango after having first become active in Baptist circles. It is not uncommon for someone undergoing mourning or building ceremonies on the "Baptist side" to experience visions and experiences that lead them further into the sphere of orisha devotions. Houk (1995:36) estimates that over 50 percent of Orisha Worshippers are also Spiritual Baptists, whereas Glazier (2001:316) puts this percentage as high as 90. Many yards across Trinidad and Tobago house both Orisha shrines and Baptist churches. These dynamics are reflected in the slang term "Shango Baptist"—discussed further in chapter 5—used to refer to people participating in both systems or, more coarsely and misleadingly, as a generic gloss on any type of African-rooted spiritism.

The growth of a complex Shango-Baptist spectrum within the subaltern sphere of Afro-creole religious culture is not without tensions. The more Christian-identified Spiritual Baptists have sought to exclude any elements of Shango, for example, especially the use of drums and offering of animal sacrifices. Mother Martha, the daughter of one of Trinidad's foremost Shango priestesses in the early 1960s, was held back from manifesting during the annual feast because people were concerned that she might undergo "improper" Baptist ecstasy (Simpson 1980:146).

Simpson's informants testified to the relatively recent rise of interaction between Shango and Spiritual Baptism, especially since the lifting of the Shouters Prohibition Ban against Spiritual Baptists in 1951 (1980:69, 99). The trend appealed mostly to younger folks; "older heads" expressed reservations about mixing the two traditions. Simpson saw these developments as a way of adapting to the changing conditions of their continued respective marginalization. Whatever the case, it is nonetheless clear that these two subaltern black religions had begun to coevolve by the mid-twentieth-century era of decolonization.

Dorothy Holland and Julia Crane (1987) confirmed these trends—based on research in the mid-1960s—finding that it was conservative rural devotees who resisted the mixing of Shango and Spiritual Baptism, whereas those in the more urban areas of the island not only exhibited hybridizing tendencies vis-à-vis Spiritual Baptism, but were also the very same persons who had begun to involve themselves in "Circle Work," a local Afro-creole form of occult spiritism also now known as "Kabba" or "Kabbalah," but seemingly unrelated to the tradition of Jewish mysticism bearing the same name. Holland and Crane observed that the "purist" strain of Shango was dying out while "the Shango-Spiritual Baptist mixtures [were] increasing" (61). Angelina Pollak-Eltz (1968), who also conducted fieldwork in the 1960s, documented not only similar evidence for the recent influence of Hinduism upon Orisha Worship, but also increasingly dynamic interrelations between Shango and Spiritual Baptism in Trinidad.

Moving forward again from the 1960s to the 1980s, ethnographic studies by James Houk (1995) and Kenneth Lum (2000) document the considerably deepened overlap and complexity of juxtaposition between Spiritual Baptism and Orisha Worship, as well as the further development of Kabba as an embedded Afro-creole ceremonial adjunct to the other two traditions. They document interrelations between Shango and Spiritual Baptism as differentiated along a continuum spanning the African to the more Christian and describe a resonant Afrocentric-Christocentric continuum within Spiritual Baptism as well. Points of connection are numerous between the African and Baptist sides of practice within the complex terrain of religious life among grassroots practitioners. Indeed, the notion of "sides"—discussed below—has emerged in full force. Both ethnographers emphasize similarities in conceptualization and practice obtaining within each tradition, as well as the phenomenon of crossover trance manifestations, such as the not infrequent appearance of Orishas in Baptist services or, contrariwise, Baptist manifestations in the midst of Shango feasts.

All of this applies equally to the interpenetrating rise of Circle Work within the Afro-creole ritual matrix and the phenomenon of crossover Kabbalistic manifestations as well. Kabba, an even more covert form of Afro-creole spiritism practiced primarily by people who are also Orisha Worshippers and Spiritual Baptists, has not received much scholarly attention. It is difficult to trace the etymology of Kabbalah, since the local practice demonstrates no connection with Jewish mystical traditions per se. Moreover, not only are the Kabba a subcultural Yoruba group on the northeastern periphery of Yorubaland, but "Kabbalah" is also the term used in reference to a sort of neomodern mysticism practiced in Nigeria (A. Apter, pers. comm., 2006). Indeed, J.D.Y. Peel (1968:136) notes that European theosophical ideas have found reception among the West African bourgeoisie since the early twentieth century. Thus it is difficult to account for the origins of Afro-creole Kabba spiritism in Trinidad and Tobago.

Circle Work has the reputation—not without reason—of being principally concerned with more diabolical spiritual forces. Many spiritists contend that Orisha Work is more powerful, yet slower; thus some turn to Kabbalah in order to more quickly deal with problems or develop their spiritual consciousness. Kabba manifestations during séances known as "banquets"—among whom Mr. Steele, Skull-and-Crossbones, and Beelzebub are prominent and, interestingly, racialized as white—may be much more aggressive and volatile than Orisha or Baptist manifestations. These "entities" or "beams" do not dance during banquets, which may be held in orisha yards or Baptist churches. Lum reports that all the mombwahs he knew were deeply involved on the "Kabbalistic side" (2000:181).

The sacred books of Afro-creole Kabba are the Bible, the two Keys of Solomon, and the Sixth and Seventh Books of Moses. The last two are important texts in European esoteric magical traditions, and Lum's informants claim local Kabbalistic connections with secret societies such as the Rosicrucians and Freemasons that developed local branches during the colonial period. He documents crossover cases of Kabbalistic manifestations at orisha feasts and returns, as well as during Spiritual Baptist prayer services and baptisms. Lum's informants claimed Kabba existed locally for most of the twentieth century, though in extreme secrecy. He seems to accept this view, noting that Circle Work was more closely related to Orisha Worship during earlier times and only came to be juxtaposed with Spiritual Baptism as the latter developed overlapping interrelations with Shango over time (2000:190).

Like Lum, Houk finds many resonances between these subaltern religious traditions, seeing their interrelations within the larger Afro-creole ritual matrix, including relations between Kabbalistic practice, known as "the white man's magic" and the other Afro-creole traditions, in terms of juxtaposition rather than blending or syncretism per se. Like its siblings within the Afro-creole religious complex, Kabba traffics in similar conceptualizations of manifestations as well as analogous practices such as stools, flags, and sacrifices. Houk believes Kabbalah has probably been practiced since colonial times but has only begun to come out of hiding since the 1970s, when a prominent southern mombwah opened his annual banquet to the public (1995:91–92). In my own turn-of-the-twenty-first-century experience, many practitioners of these Afro-creole religious traditions speak of them interrelatedly as "levels," with one common view being that you start with Spiritual Baptism and then progress toward increasingly more esoteric stages of mystical practice like Orisha Worship and then Circle Work.

Houk emphasizes the degree to which Hindu symbolism and other Indian religious elements have been incorporated—albeit at a somewhat superficial level characterized as "borrowing," rather than syncretism—within the popular tradition of Orisha Worship. He notes it is the more knowledgeable leaders who conceptualize connections between particular orishas and Hindu deities. Indo-Trinidadian researchers Mahabir and Maharaj (1996) observe the participation of Indians in Shango to have gathered momentum and become most substantial since the 1970s, though earlier forays were clearly made. They interviewed a number of Spiritual Baptist and, especially, Orisha leaders who drew clear parallels between African and Hindu divinities and ritual practices. Some of them wear Indian clothing or serve Indian food when they want to call any of the "Indian powers" within the realm of orisha ritualism.

Thus, from intraethnic creolization and inter-African as well as Afro-Catholic syncretic identifications made by the late nineteenth century in Trinidad to Afro-Indo forms of transculturation and developing interrelations with Spiritual Baptism and Kabbalah across both Trinidad and Tobago in the twentieth century, the Afro-creole tradition of Orisha Worship has demonstrated remarkable resilience and flexibility in adapting to changing sociocultural conditions. While we may never be able to definitively document each and every development, this survey of the relevant historiographic and ethnographic literatures enables a broader-ranging perspective on the tradition's evolution over more than 150 years.

A Prismatic Pantheon

A more systematic discussion of the divinities operating in the pantheon is essential to understanding the religious system as a whole. These heterodox divinities have exhibited remarkable resiliency as well as malleability over time in their adopted Antillean home.

An important characteristic of the orisha pantheon stems from the general amalgamation of worship for the entire spectrum of known powers under the same ceremonial roof within the respective spheres of each shrine compound. Though there is nontrivial secondary variation in this regard, the primary trend has nonetheless been toward the establishment of a more or less standard pantheon of popular divinity shared across separate shrine compounds and ceremonial communities. The product of this process of pantheonization is specific to Trinidad and, secondarily, Tobago. While a shrine or devotee may be especially oriented toward a particular power or two (or more), some version of the whole local pantheon is generally contained in each yard, and it is a matter of orthopraxis that all relevant powers are invoked, entertained, and supplicated during ritual activities and annual festivities. This contrasts with traditional West African tendencies whereby trance performances take place at temples dedicated to specific gods or in ceremonial contexts centered on mediumship by a few focal deities at most.

The configuration of the local orisha pantheon represents a unique constellation relative to the larger transatlantic spectrum of Yoruba religious practice, though the *processes* of clustering and consolidation which generated forms specific to the New World are not themselves new or unique. Indeed, Andrew Apter (1991, 1992, 1995) has demonstrated the plasticity of pantheonization among West African Yorubas based on dynamics of sociopolitical segmentation in his comparative study of orisha cults in the northeastern Ekiti highlands of Yorubaland. Apter shows that—contrary to the influential assumptions of Melville Herskovits (1966), Roger Bastide (1978), and Pierre Verger (1982)—orisha cults in West Africa were not formerly discrete and subsequently ruptured by the Middle Passage before becoming consolidated in specific American configurations. This means that processes of orisha clustering and revisionary dynamism are transatlantic phenomena spanning both the Old and New worlds. Going against the grain of much Afro-Americanist scholarship, Apter suggests that "the West African baseline of Yoruba Orisha Worship is much closer to its New World transformations than has generally been acknowledged" (1995:397), revealing "much greater continuity with its syncretic manifestations than Herskovits ever imagined" (1992:249). Thus flexible contingency of traditional Yoruba religious practice has been neither lost nor invented, but recontextualized within a compacted Caribbean milieu.

Since the time of Melville Herskovits (1937a, 1937b), much ado has been made about hybrid cross-identifications among African divinities and Catholic saints throughout the New World, although the same interidentifications have not generally been made from Cuba to Haiti to Trinidad to Brazil. For example, whereas Oshun—a freshwater goddess—is coidentified with St. Philomene in Trinidad, and her aquatic associations have partly expanded to include seawater (probably because her name in English suggests the sea), she is connected with the national Madonna—La Virgen de la Caridad del Cobre—in Cuba. Moreover, forms of Afro-Catholic syncretism are not always consistent even within any particular national context, such as Oshun's (Oxum) differing associations with various Catholic figures throughout Brazil.

The single most important exception to this pattern of expansive Afro-Catholic bricolage among West African–derived religions across the Americas would seem to be the pervasive popular association of the Christian Devil with Eshu—that outwardly mischievous trickster figure who is ultimately master of potentiality and messenger of the gods. Interestingly, this pan-American phenomenon echoes similar characterizations by missionaries and Yoruba Christians in Africa (Peel 2000). Despite enduring associations between Eshu and the Devil, however, many Shango devotees in the southern Caribbean also appreciate Eshu's nondiabolical significance and supplicate him accordingly. The association of Eshu with the Devil is a particular bone of contention among postcolonial Orisha purists, as we will see.

In Trinidad and Tobago, the degree to which a Catholic persona, or side, is operative for any power varies considerably from deity to deity. There are some cases—such as Peter (Ebejee), Raphael (Jakuta), and Anthony (Dada)—in which the Catholic face is typically far more prominent than the African; some cases in which the Yoruba and Catholic sides may be equivalently weighted and therefore interchangeable in practice—as with Ogun-Michael, Oshun-Philomene, Shango-John, Yemanja-Anne, or Osain-Francis; and cases in which the African face is much more salient than the Christian one—as with Shakpana (Jerome)—or when there is no salient Christian coidentification altogether—as in the case of Elofa (Olodumare). Yet even when the Christian side of the divine is most in the foreground, this hybridizing Afro-Catholic dynamic is one in which Catholicism is simultaneously affirmed and transcended.[6]

Where the mythic iconography of Catholic saints operates, elements of their symbolism have become incorporated by the respective personae of the local powers. Consider Ogun, for example, who in Yorubaland is a forceful, bivalent, "hard" god associated with ironworking and metallurgy. In TT, Ogun retains these characteristics but has joined forces with St. Michael the Archangel, and as "chief angel," Ogun-Michael is ideally the first power to arrive and receive offerings on the inaugural night of annual feast ceremonies. Since Ogun is a masculine deity associated with metal who battles evil on behalf of humanity, he has become intertwined in local orisha circles with St. Michael, who wields a sword and whose conventional iconographic representation depicts him towering above a demon, ready to lacerate the monstrous one. Thus Ogun-Michael mediums typically manifest him in trance performance through the use of swords and cutlasses as ceremonial "tools."

Ogun-Michael is one of several masculine powers—in addition to Shango-John and Osain-Francis—who are sometimes subdivided into prismatic refractions of one another and conceived as "brothers" under their African or Catholic sides. According to Houk (1995:186–87), this multiaspectuality of Shango and Osain is unique to TT, but Ogun's multiplex nature, on the other hand, is similarly operative in Haiti and Brazil as well as West Africa.

I have also encountered local identification between Ogun and St. George, who carries a spear on horseback in order to engage in battle with the forces of evil. The fact that an Ogun-George vector has not been commented upon in the past (Houk 1995:187 is the only exception) is curious and suggests several possibilities: that the playing field of orisha ritualism is so vast and complex that previous observers did not encounter such a pattern of connection during their mid- to late-twentieth-century periods of fieldwork, or that this trend is more recent.

In George's case, it seems likely that the central significance of metal weaponry fueling Ogun's symbiosis with Michael is similarly salient in relation to St. George and his holy spear, as well as Ogun's local interface with Hanuman, monkey god-man of Hindus who wields a magical *mukhtar* club.[7] Symbolism deriving from West African orisha cosmology has become intertwined with imagery stemming from the saintly pantheon of Catholicism, encountered in symbols, images, sacred objects kept on altars to ceremonial instruments, props

Figure 3.7. Ogun-Michael dances with his cutlass. Photo by author.

Figure 3.8. Conventional Roman Catholic chromolithograph of Saint Michael.

Figure 3.9. Conventional Roman Catholic chromolithograph of Saint George. This image and that of Saint Michael are widely available in Catholic bookstores.

Figure 3.10. Galloping his horse within the ceremonial arena, Ogun-George dances with spear in hand. Photo by author.

used in trance performance, and the intimacies of devotion or daily prayers. The symbolic revisionism afforded by Yoruba-based religiosity facilitates the appropriation and digestion of all kinds of initially foreign or alien cultural elements and social influences.

The following is a compilation of Yoruba-inspired powers prominent on the local scene in Trinidad and Tobago and their primary Christian cross-identifications and some of their more important tools and symbolic paraphernalia: Ogun←→St. Michael, St. George—cutlass, sword, spear; Shango←→St. John—double-sided axe, whip, cross, shepherd's rod; Osain←→St. Francis—*cocoyea* or *shesheray* (coconut frond) broom, candle, coals; Oshun←→St. Philomene—water, anchor, goblet, perfume (especially lavender);[8] Yemanja←→St. Anne—water, oar, sometimes goblet; Shakpana←St. Jerome—shesheray broom, calabash; Oya←→St. Catherine—hatchet, calabash, goblet, coal pot; Erile←St. Jonah—cane or bamboo rod, dagger. Other divinities that deserve mention include the more Christian-sided powers alluded to earlier or those—such as Obatala—whose African faces are clearly most salient.

Additionally, some powers are more obviously local contributions to the pantheon. One fascinating Afro-Catholic innovation that I have only heard about, not witnessed in person, is the manifestation of La Divina Pastora (The Holy Shepherdess)—a small, dark icon of the Virgin Mary housed in the southern parish church of Siparia—in the feasts of yesteryear. La Divina Pastora was patroness of the Spanish Capuchin missionary order that came to Trinidad via Venezuela in the eighteenth century, bringing images of and devotions to the Holy Shepherdess with them. Several older practitioners told me about mediums who used to manifest "La Divin," as she is popularly called, earlier in the twentieth century, but her votaries have apparently passed away, and there does not seem to be any activity on this front anymore. It is said that La Divina Pastora dressed in white and was mute during feasts, and she does not seem to have entertained any explicitly African pattern of identification or nomenclature.[9]

Aside from La Divin, there is also the case of Mama Lata, whose name seems to derive from the patois French for Mother of the Earth—Maman de la Terre—but whose characteristics vary to some degree. Simpson (1980:21) describes her as a quick-tempered, stubborn woman slow to forgive wrongdoings. In my experience, Mama Lata's most commonly exhibited performance characteristic involves the use of a walking stick in the course of ecstatic manifestation, upon which she puts both of her hands as she shuffles around the ritual arena, since she is often taken to be an old woman. Lum (2000:122) reports two contrasting versions of Mama Lata—young and old—but the old woman is more prevalent, typically using a walking stick and wearing a straw hat when she comes.

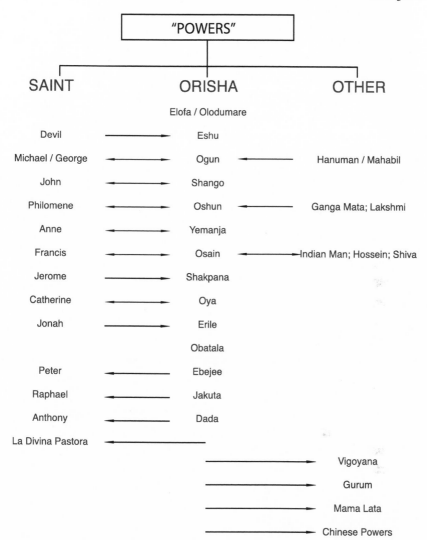

Figure 3.11. Shango-Orisha pantheon. Unidirectional arrows indicate the weight of local identification for each power; bidirectional arrows represent equivalent weighting among the African, Catholic, or other "sides" of a power. Illustration by Felipe Zúñiga.

Then there are cases of deities, such as Vigoyana, that are not well accounted for in theological or cultural terms, but that are nevertheless suggestive. Known as the "Buck"—a colloquial term to refer to Amerindians—Vigoyana is said to come from Guyana on the nearby South American mainland. Moreover, a generic set of Chinese Powers is not uncommon in orisha circles, suggesting mythopoetic tribute to the sociohistorical encounter of Afro-creole religion with Chinese people and their imagined culture in this New World neck of the woods. One prominent orisha priest sees Oshun as having a specific Chinese side called Tim Soy (Lum 2000:115). Simpson (1980:25) reported encountering a set of "Spanish Powers"—saints Amengo, Jephat, Lucy, and Louise, similar to the evolution of Chinese Powers—during his research in the 1960s; however, they have since receded.

The complexity of the orisha pantheon is clear not only from its localizing sociohistorical dynamism but also in relation to an ever-proliferating array of permutations and idiosyncrasies in practice. A more recent example of innovation resulting from the mythologization of local experience is the conceptualization of one orisha—Anthony-Dada—as Rastafarian among the heavily Rasta-oriented drummers within the tradition (Houk 1995:134).

Despite the significance of Afro-Catholic hybridity in local religious experience, then, the spectrum of Afro-Christian—in relation not only to Catholicism but also to Anglicanism and varied Baptist traditions—and inter-African syncretism is much more complex and convoluted than analytical models have heretofore surmised. All of ashé's creolized "sides" must be taken into account.

I think Shakpana's local namesake derives as much from the Fon-Dahomean Shakpata as it does from Obaluaiye-Shoponnon of the Yorubas, each of which represents cultic cognates of the West African smallpox deity. Though Shakpana has lost his primary association with smallpox in the southern Caribbean, he is nevertheless powerfully associated with healing and disease. Indeed, the honorific *shashara* broom of the West African Obaluaiye-Shakpata cult has become greatly expanded within the ceremonial arena of Afro-creole Orisha Worship in Trinidad and Tobago, where it is colloquially referred to as a "shesheray" (or "cocoyea") broom and also used by other powers. One might even say that Shakpata-Obaluaiye's African broom has become a standardized tool of the Afro-creole orishas.

Trinidad's Osain is one of the main beneficiaries of this diasporic expansion in the ceremonial use of Shakpata-Obaluaiye's broom. Osanyin in West Africa is the god of sacred herbalistic medicine. His lore depicts him as physically bizarre, he is intimately associated with ventriloquism and bird imagery, and he is deeply intertwined with Ifá, the god of divination. In the southern Caribbean, Osain seems to have lost all of these African attributes except for his central role as bush doctor. However, his creole persona has taken on a capacity never sported in West Africa: the practice of manifesting via the ceremonial performance of trance mediums. According to Robert F. Thompson (1983:43–44), Africa's Osanyin comes not via the body of a devotee but through a complex therapeutic art of ventriloquism that also resurfaced in Cuba. Thus the Afro-creole case of Trinidad's Osain not only presents us with inter-African creolization in the form of Osain's broom, but also instances innovative charismatic apotheosis in the West Indies in which a formerly *non*-ecstatic divinity took on a new sacred job description.

Moreover, Osain in Trinidad has become a prominent locus of (East) Indianization and indexes a fascinating sphere of Afro-Indo hybridity. For many devotees, Osain–St. Francis is primarily identified as the "Indian Man" or "Indian Power." Osain has demonstrated a local tendency toward fire handling or fire walking while ecstatically manifesting through mediums on feast nights, something I have witnessed on a handful of occasions (also reported by F. Mischel 1957; Simpson 1980; Mahabir and Maharaj 1996). In West Africa it is Shango who has traditionally been the main fire player (Bascom 1972). Shango's Trinbagonian avatar has likewise exhibited an appetite for pyrotechnics. Yet one must wonder whether we can easily assume that Osain was influenced solely by Africa's Shango in the southern Caribbean, as one might be inclined, or also by Hindu forms of fire walking as well. Indeed, fire walking in Trinidad is prominently associated with ecstatic Hinduism, as we will see in the next chapter.

Whatever the case, Trinidad's Osain–Francis–Indian Man is known to jharay—a folk Indian form of symbolic healing—supplicants seeking his healing power in the contexts of orisha feasts and otherwise. Trinidadian folklorist Daniel Crowley (1957) speculated that the development of a creole identification involving Osain as an Indian power may have been based on the phonetic similarity between the orisha's African namesake and that of the Muslim saint Husayn, grandson of the prophet Muhammad whose martyrdom is commemorated in the annual, well-known Muharrum (Hosay) rites of St. James, Port-of-Spain, and the southwestern state of Cedros. Indeed, Osain is often referred to as "Hossein" locally. However, in my experience, Osain's Hindu side is also now understood as Lord Shiva for some. Though there are other ways South Asian–derived elements of local Hindu and Muslim practice have been appropriated by Orisha Worship (see Mahabir and Maharaj 1996), creolization of Osain as the Indian Man seems to represent the most elaborated form of Afro-Indian symbolism in Shango cultism (cf. Aiyejina and Gibbons 1999).

The cases of both Ogun and Oshun are also significant, though less prominent. Since the mid-twentieth century at least (F. Mischel 1957; Mahabir and Maharaj 1996), Ogun has periodically incarnated himself within some orisha circles as Hanuman—the anthropomorphized monkey god-man of Hinduism—or Mahabil—a colloquial rendering of Maha Veer, Hanuman's south Indian namesake. That Hanuman wields a large, powerful club—mukhtar—in his mythical pursuits is suggestive, given Ogun's local penchant for swords, cutlasses, and spears. Moreover, Oshun has more recently undertaken a local connection with Ganga Mata (Mother Ganga), encompassing Hindu goddess of the sacred Ganges River in India whose local followers impressively span the heterodox to the orthodox, as well as Mother Lakshmi, who is nationally venerated during Divali and probably the most important orthodox goddess for Hindus in Trinidad, as well as the most well-known Hindu goddess for non-Hindus.

Overall, it is fair to say that southern Caribbean Shango has selectively appropriated dimensions of Indian symbolism into what is more fundamentally an Afro-creole sphere of practice. Appreciating the complexity of the pantheon is one of the many ways we may apprehend the resilient dynamism of this fascinating ritual tradition.

Structure and Improvisation in the Feast Script

Once Eshuing is complete, offerings of water, olive oil, incense, and so on are offered in the four corners of the palais. The group subsequently begins singing to the orishas by praising and calling them. The deities focused upon are usually dictated by which night of the feast is under way. Practitioners espouse an ideal sequence of invocations running through a series of specified powers but, other than beginning with Ogun on the opening night, one encounters variability from shrine to shrine in the "rotation" through which the powers are called.

Lum (2000:120–24) reports the following night-by-night sequence as standard, which rings more or less true in my experience: *Tuesday*—Eshu, Ogun-Michael, Mama Lata, St. Raphael, Shakpana; *Wednesday*—Osain–Francis–Indian Man, Oshun-Philomene, Erile-Jonah-Ajaja, Yemanja-Anne; *Thursday*—Shango-John and Oya-Catherine; with other, less prominent powers interspersed along the way. Live sacrificial offerings are not typically made on Friday night into Saturday morning. The last night is when any of the powers may return and manifest but usually features final climactic appearances by both Shango and Ogun.[10]

One feast night in August of 2000, in the foothills just above Tunapuna, I witnessed an incident that provides useful entrée to a more up-close discussion of orisha practice. The shrine head—known as Boysie Ben—is an older black gentleman with long, gray, matted locks. The multistoried compound flows down the crest of the hill where it is located. The labyrinth of levels and rooms is inhabited by a retinue of Ben's biological and spiritual children of varying ages in addition to his common-law Indian wife. Here I focus upon an unanticipated incident—something of a duel—that unfolded on the opening night of the feast, since it reveals the interdependence of structure and improvisation in orisha performance and a glimpse into the recursive complexity of relations between Orisha Worship and Kabbalah.

Ben patiently entertained an initial battery of questions from me while resting in the chappelle before the official activities. Members of his spiritual family prepared the ceremonial rooms, the sacrificial sites, and the animals. The feast began as usual, with perfuming, incensing, and dousing of the space with olive oil accompanied by light drumming and song. Then a long series of unaccompanied Christian prayers were said in English followed by a litany of African prayers led by Ben, his wife, the shantwelle, and their attendants in the center of the palais. Libations and obeisance were made in the cardinal directions as well as to the drummers, who proceeded to strike up their first of many rounds of more intensive percussion.

Once Eshuing was completed, the shantwelle began the first of the song-chants for the orishas while Ben paced about the palais, singing and raising the moment's élan. A woman singing and shaking chac-chacs began to convulse slightly and twist and turn in place, but she bent over and touched the earthen floor to ground the energy and not let it take her over too early. It was not long

Figure 3.12. Drummers positioned inside a palais on a feast night. Photo by author.

Figure 3.13. Set inside a circle of libations on the palais floor, offerings to Eshu on the first night of a feast. Photo by author.

Figure 3.14. Practitioners circle the offerings to Eshu within the performance space of the palais. Called "Eshuing," this enactment on the first night of a feast is meant to prevent the deity's disrupting the rest of the proceedings. Photo by author.

before Ben began showing signs of active spiritual presence in his body. His movements became stilted and abrupt; he swayed to and fro and spun in place. His manifestation gained momentum, and the transition from human to super-human, taking some five to ten minutes, was seamless and smooth. Once the power—St. Michael—had fully manifested, he was recognized with a libation of olive oil to Ben's head and feet. His pants were rolled up and a ceremonial sash in red—Michael/Ogun's color—was tied around his waist. The spirit acknowl-edged the drummers, shantwelle, and Ben's wife.

Ben's Michael purified the space with a cocoyea broom that had been fetched from the chappelle and anointed with olive oil. He drank water from a clay vessel and blew it in various directions. An assistant brought out a cutlass and anointed it; Michael then danced it around before greeting everyone present. Next a sword—another of the saint's tools—was brought out, blessed, and given to him in anticipation of his planting it into the earth in front of the drummers to "open the door of the feast." This signaled the formal entrée of legitimate ecstatic presence.

Throughout this whole sequence of activity, Ben's Michael danced with the smooth, gentle, authoritative moves that come with age and years of experience. But just on the cusp of Michael's sword planting, another man suddenly began to manifest, upstaging the flow of events. I recognized the man from another feast many months earlier, where he had taken up Erile's dagger and "tested" many people—including me—by stabbing the air around our heads. It was not typical behavior but had not been entirely beyond the ritual's frame of refer-ence, as manifesting mediums may test the faith of congregants in various ways. I later learned he was an itinerant medium with no shrine of his own. Once he began catching power that first night of Ben's feast, his female companion held his body while it underwent paroxysms. Soon she removed his hat, shoes, and pants only to reveal red short pants underneath, matching his shirt. Almost as soon as it precipitated, his manifestation broke loose from the sidelines and usurped everyone's attention, controlling the ensuing ritual action for upwards of an hour.

Now in full force, the as-yet-unidentified entity saluted the drummers and greeted those present. The shantwelle retreated, striving not to break the perfor-mative frame yet unclear how to proceed. Ben's Michael remained stoic as the manifestation secured their greetings, received libations of olive oil, and then danced with a cutlass, thrusting it forcefully under the gaze of the audience. He communicated through a series of grunted words and gestures, vigorously pointing first at the shantwelle, then at Michael, and back at the song leader, reprimanding him. The music stopped. People shifted uncomfortably, wonder-ing what the fuss was about; the shantwelle was clearly irritated.

Finally, his attendant was brought into the fray as an interpreter. The "entity"—as it was later described to me—had arrived because he thought the shantwelle slack in his duties. Michael had been present for too long without the planting of the sword, nor had anyone ascertained what kind of work or messages Michael had to offer, a serious breach of procedure in the visiting spirit's view.

Tensions rose, but eventually the medium backed down. He hugged Michael and knelt at the feet of the shantwelle. He then clapped his hands in the air; the drummers began again and people recommenced their singing. As a sign of resolution, a red ceremonial sash was tied around the medium's head.

But Ogun's sword had still not been planted. Having been legitimated with the ceremonial sash, the manifestation danced again and rearranged the drummers, motioning for Michael to plant the sword. Ben's Michael walked the sword forward and planted it with the assistance of libations from the secondary spiritual actor. The latter requested another cutlass repeatedly from the song leader, eventually receiving and dancing it about the palais. The entity then brought Ben's family into the center, lecturing them in his spiritspeak about contributing properly to the feast. As the drumming and song chanting continued, he poured milk into their mouths and poured sacralized flour on their heads and faces. Then he motioned for Michael to take his place again in front of the drummers. Michael did so, then turned and poured libations of milk onto the earthen floor in the direction of his rival, whose assertive dance continued.

What happened next was captivating. The entity singled out Mother Melody (a pseudonym)—who just happened to be the spiritual mother who had initially put me onto Ben's shrine—by blessing her on the head with the cutlass and pulling her into the center of attention. It became clear he was trying to induce her to manifest as well. She kept shaking her head and trying to look away, but the entity would not back down, repeatedly circling around and urging her into action. Eventually his attendant intervened again, as Mother Melody's irritation was on the rise. Yet, even with the interpreter and after much back-and-forthing, things remained equivocal. The manifestation again drew near Melody's face, proving the final straw. She wagged her finger, voiced her displeasure, and took leave of the palais.

The entity then blessed the drummers and called Ben's Michael—who had been unobtrusively hanging back, gently shaking and convulsing under the influence of ashé in his body—back into the center of attention. Michael picked up the pace of his dancing. Meanwhile, the entity went round blessing everyone again, including me. Then he assembled the song leader and several of Ben's sons into the center, first blessing the shantwelle and then signaling for Michael to tie red sashes around their wrists. He then put their hands on top of each other on the handle of Ogun's planted sword and directed Ben's Michael to pour libations over them so that it flowed over each hand and down the sword's metal blade.

Michael wheeled his hands in the air, something the other power seemed to understand since he responded with deferentially raised hands. Michael danced while the entity did one final lap before nodding to one of the attendants. Having done so, he turned, and immediately his entire body went stiff and he fell back into the assistant's arms. The medium was carried to a bench, where his companion eventually revived him with libations and a drink of water. With this, Michael moved toward the chappelle with his retinue closely behind, and the play and music came to a grinding halt.

Though I was unable to canvass everyone to inquire as to how they had understood the medium's unanticipated performance that night, many, like me, were unclear. He had become the vessel for some kind of power, but its identity was enigmatic. He had worn red, danced with apparent experience using one of Ogun's cutlasses, and knew the general rules of procedure. Several people speculated that he was connected to Michael himself, since Ogun (as well as Shango and Osain) is known to manifest in prismatically multiplicitous fashion as simultaneous "brothers," or "sides," of the same power at times. Yet Ben later informed me that the manifestation was a diabolical entity who had come to interfere. The terminology of "entities" comes from Circle Work; Ben pointed to the crossing of ceremonial domains by attributing the interference to a Kabbalistic spirit.

The medium in question took such a low profile during the rest of that night that I did not even realize he and his companion had left until the next morning at daybreak, when the feast was breaking up. He did not attend any more of the feast nights, so I was unable to ask whom he had manifested that night from his own perspective. I never saw him again on the circuit.

This is but a single, idiosyncratic incident from one night of a weeklong feast, yet there is much to appreciate in this episode of ritual action: the fluid interconnections between actors and spectators; the division of labor and co-orchestrated nature of trance performance; the social and semiotic subtleties of spirit manifestation; the intimate and even contested hierarchy of authority operative in the ceremonial arena; and the heteroglossia and reflexive consciousness obtaining among practitioners. I want to emphasize the relatively open-ended flexibility of the ecstatic spirit idiom for articulating and accommodating, however obliquely, differing meanings and motives of practitioners in a complex dance of divinity. This incident involved a marginal individual in an already subaltern ritual community. The man whose manifestation temporarily upstaged the flow of the feast's opening-night activities utilized the spirit vehicle to express quasi-aggressive behavior in other feast contexts and to contest the authority and ritual performance of an established local shrine head. Therefore his critique of the song leader may well have expressed a more latent conflict in relation to Ben.

This episode also reveals the degree to which feasts derive their dynamism from the lively interdependence of structure and improvisation. Trance performance in feasts is scripted, yet this schematization frames and models these forms of behavior rather than fully determines them, something crucial to appreciate when the behavior at hand involves the temporary activation of divine power in human mediums who perform and minister to an ever-changing range of supplicants with diverse interests, conflicts, anxieties, and aspirations. The feast script is generative and open-ended, making orisha mediumship and the ecstatic tradition that sustains it quite adaptive and flexible over time.

Rather than challenging things, the visiting medium could just as well have emerged as one of Ogun's brothers and fallen in line with Michael, supporting the flow of orthopraxy and embellished or improvised from within that dramaturgical position instead of contesting it from further afield. Or he could have waited until after the inaugural sword had been planted, when other spirits are welcome, in order to manifest one of the more conventional orishas and carry out its work. But he opted for a spiritual duel instead, for unknown reasons.

I have elaborated an incident here in which conflict surfaced in order to examine the play of structure and agency when pushed toward the bounds of conventional praxis. Yet orisha spiritism encompasses a wide and varied range of behavior, much of which is focused upon creative acts of healing, caregiving, and catharsis but some of which is also oriented toward spiritual entertainment and uplifting spectacle. Indeed, the talents of adept mediums, skillful drummers, and the like are highly respected within this subaltern ceremonial world and therefore are a source of esteem for performers as well as pleasure for observers.

Of course, none of these are mutually exclusive. In fact, the most compelling of spirit mediums in aesthetic terms—whether for Shango, Philomene, or the Indian Man, for example—are more effective as healers or other kinds of spiritual workers than their less accomplished colleagues. Becoming an established and effective medium whose performances come off gracefully and persuasively is no easy endeavor. It takes considerable time, experience, practice, and some natural aptitude. As the tradition is oral, performance-based, individualistic, and proceeds without explicit training, apprenticeship is informal, practice-based, and self-directed, even where spiritual lineages operate.

Orisha mediumship requires aptitude and skill, harnessed in any number of behavioral directions depending upon the personnel and circumstances at hand. Much is scripted, but this scripting affords a plethora of healing activities, devotional relations, performance practices, and improvisational flourish. In a significant sense, the orisha medium's role has become democratized and individualized in the southern Caribbean—as we will see—enabling a diversity of behavior as long as the basic ritual frame is sustained and one's ecstatic performance is felicitous. This has important implications for understanding processes of syncretism and change within the tradition, as innovations may be more easily legitimated and reproduced when introduced by persons operating under the aegis of divinities or when changes initiated by other ritual specialists are granted the seal of approval by deities temporarily manifest in human form.

This dynamic applies to the actions of leaders as a result of their authority at the popular level as well, who may introduce changes that carry weight absent among practitioners with less clout. Many leaders function as mediums on command or have spent extensive time doing so in the past; therefore their authority stems from direct contact with the powers of the spiritual world. Indeed, mediums in any community generally fall under their purview. This makes for a lively, dynamic situation on the ground, especially since mombwahs, drummers, mediums, and devotees travel the circuit widely, thereby connecting shrines to one another and circulating the flow of influence and innovation. It is not a free-for-all, of course, and any innovation is subject to negotiation and transmitted within the matrix of the tradition as a lived system of praxis. But understanding the structure of this system—as I have argued here—enables us to account for its flexibility through time and across space.

Serving the Orishas

Having highlighted the role of direct contact with popular forms of divinity in relation to practice and change within the tradition—whether via trance performance or through control of this activity by mombwahs and shrine heads—it is vital to examine the experience of orisha mediumship in greater depth. The orishas are called according to their place in the liturgy and may manifest upon one or more mediums. But they may also come independently of the rotation, depending upon those present and the energies in motion. There are specific songs for calling each power, honoring and entertaining them, accompanying their healing and spiritual work, and bidding them farewell and sending them away. If a power arrives unexpectedly—outside of the rotation—percussion and chanting may be modified to accommodate it. Manifestations may be brief but often last much longer, an hour or more, depending upon the performer and circumstances.

The orishas are thought of as having unique personalities and known for their respective areas of expertise. Yet in my experience, each may be quite variable from medium to medium, also known as *hoosi*.[11] One person's Osain may be different from another's, as long as the basic choreography and paraphernalia of that deity are taken up and maintained within the frame of ritual action. Indeed, a manifestation may have an agenda, which carries substantial weight when coming from an established medium channeling a high-profile orisha. Relations with the powers are also subject to negotiation on the ground. The fact that so much of their work is oriented toward devotional relations and healing practices means that their worldly activities must be pragmatically responsive to the concerns of their devotees and supplicants.

The performance of healing therefore takes many forms. Shakpana and other powers often use a palm-frond broom in order to "clean" the palais and yard and to symbolically treat sufferers of assorted ailments. I once witnessed an Osain medium wrap an anointed broom around the swollen neck of a woman with goiter, although I have no idea whether she experienced relief as a result. Much of orisha therapeutics might be classified in secular terms as supportive psychotherapy, in the sense that it is more effective in dealing ethnomedically with psychological, as opposed to organic, illnesses.

Tales of miraculous cures circulate within the network, and one readily encounters devotees with passionate testimonies about the efficacy of the orishas. Some specialists are more effective than others, distinguishing themselves on the circuit. Many therapeutic alliances are either initiated or reaffirmed within the context of the feast but, in fact, transpire in much greater depth privately. Depending upon the person and issue at hand, a healer may or may not call upon one's trance capacity in treating patients behind the scenes. "It all depends," I was told again and again in response to questions about these matters.

Healing is just one of several modalities within the behavioral repertoire of orisha-based mediumship, albeit an especially prominent one. The powers are also known as conflict mediators, addressing not only intrapsychic problems, but also marital, domestic, and unresolved familial issues. In addition, they may reprimand people for transgressions committed inside or outside the ritual arena, demanding a confession or repentance and disciplining them accordingly. One of Shango's implements, for example, is a dried jungle-vine whip called a pessie that he wields with stern authority. "When Shango come wid' de pessie," it is said, "yuh know is real licks yuh gettin'!"

Spirit mediumship may also operate as a conduit of reflexive feedback or self-critique. Lum (2000) reports several cases of mediums stabbing or wounding themselves as punishment for previous offenses, although I have not witnessed anything this dramatic. I have, however, observed spirits deliver messages attending congregants were instructed to relay back to the medium him- or herself after the entrancement had passed. These may be recriminations for wayward deeds, but they may also be proactive communications, such as instructions about what course of action to take in everyday life, or an injunction that one should undertake a special period of fasting in order to attain further spiritual heights.

It is therefore important to appreciate the multivocality of the spirit idiom as a vehicle for expressing thoughts and feelings along a complex continuum of valence, spanning the positive to the negative and the regressive to the progressive (McNeal Forthcoming b, Forthcoming c). Indeed, the labile contingency of trance performance as a vehicle of personal expression is what makes it such a powerful idiom of articulation. The cultivation and experience of trance is clearly cathartic for many, involving a ceremonial stepping outside of oneself—ecstasis—in which pain and anguish or joy and transcendence may come to the fore under the watchful gaze of the congregation.

It is also essential to note the sheer exuberance and pleasure involved in competent performance. Though this and their spiritual work are not mutually exclusive, the performance of the orishas is autotelic: a legitimate end in and of itself. Materializing in temporary human form offers a chance to dance and delight in the enigmatic efficacy of divine impersonation for performers and spectators alike. It is a highly esteemed talent within the subaltern community, potentially granting alternative prestige to members of the underprivileged classes.

Someone who begins to catch power more generally—at the baseline level—will shake or jerk vertiginously, abruptly twisting and turning, sometimes spasmodically falling from side to side or even onto a nearby bystander. One's head may roll around, the body may be bent over repetitively and thrown to and fro, or the medium may fall to the ground and shake convulsively. Trance behavior of this sort is exhibited along a continuum—as discussed in chapter 1—thus sometimes a person will only begin to shake with some vague sense of "energy," but this will not progress into anything more long lasting or especially prominent.

The abrupt, spasmodic, seemingly uncontrolled aspects of ecstatic trance may be unsettling for inexperienced participants and outsiders, but there is perhaps no more efficient, embodied way of signifying as well as experiencing extrahuman spiritual agency than by exhibiting precisely those kinds of behaviors and movements that signify the inverse of ordinary "human" self-control (see McNeal Forthcoming a, on embodied symbolism and visual culture in trance performance). Thus the initial behavior of persons undergoing their first ecstatic experiences is usually quite erratic and haphazard, requiring much socialization and practice before becoming anything remotely close to a competent working spirit medium.

While there may be one or more full-fledged manifestations at any particular time during a feast—especially when Shango-John, Osain-Francis, or Ogun-Michael-George comes as a prismatic set of brothers—there are also frequent cases in which a fully explicit orisha is present while accompanied by one or more others shaking and dancing secondarily within the palais, who may not be experienced mediums and do not serve any specific orisha.

The ecstatic manifestation of power therefore unfolds along a complex gradient whose poles are characterized by what I defined above as generalized ecstasy or baseline play, on the one hand, and individuated or full-fledged mediumship, on the other. These two poles are exemplified here in the case of Shakpana's medium and a generalized player dancing for a time within the palais on a feast night in southern Trinidad.

In theory, then, ecstatic mystical power may manifest upon any person. Initial activation of ashé—the cosmic energy that animates the universe in Yoruba cosmology—in a person's body is symbolized by erratic, jerky, non-"human" movements, but when the manifestation becomes that of a full-fledged power, there is a transition to the highly stylized, full-fledged performance of particular sacred personae. Since this process involves some inevitable epistemological ambiguity, there are ways of disambiguating the relationship between "human" and "spiritual" presence in the body of the medium. Put concretely, once a power has been identified, olive oil is offered onto the feet and head of the manifesting spirit; the medium's pant legs are rolled up, her head wrap is removed, or his or her clothing manipulated in other ways such as tying a ceremonial sash in the deity's associated color(s) around the medium's waist or head; and the deity is greeted by clasping hands and then touching elbows back and forth. These procedures are employed only once the power has fully "settled" on its "horse."

Once a power has become fully manifest, an experienced medium's movements take on a more controlled and highly stylized character incorporating iconic elements associated with the mythology of the power at hand—their iconography and implements, songs, and associated colors. Competent impersonation of any spiritual power requires the skillful command and stylized

Figure 3.15. A woman manifesting Shakpana greets people in the palais on a feast night. Photo by author.

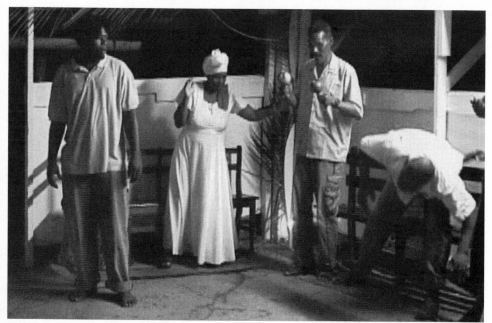

Figure 3.16. A baseline player (the man at left in figure 3.15) begins catching power after Shakpana has moved on. Photo by author.

Figure 3.17. The baseline player moves forward and dances ecstatically. Photo by author.

implementation of that deity's symbolic repertoire within the context of controlled trance performance, certainly no simple endeavor. This sort of trance performativity plays out within a complex dialectic between structure and improvisation. Orisha performance is a spiritual gift looked upon with esteem, and people pay more attention to the most experienced, well-respected mediums, who, not surprisingly, tend also to manifest the more important figures within the divine hierarchy. The more familiar the horse is to the group, the more likely the identity of a manifesting spirit will be considered a potent and more prestigious one, whereas an unfamiliar medium's or neophyte's manifestation is likely to be considered a lesser, unspecified, or even diabolical one, as we saw in the case of the upstart entity on the opening night of Ben's feast.

Thus, with progression over time and cumulative experience in their career as an ecstatic medium, individuals gradually move from initially manifesting generalized ashé to lower-ranked divinity to that of the more prominent deities as habitual practice later on, once they have honed their skills and become established within a shrine community or network. The ways one serves the orishas therefore change over time. We may better appreciate the accumulation

Figure 3.18. Shakpana returns and shares the palais with the baseline player for a time. Eventually he begins to fall back into normal consciousness and retakes his position at the palais bench in the back. Photo by author.

of experience and expertise—as well as the personal flexibility of the spirit idiom—by turning to the idiosyncratic experiences of several practitioners here.

Consider the case of a talented medium named Dexter, who, like Mother Joan, found his way into Shango through engagement with Spiritual Baptism, but unlike her, has shifted progressively from Baptist to Orisha and, more recently, to Kabba. His experience is also interesting in that he has been quite a bit more nomadic than Mother Joan.

Dexter grew up in what he describes as a "staunch Catholic family," yet his mother reports having felt "different" when he was born. When he was seven, she dreamed that a man told her to take Dexter to a Spiritual Baptist leader, which she did, despite considerable reticence. Her son and the reverend connected immediately, and Dexter experienced his first bouts of ecstasy, even performing fledgling ritual work during the church service. The Baptist leader assured Dexter's mother she had a "highly spiritual" child on her hands.

A year or so later, Dexter was taken to a Kabbalistic banquet nearby, where he "revelated" with the host, who was himself manifesting a common Kabba entity named Mr. Steele. This episode concerned the family, not least since the being gave the boy a "light to keep," that is, an injunction to light a candle weekly for protection and guidance from the power. Dexter kept the light for some time thereafter. Another year or so later, Dexter's mother held a Thanksgiving feast, during which the young teen underwent his most intense and dramatic manifestation yet. "I start to work and work and work, and do all kinda t'ing for hours," he reports. This time it was St. Francis, who would eventually become his "patron saint." Dexter began keeping a light for Francis as well.

Yet these experiences were disorientating. He hadn't imagined a future as a spiritist and was fearful about elusive mystical forces claiming his young body. His teenage years were turbulent, characterized by the waxing and waning of ambivalence regarding the spiritual call. He eventually ceased the light for Mr. Steele. After finishing secondary school, he moved to Port-of-Spain, got a regular job, and "limed" (hung out) and partied as much as possible. He vowed to run his own life, away from the spirits.

This was more or less the state of things when, not long after his twentieth birthday, he was in a maxi (a van-taxi with a set route) with friends on their way to a party in Maraval. En route, he heard drums that called him, so he got out and followed the beat to its source, an orisha feast. A brother, or prismatic emanation, of St. Francis was hard at work when Dexter reached the palais. "All I can remember is, he spin meh spin meh spin meh spin meh spin meh spin meh spin meh spin meh, and that was it—I didn't know nothing nothing nothing else until the next morning!" The spirit of Francis manifested in him too. In the wee hours of the morning, after his manifestation had passed, Dexter learned of all the power had done through him. Francis had also proclaimed that he would not be allowed to leave the feast yard until its Saturday morning closing, several days later. He was trapped. All went well that week, yet he remained ambivalent about the seemingly effortless ecstasies arising within him.

He tried moving to New York City to avoid any further development of his mystical tendencies. Still, even there, a friend took him to "a prayers" (Thanksgiving feast) and Francis took him yet again, prompting a return to Trinidad. Still, he remained conflicted.

When Dexter was about twenty-five years old, he attended a feast in western Port-of-Spain with an aunt. That night, both Francis and Ogun manifested through him, leading him to officially commit to spiritistic work. He moved to the empty old wooden house of his deceased grandmother high in the hills of Petit Bourg, where she had given feasts for seventeen years under the auspices of an "old-school" mombwah from Moruga. The powers promised that they'd "see about me and give me everything I wanted" as long as he did their work. "And so, I sink right into it—deeper, deeper, deeper."

He was formally baptized into the Spiritual Baptist faith and also "consecrated" into Orisha Work. A "Shango Baptist" leader in Tobago baptized both him and his sister. Dexter experienced an intense manifestation of St. Francis during his baptism, and he also manifested Oshun after coming up off of the mourning ground, which expresses his "feminine side," he says. Later, his head was washed and incised under St. Francis as his "one settling power" by the babalorisha who became his spiritual father "on the African side." With Francis in place, other powers came more freely. He gave feasts in Petit Bourg, which grew grander over time and deepened his engagement with the orishas.

While mourning, Dexter reports also having met with several Kabbalistic entities. Everything "came back fresh" from when he first met Mr. Steele as a kid. Once back in Trinidad, he began attending banquets and started manifesting beams and entities of various sorts, though he's an especially avid Steele medium. He also has a special relationship with an entity called Mr. Mohammed Khan.

His Kabbalistic "consecration" came in his sleep, obviating the need for any sort of formal induction by a Circle Working guru. In the years that I have known him, Dexter has been especially active on the Kabbalistic side, which he characterizes as the "flip side of Orisha."

He's always been fascinated with Hinduism, having met both Lord Shiva and Mother Lakshmi, in addition to the Buddha, during various "building" ceremonies he's undergone on the Baptist side. This makes sense, since his patron—Osain—has an especially prominent Hindu dimension in addition to his Catholic face. Dexter laid a set of stools for the Indian Powers in Petit Bourg and has kept annual prayers for Diwali ever since. "The Indian Powers did came to me and give me certain work to do. So, is from that that I started doing Diwali work—having prayers for Diwali and plantin' the flag and doin' the little puja and t'ing." He refers to his patron orisha as the "Indian Man" as often he does either Francis or Osain.

His reputation as medium, clairvoyant, and spiritual guide continues to grow. People come for consultations from far and wide. Though he ended up closing down the Petit Bourg yard in 2003, he maintains annual prayers for the powers, both Baptist and Shango. Nowadays Dexter is based out of Barataria but travels widely for his spiritual work, especially to Tobago, where his stature is even greater than in Trinidad, but also Canada and the United States. He and several others have also started a Baptist church in Maraval, where one of their first activities involved a well-attended service for Diwali. He regularly goes down on the mourning grounds for deeper rounds of "pointing," during which he cultivates already existing devotional relations with certain orishas and burgeoning new relations with others.

Dexter's complexifying experience is accommodated by his dual anchoring in both Spiritual Baptism and Orisha Worship, which interrelate and ramify one another without wholly converging. His personal élan for spiritism has ebbed and flowed, gradually gaining traction in his everyday life. His approach to African Work may seem eclectic, but it is in fact built upon a dynamic foundation in Afro-creole spiritism. His spirits influence and reflect his experience. Compared with Iya Rodney's strictly Afro-Catholic approach, or Mother Joan's more Baptist-weighted orientation, Dexter's Baptism seems to be his springboard for exploring new mystical territory and integrating it into his evolving spiritual "intelligence." While he may have come of age in the postcolonial era and his consciousness reflects the time-released popularization of Black Power ideology, Dexter's approach to Orisha Worship nonetheless stems from the increasingly overlapping Shango and Baptist local paradigm that began to evolve before the nation's political independence in 1962.

To probe the variable horizons of personal experience vis-à-vis Orisha Worship and better grasp the transformations and new possibilities of the postcolonial period, I would also like to consider a vibrant young priestess known as Queen Mother Kali, an epithet bearing both Baptist and Hindu referents. Like so many others, her initial entrée into ecstasy came via the Spiritual Baptist Church, but unlike with others, it led her into a period of time in a Sai Baba ashram in southern Trinidad, and from there into Orisha Work with a strongly Hinduized orientation.

As a young girl, Queen Mother Kali found her way from natal Anglicanism into Spiritual Baptism through family connections in Belmont, a historically black middle- and working-class neighborhood in Port-of-Spain. She first came in contact with Hinduism when she was invited to a puja in Arouca, where she exchanged words with a "swami" associated with the neo-Hindu Sai Baba movement. Several weeks later, he came looking for her in Belmont, reporting that he had subsequently gotten a message that he should seek out the church. She took him to her church and was impressed by the swami's debate with the Baptist leaders. Queen Mother soon found herself southwest of San Fernando, undergoing apprenticeship in Hinduism.

The swami and others were impressed with her sincerity and discipline. Though awkward and self-conscious initially as the only black person involved, her spirituality progressed surely and steadily. She chose Kali as her spiritual name after having become repeatedly mesmerized by an iconographic image of the fearsome Hindu goddess in the ashram where she was living and meditating. Queen Mother considers Lord Shiva as divine father and Kali Ma "the Mother of Everything—life and death."

After some years of devotional Hindu asceticism in southern Trinidad, she took up residence in the foothills of the Santa Cruz Valley, with the purpose of "laying down stands" and doing Hindu spiritual work, "to let the Mother walk on the Earth," as she put it. She teamed up with an orisha priest known as Babaluwa, who had found his way to Orisha via Rastafari, with a bit of Baptist influence along the way. He observes that the Afrocentrism of the 1970s conditioned his reception of the orishas, and he is especially articulate about the local stigma and marginalization of Orisha Worship. Queen Mother Kali now manifests both African and Hindu powers and, together, she and Babaluwa give feasts and carry out a complex calendar of ritual activities at their shrine. A small but dedicated intellectual community—many of whom have been or are currently affiliated with Rastafari—has developed around them.

Diwali is taken seriously at their shrine, after which they annually move toward their feast, which Babaluwa sees as "coming home." During feast time their Hinduism becomes more or less quiescent, although they do not hesitate if they have "something to do" for the deotas, or if the Hindu spirits require some sort of attention.

Queen Mother's discourse moves back and forth fluidly between talking about Orisha deities and Hindu deotas. "Approached in the African way," Kali is Mother Oya. Thus Shango's wife—Oya Ma—may be seen as the African side of Kali. Queen Mother Kali's trajectory into Orisha Worship is highly influenced by her neo-Hindu experiences, thereby Hinduizing her orisha praxis rather than the other way around, which is the more common vector for Afro-creole orisha spiritists such as Dexter who dabble in things Indian. Yet, though less immediate in her consciousness, this neo-Hindu foundation is itself underlain by a more diffuse and earlier experience with ecstasy in the Spiritual Baptist tradition.

Take for final consideration the case of Gopal (a pseudonym), a twentysomething Indo-Trinidadian based in Canada but who visits his homeland often and has become involved with the orishas. He found me online several years ago while doing Internet research. A year or so before that, he had been invited to a feast by someone to whom he'd been introduced for spiritual guidance. In his first e-mail, he wrote: "I had no idea what this was about, nor what was going on. It was something totally new to me. I saw many people manifest orisha spirits and thought to myself, 'is this real or fake?'" Several feasts later, he fell under the influence of Osain: "I never thought in my wildest dreams that this would happen to me."

Gopal was raised Muslim, became involved with Wicca when he moved to Canada, then later joined a Pentecostal church. Yet something was still missing, so he delved into goetia magic. This led him to the threshold of serious engagement in Orisha Work.

The man who first introduced him to Shango, and who operates as Gopal's spiritual father, often manifests "ray rays" (*re res*), known as "children" or "messengers" of the orishas. Indeed, it was his mentor's ray ray who steered Gopal toward Osain by telling him to gather items which turned out to be "relics" for Osain, with whom Gopal's relationship has been deepening ever since. He sometimes resists manifestations, but this leads to pain, especially in his shoulders and back. Gopal is also a vegetarian and has ethical problems with animal sacrifice, so he only attends the Friday night–into–Saturday morning of feasts, which do not traditionally involve live sacrificial offerings of any kind.

Gopal has also spoken with several beams from the Kabbalistic side of the spiritistic spectrum, to which he offers candles and rum at stools in a nearby shrine yard. Yet he is afraid of them and does not want to become involved in their manifestation, thereby becoming pulled even further into the underground circuit of Kabba séances.

With the guidance of his spiritual father, Gopal has begun "planting" stools for both orishas and ray rays on family property in San Juan, in northern Trinidad. Using obi seed divination, he accesses the "intelligence" of the powers in search of information for himself and others. At the time of this writing, Gopal was building a palais on the land, which gets him deeper into the tradition. But he has not yet received an official message from the orishas bidding him to start keeping feasts. In any event, he intends for his orisha yard to be free of live animal sacrifices. This reflects his age, ethnic background, and probably his experience abroad as well. Moreover, he designed an orisha-based Web site as a clearinghouse for information about the tradition.

Gopal embodies the dynamism of Shango in such a timely way: a tech-savvy, "saltwater" Indo-Trinidadian living abroad in Canada who nonetheless connects with Orisha Worship back home after a series of very different religious identifications throughout his early life, Gopal has experienced the compelling ecstasy of ashé and has already begun laying down stools as well as building his own private palais. He knows that being claimed by Osain likely means Hindu spiritual extensions and even harbors an ambivalent interest in ecstatic Shakti Puja. From dealing with ray rays to all the rest, Gopal's case may exemplify new patterns of change, but this hardly means change is something new to the local tradition.

Indeed, this examination of the personal trajectories of orisha practitioners illustrates how change has been central to the development of Shango all along; at the same time it throws into relief the historical conditions underlying temporal shifts as well as changing transcultural patterns of innovation and practice. I have focused on those whose experiences not only demonstrate the interlocking reality of personal contingency and ritual flexibility within Orisha Worship as a system of lived practice, but also point toward the complexity of interrelations between the tradition and others, from Catholicism and Baptism to Hinduism and Kabbalah.

Doing the Mother's Work

Whosoever play, let 'dem play!

Senior Pujari at the beginning of a Shakti Puja, September 2000, Pasea

You come to this Mother as a child. You go down on your knees and yuh talk to her, yuh talk to her whether you speak Greek, Hebrew, or whatever. You see, this Mother is energy and shakti and power itself. And believe me, you would feel the grace of the Mother on yuh. One of the greatest things to offer this Mother, you see, is tears from the heart.

Varun, November 1999, Tacarigua

We're here to put back the love, put back the hope, put back everything.

Pujari Krishna Angad, August 2000, Chase Village

Naziph Ali was a Muslim Indian who experienced what he described as "fits and trances" during his youth. His parents brought him to pandits and doctors, but they were unsuccessful at ridding him of what took shape over time as a full-blown spiritual affliction. During his first visit to a Kali temple as a university student, he not only was unable to "shake it off," but also was surprised to find that he harbored strong shakti energy within himself, waiting to be cultivated. Though he'd been "in love with Hinduism" since he was a child, Naziph was ambivalent about this budding ecstatic proclivity. He underwent manifestations and jharayed (healed) people for several months before quitting the temple with the intention of severing ties for good.

This proved impossible, however. He found himself feeling "haunted" again. He sought refuge in another temple—one of the first two modern postcolonial Kali *mandirs*—distinguishing himself as a medium during his first year and making a spectacular debut during the temple's annual firepass ceremony. When the temple was featured on a local television series, *Gayelle*, Naziph was interviewed as one of the "stars" of that year's firewalking.

Naziph took the spiritual name Kali Charan Dass (which he translates as Brave Servant of Mother Kali), although his followers know him simply as the Guru. He founded his own Shakti temple at his home in Penal, which had become one of the more prominent mandirs on the island when I met him in 1999. The temple's liturgical calendar revolved around ecstatic Shakti Puja services on Sundays and satsang (gatherings) for devotion to Shri Sathya Sai Baba on Thursday evenings as well. The temple's two main weekly events contrasted quite dramatically with one another. Satsang was decidedly nonecstatic though moving and heartfelt, involving seated, sex-segregated song and praise led by temple personnel and often accompanied by testimonials from congregants or visiting devotees. Their ecstatic puja was much more active and facilitated the trance activities of generalized shakti players as well as individuated mediumship for specific deities. Trance-based worship also mixed men and women. The Sai Sadhana Shakti Temple also kept an annual tradition of Christmas commemorations that brought throngs of villagers—Hindu, Christian, and Muslim, Black, as well as Indian—from surrounding areas for their Yuletide festivities.

The Guru found his way not just from Islam into Hinduism, but specifically into a somewhat subaltern sphere of Hindu practice that helped him cope with the afflictions of his youth and led him to begin ministering to others. His attraction to Sai Baba and a strict emphasis upon vegetarian (*sada*) worship reflect a more bourgeois neo-Hindu orientation, as compared with that of most of his parishioners. His temple community embodies trends and tensions within Shakti Worship throughout the island more broadly.

In this chapter, I examine the topography of Shakti Worship in terms of social organization, ritual structure, and material culture and explore its dynamic heterodox pantheon through the performances and personal experiences of practitioners. Sociosymbolic flexibility and personal contingency are built into the tradition's grassroots structure, as we saw with Shango in chapter 3. By providing an ethnographic overview of ecstatic Shakti Puja in contemporary Trinidad, this chapter establishes the foundation for an explicitly comparative consideration of Orisha Worship and Shakti Puja in chapter 5.

From the Outside In

Kali Puja and related forms of Shakti Worship have been transformed over the course of more than a century from openly practiced ritual performances observed on behalf of community groups to an amalgamated, somewhat clandestine therapeutic ritual tradition carried out weekly on behalf of individuals and families in heterodox temples dedicated primarily to Mother Kali and her local spiritual associates.

Though Kali Worship has become something of an embarrassment to "respectable" Hindus, ritualized devotions in honor of Kali have not always been so marginalized in the southern Caribbean. Indeed, during the colonial period of Indian indentureship (1845–1917), supplications in honor of the "Mother," as her devotees affectionately call her, were an important aspect of village-based pujas within the sacred calendars of many Indo-creole communities. Over the course of the twentieth century, however, Kali became stigmatized, and outsiders—both Hindu and non-Hindu alike—now commonly look upon her worship with mixed degrees of ambivalence, contempt, and fear. Thus, as with Orisha Worship on the African side, neither locals nor outsiders easily find their way into the space of ecstatic Shakti Puja held in heterodox temples throughout Trinidad.

For outsiders, Kali is considered a capricious and sinister demonness who lures people into her devotions and punishes them for neglecting her. A university librarian once furtively told me about how the well-known Scarlet Ibis Hotel had become stricken by misfortune many years before because the owners reneged on an inherited family tradition of offering animals to Kali. This was early on in my research, but I vividly remember how she got up and closed the office door before sitting back down to relate the anecdote.

In my experience, it is mainly outsiders who see the Mother as punitive and vengeful and who disparage shakti ritualism as dealing with "dark" or "diabolical" forces. Practitioners see their devotions in reverse terms: as helping them deal with problems and the forces of chaos and evil in their lives. As one person told me, "We worship Kali for protection and guidance because a lot of people in this country suffer from a lot of evil. I don't know for what reason, but we have a lot of evil forces around, and certain people get trap, and when we invoke Mother Kali, she is the one to get rid of that evil force. So we beg her when she appears on anybody."

This issue is complex, as at a deeper metaphysical level the power of shakti is morally neutral and can be utilized for varied spiritual purposes depending upon one's intention and the form invoked. As one pujari put it, "Shakti power do not have no sense," meaning that it can be used in multiplicitous ways. Indeed, since the existential polarities of the universe are paradoxically unified in the great goddess and embodied by a plurality of forms stemming from the benevolent to the ferocious, sometimes referred to as the "right " and "left-hand" sides of Shakti Work, Kali may in fact be tapped to engage in less than noble mystical activities. Even when working righteously with Kali's right hand, offering her (or any of the others) blood via animal sacrifice is considered very powerful and must be treated with care. Devotees sometimes concede that shakti may be summoned for nefarious purposes, though this is seen as a "low" form of spirituality. Most believe Kali's shakti should be sought for protection, guidance, blessing, and healing, not as a tool for mystical combat or interpersonal conflict. Anthropologist William Guinee (1992:284–89) observes that it is her ability to simultaneously bridge malevolent and benevolent forms that makes Kali such an effective symbol of healing, signifying the Otherness of both illness and well-being.

The sacrificing of goats and chickens has long been a central element of Kali Puja and has retained its significance in several of the most prominent modern temples. Moreover, the ecstatic manifestation of Mother Kali and a number of other related deotas (deities) through the trance performances of human mediums is the center of ceremonial gravity in contemporary temple-based Shakti Worship, regardless of whether a temple embraces the live sacrifice approach to offerings or not. The general public views both of these practices—catching power and animal sacrifice—as demonic, or dealing in obeah.[1]

I became acquainted with an orthodox pandit from a prominent local Indian family who had never been to a local ecstatic Shakti Puja, yet he warned me to be "very careful." During a visit to India he went to the Kali Ghat Temple in Kolkata (Calcutta) and said he'd been "lucky" he was "spared the trauma" of witnessing animal sacrifices that day, as such activity offended his sense of propriety. The problem with Kali Puja, he explained, was that it involves live sacrifice, and the taking of life is never a good thing. When I pointed out that the sada (vegetarian) offering of fresh coconuts in pujas of all kinds is also, in fact, a form of live sacrifice—since a coconut left on the ground will sprout and grow into a new tree, a point made to me numerous times by shakti devotees—he conceded that it was a complicated issue. Another pandit opined that the notion of meat-eating gods is a contradiction in terms: "Meat-eating *demons* is more like it." A lay orthodox Hindu woman went as far as to claim that Kali Puja is not even Hinduism: "We're Hindu—Kali Puja is a different thing." Shakti temples have also been attacked in the press. In 1988, for example, a prominent temple in central Trinidad almost closed after being accused in a sensationalistic weekly newspaper of engaging in demon worship, defrauding people of their money, and even of tolerating the molestation of a young girl.[2]

Not surprisingly, many shakti practitioners told me that they too initially feared Kali. One pujari's son referred to her as "Frighten Mata," to everyone's great amusement. Her dark-colored iconographic imagery, complete with a garland of skulls, incites apprehension. Yet over time followers develop love, passion, gratitude, and respect for her. I have heard it said that, even though pandits disparage Kali Puja, they themselves sometimes practice it surreptitiously in order to access its power while maintaining a respectable public face. I suspect both fact and fiction at work here but find it telling that shakti practitioners believe it so.

Just as people I spoke with outside the tradition often expressed surprise or ambivalence when they learned of my research contact with Orisha Worship, so too did they react when I mentioned my work with Shakti Puja. "Aren't you afraid?" I was asked over and over. "How did you feel?" "Did you see them catch power?" "Did they drink the animal's blood?" And so on. I began to feel like something of an apologist for both traditions, countering the stigma and misinformation associated with each of them in society at large.

From the Inside Out

Shakti Puja services are usually conducted on a weekly basis in heterodox temples ranging in size from makeshift shacks to compounds capable of holding hundreds of people at a time. There were approximately twenty Shakti temples in Trinidad at the turn of the twenty-first century. However, a handful of these hold only intermittent pujas and at least two of them were dormant in 2000. Two temples—one in central, the other in south Trinidad—hold their services on Saturdays so as not to compete with the two oldest modern Shakti mandirs in the St. Augustine area, which conduct their pujas on Sundays. There is also a temple that holds Friday night services in addition to its regular Sunday puja in order to accommodate visitors who prefer to attend under the cover of night, as well as those few who otherwise attend Christian establishments on the Sabbath.

The geographical distribution of Shakti temples correlates with the pattern of population demographics on the island. They are more or less located either along the northern east-west corridor or not too far from the main settlement arteries stretching through west-central Trinidad and down into the densely Indian areas of what is referred to as "South." Devotees and visitors may be local or may travel significant distances to attend services at chosen temples, as they may have made contact with their temple through distant family connections or by word of mouth, and perhaps also because they want to keep their participation low profile.

Though all contemporary temples may be traced to either of two prominent ones founded in the late 1970s just south of the highway in the Tunapuna–St. Augustine area, there is considerable competition and factionalism among them, which plays out primarily in terms of debate over orthopraxy. Most prominent in this regard is whether live sacrifice is conducted, but areas of contention are not limited to this issue. Competing temples may be criticized for not having "pure enough vibrations," or for having "too much *comesse*" (confusion and in-fighting), or for being involved too much for financial gain, either direct or indirect. Most people say the current situation is not like "long time" (yesteryear), when there was no thought of material gain. However, the worst offenses are usually seen as stemming from temples other than one's own. My experience leads me to believe that there may be a few cases of exploitation, especially by those who learn the Mother's work at a more established temple and then set up a private healing practice out of their own home. However, these cases are rare. And I know of very few whose temple-based income enables them to seek no other source of livelihood.

Most temples are oriented around a murti (sacred statue) of Mother Kali housed within the central sanctum of the temple compound and often based iconographically upon the popular chromolithographic image of Dakshinakali: Kali standing upon a supine Shiva, with her multiple hands offering boons and reassurance as well as signifying destruction of evil and the impermanence of the world. But there is important variability in this regard.

In her temples, statues and chromolithographs of other Hindu deotas of both orthodox and heterodox derivation accompany Kali. The most commonly found orthodox divinities include Ganesha, Surujnarayan, Hanuman, Shiva, Radha and Krishna, Rama and Sita, Saraswati, Durga, Lakshmi, and Ganga Mata (the maternal goddess associated with the Ganges River in India). The heterodox deotas that accompany Kali (Mariyamman) in local temples and who are—with the important exception of Kal Bhairo—generally not found in any of the mainstream Hindu temples on the island include a form of Shiva known as Kal Bhairo or Bhairo Baba (Maduraviran), Dee Baba (Sanganni), Munesh Prem or Muni Spiren, Nagura Baba, and Mother Katerie (Kateriyamma). Names in parentheses indicate the attributed Madrassi names of these heterodox deities for some, resulting from syncretic identifications forged over time between north and south Indian divinities.

While many mandirs are adamantly against live animal sacrifice, ecstatic rituals of spirit mediumship unquestionably represent the most salient feature of all temple-based centers of Shakti Puja on the island. The spiritual manifestation of Mother Kali through an experienced medium is a high point of temple services, and many visit the temple on puja days to consult the Mother and her associates about problems such as illness, domestic or work conflicts, infertility, and sexual dysfunction. As one devotee put it: "Yuh go to Kali when yuh have to, not when yuh want to!" Ecstatic manifestation in these contexts is conceived of as the activation of shakti, a conceptualization of cosmic energy and power within Hinduism that is especially associated with the mother goddesses. This temporary "elevation" of shakti in human mediums makes the practice of jharaying—spiritual purification and blessing—with neem leaves particularly powerful during spirit consultations in the temples. One senior pujari observed that his temple "come like a clinic," continuing: "We can heal the sick with the shakti. But it is not we that is doing it, it is God. So the divine Mother Kali and all the deities—they are using the bodies of these people, of these pujaris, to cure and heal the sick."[3]

A number of other deotas in Shakti temples—the heterodox deities such as Kal Bhairo, Dee Baba, Mother Katerie, Ganga Mata, and Munesh Prem, in particular—also manifest ecstatically via the performance of spirit mediums, offering oracular consultation and jharay sessions. Vibrating spirit mediums often take flaming cubes of camphor into their mouths as a sign that an authentic spiritual manifestation is taking place. Lay members and visitors to the temple on puja days may also become imbued with activated shakti energy and engage in shakti play, a more diffuse form of shakti not identified with a specific manifesting deity (referred to earlier as baseline ecstasy).

It is crucial to emphasize not only that ecstatic forms of Hindu religious practice now take place solely in Kali, or Shakti, temples in contemporary Trinidad, but also that the deities of the Hindu pantheon that do manifest through trance performance and spirit mediumship—such as Kali, Kal Bhairo, Dee Baba, Katerie Mata, and Munesh Prem—are also only found in these very same temples. In other words, ecstatic Hinduism is conceivable in the local cultural imagination exclusively in temples devoted to Mother Kali and her coterie of accompanying heterodox deotas. Thus Kali has become metonymic for any form of charismatic or ecstatic Hindu praxis on the island and in this regard is analogous with the name Shango in relation to popular Orisha Worship on the African side of the religious spectrum. In both cases, the name of a prominent deity from the tradition's pantheon is used to refer to the subaltern ritual practice as a whole.

"Shakti" is a Hindu conceptualization of cosmic power or energy associated with the devis, or female goddesses, who are understood as generating and animating the universe in its multifarious complexity. Shakti is conceived as feminine—whether in benevolent or ferocious form—and personified either as the dynamic, ultimate, independent goddess—philosophically speaking, the feminine ground of life itself, that is, Shakti with a capital "S" and Devi with a capital "D"—or as the divine consort of a male deity, whom she invigorates and supports (see R. L. Brubaker 1983; Kinsley 1975; Mookerjee 1988; Hawley and Wulff 1982; McDermott and Kripal 2003). As an independent divine feminine force, Shakti is refracted into a plethora of differentiated devis, each with her own individuated personality and mystical powers. Thus Saraswati and Kali, Durga and Lakshmi, Mother Ganga, Mariyamman, Draupadi, Parvati or Santoshi Ma, and so on are all metaphysical emanations of the one ultimate Devi/ Shakti/Goddess.

Shakti cosmology is relevant in the context of southern Caribbean Kali temples because these are the sole contexts in which trance performance and spirit mediumship are carried out and conceived of auspiciously as the incarnated activation of shakti. The temporary ecstatic amplification of shakti in a human body makes spiritual consultations both possible and powerful in these temples. People seek to be jharayed by shakti mediums wielding handfuls of wet neem leaves that have been ritually prepared with manjatani for the puja. Though there are other deotas that manifest in these temples, Kali has taken on an especially prominent position in the practice and its pantheon. This is why such temples, as well as the ecstatic form of puja practiced within them, may be referred to somewhat interchangeably as "Kali" or "Shakti."

Even with temples that practice animal sacrifice, orthopraxy requires that devotees and visitors alike abstain from meat, alcohol, and sex for at least three days before the puja. Many arrive on the morning of the weekly service armed with flowers, milk, fruit, and so on, which they offer to any or all of the various deotas. The temple on the morning of the puja day is therefore a hubbub of activity before the service begins, with temple personnel preparing and lay devotees making personal offerings and prayers to chosen deities whose blessing or healing power they seek. At some point those in charge gather everyone together and offer a preliminary prayer and possibly even an instructional sermon about Kali's significance or the meaning of Shakti Puja. Devotional songs are sung, and a few of the larger temples take up collections and raffle off some item of ritual paraphernalia, such as a chromolithograph blessed with *vibhuti*.

With initial announcements, songs, and discourses completed, the general structure of the ensuing puja consists of the pujaris and attending temple personnel as well as a group of participant-observers moving to each and every deity's stand—the place where the deota's icon is located—to make offerings of fruit, flowers, green and dry coconuts, incense, fire, and so forth, as well as possibly to erect a spiritual flag—jhandi—representative of each deota's power. Typically, the senior pujaris conduct the puja ritual proper at each deity's stand while being assisted by an assortment of well-orchestrated junior pujaris without whom the ceremony could hardly take place. The round of individual pujas to the various deities culminates in group devotional puja directed toward Mother Kali. If the temple conducts live sacrificial offerings, the animals are beheaded with an emphasis on a single stroke of the cutlass during the period in which the group makes offering to each deota at his or her stand.

Devotions sung in combinations of Hindi, Tamil, and, increasingly, English accompany the temple round of deity pujas and offerings performed at each stand. Hindi language-based *bhajans* (devotional song-chants) are typically sung for the orthodox deities in the temples, whereas a small, vestigial Tamil liturgical repertoire—predominantly based upon the teachings of pujaris from Guyana in the 1970s—is often used to call, supplicate, praise, and beseech the heterodox deotas that manifest ecstatically in local temples.

However, not all contemporary Shakti temples utilize the creole Tamil song base for their ecstatic puja activity. Some modify the Hindi bhajans or have developed song-chants in their own English tongue in order to orchestrate and worship the ecstatic deities. This is significant, since very few people know any language other than English at the turn of the twenty-first century, as compared with earlier times.

The rhythmic percussion of multiple *tappu* drums accompanies these song-chants. Tappu are thin, goatskin drums held between the shoulder and forearm, played primarily by males using two thin sticks, and found only in shakti temples in Trinidad. They resemble the type of drum used in the old-style Madrassi firepass ceremonies practiced on the island until the mid-twentieth century and have been revived in Kali temples under the influence of Guyanese collaborations in the 1970s. These drums were also used in colonial-era Madrassi funerary practices and are strikingly similar to the Afro-creole *tambrin* drum of Tobago. Tappu drumsticks are of different lengths, one longer, one shorter, which gives the drum a distinctive acoustic sound. Two basic rhythms are played: a slower "hand" used to "raise" the ecstatic deotas; and a faster one played to honor and praise the powers when they arrive. One large temple also uses a *woodki*—a small, hourglass-shaped, double-sided drum played by tapping on the side strings and singing through the membrane in order to praise the Mother with an ethereal voice—based on the south Indian *udakki* prototype they've seen in published literature from South Asia.

Figure 4.1. Performed only in shakti temples, tappu drumming accompanies song-chants during worship. Photo by author.

Figure 4.2. Singing through the membrane of the woodki drum produces an ethereal sound to praise the Mother. Photo by author.

The standard round of temple puja begins with the orthodox deities such as Surujnarayan and Ganesh and progresses toward an ecstatic climax with the heterodox deotas. Songs are sung and offerings made at each deity's stand along the way. Individual pujas for the orthodox figures are briefer than those for the culminating heterodox divinities. If the temple practices animal sacrifice, one of the temple's mediums will begin manifesting the spirit for whom it is being given when the time comes to make the offering. The deota must be present in the form of a shakti-activated human body in order to properly receive offerings of blood.

Along the way, any number of pujaris or lay devotees may also swoon with ecstatic shakti, their gyrating bodies congregating in front of the focal deity's stand. Many assistant pujaris orchestrate this activity, since vibrating shakti players call for manjatani to be poured over their heads and down their bodies in order to purify and fortify their manifestations. The round of deity pujas gathers momentum, moving toward a climactic display of worship for Mother Kali and her closest associates, such as Kal Bhairo. The final part of the prototypical service involves a period in which the most experienced mediums take up positions at each of the ecstatic deota's stands, usually Kali, Kal Bhairo, Dee Baba, Mother Katerie, and Ganga Mata, although temples vary in which deotas they "raise" ecstatically and offer for jharaying and therapeutic consultation. In the newer temples that emphasize sada worship and overlap with devotion to Sai Baba, these ecstatic consultations have started to include some of the orthodox deities such as Hanuman and Shiva as well as Lakshmi and Durga, perhaps a prelude to future developments.

Lines form in front of each stand whose deity has manifested. People discuss problems with the deota channeled by the medium, ask for blessings and guidance, seek the divinity's special jharay and healing power, or confess sins in need of amelioration. Though these consultations are conducted openly within the space of the temple, everyone except those directly involved stands back to create a sense of privacy for the divine interchange. The end of the puja service is also a time when severe cases of illness or spiritual affliction may be dealt with more privately by the temple's primary healers.

Leaders of some temples may also be available at other times, perhaps setting aside a weekday to "see about people" with special spiritual concerns or healing needs. I also know of several shakti devotees who run private healing centers out of their homes without holding public puja services. All these forms of spiritual healing and therapeutic consultation—being tended to publicly by manifesting mediums, privately by a temple pujari, or within the context of a private home healing center outside the purview of the temple proper—may involve the healer concluding that the supplicant should consult a biomedical doctor.

Although weekly services are the most common form of Shakti Worship engaged in throughout the year, most ritual communities also perform one or two Grand Pujas each year that take place over several days and involve weeks of preparation. The structure of the annual Big Puja is similar to that of weekly services, but the rituals, devotions, and offerings are bigger, more elaborate, and conducted with greater fanfare. Whereas weekly puja is offered on behalf of the lay temple community and the public, each temple's Big Puja represents the annual, or semiannual, climax of the primary ritual community's devotions. It is often described as a "thanksgiving" put on by the main puja personnel. The temple is repaired and cleaned; murtis are refreshed, redecorated, and reinstalled; and a special set of offerings—animals, fruits, vegetables, and flowers if the temple engages in live sacrifice, or solely sada (everything except animals) in vegetarian temples—is made on behalf of the temple community.

The ritual period of the Big Puja affords an auspicious opportunity for members to display the purity and authenticity of their devotions in two tests, which they undergo under the gaze of the temple audience while experiencing shakti: (a) receiving lashes from a ceremonial whip or chain without incurring injury, or (b) walking or dancing through a fire pit without getting burned—although firewalking may be carried out while not in a state of trance in some temples, depending upon their preferred methodology. These tests substantiate the transcendence of pain through recourse to shakti power (discussed below).

One of the most significant differences between weekly services and the Big Puja is that the latter typically involves the carrying of *kargams* from a river, stream, or the sea to the temple for its several-day duration. Kargams signify the power of shakti and are put together in an esoteric ritualized procedure using a lota (brass vessel), dry coconut, neem leaves, and several other ingredients. They are carried in and out of the temple on the heads of either children specially chosen from the temple or ecstatically vibrating devotees at the beginning and end of the puja. The presence of the kargams spiritually recharges the temple and its attendant community with the cosmic shakti of the mother goddesses. Being present for the building and carrying of the kargams is considered especially auspicious.

The other significant feature of the Big Puja of each temple that differs from their weekly events involves the conjuring of several of the core ecstatic deotas, such as Kali, Mother Katerie, Ganga Mata, or Kal Bhairo, on the road near the temple on Saturday night. This practice signifies the temple's commitment to "outreach" and may go on for hours and hours. It is said that it has been retained as a vestigial element from earlier days, when the puja was conducted before the temples existed. Devotees, laypeople, and visitors alike line up and wait patiently for an audience with the Mother or one of her associates being channeled by the temple's most talented mediums. Burning cubes of camphor line the road and are sometimes held in the manifesting mediums' hands or put in their mouths to display their power and authenticity. I found these experiences to be especially moving.

An abbreviated set of the rituals involved in temple-based Shakti Puja may also be conducted privately in homes under different circumstances and for varying reasons by a small subset of temple pujaris and mediums. Such home pujas are sponsored either by temple members and their families who keep an annual tradition of domestic supplication, for example, or on behalf of those seeking divine intervention to counter spiritual afflictions or problems plaguing the household. Home Shakti Pujas may or may not involve live sacrifice, but they do necessarily involve select ecstatic manifestations by Kali and several others in order to purify and bless the domestic space, exorcise evil influences, and jharay the inhabitants of the household to ensure well-being. In this regard, the structure of home puja mirrors in miniature that of the temple puja.

The issue of animal sacrifice is contentious for shakti practitioners and has become something of a moral flashpoint between and sometimes even within temple communities. Blood sacrifice is probably the most immediate association outsiders—Hindu and non-Hindu alike—have regarding Kali Puja in Trinidad. Yet most are not aware that many devotees and temples in fact do *not* observe or condone the practice and may be critical of sacrifice as a form of offering and devotion. Indeed, antisacrifice sentiment has in fact become more prevalent.

Temple-based Shakti Worship has attracted the majority of its devotees from the island's rural and urban Indian proletarians; it has also consistently recruited a small but significant minority of practitioners of African and mixed-African descent and a handful of upwardly mobile spiritual seekers. This demographic trend stands in contradistinction to the "mainstream" Hindu traditions and temples, which are patronized primarily by Indo-Trinidadians. Afro-Trinbagonians may attend mainstream Hindu temples or prayers, but usually as guests, not devotees. Things are different in the island's shakti temples, where black people are much more common, but still a minority.

The number of active practitioners reaches into the thousands at least, though a more specific estimate would be difficult and probably misleading given that the population using the temples is always in flux. In this regard, Shakti Puja is similar to the on-the-ground demographic dynamism of Orisha

Worship, in which affiliation is not entirely formalized and the constitution of each temple community is subject to significant fluctuation over time.

Guinee's (1990) survey data demonstrate that people involved in Kali Temples are most often poor and suffering, with nowhere else to turn. Having attempted to relieve their distress through more conventional routes without success, they often turn to an alternative community that welcomes them and addresses their problems. Once they meet with some success through Shakti Puja—accessing the healing power of the Mother and her associates—their motivation often shifts, and they become more deeply affiliated with the temple community. In time, they may even become involved in caregiving for others. Those involved in temple-based Shakti Worship are also more ethnically and religiously heterogeneous than those in orthodox mandirs.[4]

Engagement in temple-based Shakti Puja may develop idiosyncratically through time. I met Olive "Tanti" (Auntie) Lincoln Brown in 1999, just five months after her husband, the late Pujari Mootoo Brown (on which more below), had passed away, leaving her in charge of one of the biggest, most important shakti mandirs in all of Trinidad. This has been a challenging burden, as she never set out to attain such a position, and there is no local precedent for female leadership of Hindu congregations.

Tanti comes from Madrassi lines on both sides of her family. Her father converted to Presbyterianism as a young adult, then became a church deacon. Her mother converted to marry Tanti's father, taking on a "Christian" name to do so. Thus she grew up "going to church and t'ing." Yet her mother never gave up devotions to Mariyamman, though she did not get strong emanations of shakti like others in the extended family. Tanti and Mootoo met through cousins when she was eighteen years old. He wanted to marry, but she was uninterested, as he had been previously married and was a widower with three sons already. However, her mother encouraged Tanti to marry Mr. Brown, and she eventually acquiesced. The union produced several daughters. Life was hard and they worked constantly, even though Mootoo had a decent job with WASA (the national Water and Sewer Administration utility).

Brown also came from Madrassi stock and had inherited domestic shakti devotions from his forebears. His family kept an annual tradition of "Kali Puja done in the Madrassi way," as Tanti put it. The first year she was involved, "the Mother come up on me and I start to vibrate and fall down and all kinda t'ing." As she was Christian, she found it alarming. She'd heard stories about such things from her grandparents but hadn't experienced it firsthand before. "When I started to fall down, I was so frustrated to know what is wrong, yuh know! I used to feel as if my head going so [waving her finger around in the air]—all my body used to be trembling and shaking, and I wanted to know what it is." She also found it strangely compelling. She says she "loved Hinduism" growing up. Mootoo explained what was happening, coaxing her not to be afraid. They decided to "Christen" her Hindu, and they also "went back" and had a proper Hindu wedding, since their first union had been a "table [informal, common-law] wedding."

She's received shakti consistently ever since, having now "played the Mother" since the 1970s. When she becomes tired and confused, Kali comes to her in her dreams, encouraging her to keep up with the work. Though "getting the shakti is difficult," over time her body has become "lighter and lighter." As she observes, "the body come used to that shakti." Indeed, it was Kali speaking through her as an oracle who announced they should build their first temple in the late 1970s, just up the street from where the newer, more elaborate mandir is now located. The old one was smaller and less fancy, but it was peaceful, and some longtime temple members say it was more powerful. Accomplishing all of this was not easy. They "struggled, struggled, struggled."

At some point, Tanti had a dream in which she went up a mountain and met with Lord Shiva, who gave her a mala (a string of prayer beads) and instructed her to become a vegetarian. She did, which her husband, never a vegetarian except when fasting before a puja, found amusing. The only meat Tanti now eats is the Mother's *prasad*, which comes from animals sacrificed to Kali and other deotas at the temple.

Pujari Brown eventually retired from WASA, and they built a house down the road from the first temple. A loan enabled them to build a bigger, more elaborate mandir across from their home, and Brown drew on his pension funds to subsidize the ongoing temple work. Times remained difficult, yet they prayed to the Mother for assistance and somehow managed to "get through." Over time, Tanti learned that Mother Kali was the only one they could count on. "I didn't went to university, but I learnt so much from the Mother—the Mother give me so much knowledge—that I can do anything for she, and I will get her for myself. So, everything is the Mother. I love the Mother so much . . . nothing in this world is more important than the Mother now."

With her husband "gone and dead," she found herself struggling even more. When I last visited in early 2011, she was still in charge and the temple continued to thrive. But with the constant turnover of people, along with the departure of several seasoned pujaris and the rise of newer ones, the problem of temple succession is still very much alive. There is no standard convention regarding the transgenerational succession of Shakti temple leadership in Trinidad. The most likely route is through the family, but there are a number of knowledgeable and dedicated pujaris who are not kin, yet might do an admirable job carrying on the temple work once Tanti becomes too old. The issue is a source of endless tension within their ritual community and of concern and anxiety for their spiritual leader.

Colonial Precursors: Community Kali Puja and Madrassi Firepass

The most significant precursors of what is now known as Kali—or Shakti—Puja are the community-based forms of north Indian–derived Kali Puja and the old-style Madrassi firepass ceremony. Both were independently creolized before becoming reciprocal influences within Kali's current temple-based incarnation. It is only with these antecedents in mind that we may fully grasp the innovative contours of postcolonial Shakti Puja. This discussion substantiates critique of the Madrassi origin ideology of contemporary Kali Puja, which scapegoats such "unrespectable" Hindu practices as attributable to the darker-skinned, ostensibly low-caste Madrassi immigrants from south India.

What is remarkable about the local development of Shakti Puja is that Hindus of the early indentured diaspora in colonial Trinidad do not seem to have considered Kali peripheral or wayward. Indeed, evidence suggests she was in fact one of the more commonly encountered divinities within the scattered array of Hindu ritual arenas and practices operative during that period. In 1871, Anglican clergyman and novelist Charles Kingsley described an early shrine structure adorned with images and figures of Mahadeva (Shiva) and Kali—"We could hear of no other deities" (1892:300)—suggesting some degree of symbolic centrality for Mother Kali among indentured Hindus. References to Kali also appear in a series of short stories written in the 1930s by Seepersad Naipaul. Mother Kali's significance is evident in the description of a would-be pandit's efforts at cobbling together a proper Hindu place of worship (see esp. 1976:82–83). Kali is associated with Shiva, Vishnu, and Hanuman here, evincing no sign of overt stigma. This is especially interesting in light of the fact that Naipaul had "a special horror of the Kali cult," according to his son, the eminent Vidia S. Naipaul (1984:64).

The image of the older form of Kali Puja that emerges from mid-twentieth-century ethnographic reports (Niehoff and Niehoff 1960; Klass 1961) and from oral histories others (Mahabir and Maharaj 1985) and I have collected is that villagers conducted it openly on behalf of the entire community. Not everyone participated in the puja or preparations for it, but they typically contributed paraphernalia or funds in order to receive benefits from the puja. Collections were made during the preceding weeks by groups of women who would pass through all the neighboring villages in an organized group on foot, sing devotional songs accompanied by a *dholak* hand drum, and carry wooden trays on their heads to hold the offerings collected.

Each community performed its Kali Puja at the home of the *panchayati* "captain." *Panchayat* is the Hindi term, now more or less obsolescent, referring to a local village committee consisting typically of five male counselors, although the actual number varied. The puja was carried out annually or in times of special crisis to thank the Mother for her blessings and to seek her intervention. The puja seems to have exhibited a relatively standard ritual structure characterized by the sacrificial immolation of a live goat—although chickens or a pig might be offered instead—after Kali manifested.

Klass (2003) clarifies that trance mediumship for the Mother in each of these types of affairs was typically enacted solo by a medium. The ecstatic pujari operated as an oracle—answering questions about and prescribing remedies for illnesses, for example, or reprimanding people for wrongdoings but does not seem to have jharayed devotees or engaged in explicit healing performances. Upon completion of the puja, meat from the sacrificed animal was divided among families of the panchayat's jurisdiction to be taken home as prasad, food first offered to a deity and then ingested as a blessing.

Whereas those with claims to high caste tended to avoid this kind of puja, Klass emphasizes that they did in fact regularly contribute to them, even while expressing distaste for animal sacrifice. Chamars often officiated as pujaris and pandits were conspicuous by their absence (1961:173–74). Thus Kali Puja seems to have become associated with lower-status religiosity by the late 1950s. "Chamar," as noted earlier, refers to a large, low-caste group in India who traditionally worked as cobblers in the leather-working trades; however, the term has been broadened throughout much of the Indian diaspora to refer derogatorily to low-caste Hindu persons more generally. The Klasses encountered two forms of Kali Puja, known as *panchayati-Kali-ki-puja* and *ghar-ki-puja*, the only difference being that the former was sponsored by the entire community, whereas the latter was a domestic ceremony sponsored by individual families and usually held upon the birth of a child, a marriage, or moving into a new home, with relatives, friends, and neighbors attending by invitation (see also Niehoff and Niehoff 1960:126–29).

Klass (1961:176–78) also observed that all families in his central Trinidadian area of study—*including* those of high status—conducted sacrificial Di (Dee) Pujas for the health and well-being of the home and its occupants, as well as nonsacrificial Di Pujas for agricultural fertility (see also Niehoff and Niehoff 1960). This is interesting not only because it indexes sacrificial Hindu activity

Figure 4.3. Kalimai-ke-beekh, "Begging for Mother Kali," in central Trinidad, late 1950s. Photo courtesy of Sheila and the late Morton Klass.

throughout the entire status hierarchy, but also because Di has become a central deota who actively manifests in ceremonies of trance performance in heterodox shakti temples, where he has received his very own murtis for the first time.

Thus, even though mid-century Kali Puja as described by Klass and the Niehoffs points toward its ostensibly "low" status, we must take this as a sign of changing times. Consider as well that sacrificial puja for Kali was—and still is—an integral dimension of high-caste Hindu religiosity in Bengal, Orissa, Bihar, and eastern Uttar Pradesh, areas from which the most significant number of indentured migrants came to the West Indies. Brahmins are known to have taken active roles in certain aspects of sacrificial pujas for the various independent goddesses of south India as well. The fact that most high-status families

Figure 4.4. Preparing for a village Kali Puja, central Trinidad, late 1950s. Photo courtesy of Sheila and the late Morton Klass.

Figure 4.5. Performing the village Kali Puja, central Trinidad, late 1950s. Photo courtesy of Sheila and the late Morton Klass.

participated indirectly in old-style Trinidadian Kali Pujas through contributions therefore suggests a transitional phase.

Since indentured Indians brought to Trinidad were introduced at the lowest possible social stratum, it is only with progressive social change and class differentiation—facilitated by gradual adoption of Eurocentric standards of bourgeois respectability—that religious activities smacking too overtly of heathen or primitive sensibilities were castigated and gradually associated with the lower classes. Sources suggest that sacrificial Kali Puja involving the presacrificial conjuring of ecstasy was marginalized a bit earlier than domestic sacrificial offerings conducted for the diasporically recontextualized figure of Di.

The other precursor for the development of heterodox temple-based Shakti Puja in Trinidad was the old-style Madrassi firepass, or firewalking ceremony. Although it is not exclusively the case in South Asia or its diaspora, firepass among Hindus in the southern Caribbean has principally been conducted within the matrix of shakti devotion. This is significant because it represents the most prominent religious ritual of the Madrassi indentured migrants and also because it has been partially appropriated by and reframed within contemporary Shakti Puja practiced in postcolonial Trinidad. Indeed, many take the presence of firepass as confirmation of Kali Puja's Madrassi origins, though this influence has been partial, dynamic, and refracted. Clarifying the pivotal, yet also limited, Madrassi legacy with regard to Kali Worship is critical for cultivating a more nuanced historical perspective on Shakti Puja.

The nature of Madrassi influence is best understood by considering that south Indians only constituted approximately 6 percent of the 144,000 South Asians brought to Trinidad between 1845 and 1917 (de Verteuil 1990). The term "Madrassi" was used to refer to migrants of varying regional and linguistic backgrounds from south India who sailed to the Caribbean through the southeastern port city of Madras. Approximately 80 percent of these so-called Madrassis were equally divided between Tamil and Telugu speakers. Compared with those from the north, Madrassis were generally darker in skin color and subject to racialized prejudices of both colonial Europeans and north Indians. Indeed, local society quickly grew accustomed to accommodating the majority north Indian group, who could be quite hostile. The historical legacy of this conflict surfaces in the bifurcating classificatory practice among Indo-Trinidadians positing "Hindu" versus "Madrassi," discussed earlier.

Firepass and Hosay—the local name for the Muslim commemoration of Muharrum (see Korom 2003)—were the two most important festivals celebrated by Indians in the nineteenth century, even more important than the Hindu festival of Divali that is so prominent today. Gerad Tikasingh (1973) observes that

Hosay was performed by estate-resident Indians, whereas time-expired Indians celebrated firepass, which had "greater religious content." Indeed, firewalking seems to have been a cult of affliction in that its practitioners made promises to chosen deities that they would cross through the fire if their illness was cured or their problems solved.

The firepass ceremony is reported as having been held since 1867 at Cedar Grove, Naparima, and from 1868 at Peru Village, Mucurapo, in what is today St. James. Various sources indicate that firewalking was also undertaken at El Dorado, Tacarigua, Chaguanas, Curepe, Waterloo, and Boissiere Village, among other locations. Both Hosay and firepass came under direct government control in 1882 with the passing of Legislative Ordinance No. 9, which regulated processions and the use of various paraphernalia such as torches, required an application for licensed permission from the colonial authorities, and imposed imprisonment or fines upon anyone convicted of breaking these laws. Indeed, J. C. Jha (1974:5) reports that firewalking had become so popular by the early 1880s that such regulations were issued by a "frightened government" to control it. Although it is difficult to be definitive, ethnohistorical evidence indicates that the last full-scale performance of old-style Madrassi firepass took place in the early 1950s at what is now the El Dorado Shiva Mandir. That the Normandie Hotel in St. Ann's, Port-of-Spain, began offering secular fire-walking entertainment geared for tourist consumption during this very same period (Frances Henry, pers. comm., 2000) is suggestive of the complexity of sociocultural change within the broader island society at mid-century.

The local performance of firepass has clear south Indian roots. It was referred to during the colonial period as the "Madras Coolie Festival" (*New Era*, 18 August 1884), for example, and in a newspaper advertisement as the "St. James Tamil Fire Pass Festival" (*Port of Spain Gazette*, 4 December 1919). J. H. Collens's *Guide to Trinidad* (1888:191) described the rite of "passing through the fire" as an "annual one affected by the Madras people." And toward the end of the nineteenth century, missionary Father R.P.M. Bertrand Cothonay (1893:80) described the firepass as the "greatest festival of the pagan coolies from Madras." Ordinance No. 9 also indicates that Temiterna, or the firepass ceremony, was commonly referred to as the "Madrasse Festival." Oral histories collected in Boissiere Village, St. James, El Dorado, and Tunapuna (Procope 1980; Mahabir 1987; McNeal 2000, 2010a) also substantiate Madrassi origins of the local Hindu firepass.

Certain aspects of its ritual structure recur throughout oral and written sources (see McNeal 2000, 2010a, 2010b): periods of fasting and other purification disciplines; exclusive male participation; prayers recited from atop a tall pole erected near the fire pit; preparatory river or sea baths taken just before crossing the hot coals; and the use of a thin, handheld drum akin to today's tappu. Several of the features, such as fasting and purification, preparatory bathing in bodies of natural water, the type of drumming, and the firewalking itself, are related to analogous practices within contemporary temple-based Kali Worship. As for animal sacrifice and trance performance in connection with Madrassi firepass, however, the evidence is more tenuous. Though live sacrificial offerings were fundamental to the emergence of temple-based Kali Puja in the late 1970s, most sources suggest it was *not* central within old-style firepass.

As for the ritual arts of trance in relation to local firepass, the evidence is inconsistent, although it does suggest some degree of ecstasy involved. This conclusion is bolstered by the fact that festival traditions in south India and its diaspora have long been characterized by ecstatic behavior on the part of participants (Younger 2002). Collens (1888:191) described participants as "shouting or gesticulating vehemently" as they passed through the fire in late-nineteenth-century Trinidad. Cothonay observed that "the candidates rush madly" and invited the reader to "picture our hero dancing, jumping, grimacing, and making three turns around the temple" (1893:82). The *Port of Spain Gazette* (12 August 1890) likewise reported that the "dancing" sometimes continued all night, to the annoyance of the neighbors. Although trance performance may be considered a form of sacred dance, these references to "dancing"—however suggestive—cannot be taken as definitive evidence of ecstatic manifestations in the old-style firepass ceremony.

Older, community-based, sacrificial Kali Pujas involved ecstatic shakti manifestations as well. In fact, they may have even been more integral to the old-style Kali Pujas than they were in firepass ceremonies of the colonial era. And there is no ambiguity whatsoever concerning the centrality of live sacrificial offerings to the Mother in the community-based Kali Puja of yesteryear. The important point here is not only to clarify that these sacrificial Kali Pujas and Madrassi firepass ceremonies were originally part of *different* traditions of ritual performance altogether, but also to appreciate the complexities of teasing out their respective historical influences within the amalgamated contemporary scene.

Kali is nowhere near as prominent or prevalent in Tamil- and Telugu-speaking south India—the original home of the Madrassis—as Mariyamman, the great, independent, south Indian goddess whose cult is regionally paramount and who is propitiated in times of need, especially concerning problems of illness and infertility. Ceremonial firewalking in south India has not traditionally been performed under the aegis of Kali, but most commonly as a devotion to Draupadi, and sometimes for Mariyamman as well as for Shiva's son Murugan

(Younger 2010). Mariyamman was brought to the southern Caribbean by south Indian migrants and initially occupied an important position within their spectrum of ritual devotions. Indeed, ethnohistorical sources indicate that Mariyamman's murti was the largest one in the Mucurapo firepass temple during the early days, and we know that the old Boissiere Village firepass temple owned by Veerapin Swamy, a Madrassi, was called the Mariyamman Kovil, *kovil* being the Tamil word for "temple" (Procope 1980). This temple was located on the same spot as today's Ellerslie Plaza car park in Maraval, Port-of-Spain.

Thus both the community-based, sacrificial Kali Puja and the old-style Madrassi firepass ceremony of the colonial era were both dynamic traditions that adapted to their New World context and thrived for a significant period before dissipating by the independence era of the 1960s. They were also precursors of the amalgamated configuration of ecstatic Shakti Puja conducted weekly in heterodox temples under the overarching auspices of Mother Kali. The wave of new postcolonial temples has therefore provided the context for a return of the repressed, so to speak.

However, in speaking of precursors, it is important to emphasize that we are not dealing with simple continuities or influences. Each of these traditions became progressively marginalized in relation to developing class stratification among Indo-creoles and was more or less subjugated by the encroaching dominance of bourgeois-inflected "mainstream" Hinduism. The advent of alternative Kali temples and their subsequent schism and branching throughout the 1980s and 1990s allowed for the recontextualized reemergence of these castigated popular religious forms in a compacted and hybrid constellation oriented within an innovative liturgical matrix. Considering the contemporary case of firewalking underscores this point.

The first "modern" firepass was reportedly held at Bharat Moonsammy's temple in Streatham Lodge, south Tunapuna, at some point after its founding in 1977. By the time of my fieldwork in the late 1990s, the temple no longer observed the rite. People assured me that its firepass was not learned from the Guyanese, but introduced early on by several local devotees in conjunction with a businessman from India who was living and working in Trinidad. Firewalking at the temple was observed at night, involving both male and female devotees who crossed the fire pit under the influence of shakti manifestations. This is the same temple's firepass in which Naziph Ali made his national debut on television in 1991, just before the practice was discontinued. Fire walking was also practiced at a rival temple in Pasea until its leader, Mootoo Brown, decided it was too dangerous.

Meanwhile, the main offshoot from the Moonsammy temple in central Trinidad—Krishna Angad's Maha Kali Shakti Mandir on Joyce Road—has continually carried on firepass and, in turn, has passed it along to several of its institutional progeny farther south. At the Joyce Road temple some devotees cross the fire pit under the sway of trance; others cross based on their devotion and "love for the Mother" alone. Until recently, and only as a result of his tragically premature death, Naziph's sizable temple in Debe carried out firewalking in a manner similar to how he first learned it at Bharat's mandir. By contrast, a Shakti temple in Moruga conducts firepass performances in which practitioners do not vibrate with shakti energy; they simply walk across the red-hot coals in a measured and controlled manner, protected by the purity of their devotion and fasting. Still another temple, in Diamond Village, performs firepass by combining both strategies: "elevated" shakti players and nonvibrating devotees pass across the fire pit, individually as well as in mixed pairs and groupings.

The variability of contemporary firepass highlights the structural flexibility of this ritual performance and compels us to take special care when seeking to delineate relations between earlier and later iterations. Lines of connection between old-style Madrassi firepass and the firewalking of contemporary temple-based Kali Puja are convoluted. It is toward the more recent context that I now turn, delineating in greater detail the emergence of heterodox temples under the auspices of Mother Kali and dedicated primarily to the practice of regular ecstatic Shakti Puja. Clarifying this history helps to further contextualize and critique the Madrassi-origin ideology and enables us to better analyze patterns of differentiation and change among Kali temples around the turn of the twenty-first century.

Postcolonial Innovations: The First Wave and Beyond

Independent traditions of community Kali Worship and Di Puja as well as Madrassi firepass had become more or less moribund by the time of Trinidad and Tobago's first decade of political independence from Britain. Ritual practices involving trance, animal sacrifice, and firewalking had all fallen from grace within the Hindu community as a result of much wider socioeconomic change and class differentiation reflected in the moral economy of religion. This does not mean these practices had completely died out. Indeed, I have spoken with folks who testify to having been involved with, or observers of, recessive forms of Kali Puja or further truncated versions of Di Puja in the late 1960s and early 1970s.

Traditions involving trance or animal sacrifice had been suppressed down the changing local ladder of class relations and progressively associated with "lowly" religious activities. This made them morally suspect in the eyes of the gentrifying form of "orthodox" Hinduism that consolidated well into the twentieth century, but not without its own heteroglossia and contradictions. Just as Indian Christians had previously distanced themselves from grassroots Hindus and Muslims, socially mobile Hindus disassociated themselves from what came to be seen as the "common," "impure," "low-caste" ritual behavior of the lower classes. This put pressure upon the Indo-creole population at large to identify upward, even among folks with modest means, indeed, perhaps, especially among those who sought respectability but did not wield the socioeconomic power to fully substantiate it.

It is with this context in mind that we can more fully appreciate the significance of the Kali temples that arose in the late 1970s, during a time when proceeds from the oil boom were surging throughout society. The fact that Kali became the locus for the convergent reconstitution of several marginalized ritual traditions testifies to her changing symbolic significance among Hindus over the *longue durée*. Kali's mythic personage as an independent, untamed goddess made her an effective vehicle for consolidating those dimensions of Hinduism increasingly seen as the primitive Other within. Though the definitive history remains elusive, it is clear that the first, new, so-called modern Kali temple arose around 1977 as a result of collaboration between Bharat Moonsammy, Mootoo Brown, and several others in the southern Tunapuna area of north Trinidad.

Though Bharat died in 1993, an older son maintained his temple at first; it was subsequently taken over by a younger son who returned from living in Canada and was head pujari during the time of my fieldwork. Bharat was the sixth oldest of twelve children whose parents were both Madrassi. According to their eldest brother, their maternal grandfather made a vow in south India to Mariyamman after being healed from blindness. He brought this devotion to Trinidad and kept his promise for the rest of his days. This devotion was carried out annually without the use of permanent murtis and independent of any temple context. Those involved would go to the river, invoke the goddess through trance, and bring her back to the house for the duration of the puja in the form of a kargam.

The Moonsammy children were exposed to ecstatic Madrassi devotions for Mariyamman from an early age due to their grandfather's influence. The children's mother had especially strong shakti vibrations, and their father would assist but was not himself deeply involved in the practice. Bharat's older brother Lutchman (the second-oldest sibling) vibrated with shakti as a young boy, starting when he was nine years old, and would carry the kargam from the river. Bharat and another brother, Bal, on the other hand, did not begin to ecstatically manifest the deotas until their contact in the mid-1970s with Pujari Jamsie Naidoo from Guyana.

As the only child with trance experience, Lutchman took over the family tradition around the age of twenty, when their grandfather died, conducting Shakti Puja sacrificially at home. People sought his services as an ecstatic healer on an ad hoc basis at first. By the early 1980s, however, Lutchman had built both a Mariyamman Kovil and a standard Hindu *bedi* in his yard, several years after the temple was established at Streatham Lodge. From then on, Lutchman carried on weekly ecstatic pujas in the sada form on Sundays, offered private healing consultations on Tuesdays, and conducted an annual puja complete with animal sacrifices. Lutchman's shakti work was low profile and his following was small. He and Bharat mostly kept their distance from one another. It is noteworthy that Lutchman's orientation remained primarily centered on Mariyamman—as opposed to Kali—throughout his life.

In the mid-1970s, Bharat and Bal Moonsammy made a fateful trip to Guyana, where they were exposed to its flourishing Shakti temple scene and rediscovered their "roots." Neither of them had vibrated before this time. Several more trips and a series of influential exchanges with Naidoo and others ensued. The concept of a Kali temple dedicated solely to ecstatic weekly services with an especially strong healing orientation therefore stems from this Guyanese connection. Pujari Naidoo installed the first murtis at the newly established Moonsammy temple. It is said by those in Bharat's lineage that Naidoo named him the "head" of Kali Puja in Trinidad. Several years before his death, Bharat told Martin Sirju (1990) that, while he learned from his familial forebears and acknowledged the input of the Guyanese, his "true teachers" were in fact the deotas themselves.

As it happens, one of Bharat Moonsammy's most important collaborators was a neighbor, Mootoo Brown. Like the Moonsammys, Brown was also of Madrassi descent and had inherited the Mother's work from his forebears. He claimed to be a Brahmin and to have working knowledge of Tamil (Guinee 1992). It is said that Mootoo's father participated in old-time firepass held many years earlier in El Dorado and Waterloo. Yet it is unclear whether Mootoo was part of the original contingent that went to Guyana and made the first, fateful contact with Pujari Naidoo and other brethren. As I never knew him personally, it has been difficult to clarify several crucial features of this history. Mootoo was centrally involved in the founding of that first temple, yet at some point early on, Bharat and Mootoo had a falling-out, and Brown left to form his own temple nearby. The murtis for Mootoo's first temple were also established with the assistance of the Guyanese, though I do not know whether Naidoo himself was involved. After a decade or so in operation, Mootoo and his following obtained the resources to build a new and expanded temple ground a few blocks down the road. By this time, he had married his second wife, Tanti.

All Kali temples in contemporary Trinidad can in some way be traced back to either Bharat Moonsammy's or Mootoo Brown's mandirs, which have thrived in intense competition with one another since their original split. Bharat made an important move in 1984 by discontinuing the practice of live animal sacrifice, following a similar move at Pujari Angad's temple. According to his interview with Sirju (1990), Bharat was told by Guyanese pujaris that he would never be able to stop or else something bad would happen to him or his family; but this did not deter him. He prayed fervently to the Mother, asking for her blessing in dispensing with the use of blood in serving her. His prayers were eventually answered, and the deities showed him how to invoke Kali without blood in the "purer" sada (solely vegetarian) way.

Despite Bharat's authority, some of his disciples nonetheless believed terminating blood offerings was wrong. One contingent broke away to carry on the tradition on their own in the "proper" fashion (Guinee 1990:7). Another group dissented from within. By the early 1990s, as Bharat's health weakened, his son and the pro-sacrifice faction revived the practice, it is said, with his blessing. Some even say Bharat learned his lesson about the ill effects of giving up sacrifice the hard way, just as the Guyanese had warned, and that his health had suffered for it. Blood offering was the modus operandi when I attended the temple's weekly puja as well as its annual Big Pujas in 1999 and 2000.

I distinguish heuristically here between a first wave of new Kali temples established by Bharat Moonsammy and Mootoo Brown in the late 1970s and a second wave of those that proliferated in and beyond their footsteps. Krishna Angad's Maha Kali Shakti Mandir was founded in the early 1980s in Chase Village, central Trinidad, and may be seen as transitional in this scheme. Krishna had a small, non-Kali temple on Joyce Road, south of Chaguanas, before becoming a devotee of the Mother at Bharat's mandir. After a time, he established a Shakti temple dedicated to weekly ecstatic puja services by revamping his first mandir. This temple soon became the third major Kali temple on Trinidad's Hindu landscape and has been influential in the evolution of several other temples farther south. Its profile of practice may be seen in retrospect as having been portentous of future developments and contemporary patterns of innovation throughout the island-wide set of shakti temples on the whole.[5]

Because Pujari Angad had gotten his start doing the Mother's work at the Moonsammy temple, Bharat and his pujaris established the first set of new murtis at Krishna's Kali temple. Bharat and Krishna maintained a good relationship;

thus the latter held his weekly puja services on Saturdays so as not to compete with those held on Sundays at Streatham Lodge. Angad reported to Guinee (1992:176) that the idea of starting his own temple came from the Mother herself while manifesting upon his first wife. Though initially reticent, he acquiesced. Others say Krishna's family was unenthusiastic about his taking up shakti puja, which would account for his hesitance in the beginning. At some point relatively early in the temple's history, a Sai Baba medium proclaimed that Krishna should stop doing animal sacrifices, so he terminated the practice of blood offerings at his mandir (177). Soon Bharat and the heads of several other smaller temples followed suit.

Thus, while Krishna cannot claim to have built the first Kali temple in Trinidad, he takes credit for having been the first to engage in the puja "purely." This development led to the introduction of coconuts as the proper form of sacrifice and has precipitated considerable debate over orthopraxy. As we have seen, Bharat's temple suspended blood offerings for some years in the 1980s before taking it back up on the eve of his death in 1993. Mootoo's now represents the most prominent sacrificial temple, since it has maintained the practice of blood offering without interruption. While several smaller outfits carry out animal sacrifice as an essential aspect of their puja, and the Moonsammy temple continues to offer animals, the overall trend has nonetheless been toward sada worship for the Mother and her associates.

Relatively speaking, Angad's temple seems more fluid and open to change than those of Moonsammy and Brown in Tunapuna. As Guinee observed: "The temple run by Krishna Angad in particular changes its practice with every whim of the deities. During the year that I was in Trinidad, I found that if I missed going to Krishna's temple for a couple of weeks, the service would have changed radically. The deities in this temple were constantly asking their devotees to add something to the service or to change the order of things" (1990:51). Krishna's mandir attracts more young people and gives them ready access not only to baseline shakti play, but also to higher forms of individuated mediumship. Krishna also allows women to become pujaris, a trend reflected in many of the second-wave temples as well as Bharat's mandir, but not observed at Mootoo's temple. Moreover, I found Krishna's temple to involve more Christians and Muslims and more people of African or mixed-African descent than others. All of these features are characteristic of the second-wave temples.

Krishna's temple therefore represents a transition, setting the stage for a number of subsequent developments. Krishna turned the tables upon animal sacrifice, thereby opening the door to the widely prevalent antisacrificial sentiments of the majority of shakti devotees on the island at large. Both Bharat's and Mootoo's temples are associated with sacrifice, and their puja traditions are intimately associated with Madrassi heritage. By contrast, Krishna has no special connection with Madrassis, and in this regard his temple represents a fulcrum for the proliferating development of temple-based Shakti Puja more broadly. The democratization of innovation scaffolded by trance performance and intensified at Krishna's temple also seems to have paved the way for the variability of practice encountered in temples throughout the island.

Before turning to a more detailed examination of local patterns of innovation and practice, however, it is important to clarify the nature of the Guyanese influence upon Kali Worship in Trinidad. Shakti-oriented sacrificial practices have been carried out relatively continuously in Guyana since the nineteenth century, where the tradition has been strongly associated with Madrassi subculture. Yet it also gained ground in the twentieth century among increasingly wide segments of the Guyanese Hindu as well as Afro-Guyanese communities (Phillips 1960; Bassier 1987; O. Singh 1993; Younger 2002). Vertovec (1996:125) tells us that "Kali Mai Puja" became standardized in Guyana in the 1920s and 1930s, waned during the mid-century years, and subsequently experienced a resurgence, especially as a result of Pujari Jamsie Naidoo's innovations in the 1960s. There are an estimated 80 to 100 Kali "churches," or *koeloos*, throughout the country.

The most significant Guyanese influences upon the Trinidadian scene include revitalized use of the tappu drum and weekly puja services conducted in temples built especially for devotees and visitors in search of the Mother's healing power through rituals of trance performance and spirit mediumship. The Guyanese legacy represents a transnational twist of influence in the complex evolution of Shakti Worship in Trinidad and points to a unique dimension of hybridity that has been underappreciated and completely sidesteps any so-called Madrassi origin: the influence of medical psychiatry on the healing techniques adopted by Naidoo's temple community (see Singer, Araneta, and Naidoo 1976).

In 1963, Pujari Naidoo entered into a decade-long collaboration with anthropologist Philip Singer and Enrique Araneta, the director of Guyana's only mental hospital at the time. During this period, patient referrals were made bidirectionally between Naidoo's Kali Mai temple and the national asylum, located about fifteen miles apart. Naidoo's years of observing psychiatric intake assessment and therapeutic interviews conducted between doctor and patient eventually led to creative interventions in his performance of Kali Mai Puja and therefore, by extension, influenced patterns of Shakti Puja in contemporary Trinidad. In 1973, for example, Naidoo discarded the obscure sacred language used by the shakti mediums, which before that point had required the services of a ceremonial interpreter. From this point onward, devotees could speak directly to Kali Mai and her spiritual associates in their creole English during ecstatic consultations. This astonishing intervention, stemming from modern psychiatry and facilitated by anthropology, deserves serious appreciation and should expand our notions of syncretism. It also exposes yet another dimension of ecstatic shakti praxis that is not connected with Madrassi cognates in any way.

Another Prismatic Pantheon: Mother Kali and Her Coterie

A Sanskritic divinity of the high Hindu pantheon, Kali is found throughout the Indian subcontinent, north and south alike. Yet it is significant that over 90 percent of the indentured laborers from South Asia who came to Trinidad hailed from the greater Gangetic plains region of northeast India. Shaktism has long dominated areas of this region such as Bihar, Bengal, and Orissa, although they also have had strong Vaishnavite cross-currents as well. Those who came from what are today Uttar Pradesh and the Panjab left—by contrast—regions that seem to have been more dominantly Vaishnavite in orientation (Vertovec 1996:112).

By the fifteenth century, the tradition of *bhakti* devotionalism—which first emerged in south India in the seventh century—swept north and transformed worship of Krishna, and then did the same with the Hindu goddesses in the centuries that followed (McDermott 2001), all very much before the flood of indentured migrants poured through the port of Kolkata and onward to the Americas. As an urban center, Kolkata was built and driven in the early to mid-nineteenth century primarily by a Vaishnava nouveau-riche class, in counterpoint with the Shakti-identified landed classes established a century before. Thus, over the last half-millennium, Kali has become "sweetened," according to McDermott's account—"democratized, universalized, and tamed" (302)—as a result of bhakti's expansive orbit, leading to Kali's adoption of a compassionate maternal persona for the very first time. She even became a counter-colonial symbol of Indian nationalism and other political aspirations in the late nineteenth and early twentieth centuries.

This genealogy is important because imagery based on Kali's most prominent form in Bengal—Dakshinakali—is the iconographic source domain for the most pervasive symbolism of Kali in contemporary Trinidad, which circulates widely because of the influence of imported chromolithographic images. Murtis of Mother Kali in local shakti temples are often based upon the chromolithographically mediated iconography of Dakshinakali. Shakti mediums

Figure 4.6.
Chromolithograph
of Dakshinakali,
widely available in
Hindu puja stores.

who manifest the Mother do so by performing directly in front of the goddess's central temple murti, where they "consult" and tend to a wide range of spiritual seekers and therapeutic clients, as do other mediums for other deotas in front of their own icons.

The Indo-creole Kali of Trinidad is partly, but nonetheless significantly, cross-identified with Mariyamman, perhaps the most prominent south Indian goddess, who has become incarnated as Kali's Madrassi side within contemporary temple-based Shakti Worship. The only temple housing separate murtis for Mariyamman and Kali is the Moonsammy one in Streatham Lodge, though the devis are still considered two sides of the same coin there. Otherwise, all shakti mandirs revolve around a central murti of Kali, for whom Mariyamman is understood as the Madrassi side, when pertinent. I was told repeatedly that Kali and Mariyamman are the "same deity," active in different "forms," depending

Figure 4.7. Like the image shown in figure 4.6, this popular chromolithograph of Kali depicts her as dark blue, with lolling tongue, her right (dakshina) foot forward on Shiva's chest, and polydexterously sporting a sword, club, trident, cleaver, fire, severed head, and other symbolic objects.

upon how one prays to her. "In whatever form you call the Mother, she comes," according to one pujari. "Different forms have different purposes," explained another, "the same devi with different avatars."[6]

Although I am focusing here on the heterodox deotas constituting the nucleus of the Indo-creole shakti pantheon, which are not typically encountered in orthodox Hindu temples, shakti temple puja in Trinidad involves a host of divinities also active in orthodox practice: Ganesh, Hanuman, Surujnarayan (a form of Vishnu), Shiva, Durga, Lakshmi, Saraswati, Rama and Sita, Radha and Krishna, and others. Though there are recent signs of change, these orthodox deities have not been the main deotas ecstatically conjured within the sphere of Shakti Worship. They are, however, comforting to many newcomers unfamiliar with any of the temple divinities except for these mainstream ones. By contrast,

Figure 4.8. A Kali murti from a large temple in central Trinidad, flanked by smaller images of Lakshmi and Saraswati. Photo by author.

Figure 4.9. A murti of the Mother in the most Madrassi-identified shakti mandir in Trinidad. This statue is a hybrid form, combining prevalent Kali imagery with the iconography of Mariyamman from a devotional South Indian pamphlet in the temple's possession. Photo by author.

all of the powers who work through the bodies of their spirit mediums are heterodox in status and the very divinities sought by supplicants in these temples.

The ecstatic divinities making up Mother Kali's heterodox coterie can be usefully subdivided by gender. On the feminine side there are Katerie Mata and Mother Ganga, although other, secondarily significant, ecstatic goddesses operate at times in shakti temples. Katerie Mata is a historically Madrassi goddess from Tamil Nadu, and her incorporation into ecstatic puja in Trinidad seems to have been the result of transfer from the visiting Guyanese contingent in the 1970s. Her most likely origin in south India is probably in association with the Kaveri River, which runs west to east through the heart of Tamil Nadu, or possibly as the village mother goddess of the Tamil town of Kaatheri. Yet outside of the two first-wave temples established in south Tunapuna, consciousness of Katerie Mata as a south Indian, or Madrassi, goddess is rare. Indeed, Mother Katerie has also become identified with Parmeshwarie, a low-caste goddess associated with leather-working chamars from north India, whose local propitiation has traditionally involved the sacrifice of a live pig. Thus sacrificial Parmeshwarie Puja is yet another indentureship tradition that has become amalgamated within the contemporary temple-based tradition. However, devotions to Parmeshwarie have now begun to wane, and one rarely hears about Parmeshwarie Mata in second-wave temples. Katerie's face now generally eclipses her Parmeshwarie side. Chamars themselves now mostly disidentify with Parmeshwarie and her "long-time" tradition of hog sacrifice.

Katerie's shakti is especially sought after for problems related to fertility or childbearing. She is often referred to as Small Mother or Small Sister (Kali is Big Mother or Big Sister). Thus in the figure of Parmeshwarie-Katerie, we encounter a north Indian goddess coidentified with a southern one inherited via Guyana, which is then tied back to the overarching figure of Mother Kali. Katerie Mata's predominant iconographic representation in murti form is usually based upon the most common figuration of Kali, though she is often painted in a different color from Big Mother as a distinguishing visual feature.

Alongside Kali-Mariyamman and Katerie-Parmeshwarie there is also Mother Ganga—called Ganga Mai or Ganga Mata—whose mermaid-like iconography derives from her being the spiritual essence of the sacred Ganges River in India, and whose local following—exceptionally, in this case—runs the gamut from heterodox to orthodox. Indeed, even though Ganga's orthodox version may be characterized as secondary within the sphere of respectable Hinduism, her following has been growing. This is reflected, for example, in her prominent imagery on the outside of the well-known Temple by the Sea (Sewdass Sadhu Shiva Mandir) in Waterloo; devotions for her performed during the annual celebration of Kartik Ke Nehan; and the relatively recently invented tradition of Ganga Dashara, an annual pilgrimage started by a neo-Hindu organization in the 1990s in which the Blanchisseuse River in the north coast mountains of Trinidad is converted symbolically into the Ganges River for devotional observance. However, the orthodox incarnation of Mother Ganga is decidedly *non*-ecstatic, by contrast with her local heterodox incarnation, who, along with Kali and Katerie, offers her devotees tangible ecstatic access to mystical power. Notably, Trinidad's Ganga Mata has no other, alternative syncretic face or side.

On the masculine end of this pantheonized spectrum, there are three ecstatically manifesting deotas who are often referred to as the Three Dees or the Trinity, namely, Kal Bhairo, Dee Baba, and Munesh Prem. While Hinduism has its own Trinity in the divine trio of Brahma the Creator, Vishnu the

Figure 4.10. An image of Ganga Mata on the outside of the orthodox Hindu Temple by the Sea in Waterloo. Photo by author.

Figure 4.11. A young medium plays Mother Ganga and consults with devotees and seekers at the devi's stand. Photo by author.

Preserver, and Shiva the Destroyer, the Three Dees in Kali Puja are most often in fact analogized with the Christian Trinity. Consider, therefore, the irony of this syncretic Hindu configuration being conceptualized in a creole English idiom of the Christian Trinity on an island dubbed La Trinidad by Christopher Columbus in 1498 on his third voyage to the Americas, which he thought was Asia!

Kal Bhairo—or Bhairo Baba—is the most prominent form of Shiva in local shakti temples. As with Mother Ganga, Kal Bhairo is notable as a central ecstatic divinity in heterodox contexts who is nevertheless also venerated, albeit not as prominently, within the wider orthodox Hindu sphere. This orthodox avatar is anything but ecstatic in orientation, and his presence in these contexts is subordinate to the more dominant imagery of Shiva as a handsome, blue, long-haired, meditating ascetic. In addition to mediumship under the aegis

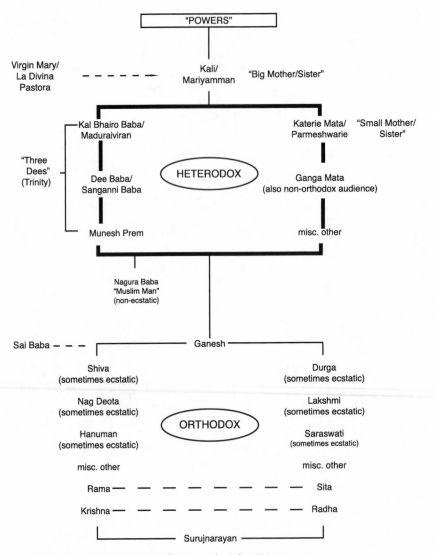

Figure 4.12. Kali-Shakti pantheon. Illustration by Felipe Zúñiga.

of Bhairo Baba, the cutlasses used for live animal sacrifice in shakti temples undertaking the practice are kept at his stand. For this reason, he is known as the Death Master. Though Kal Bhairo's iconographic roots derive in part from Tantric sources whose "dangerous" symbolism as Bhairava still lingers, he has also been "sweetened" and is commonly represented as a young, handsome god associated with a dog. Bhairo Baba also has a secondary Madrassi side, most likely derived from a postcolonial Guyanese prototype and established through cross-identification with Madurai Veeran, the Tamil demigod of Madurai.

Orthodox forms of Shiva are also generally present within shakti temples, but this latter, more socially respectable, form is less significant within hetero-dox puja practices than Bhairo Baba, described as the "brother" or "protector" of Kali. This situation is germane in light of the fact that Shakti and Shiva are consorts in the Sanskritic great traditions of South Asia. Bhairo is also known as the Gate Keeper due to his special relationship with Kali and his central role in ecstatic puja. The centrality of Bhairo Baba in contemporary Kali Worship may be seen as an index of how the tradition has become a repository for re-pressed Shaivism within the Hindu community at-large, which has privileged Vaishnavism over the long run in the West Indies.

Alongside Kal Bhairo, shakti temples also provide a heterodox home for Dee Baba or, simply, Di. He is known as Master of the Land, and some also under-stand him to have a Madrassi side called Sanganni. Several people cognizant of the founding of the first modern Kali temples in the 1970s claim the epithet "Sanganni" came from the Guyanese as a complementary Madrassi face for Dee Baba. Dee regularly manifests during weekly puja services, offering consultative jharay sessions to devotees and visitors in search of healing power. I have never encountered any image or murti of Dee outside the sphere of temple-based Shakti Worship, where his supplications are quite noteworthy, having also de-veloped his own iconomorphic representation for the very first time. In India, Di is traditionally represented as an aniconic earthen mound (J. Flueckiger, pers. comm.). "Di" is a generic category for a wide variety of protective village godlings—gramadevata—throughout Bihar and Uttar Pradesh in northern In-dia. There was typically a separate Di for each South Asian village, but Vertovec notes that "as new, isolated homesteads were founded in Trinidad following residence on estates, the propitiation of Dih came to be undertaken separately by individuals on their own plots of land" (1992:113–14).

Domestic Di Pujas in colonial Trinidad were undertaken for various pur-poses. Klass observed a distinction between private mid-twentieth-century forms of Di Puja performed without sacrifice for the benefit of agricultural fer-tility and a sacrificial form carried out for the sake of the household and prop-erty. He noted that sacrificial Di Puja was the rule rather than exception among high-status families in his primary research location, observing that it was al-ways also performed before the main part of the community's Kali ceremonies began (1961:176–78). Dee has thus been transformed from a protean rural com-munity godling in nineteenth-century northern India into a subaltern ecstatic deity summoned under the eaves of heterodox Kali temples in contemporary Trinidad, complete with his own relatively recently anthropomorphized iconic form. Importantly as well, his namesake has become metonymic for the group of the three main ecstatic masculine deotas—known by many as the Trinity—within the sphere of Shakti Puja.[7]

Figure 4.13. A young pujari-medium plays Dee Baba during a regular Sunday puja service and attends to the needs of a family, one among many other families and individuals who wait in line for a few sacred moments of direct interface with the deity at his "stand." Dee's creole murti can be seen in full view here amidst the practitioners. Photo by author.

The third "Dee" of the group is Munesh Prem, also known by some as Muni Spiren, whose heterodox creole persona is pervasive within this subaltern sphere, but whose theology is opaque in vernacular exegesis. Some see him as the "Master of Finance." Other than being a member of the Trinity, Munesh Prem is associated with the moon, a characteristic iconographically represented by murtis depicting him holding one or more moons. It is also notable that one of Muni Spiren's main mediums at one large shakti temple is a white Canadian expatriate who now lives locally with his Indo-Trinidadian wife and is raising a family within the mandir microcommunity.

Munesh Prem most likely represents a creolized derivation of the Tamil divinity Munisvaran, thereby representing a historically latent connection with Shiva. However, Munesh Prem's Indo-creole iconography bears little resemblance to that of south India's Munisvaran aside from a mustache and turban-like head covering. Indeed, the moons of Trinidad's Munesh Prem are likely local acquisitions, reflecting the lexical resonance of his name with the English word *moon*. In contrast, contemporary south Indian iconographic conventions render Munisvaran sitting on a throne with a trident in one hand and a bejeweled club in the other. Several of those knowledgeable about the founding of the first contemporary Shakti temples in the 1970s report that Munesh Prem was not known locally until the Guyanese came (see Younger 2002:135, on the Guyanese scene).[8]

Interestingly, Munesh Prem is also known to have a "Spanish" side in Trinidad, reflecting the engagement of grassroots Hindus with Spanish-creole labor migrants from Venezuela over the years. Others say it is Dee Baba—not Munesh Prem per se—who has the Spanish side. I think this transitivity can be explained by the fact that Munesh Baba is now considered one of the Three Dees; thus the emergence of a Spanish Dee could have originated in relation to either of these two deotas and then been transferred because of the Trinitarian Dee matrix. Whichever the case, the Trinidadian Spanish Dee is also considered by some to have an additional Catholic side identified as St. Anthony. In any event, the dynamism of the polymorphous side phenomenon is significant, both in terms of the prismatic set of Dees and their ability to take on a local Spanish extension (on "Spanish" as a local ethnic shifter, see Khan 1993).

Mention must also be made of Nagura Baba. Like his colleagues, Nagura is a heterodox deota found only in local shakti temples, but he is generally secondary to Mother Kali and her main coterie in that he typically never manifests via trance performance. Nagura's significance seems to derive principally from the fact that he is the "Muslim Man" or "Muslim Saint," an identity reflected in local iconographic conventions by his Muslim-styled beard. Nagura Baba's creole imagery also commonly depicts him wielding a sword in connection with the tradition of goat sacrifice—shared with Muslim tradition—associated with his propitiation. Nagura's folk theology is undertheorized, and he is present in only a subset of the shakti temples. The Guyanese may have introduced Nagura (see Younger 2002:135), but this is unclear. He represents one of the many axes of inter-Indian creolization within this popular Hindu tradition, since in his figure the community gestures toward Muslim sources of mystical power and provides a locus of worship for those harboring identifications with Islam.

Among some second-wave temples, Kali's suturing power has been directed toward the neo-Hindu sect that follows the late Shri Sathya Sai Baba, an extraordinarily popular South Asian spiritual guru who claimed to be an incarnation of God. Widespread devotion to Sai in Hindu Trinidad at large began in the 1970s. A subset of the newer shakti temples has been appropriating Sai Baba devotion—its discourses, practices, and imagery—especially within the densely Indian zone of the island running from central to south. This dynamic is so significant that Naziph Ali's Sai Sadhana Shakti temple incorporated an explicit reference in the mandir's official name and apportioned half of its weekly liturgical cycle to Sai Satsang, or devotional gathering. Given Morton Klass's (1991) finding that Sai Baba religion in Trinidad has been an ethnic-exclusive, elite revitalization movement, it is not surprising that it was Pujari Ali's temple which had become most deeply involved with Sai devotion before it closed due to his premature death. Naziph was professionally oriented and maintained a high-profile career with the Ministry of Education.

One of the most important characteristics of Shakti temples with Sai Baba connections is their vigorous and self-conscious opposition to the practice of live animal sacrifice, which they believe hinges upon a misguided interpretation of Kali's sacred mythology. As avid supporters of *ahimsa*—nonviolence—they view blood offerings as morally bankrupt. Thus the Sai Baba interface is crucial to keep in mind in relation to the predominant antisacrifice sentiment among local Shakti Worshippers.

Equally important is the fact that one is more likely to encounter murtis of Jesus Christ and other Christian imagery such as the Cross in the shakti temples that have incorporated Sai Satsang into their corpus of ritual praxis. Thus the ecumenical spirit and one-love ethos of Sai devotionalism seems to be facilitating greater absorption of explicitly Christian symbolism. Indeed, it is telling that the two original modern temples in northern Trinidad have no connections with Satsang and bear no traces of Sai imagery anywhere throughout their respective temple spaces. Nor do they incorporate Christian iconography within their puja paraphernalia, as is evident in many temples of the second wave, which tend to espouse a more self-conscious ecumenicism, preaching tolerance for other faiths and the equivalence of spiritual paths.

Pope John Paul II visited Trinidad and Tobago in 1986 and "bigged up"—as one Catholic told me—the larger island's colonial Christian etymology. Trinidad has been subjected to Catholic influence since Spanish colonization, but it was the French whose version of Catholicism became most influential. Perhaps unsurprisingly, then, many devotees employ the word *saints* interchangeably for the powers or deotas that manifest ecstatically in Shakti Puja. Temples with murtis of Jesus Christ intermittently host ecstatic manifestations of him. The temple community on Moruga Road sings Christian hymns such as "Let Heaven and Nature Sing" and "Jesus Loves Me" when they reach the stand for Jesus, during their round of weekly pujas. I know of at least three temples where Jesus manifests through shakti play, citing biblical verse in trance. (The Prophet Muhammad also appears in one of these same temples, though I have not been witness to any entranced episode.) Before he passed away in 1996, Lutchman Moonsammy used to sacrifice a sheep every year for Jesus Christ during his annual Big Puja for the Mother. Devotees in some of the more recently established Shakti temples also readily identify Kali Mata with the Blessed Virgin Mary; thus the Mother has now taken on a "Christian side," as they say. Indeed, those who favor Kali's Madrassi face as Mariyamman point out the resonance of the latter's namesake with the Christian Mary. Based on similar logic, Indian devotees with Catholic backgrounds who attend older contemporary temples in the Tunapuna area see Mother Katerie as the Hindu side of Saint Catherine.

Yet this form of Hindu-Catholic symbolic convergence is not quite so recent, having an important precedent in the Siparee Mai—Mother of Siparia—phenomenon in southern Trinidad. This is a tradition of Hindu pilgrimage to the Catholic church in Siparia that houses a dark Madonna known as La Divina Pastora, the Holy Shepherdess. She is the patron saint of the Capuchin missionary order, which brought the image to the New World. Every year the image is taken out of the church on Holy Thursday before Easter and temporarily housed in the parish hall, where it stands upon a wooden altar until mid-afternoon on Good Friday. During this twenty-four-hour period, thousands of Indians arrive to spend a brief sacred moment in front of Siparee Mai. Most importantly here, Hindus have identified La Divina Pastora with Mother Kali since at least the 1890s. Siparee Mai's earlier twentieth-century devotions are said to have included the ceremonial services of male transvestite "Kali dancers," who danced with newborn babies on the front steps of the church, blessing them during this auspicious time (see McNeal 2003:239–40 on Siparee Mai and the relevant literature).

On the more idiosyncratic and personal side of things, practitioners have described intimate visions or dreams that they've had involving hybrid or interactive Shakti-Christian symbolism. For example, one devotee told me of an intense visionary experience in which images of both Jesus and Kali merged kaleidoscopically into one another after he'd spent some time studying the Bible in search of spiritual truths. Several others, mostly women, but not exclusively so, experience dreams mixing imagery of Mother Kali and the Virgin Mary. One of these, who grew up in a Hindu home but married a man of Christian Indian background, related a dream in which she was about to enter a church, but a vision of Kali intervened, telling her not to enter and to report instead to the temple where she had begun attending puja services.

Analogies with Christianity are also commonly made in exegetical discussions of certain practices. Among those who practice sacrifice, for example, it is common to cut off the foreleg of the goat and place the severed appendage in the decapitated head's mouth. The symbolism of this act has been explained to me as a reference to the Christian cross, itself a special tribute to the power of sacrifice. Devotees also legitimate the practice of animal sacrifice by reference to Christian themes, such as the sacrificing of Jesus for the sins of humanity, or in relation to the biblical story of Isaac. Ironically, some also appeal to the Bible in order to criticize the practice of sacrifice. One prominent temple leader in central Trinidad draws attention to the Commandment "Thou shalt not kill" when discussing the topic. Another asserts that, "if you offer blood, you're breaking the covenant given in the Holy Bible."

Similarly, the practice of firepass was once explained to me at a temple in southern Trinidad by an analogy with the miracle of Jesus walking on the water. If he could do such an unthinkable thing through the power of God, so too could devotees of the Mother pass miraculously across the fire pit without getting scathed. That night the temple congregation engaged in several rounds of Christian hymns, incorporating references to Kali, Mariyamman, and Durga during the initial pre-firewalking phase of the puja.

These second-wave shakti temples interdigitating with the Sai Baba movement are the locus of interlocution with Christian imagery and practice and, equally as importantly, an arena for the innovative apotheosis of some of the orthodox Hindu divinities into ecstatically manifesting deotas for the very first time locally. For example, a relatively young temple in Moruga regularly includes manifestations of Lord Hanuman in most of its puja services. Two of the largest temple murtis are those of Hanuman and Kali, whom the temple community refers to respectively as "Father" and "Mother." This trend is on the rise, for it is now possible to encounter trance performances of Hanuman's shakti in at least a handful of contemporary mandirs. Manifesting mediums appropriately carry the mukhtar—club—wielded by Hanuman in his mythical pursuits and representative of his spiritual power. In these temples, therefore, we encounter the ecstatic apotheosis of an unquestionably orthodox divinity, ubiquitous throughout all segments of Hindu Trinidad, regardless of sect or status. Hanuman Pujas are quite common by any measure. And revealingly, Hanuman is also closely associated with contemporary Hindu nationalism in South Asia.

That an increasing number of shakti temples would begin performing ecstatic Hanuman manifestations was something heretofore unthinkable in the Trinidadian Hindu imagination. Hanuman's symbolic centrality is reflected in the name of the Moruga temple—Shri Bandi Hanuman Shakti Mandir—and his orthodox status lends legitimation within this religious microsphere. This temple conducts regular processions along the main Moruga road, including anywhere from ten to twenty shakti players—again, something almost inconceivable given local traditions of Hindu praxis and the wider abhorrence of anything smacking of obeah. In 2000, some Afro-Trinidadian onlookers came out of their houses to observe what was happening, but also in some cases to mock the simi-dimi (mumbo-jumbo) taking place practically on their doorsteps.

Hanuman may be just the tip of the iceberg. Though they are neither central nor the liturgical climax in heterodox Shakti Puja, many temples now regularly conjure unambiguously orthodox deities such as Shiva and Krishna, as well as Mothers Ganga, Lakshmi, Durga, and Saraswati in ecstatic form. While it is difficult to predict future developments, it is nevertheless clear that the trend since the founding of the first contemporary Kali temples in the late 1970s has been increasingly toward the inclusion of orthodox with the heterodox divinities.

Vibrating for the Deotas

The standard temple-based ritual script begins with offerings and supplication made to the orthodox Hindu deities. Gradually, the round of pujas for each deity makes its way toward the heterodox deotas, whose worship constitutes the center of gravity in ecstatic Shakti Worship. Spiritual seekers do not come to Kali temples to interact with the more mainstream deities, unless it is to seek their power through the subaltern method of ecstasy. Seeking the transformative power of shakti in these temples is their raison d'être.

Fruits, flowers, coconuts, incense, perfume, fire, and so on are offered to each deity at its murti, usually beginning with either Ganesha (Lord of Thresholds and Obstacles) or Surujnarayan (Vishnu's Sun-God avatar), accompanied by chants of praise along with the clanging of gongs or cymbals and the intermittent blowing of a conch shell. The round of pujas gathers an electrifying momentum as the activity progresses. The service reaches a transitional point after individual pujas for the mainstream deities have been conducted. Once this transition has been reached, some devotees and pujaris begin to vibrate in front of the stand of the deity whose shakti they serve, but just behind the zone of activity involving senior pujaris at the murti stand. Though the transitional deota varies—Shiva in some temples, but not all—the fundamental point is that the liturgy progresses from a nonecstatic to an ecstatic phase.

The bodily movements of baseline shakti play in relation to each deity and his or her stance is not unlike that of generalized trance dancing on the African side. Players quiver, spin, and contort in a manner either measured or dramatic, with their eyes typically closed. Soon they slap their heads or yell for manjantani, a substance that simultaneously "purifies" and "cools" manifestations, as they might otherwise get out of control. Assistant pujaris constantly bring lota vessels filled with manjatani, which is poured onto the heads of the players, cascading down their necks, backs, and bodies, saturating their hair and clothing. Female shakti players with long hair flail it around, creating an even more spectacular effect. Overall, baseline activity is highly dramatic and compelling for those on the sidelines.

If there are many individual offerings from devotees being made at a deity's stand that day, or if there happen to be a large number of shakti players for the deota, the congregation may linger there for quite some time. Baseline shakti dancers are never sought as oracles or healers. They are allowed to play in a somewhat circumscribed area of the temple. Pujaris, family, friends, or even bystanders assist in keeping the trancers more or less under control and out of harm's way. Eventually, the puja at a deota's stand comes to a close, and the shakti playing for that divinity dissipates.

Though most of these generalized manifestations dissolve on their own with the termination of puja activity at the murti's stand, a pujari or two may need to intervene if the vibration is especially strong or recalcitrant. Pujaris hold the trancer and press the third eye on the individual's forehead. This is known as *shantiing*, since *shanti* means peace in Hindi. Sometimes shantiing may involve a minor struggle between the attending pujaris and the player, who may thrash about and resist. But the pujaris succeed in ending the trance except in truly exceptional cases.

After the trance has passed, players may be quite dizzy or fatigued. They may be ushered to a quiet out-of-the-way place and take time to come back fully to their senses. Then, at the next stand, a new group of shakti players arises, as if the puja conducted at the deity's stand gives the murti an extra boost of energy, which is then relayed out into the temple congregation, temporarily electrifying shakti players especially tuned in to that divinity's cosmic wavelength.

As the space fills with more and more shakti players, some may call for the "whip test" by sitting and holding their arms in the air or lying on the floor with their legs held up, ecstatic vibrations pulsating through their bodies. Manjatani-soaked ceremonial whips or even chains may be used by an experienced pujari to lash their bodies. The whips and chains used for such lashings are associated with the Three Dees and are therefore kept at or near their stands.

Other than firewalking, the whip test is the most theatrical aspect of trance performance in Shakti temples. The rationale is that mere humans, without activated shakti power animating their bodies, are neither courageous enough to undergo the whip nor able to withstand the lashing without injury. The test is therefore a performance of superhuman power, testifying to the ability of the

Figure 4.14. Moved by awakened shakti energy, participants engage in baseline shakti play—a form of shakti not identified with a specific manifesting deity. Photo by author.

Figure 4.15. Shakti players gesture, bend, and vibrate as baseline play continues. Photo by author.

Mother to see her devotees through trials and tribulations. It is also an occasion to display the purity of devotion and authenticity of one's vibrations because, if one has not properly fasted, exhibits weak devotion, or fakes a manifestation, the test will expose that. While some temples do not perform the whip test during weekly puja services because it requires an adequate number of devoted practitioners sufficiently involved to undergo the ordeal, other mandirs engage in ceremonial whipping quite regularly. Those who brave the whip test gain esteem in the community and attain a higher level of practice.

The other two forms of testing in temple-based Shakti Worship involve fire, though firepass is considerably more involved than the use of burning camphor. The rationale for firepass is similar to that for whipping: one can brave the ordeal of the fire pit only because of the sincerity and commitment of one's devotions to the Mother. The more modest fire test requires little preparation or paraphernalia and may be enacted at a moment's notice. It requires putting a burning cube of camphor into one's mouth and letting it burn for a few moments to demonstrate the presence of a deota in the medium's body.

Whereas baseline shakti players may engage in firewalking, the burning camphor test is predominantly used with individuated mediums. A manifesting medium will slap his or her hands together, indicating to those assisting that the deota wants an ignited cube of camphor in order to authenticate its presence and power. Or recall the story at the book's outset in which Naziph-as-Kali demonstrated my lack of shakti by handing me a burning camphor cube, which I almost immediately dropped as it singed my palm.

What I have dubbed "individuated mediumship" is a much more accomplished and nuanced form of trance performance than is baseline ecstasy. Countless numbers of devotees or even newcomers to the temple may get swept up in currents of generalized trance-dancing not conceptualized as any particular divinity. These trancers are assisted, yet nevertheless left to play out their own states of inner-directed mystical consciousness. They are considered auspicious and in a sense divine, since they are activated embodiments of shakti. Yet they are not engaged with as spiritual agents in and of themselves; hence they do not interact directly with others. This experience is cathartic or empowering primarily for the trance dancers themselves.

Individuated mediumship, by contrast, is built upon the ceremonial foundation of baseline play but takes the practice of trance to a more interactive level. Spiritists who vibrate for specific deotas do so specifically to offer direct interactions to temple devotees and other spiritual seekers with problems in need of attention or illness in need of healing. Such mediums become vehicles mostly for the heterodox deities found solely in local Shakti temples, yet, as we have seen, they have also started to become ecstatic vehicles for the more orthodox Hindu gods as well. Manifestations of whatever deity may take place only after the appropriate offerings have been made at its stand by senior pujaris.

Once this is complete, the chosen medium and his or her ritual assistants take up positions in front of the icon. The medium bows to the deota in the form of its murti and then says a prayer while making *aarti*, the honorific circling of a brass plate with lit flame and other paraphernalia on it. Afterwards, the medium turns around and is saluted and honored by the pujaris, then closes his or her eyes and soon begins twitching, shaking, swaying, gyrating, depending upon how she or he usually catches power. The movements gain momentum, and after a relatively brief period of time, the more experienced mediums reach a full state of trance. Pujaris offer prayers and sing the deity's special songs of praise while the drummers beat out the appropriate accompaniments on the tappu. Individual mediums exhibit slight differences in personal style and in the time it takes for the deota to fully manifest. As in orisha performance, an initial, sometimes brief, period of haphazard movement signifies the onset of activated ecstatic power, then transmutes into the higher level of spiritual mediumship.

However, unlike orisha mediumship—in which baseline ecstasy morphs into an embodied iconomorphic enactment with the eyes open—individuated shakti mediums do not directly embody the iconography of the gods in human form and dance about the temple doing the deota's business. Shakti mediumship of this sort takes place directly in front of the murti whose divinity is being conjured. The vibrating body of the medium becomes interdependent and temporarily symbiotic with the chosen deota's murti, which already embodies the iconographically rendered mythology of the deity. For this reason, it is impossible to identify a manifesting deota based solely upon the medium's bodily enactments; these movements signify only the presence of superhuman energy and not the specific identity of the manifesting divinity.

What I am describing here is readily evident in images of Dee Baba and Ganga Mata discussed in the preceding section, in which their mediums play them just in front of their respective murtis. Because the eyes of the murti are permanently open—already radiating the god's vision—individuated shakti mediumship is typically enacted with the medium's eyes closed, although exceptions are possible. As a rule of thumb, the closer a manifesting medium gets to its corollary murti, the more likely its eyes are to be closed in semiotic deference to the open ones of the god's icon (see McNeal Forthcoming a for a more technical discussion).

The sequence of images in figures 4.16–4.18 illustrates the initial onset and then full manifestation of Kali Mata upon the most senior priestess at one of the largest Shakti temples in Trinidad. Wearing a special flower garland made especially for Kali, she is positioned just outside of the Mother's Room—directly in front of Kali's central murti, although it cannot be seen in these pictures—after the entire sequence of individual pujas has been conducted throughout the temple at each stand. Since animal sacrifice is practiced at this mandir, Kali is called not only in order to interact with and serve the public, but also to accept the offerings of fowl and goats. The medium has already bowed to Kali and her "sisters" in the Mother's Room behind her then turned around to be honored by the group of pujaris assembled to attend her.

Only a few moments after the tappu drumming has started along with the song-chants lauding the Mother's greatness and power, the priestess begins to flap and circle her hands in the air and to sway forward and backward with increasingly dramatic movements. Her eyes close and her head turns and twists. She falls back into the waiting arms of the assistant pujaris while throwing her hands in the air (figure 4.16). She thrashes around as they stand her back up. Her movements intensify. She stomps in place and her breathing becomes louder, more forceful. She pats her head with her hands, calling for manjatani, which is quickly brought out by a pujari standing to the side and poured on her head as she falls down backward again onto the pujaris (figure 4.17). She is brought up again and dances triumphantly. Her wet hair swings more dramatically now, scattering auspicious droplets of manjatani upon those around her and on the ground. Mother Kali is now fully present (figure 4.18). The singing becomes even more heartfelt, and the medium's enactments become more graceful and direct. All in all, the enactments depicted in this first sequence of images represents perhaps four or five minutes of ritual performance.

After Kali has fully established her presence within the temple sanctum, she slaps the back of one hand upon the palm of the other, calling for the fire test. Cubes of camphor are produced and lit by assisting pujaris, then handed to the performer. Mother Kali's medium pops the flaming camphor into her mouth, where it burns for several long moments (figure 4.19). When the fire is snuffed out, she spits out the remainder of the cube into her hand and quickly dispenses with it (figure 4.20). The fire test utilizing burning camphor is performed several more times.

Next, Kali Mata receives the "rod of correction" from a young assistant who has been patiently holding it next to her (figure 4.21). Made from a bamboo stick, this implement is accompanied by a bunch of fresh neem leaves soaked in manjatani. After receiving the rod, Kali turns toward the Mother's Room

Figure 4.16. A medium reels backward as Kali Mata begins to manifest on her.

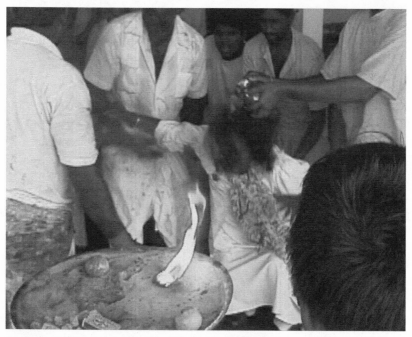

Figure 4.17. Kali's entranced medium falls, but the assisting pujaris catch and support her while one pours manjatani on her head. Photo by author.

Figure 4.18. Once Kali has fully settled, her medium dances triumphantly, hands in air, accompanied by the driving percussion of the tappu drums. Photo by author.

and salutes her main temple murti. She faces the pujaris and the congregation and dances majestically in place (figure 4.22). The pujaris continue their song-chanting while the drums continue thunderously. By now the atmosphere is electric in the immediate vicinity of the puja's climactic manifestation.

Soon the pujaris begin to collectively aarti the Mother. She raises her hands and gently vibrates in place while they do so. With the aartiing complete, the pujaris then pay their respects by touching her feet and uttering more praise to Kali in the form of her "elevated" medium. She offers commentary on the conduct of the puja that day and acts as an oracle regarding current affairs in the temple, admonishing in-group temple personnel to iron out differences (figure 4.23). Indeed, as is also the case with orisha spiritists, shakti mediums operate as conflict mediators. Their commands and opinions carry extra weight since they come from the gods and are also often delivered from the mouths of accomplished and respected mediums.

After the Mother offers her initial thoughts and sacrifices of chickens and goats are made in the earthen area just across from the Mother's Room where

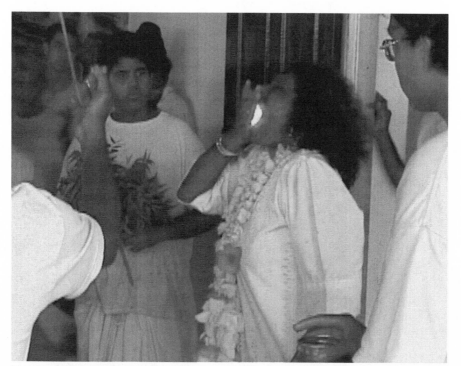

Figure 4.19. Kali's medium signals the presence of the deity by taking a flaming cube of camphor into her mouth. Photo by author.

Figure 4.20. Once the camphor cube's flame is spent, the medium spits it into her hand and soon dispenses with it. Photo by author.

Figure 4.21. Kali receives the rod of correction. Photo by author.

Figure 4.22. Kali dances in place before the congregation, rod and neem leaves in her left hand. Photo by author.

Kali manifests, the elevated medium attends to a long line of supplicants who have waited patiently, sometimes for hours, for this moment. At this temple, other deotas such as Kal Bhairo, Dee Baba, Mothers Ganga and Katerie, and possibly Munesh Prem are also conjured at their respective stands to attend to the public. Jharaying is conducted with a bundle of ceremonially prepared neem leaves, which are brushed over the head and body of the supplicant (figure 4.24). This is an auspicious and powerful gesture that transmits the power and efficacy of the Mother's shakti to seekers. Jharaying is often followed by some sort of interchange with the deota, such as making a confession, seeking advice, or receiving instructions on focusing one's devotions and "get-through" problems.

As it happens, Mother Kali had just jharayed a temple leader from Martinique on the day in question, visiting with some twenty or twenty-five devotees on a pilgrimage. This pujari is of mixed African and Indian descent and is the head of a thriving French West Indian Shakti temple whose congregation is composed mostly of Afro-Martinicans. Several years earlier, the two temples made contact with one another and have taken up regular relations. As the priestess told me, "I go and play the Mother in Martinique!" The folks from Martinique, however, tend to visit Trinidad more often than the other way around. Their visits are usually brief, consisting of a long weekend every now and then for this Trinidadian temple's semiannual Big Pujas. Most of the pilgrims speak French, and I have not connected substantially with them during their whirlwind tours, especially since they dash off on shopping trips during down times over the course of the three-day puja. They are generally much better off economically than most of the temple's local patrons. The head pujari from Martinique is also an avid tarot card reader, and some temple members solicit his services on the side.

The performance of healing is central in these temples. Guinee's (1992) illuminating study of suffering and healing in one of the largest Kali temples in Trinidad shows how the practice of ecstatic Shakti Puja operates as embodied theodicy, producing new attitudes and relationships through ceremonial enactment over time when successful. The devotee turns to the tradition against a background of stigma and fear, thereby making an agentive choice to move from one social world to another. Spiritual diagnoses of problems made at the temple offer explanations and messages of hope. The practitioner participates in a series of exchange relations with deotas mediated both by mediums and the temple community, fostering a devotional practice that alleviates helplessness by elaborating procedures for action.

Consider the case of Anushka Sookdeo (a pseudonym), who became a child

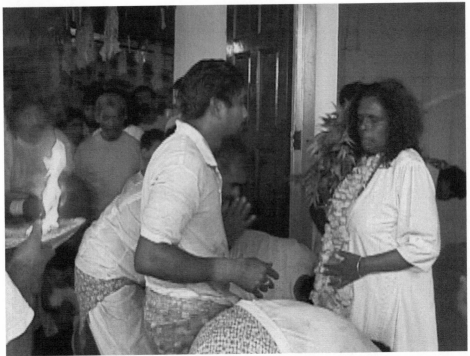

Figure 4.23. Kali offers private commentary to some of the temple's primary personnel. Photo by author.

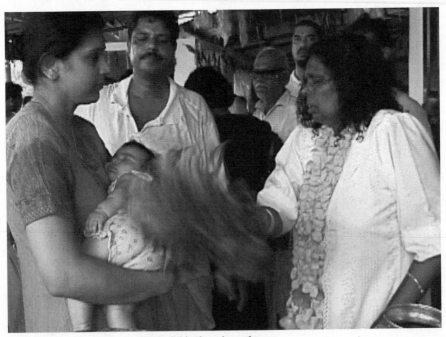

Figure 4.24. Kali Mata jharays a sick child. Photo by author.

of Mother Kali after getting very sick when she was forty years old. "I had lots of pain and t'ing. Couldn't walk, couldn't turn." It woke her at night. At first, she thought the problem was "medical," so she visited a doctor, whose treatments went nowhere. She then tried an orthodox pandit, who assured her that it was "not medical, but spiritual help" she needed. He "meditated" on her and concluded someone had "sent Kali in an evil way" to harm her. Yet his ministrations also came to naught, leading to a change in diagnosis from Kali to Mother Parmeshwarie, "you know, Mother Katerie in an evil way." But "the pandit couldn't handle that at all." Their relationship came to an end in the early 1990s.

A cousin eventually suggested going to a Kali temple for help. "I get so frustrated. I say, look, anybody tell me where to go, I'll go. When I went to the temple, when I went to the Mother, she say—'My child, you try all about, and you couldn't get through, you couldn' get better'—she said, 'but I will help you.'" Through consultations with Kali's main medium, Anushka's enigmatic illness was interpreted as obeah worked by her mother-in-law. Interestingly, the temple did not contest the pandit's prior diagnosis relating to Parmeshwarie; the point was to counter her being used for nefarious purposes. Anushka was instructed by Kali's oracle to give a blood offering by the sea to counteract the obeah, which she did. She began attending temple services weekly, continuing to this day, though she confesses to having been afraid on her first day visiting the mandir.

Anushka was healthy and strong growing up. It was not until she was married in 1982 and spent several years with her husband's family deep in eastern Caroni County (mid-central rural Trinidad) that she began having intractable and inextricable pains. She lost weight, became feeble, "felt dead to the world." When she returned to Arouca to live with her parents, her husband followed, even accompanying her at times to the Shakti temple. It was only then that both of them clearly saw it was the mother-in-law who was at fault, after hearing it directly from "small Mother" (Katerie) herself. The prognosis offered by the temple divinities legitimated what Anushka had already suspected but which her husband could not countenance.

Mr. Sookdeo attended the temple semiregularly for two years before discontinuing his visits, having become a bit disoriented by the experience. Still, he supports Anushka's continued involvement because of its beneficial effects on her. Sometimes he uses medicine made from Bhairo Baba Puja, which assuages aches and pains. And even though her own family is not keen on her relationship with the Shakti mandir—they would never dream of accompanying her there—they admit she's healthier since she began attending. Anushka comments that they don't understand what it means to be in pain, hopeless, and desperate for help. Looking back, she reflects, "You can't live without the Mother."

Anushka dreams off and on of Mothers Kali and Katerie, the temple's main Kali medium, and the now-deceased head pujari of the mandir who helped her so much. These dreams give her hope and sustenance. "You have to know from your self, from your devotion to your Mo . . . the Mother, you know. When you do your devotion, you become close to the Mother, and so the Mother contact you in yuh dreams." People at the temple often point to her as "living proof" of the power of shakti. "I does say, every extra day and time, I livin' on the Mother—Mother give me that opportunity. So the extra years is for the Mother. Without the Mother, I gone already."

Anushka's case offers a personalized window into Shakti Worship. She became a devotee of the Mother as a result of an illness cured through her involvement at the temple, but became neither a general shakti player nor an individuated spirit medium. Shakti only "came and shook" her once, briefly.

The life world of Kali Worship allows the sufferer to identify with others, realizing they are neither unique nor need be isolated. Renewed connectivity with one's ancestors, the deotas, one's family, and the temple community are all promoted, with the potential for revitalized faith in oneself and the world. The practice provides a space in which devotees reimagine themselves within a new frame of reference and restructure their sense of alienation.

This process is built upon the centrality of trance as alter-cultural praxis. Baseline shakti players experience moments of self-loss and transcendence in the course of the ceremony, developing new modes of relatedness with self, other, and spirit. Depending upon one's experience and inclination, such experiences may propel the devotee to the higher, more rarefied, level of mediumship, in which they serve the gods by serving others. Spiritual mediumship of this sort is not only a talent, but is also considered a gift. And because it represents the locus of divine intervention in the human world, ecstatic mediumship is also a locus of innovation and a source of popular legitimation.

Sides and Paths

Spirits and Transculturation in the Southern Caribbean

You have to deal with the era and walk with things in the era.

Queen Mother Kali, October 2000, La Canoa

Every spiritual people you meet is going to tell you something different, because they get things different. There's a manifestation for everything, yuh know.

Boysie Ben, August 2000, Tunapuna

Be True, Be Just, Be Aware, Be Alert, Be Pure, Be Full of Love. That's enough "Religion."

Sign in back corner of Shri Bandi Hanuman Shakti Mandir, Moruga (quotation marks in original)

All of we is God's children. Anyone get cut, the blood does be red.

Rasta Man in Blanchisseuse, July 1999

In mid-2000, I took my friend Dexter, who has vast experience within the Afro-creole spheres of Spiritual Baptism, Shango, and Kabba, to a Kali temple. His patron saint is Osain, whom he refers to equally often as St. Francis or the Indian Man, and he works with several Indian powers, keeping an annual tradition of "Prayers" during the Hindu festival period of Diwali. Yet, like many other African spiritists, Dexter's experience with Hinduism is limited. After several requests for me to "carry him," we planned to attend the weekly puja at Maha Kali Shakti Mandir in Chase Village. When I arrived to pick him up, Dexter materialized in a pale yellow, silky Indian-style pants-and-long-shirt ensemble complete with a bright yellow head wrap and flashy sunglasses.

Practitioners of both traditions are usually aware of each other, as they are similarly stigmatized. Some even perceive resonances between the two. One elder Indian man who had observed developments in Kali Worship for decades, for example, said there is a "great similarity" between Shango and Shakti Puja; they are, as he put it, "under the same heading." He related an anecdote about looking for a friend in a Shango yard, prompting him to realize that they all work with the "same powers." An inquisitive Orisha man who learned about my research pursuits on the Hindu side commented, "They do similar work to us." Yet relatively few people actually pressed for in-depth inquiry about the other tradition. Dexter's persistent desire to visit a shakti temple, then, was not typical.[1]

We arrived at the temple well before the puja began, so there was time to mull about, inspect the murtis throughout the mandir, and introduce Dexter to the head pujari. In retrospect I wish I had filmed Dexter's consultation with Kal Bhairo, though this was not a day I was videotaping. Though we chose that temple's service mainly because it is held on Saturdays, it turned out to be an interesting choice because its personnel and clientele are both quite diverse racially and religiously, as discussed in chapter 4.

The puja progressed in the usual fashion, first with singing of bhajans and a short discourse about devotion, followed by the round of individual deity pujas, which transitioned into the ecstatic part of the service once the pujaris reached the combined stand for Mothers Ganga and Katinie (the preferred pronunciation of Katerie at this mandir and those in its lineage). Generalized shakti play at this temple is especially theatrical, involving significant numbers of lay temple members as well as assistant pujaris. The puja intensified, and several sufferers were jharayed by the vibrating mass of shakti players in front of the Ganga-Katinie stand (another temple-specific innovation). Burning cubes of camphor were placed around the area where the three "patients" stood, and a group of fifteen or so baseline players swarmed around them, accompanied by the driving beat of the tappu drums. Eventually the individuated mediums of the most prominent divinities took their places in front of the murtis for whom they served as oracles. Throughout most of the puja Dexter stood silently, observing.

We exchanged our first real words once the bank of mediums had taken up their positions for the Three Dees. "It good. I feel the spirit," Dexter commented. As the players performed the whip test before taking up their respective positions for individuated mediumship, Dexter observed, "You know the power is there to take *that* lash!" He continued: "I get it. Them there [pointing to the mediums] play those powers [pointing to the murtis behind them]. How are they called?" I filled him in with names of the Dees. He drew an analogy between this convention and speaking with the orishas through their mediums at the stools for each power in a shrine yard. "They work with bush I never did see before," he noted. "What it is?" I told him about neem leaves. His commentary and my clarification continued for some time, interspersed with quiet moments of observation.

At first Dexter did not want to "talk to the powers," since the jharay with neem and manjatani would soil his clothes. He said he'd come prepared next time ready to do so, mentioning that if he were to see any of them, he would either talk with the guy playing Bhairo Baba or the woman playing Hanuman that day—the two mediums who were black as opposed to Indian in descent. Later on, Dexter mentioned how happy he was to see "Negroes" catching power, signaling the "openness" of the temple.

He eventually changed his mind about the consultation, however. Pointing to the husky medium manifesting Kal Bhairo, Dexter announced, "I have to talk to that one." He walked slowly and deliberately to the end of the line of people waiting to consult with that deota. Dexter was a head taller than most, and his bright yellow head wrap—something men do not generally wear—made him stand out even more. I hung back, but he motioned me over to join him, saying that he wanted to talk to the power about the success of an upcoming trip to Canada to visit his (now former) common-law wife and stepdaughter, since they had had a quarrel the day before, and he was worried about the state of affairs between them.

When Dexter's turn came, Bhairo told him to "focus" before approaching the medium. Dexter knelt down and prayed, after which the deota called him up. I stood off to one side, but the power called me over as well, asking if I had brought Dexter there. I replied in the affirmative, leading Bhairo to observe in guttural spiritspeak that "a friend brought a friend." The medium jharayed both of us up and down our front and back sides.

We spoke for about five minutes altogether. Among other things, the medium–cum–Kal Bhairo observed that Dexter was "spiritually high," but that he had stomach pains at times from working without eating properly, which Dexter confirmed. The power said he would "reach high" in his "spiritual work."

They also conversed about Dexter's domestic affairs and he was reassured things would work out. Afterward, we each received a *tika* of red *sindur* powder dotted on our foreheads over our third eyes, and we took our leave.

Dexter decided to go back a second time, alone, and they spoke again. He reported that Bhairo asked why he had returned, and Dexter told him that something moved him to do so.

"How did it go?" I asked.

"Good," he replied. "That shakti strong. It know me. Told me things I have to do." He smiled wryly, with a distant look in his eyes.

I later learned that Bhairo's message included a slight reprimand for Dexter's becoming too involved with the world of Kabbalistic banquets and neglecting obligations "on the Orisha side." Dexter said Bhairo Baba commanded him to fast for three Saturdays—including no salt—and that the power would assist. I suspected there was more to the story but did not pry.

Though he's never been so adamant about going to a Shakti temple again, he often refers to his experience that day as confirmation of his Hindu-inclusive "path." When questioned another time about similarity between the two traditions, Dexter commented, "Yeah, they similar because is the same brother, just on a different side. It have on the Indian side, it have the same thing on the African side—the Orisha side—and same thing on the Chinee [Chinese] side."

It was only in hindsight that I began to appreciate how swiftly Dexter had plugged into the structure of the puja and tuned into what was happening in terms of trance performance and spirit mediumship. He employed the local discourses of "play," "work," "manifestation," "power," and the like without missing a beat. Indeed, not only the rapidity with which he understood what transpired, but also the effectiveness of our interchange about what needed to be filled in pushed me toward a deeper appreciation of the resonances in how both traditions are structured and practiced despite their many differences and variant histories, what I refer to here as the "structural convergence" of Shango and Shakti Puja in Trinidad and Tobago.

By "structural convergence," I refer to the fact that they have become increasingly similar in important ways without being somehow reducible to one another, as my sociohistorical discussion in previous chapters and as my later discussion of the politics of race, religion, and diaspora in the postcolonial era attest. However, to ignore resonances would overly fetishize differences between the two and turn a blind eye to anthropological insights afforded by the comparative methodology. I became increasingly impressed with how these two subaltern ritual traditions have developed parallelisms in structure and practice that must be accounted for in terms of lateral adaptation to their convergently "glocalizing" experience in the southern Caribbean. Yet language is tricky. Though I utilize terms such as "similarity," "resonance," "likeness," "correspondence," and "parallelism," I confess to finding them insufficient for capturing the complexity and nuance the topic deserves.

The terminology of structural convergence points to the fact that, although Shango and Shakti Puja have not merged in any explicit sense on the ground, they have undergone processes of evolution specific to the southern Caribbean that have made them increasingly similar. These include resonant socio-cultural marginalization and heterodox stratification, similar transculturating dynamics of syncretic amalgamation, parallel convergence of structural form and dimensions of ritual praxis, increased individualism as well as personal flexibility of the ecstatic spiritistic idiom and corollary progressively therapeutic reorientation. I develop the notion of "subaltern liberalization" as a way of encompassing these changes and capturing the modern sensibilities of each tradition, which to an outsider may seem anything but "modern" or "liberal." Yet it is in this regard that comparative analysis serves our inquiry best.

Trinidadian sociologist Rhoda Reddock (1998) sees Orisha Worship and Kali Puja as "subordinate level interculturations," yet her analysis is brief. Local researchers Noor Kumar Mahabir and Ashram Maharaj (1996) favor a theory of "parallel traditions" in their consideration of resonances between Shango and Hinduism more generally, but they focus primarily upon Hindu elements in Orisha Worship, and their discussion of Kali Puja per se is limited to observations of similarities between the two in terms of trance performance. Houk (1995:89) also briefly observes that Shakti Puja "resembles" Orisha Worship: "There is little or no actual association between the Kali-Mai sect and the Orisha religion, but worshippers from each group are supportive of or at least sympathetic to the religious practices of the other."

The most sustained consideration of the relationship between Shango and Shakti Worship comes from a provocative essay by anthropologist Steven Vertovec (1998). He considers common beliefs concerning the local supernatural world held by practitioners of these two traditions and also Spiritual Baptism, resonant dimensions of trance performance and spirit mediumship across them all, and similar patterns of competition and micropolitics. Vertovec argues that these parallelisms have produced a sense of "perceived convergence" among practitioners that are often—erroneously—attributed to religious syncretism between them. In my own experience, however, I have encountered no one who perceives the traditions to have converged nor anyone who sees a relationship of syncretism between the two. This chapter plumbs new depths in the comparative analysis of Orisha Worship and Shakti Puja. Yet the situation on the ground is complex and my discussion does not pretend to be exhaustive.

Kali and the Transculturation of Shakti Puja

Let us first take stock of the sociohistorical development of Shakti Puja in the southern Caribbean. Consideration of this trajectory in relation to developments in Guyana as well as the deeper perspective afforded by comparison with patterns of ecstatic religiosity in South Asia bring the Trinidadian case more clearly into view.

The evolution of temple-based Kali Worship in the postcolonial era represents the amalgamation of varied elements of popular Hindu religious subculture as well as imported innovations from Guyana. Diverse sources suggest Mother Kali was not insignificant among Indians during the indenture period. In this regard alone it is interesting that she subsequently became castigated and demonized not only by colonial elites, but also by a progressively gentrifying form of Caribbean Hinduism that accelerated between the two World Wars. Thus Kali's recuperation within the space of contemporary heterodox temples indexes her transition toward greater oppositional significance within local culture.

There are several significant precursors. The north Indian Kali and Di Puja complexes, for example, as well as the Madrassi tradition, were all originally vibrant and independent ritual streams after having been transferred to the New World in the hearts and minds of indentured laborers. Though each necessarily underwent adaptation and innovation in the radically new proletarian environment of colonial Trinidad, they were conducted in separate contexts and generally operated among different groups. Their confluence within the space of postcolonial Shakti temples represents the syncretism of varied South Asian ritual lineages in a novel overseas context. They have been transformed in relation to one another as reciprocal influences within Kali's current temple-based incarnation.

The community-based Kali Pujas of yesteryear were performed to solicit the Mother's intervention in agricultural and human affairs. Preparations included "begging for Mother Kali," in which village women canvassed the surrounding areas while singing to the accompaniment of a hand drum and collecting offerings of money or materials for the puja. The ritual involved the sacrificing of goats or chickens preceded by the ecstatic manifestation of Kali upon one of the pujaris, who acted briefly as an oracle but did not engage in elaborate therapeutics. Meat from the sacrificial animal was divided up and distributed as prasad. Some families also occasionally conducted a domestic version of

Kali Puja, which followed similar scripts on a smaller scale. As late as the mid-twentieth century, community Kali Puja was supported financially by upper-status families but not generally attended by them.

Klass importantly notes, however, that almost everyone—including those of high "caste," or class—conducted sacrificial domestic Di Pujas as well as non-sacrificial agricultural Di Pujas. An offering for Di involving sacrifice of a fowl cock was also conducted before the main part of the old-style Kali Puja was performed. Klass witnessed ecstatic manifestations of Di during Kali Pujas he attended, but these were not significant as healers.

Though the community tradition of Kali Puja had waned by the era of decolonization, shakti devotees speak of it nostalgically. Some testify to the involvement of previous generations in their family, and many consider it important to revive and keep alive not only for the sake of tradition, but also because of its power. Taking up practices considered lost or abandoned by older generations has great emotional significance for some, revealing ambivalence about the disorientating effects of modernity (Guinee 1992). Others grew up under the shadow of prejudice with no immediate connection at all, yet have now found their way to Mother Kali's temple doorstep and passionately defend her honor.

In addition to the north Indian–derived forms of Kali and Di Puja, there are also south Indian traditions of Madrassi devi worship and firepass indexing another colonial vector feeding into the current dispensation. As we have seen, those who castigate it as obeah often attribute Kali Worship to the legacy of darker-skinned Madrassis. For this reason alone, it is important to reconsider the Madrassi-origin ideology in light of the many-tentacled transculturation of Shakti Puja in the southern Caribbean. The Madrassi connection is also critical since the two lead temple innovators—Bharat Moonsammy and Mootoo Brown—self-identified as Madrassis and, energized by the historical consciousness of the Guyanese with whom they consulted, adopted a heightened Madrassocentric posture in relation to the local Hindu scene. I believe this revitalizing Madrassi sensibility was influenced by the development of postcolonial multiculturalism, especially the spirit of ethnoracial revitalization brought on by the Black Power movement of the early 1970s, as discussed in chapter 6. Here I am concerned with clarifying the development of contemporary Kali Puja in relation to its hybrid origins in order to compare and contrast it with Shango at the popular level.

Of undisputed south Indian, or Madrassi, vintage, firepass in colonial Trinidad was always performed as an expression of shakti devotionalism, principally under the aegis of the goddesses Mariyamman and possibly Draupadi, *not* Kali.

Evidence suggests firewalking was carried out for ceremonial purposes as early as the 1860s, if not before, and that the last old-style Madrassi firepass ceremonies were held in El Dorado in the early 1950s, where the old earthen murtis of Draupadi and the five Pandava brothers from the Mahabharata have been preserved at the heart of the gentrified El Dorado Shiva Mandir. Ceremonial firewalking of this sort was an upregulated version of more quotidian Madrassi devotions to their goddesses.

Several aspects of Madrassi ritualism resonate with certain practices of contemporary Kali temples while other elements are quite clearly independent. In addition, some of the most prominent aspects of contemporary worship evince anything but a straightforward connection with Madrassi praxis. In the latter, animal sacrifice was less prominent, if practiced at all, whereas trance performance seems to have been more or less common.

Since Kali and Di Pujas also involved ecstatic mediumship, it would be difficult to argue that either of these or Madrassi practice was more influential within the contemporary temple configuration, especially since Guyanese influence was quite profound as well. Yet we also know that Guyanese Kali Mai Puja does not involve firewalking and that performance of firepass in Trinidad was introduced at the Moonsammy temple early on by someone said to have been of Madrassi background, resuscitating an earlier tradition that has now proliferated widely throughout the local temple-based scene.

Whatever the case, it was not firepass ceremonialism alone that served as the source of local Madrassi inspiration within the current Shakti Puja complex. The introduction of temples devoted to Mother Kali and oriented toward weekly healing services in the late 1970s was enabled by their transnational collaboration with Pujari Jamsie Naidoo and other Guyanese ritualists. This remarkable postcolonial innovation is not, therefore, simply the revitalization of dissipating local traditions, though it is indeed partly so. Shakti Worship from Guyana also carried Madrassi symbolic associations. Guyanese influence upon the Trinidadian scene is profound, the implications of which have not yet been sufficiently appreciated.

Most significantly, the Guyanese revitalized use of the tappu drum and introduced the practice of weekly puja conducted in temples dedicated to the Mother's healing power through ceremonies of trance performance and spirit mediumship. Naidoo also introduced the practice of direct communication between supplicants and trance mediums as a result of his collaboration with the director of the Guyanese mental hospital and an American anthropologist in the 1960s. He discarded Tamil as the language of communication in ecstatic consultations by switching to creole English, the primary tongue of everyone involved. These innovations—some of which represent the syncretic influence of modern psychiatry—were transferred to Trinidad and adopted as standard procedure by the first two local temples. Though ecstatic temple worship derives from the Madrassi tradition in Guyana, Naidoo's modifications also make any simplistic view of Kali Puja's Madrassi origins difficult.

Madrassis in colonial Guyana, approximately 20 percent overall, represented a larger proportion of the total Indian population compared with Trinidad. They developed a distinctive sense of identity and tradition early on, and these in fact also became stronger and more established than in Trinidad. According to Paul Younger (2010:chap. 2), colonial Madrassis formed a distinct minority with a thriving Guyanese subculture whose religious orientation revolved around the worship of Mariyamman and the eclipse of devotions to Draupadi. Their temples are located on the outskirts of circumplantation settlements originally established by emancipated Africans. An impressive "neo-orthodoxy" centered on the temple in Albion had developed by the early twentieth century, energized by a flood of fresh south Indian migrants during the last decade of indentureship. What is interesting about the Madrassi tradition in Guyana is that it combined a sense of orthodoxy with "an almost evangelical sense of social openness and willingness to share their tradition with others" (64).

Despite the strength of the orthodox Madrassi standard in worship, tensions arose as a result of efforts to modify or "reform" the tradition. The first came from Kistama Rajagopaul, who spent several years in New York City in the early 1950s. He learned to read some Tamil and became at least superficially acquainted with Tamil religious texts; he also became a devotee of Vishnu in the form of Venkateshwara, a Brahmanical branch of south Indian Hinduism quite distinct from ecstatic Shakti Puja. After returning to Guyana, Rajagopaul toured Madrassi temples and pushed for an end to animal sacrifice. Only four temple communities followed his lead, however, and the overall impact of his effort was to stimulate further consolidation of what had become established as standard Madrassi procedure from at least as early as the 1920s.

Jamsie Naidoo's efforts represent reform in the reverse direction of Rajagopaul's. Baptized and educated in a Catholic school, Naidoo operated for some years as a pujari at the Albion temple and became well known for his healing and exorcistic powers. He promoted women, including young girls, as well as north Indians and Afro-Guyanese, into the roles of pujari and medium. Younger (2002:135) notes that Naidoo's followers were, in fact, mostly people of north Indian descent or Afro-Guyanese. Since the more orthodox Madrassis resisted these innovations, Naidoo broke away, building his own larger temple complex near the coast in the late 1950s, where he introduced the changes discussed earlier. He characterized these developments quite explicitly as "creolization" in a mid-1990s interview.

Pujari Naidoo's influence has been widespread at home and abroad. Offshoots in his lineage have sprung up around Guyana and in New York City. Naidoo also went to Trinidad and Suriname to assist in the founding of temple traditions. Others trained by Naidoo but who claimed independence established temples in Guyana that now have offshoots in New Jersey. Naidoo also popularized the name Kali Mai Puja as a more inclusive moniker signifying its reach beyond Madrassi tradition, a development resonating profoundly with the Trinidadian scene, where Madrassi ritual praxis had become vestigial by the postcolonial era and Mariyamman practically forgotten.

This sketch of Guyanese Kali Mai Worship and the innovations introduced by Pujari Naidoo further dramatizes the complexity of forces that came together in the founding of Trinidad's first wave of postcolonial Shakti temples in the late 1970s. Their establishment reflects the interplay of both local and translocal developments. Under Guyanese tutelage, Bharat Moonsammy, Mootoo Brown, and their associates initiated new forms of alter-cultural practice incorporating important elements from abroad and giving new life to local dimensions of popular Hindu religious subculture that had become progressively marginalized and associated with the lower classes.

Madrassi firepass, tappu drumming, and ecstatically oriented traditions of sacrificial Kali and Di Puja were revitalized within a freshly amalgamated temple dispensation facilitating further elaboration and innovation. Several Guyanese deotas were introduced, such as Mother Katerie, Munesh Prem, and Nagura Baba, while others were syncretized with deities already known in Trinidad, such as the merging of Madurai Viran with Kal Bhairo, Sanganni with Dee Baba, and Katerie Mata with Mother Parmeshwarie. These developments involved Madrassis but also drew on the energies of many others of both Indian and non-Indian background.

Within less than a decade, new temples following in the footsteps of these pioneers emerged, starting first with Krishna Angad's in central Trinidad. Soon thereafter, the deities encouraged his temple congregation to dispense with animal sacrifice and substitute coconuts for blood offerings. This modification influenced practice at Bharat's temple in Tunapuna, of which it was an offshoot, and became the trendsetting model for most subsequent temple developments throughout the island aside from several branches in line with Mootoo Brown's stalwart sacrificial temple.

The significance of the shift toward sada worship is highlighted by the fact that similarly spirited efforts at reform of Kali Mai Worship in Guyana have never gotten very far. In Trinidad, by contrast, anti-sacrificial sentiment reflects the influence of Sanatanism, the Sai Baba movement, and other neo-Hindu influences underwritten by class-based bias against "primitive" practices of the "common" folk.

Other local innovations include the ecstatic apotheosis of some of the more "orthodox" deities such as Shiva, Hanuman, Durga, and Ganga Mata, as well as the evolution of a prismatic configuration of the Three Dees. A significant proportion of the second-wave temples have developed more or less explicit connections with the worship of Sai Baba, either offering weekly satsang—as in Naziph Ali's temple—or in the form of murti worship and even some trance performance conceptualized as the manifestation of the late global Guru. Some of these temples have also incorporated elements of Christian liturgy and symbolism into their puja praxis, and many practitioners have developed understandings of the heterodox powers based on explicit analogies with Christianity, as examined in chapter 4.

With these considerations in mind, we may better appreciate why the Madrassi origin ideology is so problematic. The issue is admittedly complex, since the postcolonial temple configuration indubitably incorporates elements of south Indian Hinduism. The head pujaris of the first two modern Kali temples were Madrassis who saw themselves at least partly as reviving familial traditions, and the historical consciousness of Guyanese Shakti Worship ties the practice to Madrassi heritage. Yet the dispensation inherited from Naidoo was in no simple sense "Madrassi." Moreover, in Trinidad, first-wave temples involved not only non-Madrassi personnel, but also a range of non-Madrassi elements and developments, most important of which is the reconfigured incorporation of north Indian–based traditions of Kali and Di Puja. Since its emergence in the 1970s, Trinidadian Shakti Worship has primarily recruited non-Madrassis and has evolved in directions wholly orthogonal to Madrassi concerns or connections.

Considering patterns of trance ceremonialism and ecstatic mediumship in South Asia fosters greater comparative perspective. Indologist Frederick Smith (2006) concludes that both good and bad forms of "possession" are far more common in South Asian culture and history than usually appreciated.[2] Culturally speaking, Smith accounts for the ubiquity of ecstatic forms as rooted in notions of South Asian personhood as permeable and fluid. He utilizes the language of "manifestation" in his exegesis of *avesha*, observing that cognate terms deriving from its Sanskrit root have found their way into many Indo-European and Dravidian languages. Furthermore, ludic conceptualization of positive possession as play emerges in a number of regional languages such as

Hindi, Panjabi, Marathi, and Nepali. It becomes clear from Smith's overview that goddesses constitute an especially prominent role within the landscape of trance and mediumship throughout the subcontinent, particularly at the non-Brahmanical level (68–75).

The question of possession in relation to Brahmanism is complex. Elite religiosity historically espoused antipathy toward the most overt forms of ecstasy. However, Smith argues that we must understand possession in both its positive and negative senses as animating the interstices of Brahmanism (2006:585). Not only does he find substantial conceptual influences of avesha and *grahana* (the negative sense of possession as affliction) in Sanskrit texts, but he also emphasizes the gap between Brahmin ideals and the reality of their practice. Indeed, a number of authors have documented Brahmin participation in ecstatic ritualism throughout India, in Karnataka, Tamil Nadu, Andhra Pradesh, Haryana and the Panjab, the Himalayan foothills of Uttar Pradesh, and so on (see F. Smith 2006:chaps. 1, 4, 13). Smith delineates a complex dialectic of Sanskritization and vernacularization in the patterning of South Asian religious forms.

With this background, we may turn to the Bhojpuri Hindi region of northeastern India, encompassing the eastern half of Uttar Pradesh and the state of Bihar, from which the majority of indentured laborers who arrived in Trinidad originated. Here I depend upon anthropologist Edward Henry's work on goddess cultism and religious culture in a Bhojpuri village district, conducted in the late 1960s. For Henry (1983), the Mother goddess cult has long been a vibrant aspect of religious culture in rural eastern Uttar Pradesh, and a fundamental theme of the goddess's local mythology concerns opposition to those who refuse her worship, especially the socially ascendant. In this regard, it is interesting that more upper-caste women than men worship the devi here. One of her annual rites—involving live animal sacrifice, ritual use of water pots associated with the goddess, offerings for Di, Kali, and Shiva, and participation by all castes—is the only local event that convenes people from all families in the area. The other main annual community ceremony in village goddess worship is Nau Ratri—Nine Nights—during which male *ojhas* (ecstatic mediums) perform at nightly séances and offer divinatory services. Henry notes that exorcism of harassing spirits by the ojha is possible, but less common.

Outside of Nau Ratri, the services of ojhas who operate as oracle or exorcist are contracted on an ad hoc basis. Henry (pers. comm., 2009) notes that these activities were carried out in the yards or homes of those seeking them out rather than in temples. Yet despite the fact that most oracular trance praxis involves manifestations of the goddesses, Bhojpuris he knew and worked among did not speak of it in terms of Shakti Worship per se. They did, however, revere a considerable number of devis, including goddesses of Bengali provenance to the east, and employ their terminologies somewhat interchangeably. Such practices, he points out, are nonetheless *not* generally considered forms of bhakti devotionalism.

McDaniel (2004) observes that "possession" in the positive sense is prevalent within the folk Shaktism of rural West Bengal, an area overlapping extensively with the Bhojpuri Hindi region in terms of religious culture (49–54). Popular goddess religion is not organized around temples, is associated with lower-caste people and especially women, and involves several modalities of ecstatic practice. Generalized, sex-segregated group possession transpires at annual festivals. In addition, individuals, most often women, may become mediums with followings, most commonly serving Mother Kali. Still others may undergo voluntary trance to fulfill vows made to the gods, who inhabit their bodies while they endure austerities such as hook hanging or carrying hot coals. Moreover, involuntary entrancement may transpire as a result of the goddess's call as a prelude to a lifelong devotional relationship. Finally, there is also spirit or ghost affliction, which requires exorcism or some other ethnopsychiatric treatment.

Pauline Mahar Kolenda (1968, 1983), moving westward from the Bhojpuri region into the central Hindi belt, reported upon practices among untouchables in a village north of Delhi. Village goddesses, whom she characterizes as the most popular folk deities in South Asia, and other tutelary spirits are avidly propitiated—including through animal sacrifice—yet never adored in a devotional sense. Most untouchable families observe Kali Puja, yet women of all castes make supplications to Kali in some form. Indeed, Kali and company are seen as controlling malevolent spirits and may be accessed through the actions of male "shamans"—as Kolenda refers to them—called *bhagats* (devotees) or *syanas* (conjurors). Generally lower in status and often young adults, these mediums operate as oracles. Their recruitment generally comes through mystical resolution of some personal crisis. Discourses of both play and shakti are used in relation to trance praxis in this Hindi context. Most ecstatic manifestations seem to unfold outside shrines or temples, either in the domestic space or in an open field.

Oscar Lewis (1958:212–13), also basing his conclusions on research in a village outside of Delhi, reported the dissipation of a tradition of popular-level ecstatic bhagats who manifested local deities—including an important local Muslim saint—in order to serve as oracles. The last one in the area, a Chamar, died around the end of World War II, after having become temporarily influenced by Arya Samaj doctrines, which compelled him to give up his mediumistic practices for a time. Such bhagats performed feats of self-flagellation to demonstrate spiritual fortitude. Lewis (295–99) also documented cases of negative possession-afflictions being exorcised by nontrance healers who invoked the power of goddesses such as Kali.

Although there are recurring motifs throughout these northern Indian cases, their variability makes generalization challenging. Turning to south India, we encounter further continuities and discontinuities in trance practice. Peter Claus (1979:29) observes that ecstatic mediumship is perhaps even more common in south India than other areas of the subcontinent. Younger (2002) emphasizes that most south Indians are goddess worshippers and that this tradition developed before the great Vaishnavite and Shaivite temples were built. Mariyamman became the most prominent independent goddess in Tamil Nadu during the medieval period (41, 95, 183). She is closely associated with village religion, and worship of the goddess remained independent of the stone Brahmanical temple tradition for many. The cult of Mariyamman has expanded to encompass other traditions in ways that continue today.

Stephen Inglis (1985:89–91) considers the variety of trance forms in Tamil communities. These include the *camiyati*—god dancer—who channels the gods during festivals and may fire walk; individuals who carry out personal vow fulfillments—*nerttikatan*—for wishes granted by the deity in the form of austerities culminating in trance performance; and vocational specialists known as *kotanki* who operate ecstatically as oracles for a fee in markets or other public spaces. Festivals involving camiyatis involve the entire community, including landlords. Rights to serve as a god dancer are controlled by patrilineal descent groups among the Velar potter community Inglis studied. Mediums are not recruited as a result of devotion, resolution of a life crisis, or some special disposition (93).

Elizabeth Fuller Collins offers the following perspective on Tamil Hinduism:

Hindu Tamil beliefs construct a hierarchy of peripheral possession cults. In relation to the worship of Brahmanical deities, who require the intermediation of ritually pure Brahmin priests, worship of the goddess and the warrior deities who guard her temple is a peripheral possession cult. However, in the Tamil village, worship of the Amman goddess is a central possession cult, whereas possession by the semi-demonic warrior deities who are deities of low-caste lineages belongs to a peripheral cult. Finally, the priests of these warrior deities are able to exorcize the demonic spirits that possess members of the lowest status groups—who are thought to attract the attention of such spirits because of their polluted and disorderly condition. (1997:110–11)

Note that ecstatic spiritism is central and public at the traditional village level, in which mediums conjure the devi in order to make offerings on behalf of the community.

Younger (2002) documents ecstasy as a prominent feature of popular south Indian festival religion cast in an explicitly ludic register. Most frequently, this involves the practice of trance as a fulfillment of vows, in which promises have been made to the goddess to undertake austerities and penances, and climaxes in trance performance during the festival period should the deity grant the supplicant's wish. At the annual festival for Mariyamman at Samayapuram, supplicants shave their heads, wear bright yellow clothing, take an exhausting walk from home, and then dance ecstatically along the crowded roadway leading to the temple. The scene is dramatic and intense. Yet when people reach the inner sanctum of the temple, the drumming ceases and the penitents approach the devi quietly and nonecstatically. Out in back, however, the trance performances arise again. For many, this is a brief reprise, but a few become oracles and attend to the public.

Alf Hiltebeitel's (1988, 1989, 1991) study of the Tamil Draupadi cult and festival cycle demonstrates an explicit conceptual differentiation between demonic possession and positive oracular manifestations as vehicles for bhakti. He uncovers not only an ecstatic continuum within the ritual dramas, but also a continuum between trance praxis and bhakti devotionalism. A close reading of Hiltebeitel's work on Draupadi cultism and that of others on Tamil religious culture more generally discloses a range of practices and paraphernalia characteristic of trance performance of significance for the southern Caribbean scene: animal sacrifice; the use of water pots and *karakams* associated with the devi; *tulsi* and neem leaves; the *utakki* drum; sword dancing; firewalking; and the use of saffron water on trance dancers.

Ecstasy seems almost exclusively associated with Shakti Worship in south India, and with what seems to be greater bhakti emphasis than in the north. Karin Kapadia (2000) studied trance under the influence of Murugan among middle-ranking non-Brahmins in Tamil festivals and found the experience conceptualized in terms of both shakti and bhakti. Isabelle Nabokov (2000:16) observes the recent rise in bhakti-oriented trance praxis more generally in Tamil religious culture: "Over this century south India has undergone a revival of devotional fervor (*bhakti*) first popularized by the Tamil poets and saints between the seventh and the ninth centuries. Increased participation in practices such as firewalking, flesh piercing, and pilgrimage have moved devotee to experience deities directly, intimately, and intensely."

Returning to the West Indies with South Asia in mind, the supplication of goddesses through trance-based performance is central within both regional contexts at the popular level. Moreover, these traditions differentiate between good versus bad possession in the form of mediumship versus affliction. Though the line between these poles may be protean in practice, the distinction is critical. Another recurrent theme is the ludic motif in which trance praxis—especially at the positive or oracular end of the spectrum—is conceptualized as play.

In a more intermediate sense, the status of trance performance as a form of bhakti devotionalism seems to have been considerably enhanced in the Caribbean Hindu case, although this is a relative comparison that varies depending upon which South Asian iteration is used as a point of reference. North Indian ecstatic ritual forms are less bhakti-oriented than south Indian genres. This is significant given the fact that the vast majority of Indians who migrated to the Caribbean did so from the greater Gangetic plains area of north India. Contemporary Indo-Caribbean Shakti Worshippers emphasize personal sincerity and devotion in relation to the ecstatic deities, perhaps even more so than in popular south Indian religious culture.

Moreover, the emphasis on healing as central in West Indian Hindu Shakti Puja seems intensified when compared with South Asian cognates. Frederick Smith (2006:97) observes that the therapeutic dimension of Indian mediumistic healing most commonly concerns the ecstatic conjuring of divinity in order to exorcise wayward spirits or malevolent afflictions from the sufferer's mind and body. He also notes that oracular mediumship has rarely been conceptualized as a vehicle of personal growth in South Asia, although there seem to be signs of recent change in this regard (98–105). Additionally, Smith shows that classical Sanskritic conceptualizations of divine incorporation primarily concerned the past, not the future. Hindu ecstasy in the Caribbean, by contrast, has become related to personal growth and a decidedly more futuristic orientation.

Also intermediate in comparative perspective is the unambiguously low status of ceremonial trance in the West Indian context, where Sanatanist and other neo-Hindu streams bear little trace of the avesha Smith finds in the interstices of South Asian Brahmanism. Hindus of high status in the Caribbean have unambiguously disassociated themselves from ecstatic traditions since at least the mid-twentieth century.

Even more distinctly different from India in the Caribbean context is the fact that ecstatic Shakti Worship has become more privatized, as discussed below. The current scene reflects long-term processes in the West Indies by which earlier traditions of public observance were carried out in progressively eclipsed forms during the colonial period. Ecstatic puja in the southern Caribbean has become confined to privately owned temples dedicated solely to devotional and therapeutic purposes.

Having taken stock of Kali and the transculturation of West Indian Shakti Puja in relation to South Asian past and present cognates, I turn to the analogous case of Shango and Orisha Worship vis-à-vis West Africa. Doing so enables an analysis of the ways they have undergone structural convergence in the southern Caribbean.

Shango and the Transculturation of Orisha Worship

Though Yoruba religion has often been foregrounded in the study of African "survivals" throughout the Black Atlantic world, Trotman (1976) observes for the southern Caribbean that, even though indentured Yorubas were similarly settled in both Trinidad and Guyana in the decades after emancipation, Orisha Worship took hold only in the former. Though a larger number of Yorubas found their way to British Guiana, in fact (approximately 14,000 as compared with 9,000 in Trinidad), various factors affected their ability to adapt and reproduce their religious practices within each context.

Constrained circumplantation conditions along a thin coastal strip and lack of access to viable peasant holdings made for the difficulty of group cohesion among liberated Africans in Guyana (Trotman 1976:7–9). Small traders of various backgrounds downplayed ethnicity in order to compete with the dominance of Portuguese merchants. Additionally, the absence of Anglo-French rivalry among European elites meant a more pervasive and systematic process of Anglicization in British Guiana than Trinidad. Trotman (11–13) argues that patois French and popular Catholicism became not only sociosymbolic refuges for Yorubas in resisting colonial domination in Trinidad, but also in fact vehicles of Yoruba-creole religious and cultural reproduction. With a weak economic base and surrounded by a Protestant majority, Guyanese Yorubas found themselves vulnerable on all fronts and had little room to maneuver. They were more rapidly and thoroughly absorbed within the locally evolving Afro-creole cultural matrix.

Many Yorubas in colonial Trinidad congregated in ethnolinguistic enclaves, enabling them to reproduce aspects of their cultural identity and ritual practices within modified local configurations. They became peasant landholders and successful marketers. Yorubas established patterns of solidarity through extended kinship and social support networks, such as the informal cooperative banking institution known as susu. Though their language began a gradual process of becoming obsolete, they produced a creole dialect mixture that persisted for several generations and has been retained to a remarkable degree within the liturgical repertoire of Orisha Worship. Indeed, Yoruba religious subculture endured in a compacted and reconfigured form, becoming an expansive vehicle of ritual creolization among Blacks more broadly.

I examined colonial historiography pertaining to Yoruba experience in nineteenth-century Trinidad above, in which the layering of several modalities of creolization was critical. First was intraethnic transculturation among folks from various areas of Yorubaland, reflected in a range of novel linguistic and ritual interactions and resulting in sociocultural configurations specific to the southern Caribbean. Second, despite relatively significant clustering, Yorubas of colonial Trinidad nonetheless began interacting with Africans from other backgrounds—Mandingo to Fon to Hausa to Kongo and beyond—in a process of inter-African creolization. Additionally, liberated African Yorubas also began to mingle both culturally and biologically with Afro-creoles of much longer standing on the island, who had already adopted some Christian dispositions and Eurocentric biases. Finally, all groups—no matter their positioning within this complex, evolving matrix—were subject to colonial subjugation and domination; hence they were all becoming acculturated to the prevailing socioeconomic winds and political institutions of transatlantic capitalism as engineered by Europeans.

Any assessment of the evolution of the popular tradition of Orisha Worship must attend to the recursive effects of these dynamics. For example, they help account for the sociolinguistic state of affairs in the realm of orisha song-chanting. On the one hand, the liturgy represents an astonishing informal archive of Yoruba-creole language. More than half of the songs are in Yoruba, and the percentage has even been recently increasing because of the efforts of Afrocentric activists. On the other hand, most people do not understand the meanings of these songs even when they know them by heart. The xenoglossic nature of Yoruba language in this context lends it an aura of mystical power, but it does not lead to generative linguistic production within or beyond the ritual arena. The repertoire also contains vestigial patois French retentions, various Englishisms, and a range of nonsemantic improvisation.

Earlier, I examined the historical significance of social interaction and ritual reciprocity between Yorubas and Dahomeans by the late nineteenth and early twentieth centuries. We know of ongoing interconnectivity between prominent ritual communities of each type in Port-of-Spain, and a number of Fon-based influences are evident within the ceremonial sphere of Shango. Resonance with and inputs from Dahomean ritual subculture would have buttressed important aspects of Yoruba-creole religiosity, such as trance performance and animal sacrifice. Warner-Lewis believes the evolving tradition of Orisha Worship not only absorbed Rada activity over time, but also incorporated elements of Kongo religious culture too. Shango came to reflect processes of Yoruba creolization and interculturation among Yorubas, other Africans, and Afro-creoles as well. Over time the "Yoruba" ethnonym was transmogrified into a privileged term of "African" ritual reference associated with the Afro-creole tradition that became widely known as "Shango," "Yoruba Work," "Orisha Work," "African Work," and so on. In other words, "Yorubaness" became progressively more based upon ritual kinship established through participation in the cult's ceremonial life, as opposed to an ethnic identity per se.

This flexibility of Orisha Worship is also crucial for understanding its incorporation of Catholic saints and a host of other "Christianisms" (Hucks and Stewart 2003). Nineteenth-century Yorubas embraced Catholicism, taking baptism seriously and garnering accolades from colonial observers for their upstanding character and respect for "civilization." Yoruba-creoles not only accepted the significance of both Christianity and their traditional ethnic religion, but also drew spiritual parallels between the two domains. A creative analogical process generated the plethora of orisha-saint identifications so common on the ground. Also widespread is the tendency to compare Olodumare, Oduduwa, and Obatala of the Yoruba pantheon with the Christian Trinity of Father, Son, and Holy Ghost, which has been explained to me countless times—including by leaders such as the late Babalorisha Sam "Baja" Phills. One finds similarly spirited analogies moving in new directions, such as the late Babalorisha Clarence Forde's likening of the Nigerian *Ooni* of Ife to the pope of Roman Catholicism.

The process by which Orisha Worship became animated by a host of Afro-Catholic spirits and practices, then, is part and parcel of the same process turning Yoruba-creole into Afro-creole. Though we have no direct access to what happened and when, the legacy of their cultural creativity is evident. Afro-Catholic hybridity seems to have become fully ensconced by the 1930s, such that the Herskovitses concluded that terminology of "saints" was paramount. The now-standard pattern—involving trance performance and animal sacrifice in a palais-chappelle-perogun shrine complex—had been established by that time. This pattern is also tellingly similar to the late 1940s Rada Vodou community of Belmont investigated by Andrew Carr.

Further complexifying these developments was the steady stream of British West Indian labor migrants to Trinidad—especially from Tobago, Barbados, and Grenada—in the latter nineteenth and early twentieth centuries. The historical and ethnohistorical materials of several researchers are full of references to Grenadian immigrants and their contributions to Shango, Spiritual

Baptism, and other aspects of Afro-creole popular culture in Trinidad such as *bélé*, *saraka*, and related forms of "thanksgiving" feasting (discussed below).

The Grenadian case is significant since indentured Yorubas were also brought there during the postemancipation decades, and their religious subculture soon trumped the earlier established "Nation Dance" and "Big Drum" ceremonies associated with "Kromanti" slaves from the Gold Coast (M. Smith 1965), preserved on the smaller island of Carriacou (McDaniel 1998). Though shrine compounds are uncommon in Grenada, Orisha Worshippers maintain private altars and build temporary palais for ceremonies. Few worship the orishas exclusively, instead espousing multiple religious affiliations and engaging in hybrid ritual practices. Patrick Polk (2001:129) believes ecstatic mediumship is likely responsible for the expansion of Afro-Grenadian Shango. Spiritual Baptists are also numerous in Grenada, and the phenomenon of "Shango Baptism" is pertinent among those active on both sides of this ritual continuum (Pollak-Eltz 1968).

The important point here is to appreciate how Grenadians have contributed to the development and consolidation of Afro-creole religious life and popular culture in Trinidad. Already-creolized Yoruba religious culture in Grenada was in turn carried farther south, where it encountered resonant concepts and practices, thereby contributing to ritual creolization.

Overdetermined by many sources and processes, then, what became routinized as Shango was documented by Frances Mischel in Port-of-Spain and the southern company towns of the mid-1950s, as well as by Jacob Elder for the Yoruba-creole communities of Gasparillo in west-central Trinidad in the 1950s and 1960s. Aside from a few antisyncretic stalwarts interviewed by Elder, most devotees in these reports espoused no consternation over Afro-Catholic hybrid forms. If anything, the Catholic side seems to have been ascendant in the consciousness of many practitioners. This documentation is also notable in that neither researcher reports flags in any of the compounds studied. However, Mischel (1957) makes the first published reference to an orisha with an Indian side and also quotes an informant regarding the subaltern significance of Circle Work within the Afro-creole ritual sphere.

By the time George Simpson entered the field in the early 1960s, the practice of planting flags for the powers in both Orisha shrines and Spiritual Baptist churches had clearly emerged. It is impossible to know exactly when this pattern was adopted by ecstatic Afro-creole ritualism, but it may plausibly be seen as a post–World War II development influenced by local observation of Hindu puja praxis, in which jhandis are planted in honor of the deity being supplicated during ritual devotions. Yet it is also possible that Orisha and Baptist flags derived from deeper Afro-creole sources not previously commented upon, since ceremonial flags are important objects in many African and Afro-American cultures and represent one of the most significant ritual and aesthetic continuities within the Black Atlantic world (R. Thompson 1993; Polk 1997).

Simpson also observed the first trickle of Indo-Trinidadian Shango practitioners, including at least one trance medium, and noted the use of various Hindu implements in both Shango and Spiritual Baptist ritual spheres. He also encountered increasing overlap and reciprocal sociosymbolic influences between these Afro-creole traditions. Indeed, the significance of Baptism for Shango was such that Simpson even characterized the latter as resulting from the fusion of Yoruba, Catholic, and Baptist elements. He encountered mixed-use compounds and hybrid ritual events, as well as the development of multifunctional "mourning" and "fasting" practices on both "sides" of the Afro-creole spectrum. Moreover, he noted the specter of Circle Work, though it does not loom large in his account. In the 1960s, Holland and Crane confirmed the trend toward Shango-Baptist convergence and the encroaching significance of Circle Work. Pollak-Eltz echoes these findings, also noting the rise of Hindu elements within Shango.

In turn, the respective investigations of Houk and Lum in the 1980s and early 1990s document continuing momentum on all fronts: intensification of the overlapping juxtaposition between Shango and Spiritual Baptism; continued incorporation of elements of Hinduism and other forms of Indian symbolism into grassroots Orisha Worship; and the surfacing of Circle Work, also becoming known as Kabbalah. The interdigitation of Baptism, Orisha, and Kabba had become so substantial that Houk (1995) refers to them as a composite "Afro-American religious complex." Many practitioners invoke the concepts of "side" and "levels" when referring to their overlapping affiliations. While the spectrum spanning from Spiritual Baptism to Orisha Worship runs from the Christocentric to the Afrocentric, the field of Baptist churches is also differentiated along a congruent gradient.

This pattern is complexified in Kabba, which practitioners consider a tradition of European magic characterized by interaction with spirits racialized as white. Some ritualists I know who have become deeply involved on the Kabbalistic side maintain that it is the highest level of all. In this scheme, one starts out under St. John in the Baptist realm, which leads to Shango—St. John's African equivalent—in Orisha Worship, and then eventually to the mystical planes accessed by the select few within Kabba. However, many others castigate Kabbalistic work as too quick and dirty, as compared with what they see as the more patient, deeper religiosity involved in the path of the orishas.

Though traffic between Trinidad and Tobago was slight throughout the nineteenth century, it picked up after the two islands were unified in 1899 as a joint Crown Colony. Laitinen (2002a:43–44) believes Spiritual Baptism spread to Tobago from Trinidad in the early twentieth century, possibly also with inputs from St. Vincent and Grenada. Though elements of Shango ceremonialism have presumably also been transported to Tobago through association with Spiritual Baptism, this would not have happened until the post–World War II period, when the two traditions began interacting and increasingly overlapping in Trinidad itself.

The majority of Afro-creole religious practitioners in Tobago are Spiritual Baptists, and the only two full-fledged orisha compounds were established relatively late in the twentieth century. Most come to Shango through Baptist work. I participated in a pilgrimage for Yemanja conducted by a neotraditional shrine from southern Trinidad in the summer of 2005, for example, which focused upon her Africanity and involved no Christian liturgy. However, a number of Tobagonian Baptists also turned out, intermittently singing Christian hymns and making their own prayers throughout the afternoon. The two groups coexisted more or less respectfully on the beach that day.

As in Trinidad, Afro-creole popular religion in Tobago reflects a complex matrix of practices and beliefs; however, its center of gravity is clearly more weighted in the direction of Spiritual Baptism (Laitinen 2002a, 2002b). Even Baptist churches emphasizing a strong orientation towards the "African Nation" and entertaining a host of "African Powers" nonetheless often actively disidentify with Orisha Worship. Still, Laitinen observes that Baptist churches in Tobago are nevertheless generally quite eclectic, incorporating many more deeply Afro-oriented symbols and practices at the tacit level when compared with the most orthodox of their Christocentric counterparts in Trinidad.

The more time I have spent throughout both islands, the more I have become impressed by the depth and complexity of interrelations between these two most prominent Afro-creole ritual traditions. I believe the Christocentric emphasis of the most orthodox of Baptist churches combined with the Afro-centric revitalizing trends of the postcolonial era—especially vis-à-vis Orisha Worship, but also in relation to Spiritual Baptism to some degree—have fostered an ideological climate encouraging us to overlook the depth and degree to which these traditions have interpenetrated and influenced one another. This point may be made in relation to "Shango Baptism," a term commonly used by outsiders as a generalized catchall for anything smacking of subaltern African religiosity. The name is highly problematic, as it glosses over important historical and sociosymbolic differences in ritual life and the varying identifications of practitioners differently positioned with the Afro-creole matrix. For this reason, some understandably eschew use of this terminology. However, the notion of Shango Baptism captures something dynamically real on the ground when understood *not* as an essentializing rubric that collapses differences, but as recognizing complex processes of subaltern hybridity. Indeed, some practitioners themselves use the term nonpejoratively.

The reality of the Shango-Baptist interface was dramatized for me in October of 1999 at a funeral service for the late Philip Jeff Guerra at the Belmont shrine originally belonging to Tanti Silla and Shepherd Breton and which Frances Henry visited in the mid-1950s. Now known as St. Ann's Spiritual Baptist Church, the compound houses an impressive palais alongside a line of orisha stools and a boat just inside the entrance gate. Lithographs of Jesus adorn the Baptist hall as well as the main house's porch.

The service drew a large crowd, reflecting the deceased's involvement in both Orisha Worship and Spiritual Baptism. Guerra's body was dressed in white and lavender-colored Baptist robes in the coffin, yet the service took place in the yard's palais, where a Baptist-style chalk cosmogram was drawn on the floor, and above which the casket was placed. A Spiritual Baptist preacher offered a brief sermon about life and death and then led several rounds of hymns. Half of the printed program was devoted to the lyrics of six hymns—including "Amazing Grace," "What a Friend We Have in Jesus," and "How Great Thou Art"—which were movingly sung by throngs of Baptists. The eulogy, given by another Baptist, remarked upon Guerra's involvement in Shango in a way that tacitly affirmed a Baptist orientation among the majority of those present.

Two prominent Orisha elders took turns with remarks. The late Sam "Baja" Phills, chairman of the Orisha Council of Elders at the time, began by announcing that Guerra was "both a Christian and an Orisha man," invoking Olodumare in this time of need. He offered reflections on Guerra's life and some of their shared experiences many years before. Olori Jeffery Biddeau offered another discourse on life and death, which invoked a more strictly Yoruba perspective. Baja Phills and Olori Biddeau then initiated a period of orisha song-chanting—which many seemed to know—accompanied by slow ceremonial circling around the coffin. The burial was not elaborate, yet profuse libations of olive oil—reminiscent of orisha feasts—were repeatedly offered around the grave site.

I now understand why I so commonly heard people mention that they had recently been to a "Shango Baptist" funeral. Though I initially found this refrain somewhat inscrutable, it now makes sense that mortuary commemorations for people with complex and elaborate Afro-creole religious engagements would involve elements of both Orisha Worship and Spiritual Baptism. Whereas their spiritual practices may remain spatially separate while they are alive, these necessarily come together at a funeral. Further, practitioners evince diverse views concerning the relationship between Shango and Spiritual Baptism: there are Baptists who disparage Orisha Worship; those who enthusiastically embrace and practice both; Shangoists uninvolved with Baptism; and purists who distance themselves from any form of Christianity. The complex and shifting ritual terrain captured by the phrase "Shango Baptism" therefore seems to be a reality, even if imprecise.

I attended a number of orisha feasts in Baptist churches, such as that of Spiritual Baptist bishop Eudora Thomas—known as Mother Eula—in Tunapuna. She holds important bureaucratic offices on both the African and Baptist sides and is the author of an Afrocentrically oriented history of Spiritual Baptism in Trinidad and Tobago (E. Thomas 1987). Like those of Mother Joan and many others, her church doubles as a palais during feast time.

To take another case: the multipurpose palais of St. Anthony's Baptist Church in St. Helena, Piarco, is adorned not only with Catholic iconography, but also with extensive Baptist paraphernalia. Its feast attracts Indo-Trinidadians involved in Spiritual Baptism, with a smaller subset also associated—but not exclusively—with Orisha Worship.

Related to the phenomenon of multiplex shrine-and-church compounds discussed earlier, in which palais may serve as churches and chappelles as mourning rooms, and vice-versa, is what now seems to be the convergent practice known by Baptists as "mourning" and Shangoists as "fasting." Increasing numbers of practitioners see this period of ascetic withdrawal and ritual fasting as analogous in both the African and the Baptist domains, the primary difference being which side one is cultivating.

Baptist and Shango terminologies may be used interchangeably by those involved with both, who said it was a question of "levels" when I probed for specificity. "It all depends," I heard repeatedly. I know of cases in which Baptist mourners travel to Mother Africa in the spiritual world, meeting with Shango or other "African" deities who lead them toward orisha praxis. Likewise, I know of Orisha Worshippers who fast and discover, or reestablish, connections with Baptism. Such crossover activity is facilitated by polysemic symbolism such as the anchor, shepherd's rod, keys, or the steering wheel.

"Thanksgiving feasts" or "tables" may be offered that are described as "half African and half Baptist." However, thanksgiving and feast practices are widespread in black popular culture beyond the realms of Spiritual Baptism and Orisha Worship. Indeed, the feast might be seen as a generic vehicle of Afro-creole interchange overall. A plethora of evidence points to the pervasiveness of Afro-creole "drum dances" throughout the late nineteenth and early twentieth centuries. These were held at wakes, ancestral commemorations, thanksgivings, community celebrations, fund-raisers, and so on, and were the activities that many of the mid-to-late-nineteenth-century musical ordinances and much antiobeah legislation were designed to regulate and suppress. Elites saw drum dances as the obscene, déclassé diversions of an insufficiently civilized people, especially since they involved intense physicality and dancing, revolved around the percussive rhythms of African drums, and often included animal sacrifices. Catholic missionary R.P.M. Cothonay (1893:62–65) described a lower-class black festival held at Carenage in the early 1880s to commemorate emancipation half a century before. After attending Mass and staging a public procession, those involved built a bamboo hut they called a "palace" in which to carry out their drumming and festivities. References to the palais and the combination of both African and Catholic dimensions are especially noteworthy in the context of this drum dance.

Commemorative feasts came to feature various dances such as the bélé, an Afro-creole variant of a French courtly dance performed to drummed accompaniment. The concept of bélé expanded into an all-encompassing rubric for feast occasions sponsored upon recovery from sickness or the advent of some other good fortune. Over time, the term also came to partially absorb the Yoruba-based saraka, another tradition focused upon religious worship and animal sacrifice. The terminology derives from African Yoruba linguistic borrowing from the neighboring Hausa Muslim word sadaka—itself borrowed from Arabic—referring to a ceremony in which alms are given to the needy (Warner-Lewis 1991:115–16).

Thus the amalgamating complex now known simply as "feasts" or "thanksgivings" includes both secular and spiritual iterations and has become incorporated into the language and operation of Orisha Worship and Spiritual Baptism in multiple forms. Warner-Lewis's older informants (1991:31–32) used the French for "service" interchangeably with saraka and testified to the commonality of attending church as a preliminary aspect of the festivity. Warner-Lewis (116) observes that the religious saraka gave way to the greater popularity of "Shango feasts," in fact, bolstered by the practices of incoming migrants from Grenada (116). This connection is especially suggestive given that sarakas in Grenada historically involved trance performance (Pollak-Eltz 1993:19–20).

In Trinidad, then, Shango seems to have come to embody the religious dimensions of Afro-creole feasting, whereas bélé inherited the more secular occasions. The latter was domesticated for the national stage—and therefore circulated widely in public culture—in the televised "Best Village" competitions promoted by Williams's nationalist government in the 1960s and 1970s. Still, bélé has diminished as a secular practice, and most feasts and thanksgivings are now associated with Orisha Worship and Spiritual Baptism. Significantly, shantwelle is shared across all categories of Afro-creole feasting.

This discussion cannot avoid the problem of syncretism, which refers to hybrid religious forms produced through the interaction and interpenetration of differing social groups and cultural traditions (see Appendix). Popularized as an analytical concept in anthropology by Melville Herskovits, the concept of "syncretism" has been subject to critical scrutiny for carrying pejorative connotations or too easily implying that the mixing "cultures" or "traditions" are pure prior to their hybridization. There is also the problem of emic and etic points of view, as there may be a critical difference between the view of social actors and that of the analyst. For example, though the most orthodox of Spiritual Baptists see their practices as authentically Christian and strongly reject African roots, many observers view their religion as rooted in Africanity to the extent that they engage in mystical chalk-drawing, ascetic ordeals of mourning and visionary travel, and practices of trance performance that seem clearly derived from African sources.

The debate over syncretism in Afro-Trinbagonian Orisha Worship largely turns upon one's stance with regard to what has become known as the "camouflage theory" in the study of Afro-Atlantic religions. This is the view that African and Afro-creole slaves and, by extension, indentured laborers strategically employed symbolism and aspects of Christianity in their ritual activities to create the illusion that they were engaging in respectable religious worship in the eyes of the Euro-colonial establishment. In this regard, Afro-Catholic hybridity in the case of orisha-saint identifications is seen as a crafty subaltern black ruse for evading domination through symbolic disguise. This perspective has been espoused by numerous analysts, including Roger Bastide, who not only acknowledged "parallels" between West African religions and Roman Catholicism (1978), but also adopted the camouflage point of view regarding Afro-Brazilian Candomblé: "Syncretism by correspondence between gods and saints . . . can be explained in historical terms by the slaves' need, during the colonial period, to conceal their pagan ceremonies from European eyes. They therefore danced before a Catholic altar; and although their masters found this somewhat bizarre, it never occurred to them that these Negro dances, with their prominently displayed lithographs and statuettes of the saints, were in fact addressed to African divinities" (1972:156). Pollak-Eltz (1993:15) puts the matter similarly concerning Shango in Trinidad: "The outward identification of African deities with saints had the purpose of protecting adherents from persecution; as they could always show their altar decorated with lithographs and statues of saints, they could claim to be practicing Catholics" (also see Pollak-Eltz 1968:425). Statements such as these are common in the literature (e.g., Walker 1980).

This camouflage view is not just an interpretive framework adopted by social scientists, however. It circulates more widely, such as in David Tindall's otherwise informative article "Drums and Colours" (2000) on Orisha religion in Trinidad and Tobago for *Caribbean Beat*, the hip in-flight magazine of the former British West Indian Airlines. He writes: "In the early nineteenth century West African slaves in Trinidad were sometimes baptized into Catholicism en masse; it seems likely that many Orishas [i.e., practitioners] used the paraphernalia of the Catholic Church as camouflage behind which they hid their African beliefs and practices. Their faith was not to be diminished by oppression" (41). Note the focus on slavery in lieu of the reality of postemancipation Yoruba labor migration.

This point of view is also put forth at the popular level. Houk (1995:68–69) documents the view of an influential spiritual leader clearly espousing the camouflage interpretation of Afro-Catholic syncretism, and I have encountered similar sentiments among some devotees, yet not in fact so frequently. Indeed, this perspective is most commonly held by the more Afrocentrically oriented practitioners associated with the self-identified "Orisha Movement," which seeks to dispose of Christian influences as corrupting impositions—a thorny topic to which I return in chapter 6.

Though there are certainly limitations to our historical knowledge that trouble the debate, the camouflage paradigm must be reframed. Trotman (1976) finds the camouflage view "more romantic than logical" on two grounds: first, antiobeah programs did not gather serious momentum until the last third of the nineteenth century, before which time Yorubas would have begun reproducing their ritual forms; and second, African religious activity was so distinctive as to in no way be mistakable for Christian worship. Trotman emphasizes the nineteenth-century alliance between the Catholic Franco-creole plantocracy and patois-speaking Afro-creoles in relation to their common British enemy as another factor motivating syncretic processes on the part of Yorubas and their descendants. "Rather than serving the function of fooling the authorities," he concludes, "Catholic saints were a conscious and deliberate inclusion of the Yoruba" (13).

Most Yorubas were brought as indentured laborers to the West Indies, a pertinent fact given that the camouflage view has been advanced primarily with regard to slave religion. Insufficient attention has been paid to the differences between slavery and after. Trotman's view is that Catholicism was not just an agent of domination, but, paradoxically, also a vehicle of Yoruba-creole sub-cultural reproduction, what he refers to elsewhere as a "transcultural bridge" (2007:219). His perspective accords with Warner-Lewis's conclusions that Yoru-bas more or less embraced Catholicism and generated hybrid ritual forms that were supple and genuine, not simply the result of sheer domination, though dominated they certainly were. Elder's ethnohistorical work likewise suggests the authenticity of Afro-Christian syncretism within Orisha Worship, repre-senting creative resistance by resilient people.

Yet Elder also notes the mid-twentieth-century presence of a handful of folks who adopted an antisyncretic posture in relation to Catholicism, endeavoring to keep the tradition "pure." Indeed, the picture is more variable on the ground than usually appreciated in debate about syncretism. Frances Henry (2001, 2003) takes the position that camouflage-oriented Afro-Catholic syncretism probably first arose for purposes of adaptation to the colonial milieu, but then grew into a more authentic and elaborated hybrid configuration. Houk agrees that a temporal dimension is crucial, but he seems equivocal about just how to parse the matter. At one point (1995:70), he sees things the other way around, suggesting that "the incorporation of Catholic elements may have been volun-tary at first, only later giving way to the camouflage stratagem as the govern-ment began to legislate against African religious practices." Yet later, he seems to do a U-turn:

> Although there is little documentation on the origins of *orisha* worship in
> Trinidad, my research supports the contention that the initial syncretism
> of Catholicism and the Yoruba-derived African religion occurred on the
> level of form only. As one of my contacts explained, his ancestors in earlier
> times in Trinidad would simply use a statue or some other representation
> of a Catholic saint to stand in the place of an African god so as not to draw
> attention to their African religious activities. As far as the Africans were
> concerned, the shrine was devoted to, say, Ogun and not Saint Michael.
> In time, however, the initial synthesis of form gave way to elaboration on
> a broader scale involving the fusion of ideology and meaning, and many
> *orisha* worshipers now view the two figures as aspects of the same deity.
> (1995:182)

All of this presents serious empirical and methodological challenges. What is clear is that elements of Catholicism were incorporated into local orisha tradi-tion by the turn of the twentieth century, if not before.

I acknowledge both temporal dynamism and individual variability in the evolution of hybridity, as the reality is an overdetermined and highly complex field of sociocultural change. While camouflage undoubtedly occurred, it was not the sole factor in syncretizing processes. Indeed, I see the interpretive flexibility and hybridizing dynamism of Afro-creole religion as testaments to its Africanity. The camouflage debate is also overly preoccupied with Afro-Catholic hybridity to the exclusion of other vectors of transculturation. The reconfiguring relationship of Orisha Worship and Catholicism is but one, albeit an important, dynamic. It has generated its own local creole innovations and also incorporated elements of Hinduism not easily attributed to camouflage motives. Multifarious reconfigurations within the Afro-creole sphere of Shango illustrate its many-splendored ingenuity and resilience across space and time, attributes that can be accounted for only in terms of its African-inspired hermeneutic roots.

Here the work of Andrew Apter (1991, 1992, 1995, 2002) on the cultural principles of West African Yoruba orisha ritualism—which he sees as part of a regionally coherent set of ritual schemas and political forms underlying Yoruba, Fon (Dahomean), and Ewe variations alike—is indispensable. Resuscitating a neo-Herskovitsean line of argumentation within a more empirically nuanced formulation, Apter demonstrates how an understanding of West African cultural hermeneutics illuminates the study of creolization in the New World. He argues that revisionary principles of Yoruba "deep knowledge"—*imo jinle*—have enabled Orisha Worship to extend its interpretive horizons in diaspora and embrace colonialism, modern class formations, and the postcolonial state by ritually bringing the "outside" in.[3]

Apter reconsiders the assumption of earlier scholars that West African spirit cults represent discrete organizational entities that were fragmented by slavery in the Americas. He shows not only that no pure theological Golden Age ever existed in Africa, but also that Yoruba-Dahomean hermeneutics embodied in ritual praxis have been more coherently operative in their admittedly compacted and truncated New World forms than heretofore appreciated. Materials from the Ekiti highlands demonstrate that orisha cult pantheons are dynamic and never entirely discrete (also see Barber 1981, 1990). Dialogically related to political forms, West African Orisha Worship traditionally both reflected the distribution of power and opposed that power from below. Thus the variability of orisha clustering is a transatlantic phenomenon reflecting a more widely shared cultural dynamic. New World cult organization may not be as radically novel as earlier scholars surmised, and polyvocal processes of syncretic reformulation must be taken more seriously as signs of perduring African inspiration.

This line of analysis requires accounting for the ways Black Atlantic orishas and their votaries have adapted and reconstituted themselves in relation to changing sociocultural conditions. Though the process of pantheonization is not unique to the southern Caribbean, what is distinctive is the fact that the range of local powers is collected together within each compound. In this regard, the Afro-Trinbagonian pantheon is dialectically related to political segmentation, but through total subordination, by contrast with precolonial West Africa. Trinidadian shrines share a more or less standard set of divinities praised and supplicated during feasts. The pantheon is therefore amalgamated into one specific to TT, and all of the powers also generally materialize through the ritual arts of trance within each shrine arena.

Though one must be careful in drawing too hard a contrast, the impression one gets from the West Africanist literature on Yoruba religion, on the other hand, is that trance performances take place at temples or shrines more prominently devoted to specific gods or in ceremonial contexts featuring mediumship by a few focal deities at most. Indeed, in traditional Yorubaland (Olawaiye 1980:89–90), many of the major orishas receive their own rituals of worship—often by a specific lineage or village—in which they alone manifest upon devotees. Mediumship for multiple orishas is also practiced, but this still seems more or less centered upon the manifestation of but a handful of deities, by contrast with Trinbagonian Afro-creole spiritist circles, where all of the locally known gods are conjured throughout the ceremonial period as part of standard practice.

More important, perhaps, is the upregulation of trance performance and spirit mediumship as focal for Orisha Worship in this area of the diaspora. Pollak-Eltz, drawing on comparative research in Yorubaland and throughout the Afro-Americas, writes, "In Africa, the cult members fall in trance occasionally in order to receive their deities, but the trance is not very important. The will of the gods is rather expressed through Ifá, the elaborated kola-nut oracle, cast by special priests. In the Americas, where the complicated system of Ifá was lost for the most part, the trance becomes all-important as a means of communicating with the deities. The gods descend upon their 'horses' and speak from the mouth of the devotees" (1968:425; cf. Simpson 1980:78–79). West African mediumship for the orishas is in fact relatively marginal in the scholarly literature. Reviews of Yorubanist scholarship (Pemberton 1987; Olupona 1993) hardly mention trance performance. McKenzie's (1997) study of nineteenth-century materials barely mentions trance and mediumship, restricting them to ten pages out of a 550-page tome. Àjàyí's (1998) study of Yoruba dance traditions is interesting in that "possession"—as she refers to it—appears to be deeply embedded within many other layers of nonecstatic ritual processes.

Similarly, Drewal's (1992) magisterial study of Yoruba ritual performance deals with trance mediumship only briefly.

While I do not mean to downplay the significance of trance and ecstasy in West Africa, it is crucial for comparative purposes to appreciate the relative weighting and contextualization of these practices across the Black Atlantic world, especially when they have become so paramount within the sphere of Orisha Worship in Trinidad and Tobago. If the trend is, or was, more toward singular ecstatic patronage for specific orishas by devotees in Africa, in Trinidad and Tobago, by contrast, practitioners tend to accumulate trance experience with multiple deities over time, becoming hoosis (mediums) for increasingly broad sets of divinities throughout their spiritual careers. And whereas people often come into the service of the orishas in West Africa through their families, lineages, villages, or polity, those in the southern Caribbean most often become devotees as a result of personal experiences that compel them to seek guidance or healing from orisha religious specialists—not for political or sociological reasons per se.

Thus, related to the upregulation of trance praxis is the corollary increase in the therapeutic orientation of ecstatic orisha cultism in TT. A survey of literature on Afro-Yoruba trance and dance (e.g., Drewal 1975, 1986, 1989, 1992; Simpson 1980; Àjàyí 1998) suggests that healing is not especially central to practices of ecstasy in traditional ritual forms. In his discussion of trance and convention in Yoruba mediumship, Pierre Verger specifically observes that Yoruba and Fon trance cults do *not* represent therapeutic systems (1969:51–52). He notes that the traditional performance of trance derives primarily from societal pressure and ritual scripting, not from individual expressive needs or initiative. West African healing arts have more traditionally been carried out by diviners and herbalists than ecstatic mediums. Indeed, the eclipse of Ifá divination in the southern Caribbean is profound and should not be underappreciated. Peel (2000:114–15) notes that the elaborate cult of Ifá in Yorubaland was the most widespread aspect of traditional religion, involving highly trained specialists as well as laity and operating as the interpretive linchpin of the entire ritual system.

This transatlantic expansion of Orisha Worship's therapeutic orientation may be understood partly in relation to the demise of its political significance in continental practice. Historically speaking, Dahomean and Yoruba ritual groups were not marginal healing societies—"peripheral deprivation cults" in Lewis's terminology (1989)—but linked to the established power structure at several levels of resolution (Bascom 1944; Parrinder 1953; Verger 1957; Beattie and Middleton 1969; Apter 1992, 1995; Peel 2000). The cult of Shango played a vital role in the imperial Oyo administration that developed in Yorubaland in the seventeenth and eighteenth centuries (Matory 1994). This was an expansionary state drawing great economic strength from the transatlantic slave trade. We might say that the vertical continuum ranging from central to subordinate in traditional Yoruba cultism was flattened because of the colonial Atlantic experience, driving the practice underground into compacted Afro-Caribbean subaltern cults of healing, divested of their former political significance and relegated to the margins of public culture.

Thus Trinbagonian orisha cultism represents the coalescence of important features of traditional Yoruba religion accompanied by the truncation of other central elements. This is reflected, for example, in the recessive concatenation of song-chants in the subaltern liturgical repertoire (see Warner-Lewis 1994). It is also evident in the local condensation of ceremonial personnel, in which the mombwah takes special precedence whereas the roles of diviner and communal priest, so significant in traditional West Africa, have been left behind. The Afro-creole mombwah is somewhat different in character from its ancestral precedent, the *màngbà* of Yorubaland, an office of hereditary priesthood associated with Oyo state administration. Aiyejina and Gibbons (1999) observe that women in Trinbagonian Orisha Worship have come to garner stronger leadership positions than in West Africa, even though they do not usually operate as mombwahs. What Orisha Worship on both sides of the Atlantic does have in common, however, is that the bulk of active, regular worshippers are women (Peel 2000:103).

Another central aspect of Afro-Yoruba religion concerns the ancestors, for whom much ritual and offering take place. Indeed, Yorubas have traditionally endowed some ancestors with the qualities of orishas. Orishas and ancestors are therefore both complementary and convergent (Peel 2000:94–97). By contrast, only the orishas manifest upon devotees within the southern Caribbean tradition of Shango. Eastman and Warner-Lewis (2000:414) point to the decline of ancestralism within the Afro-creole matrix. Yet though the centrality of ancestral veneration has subsided, subtle traces remain, and it is being revived more recently by one Afrocentric *ile*, or "house," in southern Trinidad (see chapter 6). Masking traditions were separated from their religious moorings through secularization and incorporation into Carnival.

Though I have explored the ways traditional Afro-Yoruba religion has been transformed as a result of the transatlantic experience in order to clarify the form and function of southern Caribbean Orisha Worship, the situation is less different in comparison with Yorubaland today. Indeed, the advance of colonialism and Christianization also progressively subjugated the orisha cults of West Africa. Christianity and Orisha Worship also intermingle and are not mutually exclusive at the popular level. The persistence of orisha cultism reflects the dynamism of realignment in relation to dramatically changing forms of economic and political power not unlike what transpired more radically and precociously across the Atlantic in the Americas. It is for reasons such as these that Stephan Palmié (2007c, 2007d) argues we should better attend to coeval cultural and historical developments throughout the Atlantic matrix, in all of which "Africa" operates as a complex, layered, contested, and shifting chronotope.

It is also important to appreciate the longstanding urbanism of Yoruba civilization, arising in the latter half of the Common Era's first millennium (Wheatley 1970). Henry Drewal (1989:47–49) notes the development of domestic and communal altar traditions at Ile-Ife, the sacred mythological center of Yoruba civilization, where Olodumare's son Oduduwa climbed down from heaven and became the first king, fathering future generations of Yoruba royalty through his sixteen sons. This is relevant here because the web of traditional Yoruba religion is spun within a network of shrines differentiated between urban and natural landscapes. In Trinidad and Tobago, however, this pattern has been compacted by the bifurcation of "inside" and "outside" stools *within* the private orisha compound. This transposition exemplifies how continuity and change comingle in Black Atlantic ritual forms. Indeed, I found the inside-outside distinction puzzling before understanding it as a recontextualized transformation of the urban-bush pattern of spatial and symbolic differentiation in Yorubaland.

Though I have explored a plethora of substantive changes and creolizing transformations, the resonances are also compelling. James Adeyinka Olawaiye—a Nigerian priest—wrote this about a feast he attended in Trinidad in 1977: "At the various ceremonies I attended, the songs were so clearly sung in the Yoruba language that any Yoruba person would have felt he was listening to Yoruba worshippers. The dances, the participation of the worshippers and the leadership and control of their congregations by Father Isaac and Reverend Fitzroy Small were also very much what you would expect of a priest and the devotees of Yorubaland" (1980:59).

I have made the case for other compelling continuities in the black Yoruba Atlantic. An example of this is the transatlantic conceptualization of Yoruba ritual in general, and trance performance in particular, as "play." Yoruba performance culture emphasizes the underlying principle of *ere*—play—in all forms of ritual, festival, and spectacle. Yoruba performative play is deep, not frivolous. A central thread in Yoruba culture, it is given theological expression in the figure of the trickster deity Eshu-Elegba. To play a situation is to intervene in and transform it by exercising agency and power. Indeed, when Yorubas "perform ritual" (*se etutu*) they often say in English that they are going to "play" (M.

Drewal 1992:19). Yorubas understand ritual behavior to be dynamic and not inherently stable: "Innovations in ritual do not break with tradition but rather are continuations of it in the spirit of improvisation" (23). The malleability of Yoruba ritual praxis has therefore enabled it to adapt to the encroachment of two world religions, surviving and sometimes even subverting colonial and postcolonial domination.

Small wonder, then, that devotees of the orishas in TT speak of their ritual practices through Anglophone discourses of "play." This ludic conceptualization represents one of the most salient transatlantic continuities of Yoruba hermeneutics, helping to account for the syncretic flexibility of rhizomatic extensions in diaspora. What makes Yoruba religion so resilient in West Africa obtains in the New World as well, though perhaps less obviously as a result of its ostensibly non-"African" symbolic refigurations in the latter. I have argued against the camouflage perspective, showing how the transculturating potential of Orisha Worship in the southern Caribbean in fact signifies its transgressive subaltern Africanity. Thus, despite formidable changes, we are confronted with an underlying continuity within popular practice, albeit in a recontextualizing form that makes it elusive on the surface.

Structural Convergence and Subaltern Liberalization: Shango and Shakti Puja Compared

Having considered the development of Orisha Worship and Shakti Puja in relation to precedents and cognates in West Africa and South Asia, as well as regional crosscurrents and deeper local dynamics in the southern Caribbean, we may now turn to the two ritual traditions vis-à-vis one another. This enables us to clarify what is distinctive about each and to identify processes of sociocultural change common to both that might otherwise be overlooked. Despite the fact that these religious subcultures have not explicitly intersected, they have undergone parallel processes of structural convergence, by which the lateral experience of adapting to colonial society in the southern Caribbean has led them to become more alike over time. I pursue this line of analysis in relation to resonant marginalization and heterodox stratification, increased individualism and therapeutic upregulation, parallel differentiation of ritual praxis, and analogous privatization as well as petit bourgeois orientations to land and property. Needless to say, my focus on similarities in no way obviates the innumerable differences between the two.

Both traditions have—along with the society around them (see Winer 1993, 2007)—become progressively encoded within a local creole English tongue. I have examined concepts used similarly across both domains concerning "play," "work," "manifestation" as positively cultivated ecstasy, generalized cosmic "power" and the individual "powers," "possession" as affliction, and so forth. It is easy to overlook the significance of this convergent Anglophone evolution, yet this is what made it possible for Dexter to attend an unfamiliar ritual and efficiently plug into the scene, as well as ask appropriate questions to fill in the gaps. It was not just the differentiated structure of baseline ecstasy and individuated mediumship that made for ready translation, but also shared metapragmatic conceptualizations alive in both traditions.

Of course, sociolinguistic convergence does not mean the historical trajectories of these traditions mirror one another in any simplistic way. Blacks became creole Anglophone speakers earlier than Indians, resulting from the later introduction of indentured South Asians and the successive in-migration of speakers of Afro-creole Englishes from throughout the eastern Caribbean along the way. Though Trinidad became a British colony at the turn of the nineteenth century, Anglicization of language and popular culture did not become widespread for another century, judging from changes in calypso by the time of World War I. By then, the more popular French patois had begun to dissipate throughout the Afro-creole population. A Hindi patois persisted longer among Indo-creoles, by contrast, even though processes of creolization and "douglarization" (Afro-Indo mixture) were certainly under way. Indians also came to benefit en masse from education much later than Blacks.

These demographic trends influenced the linguistic rendering of subaltern ritual practices. Aside from their differently encoded song-chant repertoires— a mix of Yoruba, French, English, and a pastiche of nonsemantic utterances in Shango versus a blend of Hindi, Tamil, and English in Shakti Puja—each tradition otherwise came to be understood in terms of the local English argot that gained ground in the twentieth century. Indeed, this is how English seeped into the liturgies of each. Thus, even though they took different routes getting there, both converged upon the seamless Anglophone rendering I encountered at the turn of the twenty-first century. It was only after the experience with Dexter at the Kali mandir that I began to truly appreciate the significance of these shared discourses, which capture the spirit of what I mean by "structural convergence."

Let us therefore turn to the resonant historical marginalization and heterodox stratification of Orisha Worship and Shakti Puja as popular traditions of trance performance. Both suffered from colonial Christian critique and have offended middle- and upper-class notions of social respectability up to this day. This is the case despite the differently positioned relationships of Blacks and Indians to Christianity and the varying temporalities of ethnoracial stratification in the nineteenth and twentieth centuries. I have suggested that Yoruba-creole religious practices became increasingly compacted in adapting to the structures and strictures of colonial society, and that the orisha-based tradition progressively incorporated aspects of Dahomean, Kongo, and other African ritual cultures extant on the island. Moreover, early Yoruba adoption of Catholicism and a nonexclusivistic relationship with Christianity set in motion a pattern of Afro-Catholic bricolage animating the popular tradition of Orisha Worship. Further into the twentieth century, the tradition known by many as Shango has developed dynamically complex interrelationships with both Spiritual Baptism and Kabba and has incorporated elements of Hinduism and Indian culture.

The Afro-creole ritual complex centered on Orisha Worship involves an assemblage of activities—especially trance performance and animal sacrifice—considered common and primitive in relation to dominating liberal bourgeois norms. Yet, despite modernist assumptions at-large, Shango has not disappeared. It has become suppressed down the ladder of social relations, where it continues to adapt, transform, change, and recruit devotees of varied ethnic backgrounds. The localizing stream of Orisha Worship has been progressively marginalized since its transoceanic transfer and local reconstitution in the mid-nineteenth century. Yet with the formation and mobility of the colored—followed by black—middle classes, and their cumulative Christianization in relation to the developing matrix of class-stratified denominationalism, popular Afro-creole orisha ritualism became ensconced at the lower level of a more fully differentiated national social structure, reaching something akin to its structural configuration between the two World Wars, if not earlier, and reproducing itself quite resiliently into the present.

Though arising later and in relation to the Indo-Trinidadian experience, similar processes of class stratification and social marginalization have likewise affected the trajectory of what coalesced as temple-based Shakti Worship in the 1970s. Even though anything "Oriental" was castigated by colonial elites during the period of Indian indentureship, evidence suggests that Kali, Di Puja, and Madrassi-based forms of goddess devotionalism and firewalking were not especially peripheral early on within the Indian community. Over time, however, Presbyterian missionization made a small but significant impact among Indo-creoles, producing an incipient professional class that came into ascendance in the wake of indentureship. By the mid-twentieth century, popular religious culture involving animal sacrifice and trance performance had become progressively pushed down the internal status hierarchy, echoing earlier trends among Afro-Trinbagonians.

This was more or less the state of things when Bharat Moonsammy, Mootoo

Brown, and their brethren made contact with Jamsie Naidoo's Guyanese Kali Mai circles in the 1970s and established the first full-fledged shakti temples in the second decade of the postcolonial period. Though the majority of Indo-Trinidadians did not convert to Christianity, the development of an orthodox West Indian Hinduism reflected the partial incorporation of bourgeois values and Christian norms. The conceptualization of Kali Worship as "unrespectable" therefore mirrors that of Afro-creole Shango. The innovation of temple-based worship in an Anglophone tongue provided space for the resuscitating amalgamation and hybrid realignment of formerly independent substreams of Kali, Di, Madrassi, and other forms of subjugated puja praxis. That this new system largely converted itself to vegetarianism reflects dominant Hindu ethical concerns and gentrified biases; yet it nonetheless remains marginalized by Hindus and non-Hindus alike as "backward." Shakti Worship has also recruited a small but steady stream of devotees of black descent, dramatized by their absence in orthodox Hindu circles more broadly.

The larger point here is that Orisha Worship and Shakti Puja have both been structurally marginalized and conceptualized as beyond the bounds of respectability. Orisha Worship has suffered more longstanding castigation as a result of its longer history and explicit interlocution with Christianity, whereas Shakti Puja has weathered a differently timed yet resonant fate also conditioned by Hinduism's less overt relationship with Christianity. Each represents a sort of subaltern grassroots archive of rituals and deities that may have otherwise been lost to the mists of time (McNeal 2010c). Each tradition has similarly come to be known metonymically by prominent divinities from its respective pantheon: "Shango" for Orisha Worship and "Kali" for Shakti Puja.

It is important to emphasize the nonexclusivism of practitioners in each popular tradition in relation to the dominant religious formations that marginalize them. The majority of orisha devotees consider themselves Catholics or Anglicans or Baptists despite the fact that these denominations generally find the Shango religious complex anathema. Similarly, most shakti devotees identify with the larger universe of Hinduism and participate in a range of more orthodox practices and conventional rites of passage. This puts votaries of both traditions in a complex relationship of both opposition and accommodation to local religious macrostructures. Their participation fulfills desires unmet by orthodox engagements in a complementary rather than a mutually exclusive manner. An appreciation for this may be had by considering the concept of "side," not only prevalent within the understandings and discourses of practitioners in each, but also exemplifying and tying together a number of dynamics under discussion here.

This dynamic concept is critical for appreciating the syncretic dynamism of both traditions. Recall that the popular gods and goddesses of each pantheon have developed prismatic sides. For example, Mother Kali has a Madrassi side, Mariyamman; or, if one identifies primarily with Madrassi heritage, Mariyamman has her north Indian, or "Hindu," side, Kali. For those with Christian orientations, Kali has a less prominent, yet nonetheless significant, secondary Catholic side as the Blessed Virgin Mary within Shakti Puja. Hybrid cross-identifications conceived as sides have likewise been forged between other north and south Indian deities—such as that between Mother Parmeshwarie and Mother Katerie—and between Guyanese and Trinidadian deotas—such as Madurai Viran and Kal Bhairo, or Sanganni and Di Baba. We have also witnessed local proliferation of plural creolizing sides for Dee himself, tying him to Bhairo Baba and Munesh Prem together as the "Trinity"—or the "three wise men," as one person put it—each aspect of which has taken on even further extensions, such as Spanish sides. This generative conceptualization of "side" enables spirits to operate as loci of transculturation, reflecting demographic crosscurrents within each ritual tradition as well as wider social trends.

A similar dynamic operates within the sphere of Orisha Worship as well. The development of syncretic Afro-Catholic cross-identifications—in which many of the local powers sport both African and Catholic sides—is only the most prominent example. Some orishas with Catholic iterations are divided even further into subsets. For example, Osain has three "brothers," each linked with a different form of St. Francis: Osain Kiripiti associated with St. Francis of Assisi; Osain Demolay identified with St. Francis Xavier; and Osain Metaphi, known simply as St. Francis. Shango has seven Catholic sides, or brothers, such as St. John the Baptist, St. John the Divine, St. John of the Cross, St. John the Evangelist, and so forth. Moreover, Ogun has taken on two wholly separate local Catholic faces, with St. Michael on one side and St. George on the other. Moreover, some orishas have also taken on "Hindu" or "Indian" sides, such as Ogun's incarnation as Hanuman, the Hindu monkey-god, or Osain's prominent figuration as Hossein or the Indian Man.

Even when looking for evidence of such phenomena, I was nonetheless still sometimes surprised upon learning of a deity's proliferating sides. Devotees found it much less surprising, however, given the omnipotence of the powers themselves. One captured the matter succinctly by characterizing the orishas as "living entities," whom we should expect to develop and morph over time. "Beauty," she observed, "consists of variety and changes," reflecting the "ultimate energy of life, which recognizes us all." One of Warner-Lewis's (1996:81) informants asserted that the more appellations addressed to an orisha, the more flattering to the deity. She writes: "In Trinidad, it is recognized that the same deity may manifest itself with slightly different personalities, though no term is applied to this concept, which is similar to the Hindu concept of the *avatar*. In Yorubaland, the term used is *ona*, in Cuba *camino*, both words meaning 'road, path'" (249). Here I propose that in Trinidad and Tobago there is indeed such a term—"side"—which applies not only to the African but also to the Hindu materials as well.

The side concept also facilitates idiosyncratic renderings. Whenever Dexter fasts or mourns and discovers new dimensions of his tutelary spirits, he readily conceives these to be prismatic sides of the better-known deities. The orisha Vigoyana has a personally esoteric Indian side with whom he works at times, for example. Mother Joan communicates and works with "a woman on the Francis side," that is, an idiosyncratic sister of St. Francis whom no one else knows. Within Shakti Worship, the Blessed Virgin Mary is most often seen as Kali's Catholic side by those with Christian leanings; in chapter 4, however, I mentioned someone who sees Mary as the Catholic side of Katerie Mata, instead of Kali, as a result of her personal revelations. Another sees Mother Katerie's Catholic side as St. Catherine, by contrast, premised upon lexical similarity.

Yet the "side" phenomenon is not limited to prismatic refractions of popular deities. It is invoked to conceptualize differing positionalities within these complex fields of ritual action. Practitioners with multiplex involvement in subaltern Afro-creole ritual subcultures speak of them in terms of "sides" as well as "levels." For example, an orisha shrine leader may also be said to work on the Kabbalistic side. Or one may become initiated on both the African and Baptist sides. I know a woman whose daughter had been contemplating getting married on the Orisha side after the passage of the Orisha Marriage Act into law in 1999. Here the notion of "side" is utilized to distinguish between the newly established nuptial route as opposed to a Christian wedding. Yet the couple was in a hurry and Orisha nuptials had not been fully institutionalized, so they opted to tie the knot quickly in a Pentecostal church instead.

Thus the "side" concept not only reflects and facilitates complex interrelations among various dimensions of ritual traditions and subtraditions, it also captures the complexity of individual trajectories in and across these domains. Within the Hindu sphere, I sometimes heard people characterize others as being "more on the Sanatanist side," meaning their involvement in Shakti Puja was secondary as a result of their identification with the more orthodox version of Hinduism on the island. I also know one woman who runs her own small temple outfit in Caroni that is divided into two sides, one for sada forms of worship and the other for blood sacrifice, reflecting her circuitous connections with competing iterations of Shakti Worship. The polymorphous "side" conceptualization embodies the highly individualistic orientation of each tradition, indeed actively enabling this individualism within each sphere.

Each has not only become more individualistic and flexible as compared with ancestral precedents in West Africa and South Asia, but has also become progressively more so through time in the southern Caribbean as well. In earlier chapters, I offered case studies demonstrating the varied recruitment patterns and pathways into, through, and out of each tradition. That the deities develop different sides reflecting the interface and coalescence of demographic trends and processes of change is but the flip side of the notion of "side" applied to the variability of personal practice.

In this regard, the concept of "side" connects with the notion of "path," also frequently invoked in these religious subcultures and deployed in a range of overlapping ways. It may refer to having found a "spiritual path" in general, regardless of the tradition in question and for involvement in any religion, orthodox or heterodox. Khan (1999) discusses the ecumenical idea among Indo-Trinidadians of being on the "right path"—regardless of Hindu, Muslim, or Christian affiliation—referring to moral principles regarding temperance, faith, propriety, fidelity, charity, civility, and not being "racial" (racist), though it may also operate as a tacit critique of Afro-Trinbagonian patterns of cultural behavior. Similarly, some within the subaltern sphere of Afro-creole spiritism who disparage involvement in Kabba describe Orisha Work as walking on the "pure path." In Shakti Puja, practitioners who favor the sada form of worship likewise characterize it as the "pure path," in contradistinction with that of animal sacrifice. Yet there are those on the Madrassi side, championing blood offerings as the traditional and therefore most efficacious approach, who conceive it as the "Madrassi path." In all these cases, a "right" or "pure" or "correct" path is pursued by someone in the know.

Perhaps unsurprisingly, the concept of "path" has individualistic applications as well. One's spiritual path in this sense often traverses a series of different institutions and identifications over the course of one's life, reflecting cumulative experience in an environment of religious pluralism. This notion of one's path is therefore highly individualistic, subject to the vicissitudes of personal experience. Dexter's patron spirit, St. Francis—whom he refers to as the Indian Man as often as he does as Francis or Osain—and his attraction to things Indian substantiates what for him is his Hindu path. Mother Joan emphasizes her own path as primarily Baptist, though for her this necessarily means intimate connections with Shango, since he is the African side of St. John the Baptist. Naziph's path included an intense devotional relationship with Sai Baba. Another's path, by contrast, led him in and out of temple work several times before steering his shakti devotions in the more private direction, which characterizes his current posture.

The notion of "path" therefore invokes individual development and a sense of fate, though not in any overly fatalistic way. One's path is cultivated and reflects personal effort, though it also incorporates the vicissitudes of life experience beyond one's control. Thus the concepts of "path" and "side" are intrinsically related, reflecting and refracting variable dimensions of personal devotion and ritual practice through time and space. This understanding compels us to more directly consider the individualism and personal flexibility and psychologization of the ecstatic spirit idiom in the traditions under discussion here. West Indian spiritisms have become more individualistic than their precursors, reflecting their experience in the Caribbean. Most importantly, though exposure and experience may run in families involved in ecstatic work to some extent, recruitment is largely based upon the vicissitudes of personal motivation, especially the devotional and therapeutic effects offered by involvement in each tradition. If comparable practices in Africa and India are changing in similar directions, we should not be surprised.

Recall from earlier examination of South Asian materials that trance performance on the subcontinent (bhakti) has traditionally been less exclusively therapeutic in orientation, as well as rarely devotionally based. When it is therapeutic, Indo-Indian trance praxis seems most often geared toward summoning an extrahuman source of power for exorcism; otherwise, ritual ecstasy is cultivated for oracular purposes, or in order to conjure the presence of divinity as a ceremonial placeholder for conducting puja. West Indian Shakti Worship, by contrast, is predicated upon cathartic forms of shakti play at the baseline level as well as individuated mediumship oriented in a more supportive psychotherapeutic direction. Oracular communication is relevant, but far more concerned with people's existential trials and psychological tribulations than with fact-finding or soothsaying. Potential devotees come to the temples seeking personal empowerment and healing efficacy. When they find it there, they become integrated into the temple's microcommunity and its alternative network of social support and ritual kinship. This process is entirely voluntary—involving individuals and sometimes families—and not an expression of "community" beyond the walls of the temple.

Turning to West African cognates, my reading of the literature suggests that the individualism of the southern Caribbean scenario is an intensification of certain precursor ritual forms accompanied by the diminution of others. Comparatively speaking, trance performance and spirit mediumship have undergone general overall upregulation as focal ritual activities, and it is clear that West Indian Orisha Worship in this context has become more cathartic and therapeutic in orientation—taking up functions addressed in other religious spheres and traditionally performed by altogether different personnel in Yorubaland. Akin with its correlate on the Hindu side, southern Caribbean Shango is more individualistic and voluntary, recruiting practitioners based on its capacity to meet their devotional and therapeutic needs.

The constant flux of people in and out of these ritual subcultures also reflects their individualism. These ritual communities reproduce themselves through the efforts of a small core of leaders, performers, and assistants counterweighted by expanding circles of devotees and practitioners who are much more inconsistent and mobile. Most participate only as long as it serves their own needs. Otherwise, they tend to disappear and move on. If one of the marks of modernity has been "the triumph of the therapeutic" (Rieff 1966; de Zengotita 2005), then Orisha Worship and Shakti Puja have not been spared this form of modernization any more than have the secular psychotherapies. Indeed, the influence of the latter was syncretically folded into the practice of Kali Worship, as introduced by Pujari Naidoo as a result of his interdisciplinary collaborations in the 1960s. Yet even without this intervention, the center of gravity in each tradition has become decidedly therapeutic in orientation.

These developments are reflected by the personal flexibility and psychologization of the ecstatic spirit idiom in both the subaltern African and Hindu spheres. People constantly spoke to me about the significance of their "devotion" and "feeling" in the development of their spirituality. "Yuh have to have love in your heart and be true to yourself in order to seek God for true," I was told. "When you do it from your heart, it is well done," one Shakti temple leader announced to the congregation at the beginning of that day's service. One's devotions must be "sincere" in order to get shakti. Another devotee related that, no matter what way one serves God, "yuh have to be true to yourself, worshipping with true love and devotion." An orisha leader explained: "Once you pray sincerely, things will come right. This makes true manifestations or not. Yuh can't do nothing right if you're not true to yourself." He emphasized sincerity as central to the pursuit of one's spiritual path. Several practitioners on both sides of my study also mentioned sincerity in devotion and purity of intention as compensating for what they experienced as the lack of sufficient theological exegesis or adequate training.

These may seem obvious or unremarkable statements to moderns weaned in psychological culture, but overlooking the similarities would be insensitive and belie the very point I am making here. Subaltern spiritisms are not premodern or illiberal. Devotees of both traditions also commonly emphasize the centrality of "belief" in a way that echoes Protestant-inflected modernist notions of what constitutes religion (see Asad 1993, 2003; Klass 1995; R. Smith 1998). "You have to have belief in what you're doing," one shakti devotee in Penal told me, "if you does not have belief, yuh can't make any progress on this path." Another practitioner put it similarly: "Everybody need de Mudda and everybody need help. If yuh don't believe on the Mother, yuh wouldn't get help." Recall as well what Erile's medium asked me that fateful night in 1997 during my first feast experience: "Do you believe?" Indeed, the emphasis on belief is pervasive and strong within these ceremonial subcultures.

By contrast, the literatures on trance and mediumship in West Africa and South Asia rarely depict such a concern among indigenous practitioners. While it is important for scholars to critique modernist assumptions about "purity" and "belief" in religion, we should not engage in a doubly obscured form of ethnocentrism by refusing to recognize the ways the popular religious cultures we study may be as "modern" or "Western" as those in the prototypical metropoles. Modernist presuppositions about religion may have arisen in the "West," but that does not mean they do not travel outside the North Atlantic.

Another aspect of the psychologization of the spirit idiom stems from the paramount emphasis on experience in each tradition. The repeating refrain I heard was the significance of "spiritual" over "book" knowledge as the foundation for existential pursuits in this pluralistic context. Though he sometimes appealed to the Bible in explicating certain points about the rationale for animal sacrifice, for example, Boysie Ben generally opined that one should not trust books: better to communicate directly with the spirits to gain knowledge and wisdom. Pujari Krishna Angad expressed the same sentiment in conversations with me as well as in sermons to his congregation on puja days. Queen Mother Kali emphasized the importance of "knowledge from the spirit" versus "knowledge from books" during a conversation in which she and her partner argued that I should directly experience the traditions I was studying in order to truly understand them, not just report about them—a refrain I heard over and over from practitioners of both Orisha Worship and Shakti Puja. This was the very issue taken up by Naziph's Kali during the puja that day in 2000, related in the Prologue.

This emphasis on spiritual knowledge based on direct experience is intimately related to the significance of dreams and visions in people's religious lives. Many spoke of seeing with their own "spiritual eye." Often such experiences came during periods of fasting or mourning, but not exclusively so. Dreams are taken seriously and may be interpreted as messages from the spirit world. This open-ended envelope of individual experience and mystical communication plays a central role in the development of innovation within the traditions as well as idiosyncrasies in personal practice. A modification introduced as the will of the gods—especially when performed publicly through respected trance mediums—is one that garners special attention and carries considerable weight. Recall the tremendous transformation in postcolonial Shakti Puja toward sada (vegetarian) worship introduced through the mouth of a medium at Krishna Angad's temple in the early 1980s. Naziph Ali emphasized the significance of "shakti-gifted" communications given to him through his trance experiences in influencing his own evolution. He claimed to have inaugurated his temple's firepass through a vision he received. He also highlighted spiritual travel to Sai Baba's ashram in India: "India is far and one can't go all the time, so spiritual communication is important." Downplaying the tradition's Guyanese and Indian heritage, another shakti devotee noted, "Some people say this worship is from Guyana, from India, but what it is—basically—it's really God-guided." Bharat Moonsammy expressed a similar sentiment, emphasizing that his "true teachers" were the deotas themselves, thereby minimizing the influence of both Jamsie Naidoo's group and his own forebears (Sirju 1990). Another pujari astutely observed that this orientation not only leads to a high level of variation—"this and that"—among practitioners, but spawns "confusion" as well.

On the African side, Dexter was moved to found a new Spiritual Baptist church during the course of a fasting. Some orisha mediums explained the meanings of song-chants not based on their literal understanding of the liturgical language, but as a result of their experiences under the ecstatic sway of ashé, which empowered and legitimated their own inspired interpretations. Baba Forde received an initiation directly from Ogun in a vision, rather than through the more traditional method of being inducted by a spiritual mentor. A number of people I know received similar sorts of "initiations," and I am inclined to think that this sort of self-initiated agency accomplished through personal spirit idiomata is in fact on the rise. Messages relayed through ecstatic performance as well as received in visions and dreams constitute compelling vectors through which innovations and idiosyncrasies are introduced. After all, an innovation is an idiosyncrasy that takes root and spreads.

These considerations bring us around to parallel dimensions of ritual praxis in both Shakti Puja and Orisha Worship—the differentiation of trance performance into a generalized level of baseline play and a higher level of individuated mediumship—examined variously above. Here I emphasize these analogous fields of ritual action in each tradition as yet another dimension of their structural convergence in the southern Caribbean. I think this laterally dual differentiation in ceremonial activity represents a sort of democratizing expansion of ecstasy at the baseline level accompanied by an avenue for advance and the development of esteem and proficiency at the higher level of performance. Cases of what I call "generalized" ecstasy here—cathartically inner-directed ecstatic activation by cosmic energies, whether ashé or shakti, within the shrine or temple context—are less elaborately developed in the relevant West African and South Asian contexts. The Caribbean experience seems to have popularized the environment for baseline ecstasy, not only including more people, but also involving practitioners of all ages and sexes at the same time. Generalized trancing is voluntaristic in psychospiritual terms, arising primarily out of personal motivation and not out of political or other extrinsic needs or concerns. In turn, this space of ritual praxis constitutes an ecstatic reservoir of mystical energy from which individuated mediums materialize in order to perform their trance-based renditions of the deities. We must appreciate the recursive levels of individualism operative in both of these subaltern religious spheres. Both traditions have "structurally converged" in that they involve similar overall patterns of differentiation in the forms and functions of trance performance.

Becoming a respected medium is one of the ways one distinguishes oneself, gains legitimacy, and may develop an independent group of followers. When this happens, tensions may arise with the leader(s) of one's home temple or shrine. Those who become confident in their abilities not infrequently break away to form their own group, sometimes maintaining an affiliation with the original community, but equally often under schismatic conditions. A similar scenario develops with nonmediums who apprentice under mombwahs or head pujaris for a time and then break away to establish their own independent group. Complex and changing webs of identification and disidentification become the basis for persistent intertemple or shrine conflicts as well as battles over followers and influence.

These are the sorts of micropolitics Caribbeanist Peter Wilson (1973) once dubbed "crab antics," by which people of modest means and little overall power squabble over subtly rendered differences in attempts to establish and consolidate their humble spheres of influence. For this reason, traversing between African and Hindu ritual subcultures was often politically easier for me than circulating internally within one or the other. People at one temple, for example, badgered me about spending time with competitors, cautioning me against being misled. At times, I kept my activities to myself unless I was pushed on the matter. Some folks appreciated the "sociological" rationale for my study and they were the most open to my moving about within these subcultures, though it took time to clarify who was sympathetic to this approach.

The final dimension of structural convergence up for discussion is the privatization of these ritual traditions and their respective orientations toward land and property. Unlike those Christian churches incorporated and supported by the colonial state, the subordinated African and Hindu subcultures that reconstituted themselves under conditions of domination throughout the nineteenth and early twentieth centuries did so by turning inward and developing ritual structures operative within increasingly private contexts. If the privatization of religion is taken as an emblematic modernist development (Casanova 1994), we cannot overlook the significance of this phenomenon among subaltern spiritisms, which were in fact privatized earlier than the Catholic, Anglican, and Presbyterian churches condoned by the colonial state. The Maha Sabha was not incorporated until the early 1950s, representing the confluence of two Hindu organizations established in prior decades, but following the explicit precedent of the Catholic Church. Grassroots traditions, by contrast, adapted to the colonial situation by receding into the private sphere and serving the needs of their practitioners in that context. This process was especially facilitated by land ownership.

Afro-creoles were involved in landing schemes introduced by Ordinance 8 of 1869 under Gov. A. H. Gordon, which made Crown lands available to squatters. The rationale for this policy change was that property ownership was the best stimulus for industriousness and stability in the labor pool. In many areas of Trinidad in the last decades of the century, many had in fact become peasant proprietors, signaling the success of the project. Yorubas and their descendants benefited from these developments, gaining access to land on which they could not only carve out their livelihoods, but also configure their religious and ritual practices in ways that suited them. Owning a plot of land and "independence" based on wage earning were supremely important for Africans and Afro-creoles. The Yoruba-descended ritual communities of Gasparillo studied by Elder in the 1960s are a direct legacy of landing schemes initiated a century before. The shrine compounds studied by the Herskovitses and Henry in the late 1930s and mid-1950s, as well as the Rada compound documented by Carr in the late 1940s, all similarly reflect the privatization of subaltern Afro-creole ritual practice.

Privatization of Hindu religious forms proceeded throughout the indentureship period. Again, access to land proved consequential for maintaining puja traditions castigated by colonial planters and Christian elites, making Hinduism a decidedly domestic affair (Vertovec 1992; Khan 2004). Though community forms of Kali Puja were practiced well into the twentieth century, they were becoming increasingly stigmatized and pushed down the ladder of social status by the time Morton and Sheila Klass conducted their 1950s research in Felicity. More prevalent were domestic iterations of the devotion—ghar ki-puja—observed by the Klasses. By that point Di Puja had become an entirely private affair.

On the Madrassi side, though firepass remained a high-profile spectacle until the mid-twentieth century, it was conducted on the premises of temples or pieces of land unincorporated by the state. Other than firewalking, various forms of Madrassi ritual practice had become almost wholly restricted to the private sphere and passed down within individual families. Thus, although the postcolonial advent of full-fledged Shakti temples was a momentous development in sociohistorical terms, it only served to consolidate the further privatization of the newly amalgamated tradition within institutions owned and run by private citizens. Those without land and resources are unable to launch such mandirs. Mootoo Brown had to take out a loan from the local credit union for which he alone was responsible in order to expand and refurbish his first temple, established in the late 1970s.

These developments are reflected in the fact that contemporary Orisha shrines and Shakti temples are all located in domestic compounds often simply referred to as "yards." In this regard it is notable that each tradition takes part in the local system of flying spiritual flags associated with deities on tall bamboo poles planted throughout the shrine or temple compound, thereby signifying the presence of subaltern ceremonial space behind the walls of the yard. These flagpoles—called jhandis in Hinduism, Orisha or Baptist flags on the African side—are significant in that they mark spots on the earth where each of the powers is grounded and installed in the form of Afro-creole stools or Indo-creole stands, representing a sacred locus of heterodox spiritual power. This sacralization of the land must be understood in relation to the overall meaning of landed property in West Indian experience.

Mintz (1960) pointed long ago to the significance of yards in Caribbean societies, in which one's freedom is thought to begin inside the fence, within the private sphere. This sensibility derives from a past rooted in plantation slavery, in relation to which access to land for extra-plantation agricultural activity not only constituted a means for the accumulation of resources and even capital, but also became the anchor for the development of reconstituted peasantries (Mintz 1985a). Indeed, the Slave Ordinance of 1800 affirmed the right of slaves to their provision grounds (Yelvington 1995:47). Moreover, the interrelationship of freedom and land rooted in traditions of slave resistance and proto-peasant adaptation represents a theme extending well beyond emancipation (Besson 1992).

The early-twentieth-century transformation of the plantation system through corporate capitalism as well as post–World War II developments in the mining, petrochemical, and tourist industries have reinforced the oppositional significance of landholding and property ownership for the petit bourgeois and lower classes.

We must appreciate the significance of socioeconomic differentiation within lower levels of the national hierarchy in terms of land, property, and resources for attaining status and clout within these religious subcultures. Recall the confrontation between the uninvited ecstatic entity and Boysie Ben's Ogun along with his mombwah during the opening feast night described in chapter 3. Though it transpired in the idiom of spirit personae, the upstart was an itinerant medium on the circuit with a very small following and no shrine base of his own. I hypothesized that the public reprimanding of Ben and his mombwah represented a status conflict motivated by envy of Ben's stature as an established shrine head.

Shakti Pujas as well as Orisha feasts require the mobilization of considerable resources. Those who are able to do so are more likely to establish prominence. Having one's own temple or shrine facilitates independence and provides the context for maintaining a congregation or following. In other words, class matters just as much at the lower levels of the socioeconomic pyramid as it does at the top, driving much of the crab antics carried out in terms of local debates over aspects of orthopraxy and so on. Having followers makes possible the corollary "independence" of leadership.

All of this stems from the political culture of the Commonwealth Caribbean, in which private capitalist interests have long been paramount in shaping the social and political order. Indeed, British colonialism privileged the defense of property as more important than that of human life from the beginning in the southern Caribbean. As political scientist Paul Sutton observes: "The roots of that order are to be found in the colonial past, particularly in the reaction to chattel slavery, apprenticeship, indenture and the ordeal of 'free labor.' The denial or restrictions on liberty and mobility have put a premium on freedom and invested that freedom with a positive association to private property, especially in land, and the practice of a lively religiosity, witnessed individually or in joyous free association with others" (1991:110).

The "benevolent" mythology of the Crown Colony government system masked the fact that it expressed the will of rich and powerful local property-owners and transnational capitalists, who exercised their influence over policymaking through heavy unofficial representation on the Legislative Council (Brereton 1981:chap. 8). An iniquitous tax system favored the interests of elites:

few property taxes, heavy import duties on items of mass consumption, no income tax, and exemption of sugar-manufacturing facilities from the building tax. Lower-class punishments were harsher for property or labor infractions than those involving bodily harm (Trotman 1986:138). Even the incipient "radicalism" of late-nineteenth- and early-twentieth-century local reform movements was co-opted by bourgeois interests in the end.

Anthropologically speaking, it is unsurprising that the dominant political and economic institutions of colonial society should have so fundamentally impacted the growth and trajectory of religious institutions in the southern Caribbean, both orthodox and heterodox. My analysis of varying dimensions of structural convergence concerning these two ritual traditions substantiates this point. Their subaltern status should not blind us to seeing the generative effects of capitalism and liberal political culture within each sphere.

I capture this insight with the notion of *subaltern liberalization*. The historical development and ideological contours of liberalism are a complex topic beyond my purview here (see D. Smith 1968; R. Williams 1983; Hall 1986; Wallerstein 1995; Leach 1996; Sedgwick 2002). Thus I must explicate what I mean by "subaltern liberalization" in the comparative analysis of our focal religions. It may be imperfect, but if it spurs further conversation and debate, then it will have been a useful contribution. The friction between notions of "subaltern" and "liberal" is productive in grappling with the ways these materials slip between the cracks of conventional analytical categories.

Liberalism—a political philosophy valuing liberty and individual autonomy—developed most fully in England between the Glorious Revolution of 1688 and the Reform Act of 1867. Incorporating the legacies of Renaissance humanism and the Protestant Reformation, as well as Enlightenment thinking and the rise of capitalism and the bourgeoisie, liberalism in England first took the form of a demand not only for constitutionalism and political rights, but also for religious liberties and toleration (D. Smith 1968:278). This early liberalism was essentially negative in character, spawning such principles as the right of opposition, the rule of law, and separation of powers. These developments, in turn, gave rise to economic liberalism based on the laissez-faire doctrine of the self-regulating market. The rise of utilitarianism represented the fruition of earlier trends, with an emphasis on education, free speech, inclusive representation, expanded suffrage, and accountability of the governors to the governed—that is, politics organized on the model of the free economy—as providing constitutional security and good government to the greatest number. It is this strain of British political thought that made common cause with the abolition movement, leading to emancipation throughout the Empire in the wake of liberalizing parliamentary reforms passed in 1832.

Of course, these developments should not be idealized, for they were riven by conflicts and contradictions at every turn. Because John Locke celebrated the importance of "natural" liberty, he had to justify slavery by placing it outside the social compact, which was ostensibly designed to protect man's inalienable rights (Davis 1998:xvi). Not just slavery itself contravened liberal principles; emancipation was accompanied by massive compensation for the colonial plantocracy and related metropolitan interests, for example, leading in turn to new forms of "liberal" domination. The postemancipation program, involving a remarkably functionalist view of religion, looked toward Christianity in order to turn former slaves into docile, dependable wage laborers (R. Smith 1976:320–21).

If liberalization of civil society took centuries to "trickle down" in the metropole, it took even longer in its overseas colonies. Many historians believe liberalism climaxed in mid-nineteenth-century Britain as it wrestled with reconciling two ultimately conflicting values: earlier emphasis on political and economic liberty protected by the state—"freedom from"—and efforts to mitigate the tendency toward inequality in this approach by equalizing opportunity for the disenfranchised and dispossessed, also through the actions of the state—"freedom to." Prior to the nineteenth century, liberal aspirations were in fact restricted to an elite of birth and wealth (R. Williams 1983).

The resilient reproduction of ecstatic traditions at the subaltern level must be seen as reflecting the oppositional assertion of religious autonomy over a considerable period of time: a will to cultural expression in the face of great odds involving official suppression as well as informal stigma and marginalization. It is difficult to say when devotees of each tradition came to think about their religious subcultures in terms of the prerogatives of "freedom." Yet it is this very persistence in the face of daunting odds that has been celebrated by cultural activists of the postcolonial era. I emphasize the time-released impact of liberal values such as individual liberty and personal autonomy within the colonial religious underground. The Spiritual Baptist fight to bring down the Shouters Prohibition Ordinance of 1917—which succeeded in 1951—is the best known subordinate effort to dismantle an illiberal policy of the colonial state. It exerted powerful effects more broadly.

The blossoming of Trinidad as a result of the late-eighteenth-century liberalizing age in the Atlantic system prompts an appreciation of subaltern religious resistance and local understandings of it as an expression of the "right" to autonomous expression in at least partly liberal terms. This insight is not meant to chalk up the spirit of African or Indian cultural resistance to liberal acculturation in any simple sense. However, if we take argumentation concerning the precocious modernity of the Caribbean seriously, then we are obliged to consider the ways subaltern ritual traditions, which seemed so "primitive" to the colonial imagination, have in fact become modernized and Westernized, if not entirely Europeanized per se.

This brings us to the second element at work in understanding the transculturation of these traditions in terms of subaltern liberalization: the development of a strong individualistic orientation. Peter Sedgwick observes that liberalism espouses an "ontology of the individual" (2002:214): a metaphysical conception of the individual as an irreducible entity endowed with a transcendental, extrasocial essence, the basic unit of politics and social life (also see Lukes 1973). Such a view originates as early as Locke's conception of the individual premised on freedom of action and equality of rights in his *Two Treatises on Government* (1690), in which government's principal role is to arbitrate conflicts arising between self-interested individuals. John Stuart Mill's *On Liberty* (1859), which many see as the greatest single statement of liberalism, takes the individual to be an autonomous entity with an absolute right to independence. For him, civil society should be premised upon a regulative model of negative freedom, conceived as the freedom to act according to one's interests as long as it does not infringe upon the liberties of others. Twentieth-century theorist John Rawls (1972) concludes that maximizing the liberty of individual interests is the bedrock political issue.

Espousing an underlying commitment to individualism, liberalism has nonetheless changed with the times. Liberalism since the late nineteenth century has come to emphasize positive rather than negative aspects of liberty: the opportunity to form and accomplish self-appointed goals, rather than simply freedom from the state per se. David Smith (1968:281) observes:

> The earlier liberal view of human nature was two dimensional and overly rationalistic. Nineteenth-century sociology and psychology destroyed that view thoroughly. Modern liberalism has assimilated much of the critique. Liberals today see man not only as an individual in society but also as a person with a continuing need for self-expansion and reintegration. For this reason the emphasis of modern liberalism is less upon external impediments to motion and more upon the individual person's subjective feeling of freedom and those circumstances that give to this feeling an objective reality in the experience of the individual. If a man does not feel free, he is not free.

These changes are connected with the development of industrial capitalism and forms of mass culture every bit as relevant to the Caribbean as to the metropoles.

Thus the second substantive dimension of subaltern liberalization in Orisha

Worship and Shakti Puja pertains to the rising prominence of individualism within each practice over time, especially when considered relative to ancestral traditions in West Africa and South Asia. Mintz has shown how transplanted peoples of the West Indies were homogenized by the economic demands imposed upon them, as well as individualized by the erasure of the institutional underpinnings of their pasts: "Caribbean social history gave to its peoples a life-style adapted to the anonymity, depersonalization, and individualization of modern life, but did so when such phenomena were by no means yet recognized for what they were" (1974a:257). Elsewhere, he observes that the region's precocious modernity brought "the growth of individuality on a new basis" (1996b:301). We must appreciate not only the paramount significance of voluntarism in the recruitment patterns and reproduction of these traditions, but also the progressive personalization and psychologization of the ecstatic spirit idiom. In this regard we encounter the triumph of the therapeutic here as much as in the more "obvious" contexts of the North Atlantic.

Finally, I want to focus upon the significance of property ownership, possessive relationship to the land, and the significance of privatization linked with the development of capitalism as a third component of subaltern liberalization characteristic of the religions studied here. Raymond Williams (1983) observes that liberalism, as a philosophical doctrine based on individualist presuppositions about humanity and society, is "the highest form of thought developed within bourgeois society and in terms of capitalism," "a doctrine of certain necessary kinds of freedom but also, and essentially, a doctrine of possessive individualism" (181). In his classic *The Political Theory of Possessive Individualism*, C. B. Macpherson (1962) shows that a set of seventeenth- and eighteenth-century assumptions about property, ownership, the market, and individualism bears a strong resemblance to what nineteenth-century English liberals and their critics alike called "capitalism." A central tenet of bourgeois possessive individualism posits liberty as freedom from dependence; thus individual existence turns upon the possession of private property, which in turn creates the conditions for independence from others. To be dependent upon another is to be incomplete as a human being in British political thought. The truly realized individual is autonomous, defined not only by the degree of independence, but also by the property and resources possessed. All of this was consolidated with the late-eighteenth-century Enclosure movement in England, by which large estate owners backed by Parliament aggressively claimed title to "common" land formerly exploited by small cultivators based on customary rights. There is an intimate connection here between the political ideology of possessive individualism and the rise of the bourgeoisie.

Though differently positioned, developments in overseas colonies were related to such changes at "home," with the winds of transnational capitalism generating change throughout the entire system. We have seen how capitalism brought the modern Caribbean into being, structuring patterns of stratification premised upon race and class, as well as influencing the evolution of religious pluralism and patterns of political culture. Dominant institutions conditioned the horizons of possibility for the region's cultural practices and social forms in complex ways. Subaltern actors have resisted and opposed domination in a host of ways that need not be discounted in order to appreciate the dominating effects of colonialism. It was very difficult, if not impossible, to get outside the system in order to resist or overturn it.

Since we are dealing with marginalized ecstatic ritual traditions, a last comment regarding the ideology of liberalism is apropos. Locke's labor theory of value argued that each individual has a "natural" right to possession of her or his own body and all the products of its efforts. The proper function of government is to protect the rights of individuals and their property, a privilege of the landed and moneyed classes. Ritual practices involving the ecstatic body conceptualized not as one's own agency but as that of spiritual alters may therefore be seen as a sort of oblique reclaiming of the alienated labor and body of the dispossessed classes. Burton (1997) makes a related argument: that the descent of power in Afro-Caribbean rituals of trance performance obliquely mirrors the externality of political and economic power, which also descends, godlike, from elsewhere.

These remarks are made in order to clarify the ways capitalism and its attendant ideologies have not simply framed, but also seeped their way into, less evident areas of sociocultural life such as subaltern spiritisms. Access to land and property ownership have been critical for the cultural reproduction of these focal traditions, providing a "private" sphere in which to retract in order to carry out chosen devotions and preferred ritual practices. This process necessitated the privatization of these religious systems in order to ensure their viability and resilience in a hypocritically liberalizing context. This interpretation is reflected in the sociosymbolic centrality of the yard within each tradition and substantiated by the significance of property, possessions, commodities, and financial resources in establishing not only shrine or temple compounds, but also legitimacy and status within each sphere.[4]

These three characteristics—an insistence on religious autonomy, a strong individualistic orientation, and capitalist-inflected orientations toward property and privacy—are important vectors of structural convergence leading me to the concept of "subaltern liberalization." I am aware of the ironic juxtaposition of "subaltern" and "liberal" in one phrase; however, this tension makes the concept productive. If we focus on the subaltern without the liberal, we risk misrecognizing the ways these traditions have become "modernized" and, indeed, even "liberalized" to a significant extent. The fact that these processes have unfolded at the subordinate level means we must attend to the ways dominant trends in liberal culture find their way into and become recontextualized within lower social strata (see S. Hall 1986 on stratified variants of liberalism). The social forms and cultural practices of subaltern peoples must be understood in relation to dominant translocal institutions and social structures. These are not mutually exclusive endeavors.

There are doubtless other ways in which Orisha Worship and Shakti Puja have become structurally convergent in the southern Caribbean. I have outlined some of the more significant dimensions of this process evident through controlled comparison. This analysis helps account not only for the conceptual accessibility of Dexter's fateful visit to a Kali mandir, but also for how and why practitioners within each tradition may see them as so resonant, despite the fact they have not explicitly intersected or merged on the ground in any substantial way. Though this does not lead devotees to perceive convergence or syncretism between the two subcultures (cf. Vertovec 1998), it does prompt perceptions of congruence or parallelism characterized here as resulting from their structural convergence and subaltern liberalization.

When she learned that I was doing comparative research on Shango and Shakti Puja, one longtime participant at the Moonsammy Kali temple observed that both religions "work with the same powers, just in different forms." A *dougla* assistant pujari at another large Shakti temple once made a similar observation, yet in a starkly different way. When we first met while cleaning the mandir one day and chatting about my research activities concerning both Orisha and Shakti Worship, he said, "Oh, I see, yuh wanna know about things on the other side of Christ." It took me a few moments to digest the meanings of his words, but I realized he was characterizing the two traditions as similarly stigmatized vis-à-vis the Christian-dominated institutions and elite structures of local society, hence "on the other side of Christ."

Relatedly, in a conversation in which I once asked Mother Joan about Osain being known as an Indian power, she responded by saying, "Well, you know, Africa and India are very close. We deal with different sides. The power an' dem are all the same person, but they come in different forms—they're called by different names." In a peculiar sense, "Africa" and "India" have become very close indeed in the southern Caribbean.

Religion and the Politics of Diaspora
in an Era of Postcolonial Multiculturalism

There can be no Mother India . . . no Mother Africa . . . no Mother England . . .
no Mother China . . . and no Mother Syria or Mother Lebanon. A nation, like an
individual, can have only one Mother. The only Mother we recognize is Mother
Trinidad and Tobago, and Mother cannot discriminate between her children. All
must be equal in her eyes. And no possible interference can be tolerated by any
country outside in our family relations and domestic quarrels, no matter what it
has contributed and when to the population that is today the people of Trinidad
and Tobago.

Eric Williams, The History of the People of Trinidad and Tobago

Many in society, fearful of taking the logical step of seeking to create a culture
out of the best of our ancestral cultures, have advocated rather that we forget that
ancestral root and create something entirely new. But that is impossible since we
all came here firmly rooted in the cultures from which we derive. And to simply
say that there must be no Mother India or no Mother Africa is to show a sad lack
of understanding of what cultural evolution is all about.

Brinsley Samaroo, Express *newspaper, 18 October 1987 (following the victory
of the NAR in December 1986)*

I have documented and analyzed the maritime colonial transfer and "glocal"
transculturation of subaltern African and Hindu spiritisms in the southern
Caribbean, so in this chapter I turn to the question of why each tradition has

undergone an inverse political trajectory in the postcolonial era. Shango has become highly politicized by a vocal vanguard of Afrocentrists as a vehicle for reclaiming and rehabilitating blackness in response to the legacy of colonial racism and the hegemony of Christianity in Afro-Trinbagonian experience. Shakti Puja, on the other hand, has not been politicized, though Indian nationalists have nonetheless embraced Hinduism for the revitalization of Indian ethnicity and articulation of Indocentric politics.

In light of their structurally convergent resonances at the popular level, it is important to consider the very different political fates of each tradition in national political culture around the turn of the twenty-first century. I account for this divergence by extending the analysis of differing colonial ideologies of racial subordination regarding Africans versus Indians in the articulation of hierarchy and religion in the southern Caribbean. Each case reflects the continued spell of these ideologies within the national imagination, albeit in tellingly recontextualized forms in an era of postcolonial multiculturalism.

Colonial imagery of the "culturally naked African" prefigured a vision in which West Indian Blacks were compelled to hybridize their religious beliefs and practices with Christianity. Antisyncretic trends among Orisha Movement reformers—who favor a camouflaged view of syncretism and seek to exorcise Christianisms from the practice—reflect the dominance of colonial racial ideology even when contesting its hierarchical valuing of Christianity over Africanity. Postcolonial "Africanizing" reformism tacitly accepts certain colonial terms of the debate even while ostensibly subverting them. Ironically, such reforms adopt Eurocentric models of what makes for a "legitimate" and "pure" religion along the way.

The colonial ideology of the "culturally saturated Indian," by contrast, framed Indo-Trinidadian culture as static and unable to become creolized. In this view, Hinduism is considered forever and always East, rather than West, Indian. The emergence of Indian nationalism has therefore not made recourse to rehabilitating heretofore-marginalized religious practices such as spiritism as the "Other Within," since Indians have been ideologically positioned as outsiders to the nation, and Hinduism, the quintessentially Oriental religion, is already seen as essentially diasporic. The recuperation of Hinduism is different than that of African religiosity, proceeding through the construction of a Sanatanist orthodoxy concerned with respectability and critical of ritual practices smacking too overtly of the more "primitive" Indian past.

TT's population is conventionally understood as consisting of demographically equivalent groups of people of African and Indian descent—approximately 40 percent each—along with a significant minority of mixed-descent persons and small groupings of people of Chinese, Portuguese, Syrian, and European origin. As with many New World nationalisms, that of Trinidad and Tobago embraces ancestral diversity and signs of polygenesis as central to the nation's body politic. Its national anthem proclaims a country "where every creed and race finds an equal place," and a popular national motto espouses that "all o' we is one." Yet Williams was a "Racial Messiah" (Oxaal 1982) primarily for the Afro-creole sector.

Conceptualizing ideology as a regulating discourse that organizes social relations and disciplines understanding of them, Segal (1989, 1993) demonstrates the enduring significance of colonial mythologies of racial subordination regarding the culturally naked African and the culturally saturated Indian in the structuring of social relations from colonial times into the postcolonial period. Through an analysis of the dialectics of positive and negative visions of nationalism in politics and public culture, Segal (1994) also shows how both perspectives take the nation to be populated by distinct racial archetypes, *notwithstanding* their social and biological mixture.

Building on my historical anthropology of capitalism and religion in the southern Caribbean, I show how subaltern African and Hindu spiritisms have undergone contrasting postcolonial trajectories of politicization. Extending Segal's work on these racial ideologies, I explore their continued legacy in relation to the politics of religion in the era of postcolonial multiculturalism. My aim is akin to the historiography called for by Pierre Bourdieu: "a form of structural history which finds in each successive state of the structure both the product of previous struggles to maintain or to transform this structure and the principle, via the contradictions, the tensions, and the relations of force which constitute it, of subsequent transformations" (quoted in Wacquant 1989:37).

Put otherwise, the postcolonial politicization versus nonpoliticization of lower-status religious traditions may be accounted for in terms of differing interlocking dynamics of racial and class stratification. Donald Donham reminds us that the productive inequalities of capitalism such as gender, sexuality, race, and nationalism are *not* limited or determined simply by class relations, even as class "provides the dominant inequality, the low note that anchors the chord" (1990:204). The point is not to overly essentialize racial ideologies but to consider their repeatedly privileged logic and the ways they have been reproduced over time in the midst of ongoing sociocultural change, conflict, and transformation. Examining the complex nexus of race-class-religion has been important for understanding not only the long-term transculturation of the two grassroots traditions, but also their differential politicization in the postcolonial era, which I take up here. Late-modern diasporic political projects—understood as alter-nationalist postures vis-à-vis the politics of postcolonial statecraft—recruit religions in new ways, with variable local implications for the politics of culture.

The two traditions at the center of this study experienced resonant sociohistorical trajectories from the mid-nineteenth to the mid-twentieth centuries in the southern Caribbean due to colonial experiences of domination and adaptation, even as these trajectories have unfolded under the influence of differing ideological frameworks regarding race and religion. Yet the advent of nationalist independence in 1962, the emergence of a Black Power Movement in the early 1970s, and the subsequent oil boom-and-bust cycle of the mid-1970s to the early 1980s set in motion dynamics that have transformed the locally intertwined fields of religion and politics in revealing ways.

Religion and the Maze of Color in an Era of Postcolonial Multiculturalism

A useful entrée to my analysis here is Selwyn Ryan's *The Jhandi and the Cross: The Clash of Cultures in Post-Creole Trinidad and Tobago* (1999), by one of the country's leading political scientists, demographers, and cultural critics. Ryan considers the intensification of conflict among Hindus and Christians following the demise of the PNM's monopolistic hold on power in the 1980s, tension energized by currents of ethnic revitalization and religious fundamentalism across society as a whole. Christianity has therefore become an increasingly visible interlocutor in relation to local Indian culture and especially Hinduism, as compared with the earlier colonial scenario.

Demographic data from a 1998 survey by Ryan's research group suggests that religious affiliation is as significant as race in determining people's political attitudes and voting patterns (1999:113–23). Ryan's discourse concerning the "clash of cultures" therefore operates polysemically, referring to Christian-Hindu as well as African-Indian axes of ideological terrain. He argues that schismogenesis between "Hindu" and "Christian" in postcolonial cultural politics may only be understood in relation to the intensified and changing field of contestation over political power in the postindependence period. He emphasizes the fertilizing effects of the oil boom, which prevailed from the mid-1970s to the early 1980s, on social mobility, ethnic revitalization, and socioreligious involution (54). The emergence and triumph of the NAR over the PNM in the wake of the oil boom's crash, for Ryan, signaled the end of the "Creole" nationalist period and ushered in a precarious new era of multiculturalism in "post-Creole" Trinidad and Tobago.

Yet what does "Creole"—and therefore "post-Creole"—mean here? "Creole" terminology was first used to refer to people born in the New World: of European or African descent, for example. Then, through extension, "creole" came to encompass the Afro-Euro "color" continuum of racial mixture in the West Indies, adding a new layer of meaning to the term. Thus "creole" connotes locality and rootedness without autochthony and has therefore been subject to a range of charged meanings and contested politics. Conceptualizing people of African and mixed-African descent as "Creoles"—and hence more readily as authentic West Indians—loaded the ideological bases in their direction throughout the nationalist period of decolonization and independence. Premised on colonial imagery of the culturally naked African, "creole" was applied to the continuum of skin color signaling racial mixture between Europeans and Africans that transpired in the Caribbean, the ends of which were defined by the ideal types of "black" and "white." As Segal writes, "the 'African' and 'European' were placed within a system of 'color' which imaged them as physiological opposites and, at the same time, as the defining endpoints of a continuum of locally produced 'mixing.' Thus the idiom of 'color' affirmed the 'natural' difference of these kinds, even while expressing their shared 'localness'" (1993:100).

Ideologically, Africans became civilized to the extent that they intermixed with whiteness and were "lifted" and "educated" by contact with European civilization. This sociosymbolic space of "creole" was therefore deeply intertwined with Christianity, given its paramount status for Whites and its increasingly central role in the lives and identifications of Blacks during emancipation and after. Indeed, the significance of this Christian-Creole nexus helps account for why persons of Portuguese, Spanish, French, Syrian, and even Chinese descent have all come within the emically *creole* orbit, as in "Portuguese Creole," "Chinese Creole," and so on. Arriving already Christian or becoming Christianized locally, as with the Chinese, served to fold these groups into the creole matrix. Though they hailed from another Oriental civilization, the fact that Chinese soon intermixed with Afro-creoles, became Christianized, and entered creole social space reflects the sociohistorical contingency of racial ideologies.

By contrast, South Asians have been conceptualized within the dominant framework as East, not West, Indians; thus they have been historically excluded from national culture in a range of ways. In marked contrast to the elaborate distinctions of color among Afro-creoles, there was no colonial terminology produced for persons of mixed Indian and European ancestry, a lexical absence—Segal (1993:93–94) notes—that was not mimetic of actuality, but generative of classificatory erasure. "Immigrants from South Asia and their descendants were neither part of a locally-created 'white-Indian' continuum nor part of a locally-created 'black-Indian' continuum. In the socially constructed absence of local connections, 'East Indians' never became 'Creoles,' and had no place on the creole scale of color: they were emphatically 'East' and not 'West Indians'" (97). The reigning imagery has been that of the culturally saturated Indian.

This contrasting ideological imagery of the deracinated African versus the unassimilable Indian rationalized varying patterns of labor exploitation and was taken for granted by most as a result of political domination and colonial subjugation, even among those who rejected claims of European superiority (Segal 1993:95). Such ideological presuppositions were assumed not only under colonialism but also within the nationalist contestation of colonial power and political sovereignty that emerged after World War I and gathered force after World War II.

The passing of Creole nationalism into post-Creole multiculturalism is therefore a multifaceted process conditioned by many factors: the political, if not wholly economic or cultural, denouement of whiteness with the rise of nationalism and decolonization; the emergence of Black Power in the wake of independence as a form of internal critique connected with wider hemispheric currents; the rise and fall of an oil boom, which wrought unforeseen transformations in economic differentiation, social mobility, and ethnic and religious revitalization across the society as a whole; the death of Eric Williams and subsequent fall of the PNM in the wake of the boom; the rise of the NAR, a coalition of Africans and Indians headed by A.N.R. Robinson, a black Tobagonian, which obtained a plurality of support under a banner of "One Love" from all racial groups, religious denominations, and social classes, but which soon fractured because of internal racial politics and fierce debate regarding "culture" and the state; then, after a one-term return of the PNM in the early 1990s, the ascent of a more forthrightly Indian-based political party, the United National Congress (UNC), in 1995.

In other words, the symbolic European head of the Creole color continuum was decapitated and whiteness de-idealized with the advent of nationalism, decolonization, and independence, developments which ultimately led Indians to challenge their position as ideological outsiders (Vertovec 1992; Khan 2001, 2004; Munasinghe 2001a, 2001b). If the victory of the NAR was hailed as a triumph of democratic pluralism, then its rapid and contentious demise suggests that an equally precarious post-Creole multiculturalism has replaced the paradigm of Creole nationalism.

Yet capitalist interests remained paramount through these transformations. The NAR pursued an unambiguously neoliberal economic agenda of "structural adjustment" spurred by the end of the oil boom, for example, a context in which TT fell victim to statistical malpractice by the International Monetary Fund, which exacerbated its financial crisis and economic vulnerability (see Klein 2007:259–62 on the latter).

Ironically in light of the local creole ideology, yet unsurprising given the persisting virulence of racism and classism, the first real challenge to PNM dominance came toward the end of TT's initial decade of independence as a result of the Black Power Movement (Oxaal 1982; Sutton 1983, 1984; Bennett 1989; Ryan 1995a). By the late 1960s, the inadequacies of industrialization by invitation and import-substitution "development" models had become increasingly apparent, reflected in underemployment, labor unrest, intensified inequality, public debt, escalating inflation, and enduring foreign dependence. The National Joint Action Committee (NJAC) launched a high-profile critique of these conditions, including discrimination by state and private sectors, which it attributed to continued multinational domination of the national economy chaperoned by local elites. Colonialism, in other words, had led to neocolonialism. The nationalist project had been hijacked by "Afro-Saxons." NJAC staged high-profile and controversial marches and demonstrations in 1970, including at the Roman Catholic cathedral in Port-of-Spain, where members draped its icons with black cloth.

However, the movement alienated Indians by referring to the underprivileged as "black" and embracing "African" symbolism, because its leadership was primarily Afro-creole, and by concentrating its efforts in predominantly black urban areas. Contrary to popular perception, NJAC's vision was quite explicitly *not* a Marxist one, but anti-imperialist fused with ethnic nationalism (Bennett 1989). By declaring a state of national emergency, Williams's government was ultimately able to co-opt the movement's critical energies by conceding some of its demands while stealing some of its thunder, in addition to quelling a mutiny within the National Regiment. Still, NJAC succeeded in pushing the PNM into a redistributive stance, enhanced by the rising tide of oil in the early 1970s.

Thus the demise of Black Power became the PNM's gain, leading to a program of "National Reconstruction," a (later aborted) move toward constitutional reform, revision of the third national Five Year Plan for development, and a revivified nationalism leading to full sovereignty as a republic in 1976. NJAC raised political consciousness among the poor—especially black urban youth—and generated some public support, but it ultimately frightened away many with its radicalizing agenda. Paul Sutton (1983) argues that the events culminating in 1970 were indeed less than the "revolution" claimed at the time. Yet, as Ryan observes, "NJAC was a 'midwife' to the new society" (1995b:703). These events are important not only for understanding the development of cultural politics in the emergent era of postcolonial multiculturalism, but also because Black Power affected subsequent efforts of black activists and socially mobile spiritual seekers to transform grassroots Shango into the self-consciously politicized Orisha Movement examined below.

Twenty years after Black Power, the government and state media were taken over in what has often been called a "coup" staged by a predominantly black Islamist sect: another attempt to right old wrongs in the name of the dispossessed. Indeed, the links between 1970 and 1990 may be seen in the reappearance of activists from 1970 as well as the ideas informing the protests of 1990. The critique of black inequality and powerlessness was clearly articulated within the idiom of Islamism (see Ryan 1991; Forte 1995a). Led by Imam Abu Bakr, the Jamaat-al-Muslimeen sought to overturn the neoliberal policies of the NAR by forcing new elections. A car bomb was driven into police headquarters while insurgents stormed Parliament, taking cabinet ministers, parliamentarians, Prime Minister Robinson (who suffered a gunshot wound to the ankle), and a number of journalists and civil servants hostage. A national state of emergency with curfew was put into effect.

Despite looting and destruction in Port-of-Spain and along the east-west corridor, the public did not rise in support of the Muslimeen. Unlike during the 1970s Black Power demonstrations, the army remained firmly on the government's side in 1990. Hostages were released. Robinson emerged from Parliament several days later after negotiating an agreement in which the Muslimeen would lay down arms in exchange for capitulation to six demands, including amnesty. Further spurring the politicization of religion in an era of intensifying multiculturalism, the Muslimeen insurrection ensured the demise of the NAR in the 1991 elections.

Yet the rise of the NAR was already an index of Indians having come into their own politically; thus the fracturing of the coalition further energized Indo-creole critique of ethnic prejudice in society and political hypocrisies of governance, fueling patterns of revitalization that have been seen by many as an "Indian Renaissance" of sorts. While these trends have much deeper taproots in cultural history, it is still the case that the waning of colonialism and succeeding crises of nationalism have continued to stimulate refigurations and retrenchments in public and political culture. The rise to power of the UNC in 1995–96 spurred many of these social dynamics and cultural politics even further.

The effort to revitalize Hinduism has therefore been stimulated by many factors, including a concern with Pentecostal conversion across racial lines. Pentecostalism is the fastest-growing religion in TT, and Ryan goes as far as to characterize central Trinidad—an area historically emblematic of Indians—as the country's new "Bible Belt" (1999:92–93). North American mission groups constantly visit Trinidad and Tobago, and local church communities have developed considerable interlinkages with them. Ethnomusicologist Timothy Rommen's (2007) study of popular gospel musics and their "ethics of style" shows how local Pentecostalism is characterized by internal dialogue and lively debate concerning orthodoxy, race, nationalism, and generation. Looking outside themselves, however, evangelicals have been the most vocal critics of Hindu "idolatry" and "paganism," spurring rebuttal and countercritique.

Indeed, Indo-Trinidadians, preoccupied by the meaning of beliefs and practices in light of a late-modern, globalizing world and in response to socioeconomic changes in mobility and class identification connected with the oil boom, hold polylogues within their respective religious communities as well. Hinduism in particular is embraced in the late twentieth century as an expression of Indian prosperity. New wealth earned by Indo-Trinidadians facilitated the construction and maintenance of temples, the sponsoring of ceremonial and organizational activities, the pursuit of doctrinal or religious knowledge, the proliferation of Bollywood films and Indian radio stations, and more active interest in connecting with and traveling to Mother India. Morton Klass's (1991) study of the neo-Hindu Sai Baba devotional movement, for example, suggests a respectably revitalizing alternative within the Hindu fold: an elite, ethnically exclusive spiritual movement mediating tradition and modernity.

Meanwhile, some Presbyterian Indians have become re-Hinduized. As Premdas and Sitahal write: "The capture of power by the PNM and its perceived discriminatory policies against Indians released a powerful motivation for Indian unity. After thirty years of such a regime, Presbyterians found solace and security not with their Christian Creole and mixed-race confessional compatriots but with other Indians. Many seek their roots within ancient Indian culture in reaction to Creole assertion of a rediscovered African identity and the subsidies and biases of the state for calypso" (1991:347–48). Hinduism has therefore become the privileged vehicle of diasporic identification for a revivifying glocal Indian ethnicity.

Ryan (1996, 1999) observes that the UNC defeat of the PNM in the mid-1990s was brought about more by political action in mandirs and mosques than in the public square. At the forefront of these efforts has been the Sanatan Dharma Maha Sabha, the largest and most assertive Hindu organization in the country. The SDMS sees itself as the representative of orthodoxy, "the vanguard of the movement to 'answer back' those whom they believed gratuitously denigrated the Hindu religion" (Ryan 1999:58). It has sought to bolster local support and internationalize its linkages in the globalization of Indian ethnicity and Hindu nationalism in India, represented by the rise of the Bharatiya Janata Party (BJP). It took up the mantle anew regarding the politics of the state, pressing for public culture to be de-Christianized—echoing Black Power in 1970 and the Muslimeen in 1990—to more adequately reflect Trinidad and Tobago's multiethnic reality.

Yet the resurgence of Hinduism and further development of Indocentric politics by the 1990s was hardly unified, and the UNC government and SDMS diverged in many ways. Indeed, the SDMS hardly speaks for all Hindus, much less all Indians; some even believe things were better under the PNM.

The larger point is that the transitions from colonialism to independence and from creole nationalism to postcolonial multiculturalism have transpired in terms of ethnoracial politics and interwoven and contested religious lines as well. These developments have spurred dialogue and debate within and between "racial" and "religious" groupings that ebb and flow (Khan 2004). Some Blacks have responded through the popular medium of calypso, and Ryan even argues that calypsonians were, in fact, a more effective opposition to the UNC than the PNM while in office (1999:164–65). Yet responses to the rise of Indian cultural and political assertion have taken forms ranging from Christian fundamentalism to black Islamism and from retrenched nationalism to pro-dougla cultural activism and aesthetics.

It is within the context of black response to Indian revitalization that Ryan notes the postcolonial politicization of historically marginalized Afro-creole traditions such as Shango and Spiritual Baptism. "As a parallel development," Ryan argues, "there was also evidence of an Afrocentric religious awakening" (1999:216). Yet while there is no reason to dispute the influence of intensified Indo-Afro cultural politics in the wake of social and political developments of the late 1980s and early 1990s, Ryan's analysis seems to underestimate other sociohistorical currents, especially the impact of Black Power, which represented the surfacing of deeper racial tensions, economic conflicts, and ideological contradictions.

Black Power and the Transformation of Shango into Orisha

Orisha Worship has experienced a range of "anti-syncretic" (Shaw and Stewart 1994) developments since the 1970s in counterpoint to the flexibility of the Afro-creole tradition of Shango. A decade into independence, national perceptions began to change dramatically in relation to black spirituality, leading to what Frances Henry (1983) referred to as the "resurgence" of Shango after she earlier predicted the religion's demise. This period catalyzed a shift in nomenclature from Shango to Orisha among new practitioners, a change that has by no means been complete or systematic. Shango's association with blackness and African religiosity made it an object of scorn and derision for many in the colonial period; that association has also now legitimized it in the postcolonial era as an institution for Afrocentric revitalization, an arena for recuperating blackness.

Black Power responded to racial and class prejudice in the political-economic culture of the newly independent nation-state, drawing its most ardent followers from the younger and university-educated elements of society. Turning to the religion as much for political as religious motives, they sought out shrines and feasts as a means of reclaiming black selfhood. As one of the movement's most eloquent spokespeople, Pearl Eintou Springer, writes, "Any people that does not possess, for whatever reason, the ability to conceptualize God, the giver of life and therefore the ultimate life force, in its own image, must clearly suffer seriously from a crisis of self" (1994:86). Similarly, Tobagonian folklorist Jacob D. Elder claims that, "considering the crucial status of religion in African politics there seems to be nothing illogical in our prediction that in time the Shango cult will be embraced by young black radicals in their drive for the creation of a politics whose base is truly African in culture in Trinidad and Tobago" (1996:36). In what amounts to a sort of neo-Herskovitsean spirit, Shango is seen as the subjugated, yet premier, local repository of African culture.

Yet interfacing with the complex Afro-creole grassroots reality of Shango is no straightforward endeavor. The movement has responded by seeking to "Africanize" the practice by exorcising the popular tradition of its Christian "impurities" while simultaneously "Yorubanizing" its praxis. The trend toward African-styled clothing reflects this sentiment. These and other changes discussed below are taken to be the logical way of "returning" to more traditional, ostensibly "pure," West African ritual habits and structures of devotion.

Here I offer an overview of sociopolitical developments in what has come to be known as the Orisha Movement in the wake of the Black Power revolution, consider several trends encountered on the ground in my fieldwork, and discuss my experience with the Sixth World Congress of Orisa Tradition and Culture in August of 1999, an event which dramatically concretized the class divisions and differential interests of Shango at the popular level versus Orisha as a politicized movement.[1] Finally, I analyze these developments in terms of the politics of religion in TT's era of postcolonial multiculturalism, clarifying some of the ironies and tensions embodied by the movement to "Africanize" a problematically "African" tradition.

The Black Power revolution continues to have reverberating effects. Segal notes the relatively recent use of the phrase "black middle class" in Trinbagonian discourse: "I have never found this phrase in a document from the pre-inde-pendence period, and its identification of 'black' with a status other than 'lower' fits with the politics of meaning of the post-independence period, and in par-ticular, of the period following the Black Power Movement of 1970" (1993:112). Likewise, Emancipation celebrations have become more Afrocentric. Segal ob-serves that the centenary of emancipation in 1934 explicitly commemorated the "enlightened" and "benevolent" Emancipation Act of British Parliament in 1834, as opposed to highlighting the agency of Africans and Afro-creoles who has-tened the end of the transitional "apprenticeship" period by two years, in 1838 (104–5). Indeed, contrary to popular perception, Brereton (1983:73) observes "absolutely no evidence, for the post-1838 years, of any popular celebrations by the ex-slaves on August First" (Emancipation Day) in Trinidad.

Fast-forward to my first Emancipation Day celebration, in 1997, in which the year's theme was "Renewing the Vision of African Redemption." In 2005, the official Emancipation Day theme was "Discarding Broken Chains, Discovering Unbroken Connections." Each year there is a week's worth of galas, processions, presentations, concerts, lectures, performances, and the like along with mate-rialization of the Lidj Yasu Omowale Emancipation Village, featuring African cuisine for sale and a market of African clothing, jewelry, pottery, accessories, and so on.

The ideology of Black Power also exerted powerful effects in the arts and popular culture. Though Africanist imagery existed in Carnival band produc-tions before the 1970s, it hinged on tropes of exotica and fantasy. Since that time, however, masquerade themes reflect the postcolonial Afrocentric mo-ment in myriad ways. In 1969, fifteen bands with names such as Tribute to Africa, Great Faces of Africa, Afromania '69, and Psychedelic Afro played the streets, featuring "African" masquerade. Then, in 1970, protest *mas* foreshad-owed the disturbances that would erupt just afterward, with one band parading in black outfits and holding up clenched-fist Black Power salutes and carrying placards of Malcolm X, Huey Newton, Eldridge Cleaver, and Trinidad's own Stokely Carmichael (Anthony 1989:343–44).

More positive images of both Shango and Spiritual Baptism also emerged in calypso, accompanied by open identification with these religions by some artists (F. Henry 2003:166–82). This has been accompanied by increased his-torical consciousness of African and Afro-creole influences in the local history of Carnival, calypso, and steel band, already apotheosized as sacred nationalist iconography of the independent postcolonial state.

Similarly, Black Power stimulated government to capitalize on pride in the African past by encouraging other cultural manifestations, such as creation of the annual Best Village Program and its competitions for best plays, poems, dances, and so forth. The finals were telecast nationally, and winning villages received cash prizes. Many productions were based upon Afro-creole folkloric materials such as Shango subculture (F. Henry 1991), adding to the growing legitimacy of Shango-Orisha in mainstream public culture.

Nationally televised local series such as *The African Presence in Trinidad and Tobago* (1983) ramified these developments, along with programming in the independent *Gayelle* series in the mid-1980s focusing, among their varied features, on local black cultural traditions. One of Banyan, Ltd.'s (the producers of *Gayelle*) documentaries—*Crossing Over* (1988)—brought together Ghanaian musician Koo Nimo and the formerly high-profile southern Trinidadian shrine of Isaac "Sheppy" and "Queen" Pearlie Lindsay (known as the United Brotherhood of Time Spiritual School, where Spiritual Baptist, Orisha, and Kabba ritual work were all practiced) for experimental music-making and cultural exchange. It was Sheppy's sister's feast, on land just adjacent to the UBOTSS, which I describe in the Prologue.

As an expression of their cultural nationalism, many of those influenced by Black Power have turned either to Orisha or Rastafari in racially self-conscious spiritual quests. Perhaps not surprisingly, Rastafari and Orisha have even begun to interrelate distally. Many drummers on the orisha circuit are Rastafarians and some of them see the orisha Dada–St. Anthony as a "Ras," for example. A shrine in Santa Cruz is patronized predominantly by Rastas or former Rastas amenable to the main (black) priestess's Sai Baba–influenced Hinduism, yet another twist in the many-tentacled evolution of popular religious pluralism at the grassroots level.

Transforming Shango into Orisha

Establishing official recognition vis-à-vis the state and combating the popular stigma surrounding Shango has been spearheaded by a small coalition of activists and spiritual leaders. Indeed, one outcome of Afrocentrically oriented revitalization has been the effort to formally legitimate "Orisha Worship," which has in turn spurred bureaucratization. The first major step toward erecting a national movement upon the shoulders of grassroots Shango came in the early 1980s with the official incorporation of the Orisha Movement in 1981 under the leadership of Iyalorisha Melvina Rodney, whose shrine in southern Trinidad came to be known as Egbe Orisa Ile Wa (see note 1 on orthography). According to Tracey Hucks (2006:33–34), this was the first legal enactment to legitimate the status of an African-derived religion in the black diasporic world. In 1985, the Orisa Youth's Cultural Organization circulated a printed collection of Yoruba prayers with English translations, an effort to standardize and disseminate Africanized knowledge about liturgy that has been followed by many others (Houk 1995:159–61, 189).

Also pivotal was a government-sponsored visit by the fiftieth Ooni of Ife—Oba Okunade Sijuwade Olubuse II—as a guest of the Confederation of African Associations (COATT) for Emancipation Day celebrations in August of 1988.[2] Greeted by government officials upon his arrival, the Ooni traveled the country, visiting the historical slave burial site at Lopinot Junction, off the Eastern Main Road, where he laid a commemorative stone honoring the late Isaac "Sheppy" Lindsay. He also visited the shrine of Iyalorisha Rodney in Marabella, which he reconsecrated, and whom he then anointed the spiritual head of orisha in Trinidad and Tobago. A celebration was also staged at the Jean Pierre Sports Arena Complex in metropolitan Port-of-Spain, attended by the prime minister, the president of the republic, and other officials. Prime Minister A.N.R. Robinson was bestowed the title of Chief *Olokun Igbaro* during the Yoruba king's sojourn.

The Ooni declared himself pleased with TT, claiming that local tradition might in fact be *more* authentic than that contemporaneously practiced in Nigeria (Frances Henry, pers. comm., 1999). He urged local religionists to organize a centralized apparatus for administering affairs and also advocated for a National Council of Orisha Elders with representation from major local shrines, which was accomplished a decade later, in 1998. Perhaps not surprisingly, the visit also exacerbated local factionalism, since the Ooni aligned himself with one group in particular.

Soon thereafter, Babalorisha Clarence Forde and Iyalorisha Molly Ahye of Opa Orisa Shango (OOS)—who had organized the Ooni's event at the Jean Pierre Complex—launched the first Oshun Festival at Salybia in 1990, on the northeast coast of Trinidad (televised as part of the *Gayelle* series, program 20, 30 August 1990). This is a spot where a freshwater river meets the ocean in a somewhat out of the way yet accessible location. Drawing practitioners from multiple shrines in the bright light of day, the Oshun Festival established a new local tradition of offering a federated public "table" for the feminine orisha of beauty, fertility, and water, including cakes, fruits, olive oil, flowers, and so on, to be washed out to sea at high tide. Leadership of the festival was in slow flux over the 1990s, and some micropolitical tensions were evident, but the festival has gained momentum all the same and—unlike traditional feasts held at local shrines—takes place publicly. Iyalorisha Ahye is no longer involved.

I observed a similar pattern at the festival in 1999 and 2000, including the gathering of varying shrine community groups, *not* an especially common occurrence in local orisha circles; an invocational and divination ceremony leading to Salybia beach by the most prominent elders and leaders, followed by a procession down to the sea; the planting of a pink flag for Oshun on the beach after more seaside rituals; a large set of offerings on the sand around the flag, which (ideally) get carried out to sea with the rising tide; and singing, celebration, and general fellowship. There was but one ecstatic manifestation of Oshun each year, which took to the sea and was attended by several ritual experts for most of its duration.

Though formed in the 1980s as an umbrella organization inclusive of Sheppy Lindsay's "Shango Belief System," OOS was not officially incorporated until 1991, with Baba Forde and Iya Ahye in charge. That year Molly Ahye was publicly enthroned in a government-supported, nationally televised ceremony as the official head of OOS, though the event was not especially popular at the grassroots level (F. Henry 2003:81–82). When I told people about my research while circulating in middle-class networks, I repeatedly heard the refrain, "You have to talk to Molly Ahye! You have to talk to Molly Ahye!" The fact that her case becomes better known the farther one moves up the local class ladder is significant.

Ahye earned a Ph.D. from New York University and is an expert on Afro-Caribbean dance (Ahye 1978, 1983). Born to an urban middle-class family, she was nonetheless exposed to Shango while young. She established connections with the Puerto Rican cultural activist Marta Moreno Vega and the Caribbean Cultural Center in New York City in the late 1970s and early 1980s, where an international group with regular meetings was first hatched. Ahye attended the first World Congress of Orisa Tradition and Culture in Ile-Ife, Nigeria, in 1981, cultivating transnational spiritual contact with specialists in Nigeria, then Brazil. Indeed, her initiation took place abroad, not in Trinidad. In addition to spearheading OOS, facilitating the Ooni's visit (though she subsequently criticized him for "creating confusion"), and launching the annual Oshun Festival at Salybia, Ahye's organizational efforts were also directed toward pressing for official orisha marriage legislation in the early 1990s.

A resident of metropolitan Port-of-Spain, Iya Ahye neither has a shrine nor moves widely on the circuit. Indeed, she is relatively inaccessible, as compared with most Iyalorishas and Babalorishas. In an interview granted to Hucks (2006:35), Ahye commented, "I was looking for structure, looking for [Orisha] to have a voice and the only way we could have a voice [was] for us to go to Parliament." These efforts paid off. In 1992, representatives from OOS were invited for the first time by the government to attend the opening of the new Parliament (Houk 1995:126). Further efforts at unifying the shrines into a federated movement and clarifying a national agenda continued throughout the 1990s.

In 1995, Egbe Onisin Eledumare (EOS)—another contemporary, intellectu-alized, back-to-roots activist shrine group led by Black Power offspring Oludari Massetungi and based in Petit Valley, greater Port-of-Spain—held a weeklong conference at the Royal Palms Suite Hotel in Maraval entitled "Orisha: Towards a Common Theology." The conference involved plenary sessions, workshops, various presentations, and special performances featuring native social scien-tists J. D. Elder and Maureen Warner-Lewis, Iyalorisha Molly Ahye, a Ghanaian researcher, a Cuban *babalawo*, and an academic from the University of South Florida. Addresses were given by the secretary of the Nigerian High Commis-sion and by former mayor of Port-of-Spain, Ethelbert Paul, who stressed the importance of Orisha religion reaching out to the black youth of TT in order to make them "better citizens" and "very conscious of their color" (from Ban-yan, Ltd., archival video footage). The conference concluded with calls for the Ministry of Education to incorporate Africanist pedagogy into its curricula and for the government to establish an Institute of African Studies at the University of the West Indies at St. Augustine in Trinidad. Several religious events were staged at the Little Carib Theatre in Port-of-Spain.[3]

EOS also launched an annual Shango Day celebration in 1996 and has even lobbied for it to become an official national holiday. In 1999, I attended a press conference held by EOS at the Queen's Park Savannah, the largest park in the country, located in central Port-of-Spain. They outlined their rationale and itinerary for Shango Day that year, passing out information about their com-munity's practice of "African Sacred Science," as well as complimentary copies of their print and online publication, *Ifá Speaks*. That year the event was held in the Savannah across from the national zoo and president's house and attended by around fifty people affiliated with the shrine.[4]

Throughout Shango Day 1999, there were periods of drumming and chant-ing, yet there was only one relatively mild ecstatic manifestation among dev-otees. Oludari framed the observance in service to the nation, beseeching Shango to bestow his blessing upon the twin-island republic. At one point the police approached and asked for a public meeting permit, which had not been arranged beforehand, so the group's leader and several of his assistants piled into my used car and we drove to the St. Clair Police Station to take care of the necessary paperwork. The authorities were respectful, but this experience dramatized the long arm of the law. Indeed, that colonial legislation requiring a permit for religious activities involving drumming and other related aspects of African religion remained on the books in the postcolonial period was a bone of contention for the Orisha Movement, motivating the effort to have these statutes permanently excised from the national legal code.

Most memorable that day for me was my conversation with an eighty-year-old woman who described herself as "African conscious, not racist." In 1979, she started a nursery called Kilimanjaro and then a kindergarten in metropolitan Port-of-Spain. The Creator made animals and flowers to beautify the earth, she commented, yet she also repeatedly invoked the notion of "choosing sides," emphasizing that she had embraced her "African side." Pointing out the light, "red" skin of the shrine's leader, she observed that he is "mixed" and yet nonetheless has "also chosen a side." Revealing some "white ancestry" of her own, she knew she would be "rejected in Scotland." Embracing Orisha helped her shed the ostensible stigma of "Negro" blood.

Shango Day 1999 ended with a well advertised, pay ticket–based concert featuring local performers either directly associated with, or supportive of, the Orisha Movement. Several percussion bands performed at Port-of-Spain's city hall. Abbi and Shanaqua sang an Afrocentric calypso. Baba Forde's Tunapuna group took a turn chanting and drumming. Judging by audience response, the highlight of the evening was the final performance, by Ella Andall, a prominent orisha devotee of Grenadian background well known in the local art and music scene. She had a smash hit entitled "Say My Name, I'm an African" and has released several compact discs of her orisha song-chanting accompanied by a youth choir. The same mildly trancing woman from earlier in the day at the savannah began to manifest near the front of the auditorium but was ushered out of the concert hall, perhaps because the event was held at such a high-profile venue. The concert was the only time during Shango Day in which shrines in addition to the hosting EOS were present.

Meanwhile, other efforts relevant to the national status of African religions were coming to fruition. Spiritual Baptists had long been agitating for a national holiday on 30 March, the date in 1951 on which the colonial Shouters Prohibition Ordinance (originally legislated in 1917) was repealed under the interim ministerial government of Albert Gomes, a decade before independence. According to Sen. Barbara Gray-Burke—the first Spiritual Baptist appointed to that post, by Basdeo Panday in the early 1990s, as part of the parliamentary opposition to the PNM under Patrick Manning—Spiritual Baptists had repeatedly suffered broken promises made by the PNM under Williams and his successor, George Chambers, as well as NAR prime minister Robinson (F. Henry 2003:66–67). The final straw came when Manning also reneged once attaining power in 1991.

Parliamentary debate was intensified by similar efforts of Indian cultural activists for the establishment of a national Indian Arrival Day on 30 May, commemorating the 150th anniversary of the arrival of the first wave of indentured

South Asian laborers in 1845. The matter of public holidays was quickly swept up in the country's racially polarizing politics and into national headlines. It is within this context that opposition leader Panday had appointed Burke to the Senate. Manning's government eventually established a parliamentary committee to consider the question of public holidays and report back by the end of March 1995.

Manning believed there were already too many national holidays and that granting African religions a less official "festival" day would sufficiently recognize them. He opposed removing a holiday associated with Christianity—the most likely candidate for the chopping block—in order to make room for what many saw as an ambiguously Christian holiday at best. Thus Manning advocated official sanctioning of a generic Arrival Day rather than a specifically *Indian* Arrival Day, claiming it was too racially divisive, even though everyone knew an Arrival Day celebrated on 30 May made it an ethnic holiday.

The joint bipartisan committee reported after some delay yet reached no consensus. The majority report reflected Manning's view, whereas a minority report called for the granting of national holiday status to Spiritual Baptists and the Orisha religion, as well as an Indian Arrival Day on behalf of Indo-Trinidadians. No legislative action was taken. As a compromise gesture, however, Arrival Day was declared a one-time public holiday on 30 May 1995 by presidential order, in order to commemorate 150 years of local Indian domicile. The celebrations were well attended, especially in Indian communities.

By the end of 1995, the tables again turned. The PNM was defeated and the United National Congress—a predominantly Indian-based political party led by former opposition leader Panday—elected into power. In one of his earliest moves, Panday called for establishment of a public holiday for Spiritual Baptists to be held on 30 March and the granting of land to Baptist groups for celebrations and the building of a school and other facilities. Subsequent legislation, in February of 1996, formally institutionalized Spiritual Baptist Shouters Liberation Day as an official national holiday, removing Whit Monday in order to do so. At the same time, Indian Arrival Day was made into a permanent holiday. Granting an Afro-creole religious group a national day accompanied restoration of the "Indian" in Arrival Day.

Building on efforts at incorporation and legitimation, a high-profile conference of Spiritual Baptist groups was held later in 1996 at the Central Bank auditorium in Port-of-Spain. It called for institutional development of the land granted for an African Religions Spiritual Park at Maloney and resulted in the formation of a National Council of Spiritual Baptist Elders. Deeds of ownership of the dedicated twenty-five acres of land at Maloney were not handed over until July of 2000; three five-acre parcels went to Spiritual Baptist organizations, while the other two were bestowed upon the Orisha Movement.

With these developments, the holiday calendar had taken the shape I encountered in the late 1990s, a contested national liturgical cycle embodying what I call Trinidad and Tobago's field of "postcolonial multiculturalism": New Year's Day (secular); Spiritual Baptist Shouters Liberation Day (Afro-Christian); Good Friday and Easter Monday (Christian); Indian Arrival Day (Indo-secular); Corpus Christi (Christian); Labour Day (secular); Emancipation Day (Afro-secular); Independence Day (secular); Eid al Fitr (Muslim); Republic Day (secular); Diwali (Hindu); Christmas and Boxing Day (Christian). Though Carnival Monday and Tuesday are not official holidays, they are treated as such by many.

Though the idea was floated much earlier, it was not until 1998 that a formally incorporated National Council of Orisha Elders was brought into being under the Companies Act. Its formation was finally precipitated by the experience of several Trinbagonians having attended the 1997 World Orisha Congress held in San Francisco, and in anticipation of Trinidad and Tobago's hosting of the next Congress in 1999. The council seeks to bring unity and direction to the Orisha Movement. It consists of an Executive Committee of six elders also known as "directors," one of whom acts as chair; regional district coordinators, including for Tobago; a general secretary; a public relations officer; and an administrator. Membership in the council is open to all shrines, but participation thus far stems largely from those belonging to Egbe Orisa Ile Wa, Opa Orisa Shango, or Egbe Onisin Eledumare. During my fieldwork between 1999 and 2005, two of the council's elders were also Spiritual Baptist leaders.

The Council of Elders created an annual Orisha Family Day (OFD) in 1998, which puts yet another event on the local calendar for public attendance and media consumption. It raises consciousness about the religion, fosters solidarity among shrines and practitioners, and seeks to reinforce the value of family. The event is held at Lopinot, a slave burial site that was consecrated by the Ooni of Ife during his visit in 1988, and brings together several hundred people— most decked out in lavish African garb—for a day of invocation and prayers, addresses and updates, music and performance, and food and fellowship.

The first two years of OFD saw the attendance of Chief Patricia Oluwole from Nigeria as an emissary on behalf of the Ooni. The second year's observance, in 1999, brought even greater national recognition due to the participation of UNC prime minister Panday, who honored the commemorative stone laid at Lopinot—which has come to be known as an African Heritage Site—with libations and affirmed his support for the Orisha Movement. In 2000, OFD was attended by then-president of the republic A.N.R. Robinson, upon whom had been bestowed the Yoruba title of Chief Olokun Igbaro by the Ooni more than a decade before. The event has become an important day of solidarity and public recognition for the movement.

During its first year, the Council of Orisha Elders also held its inaugural convention in conjunction with the launching of OFD. I attended its second annual convention in June of 1999, held in the community hall of a secondary school in southern Trinidad, after the convention was disentangled from Family Day. After preliminary incantations and invocation, then-chair—the late Sam "Baja" Phills—praised past elders and invoked a genealogy of Orisha Worship stemming to Ile-Ife and the "Golden Age in Africa." He claimed the religion must be proud, not "ahow" (embarrassed), that "being ashamed of who and what you are makes you subservient." He called for recognition, the convention's theme. Orisha Worship had been stigmatized for too long, but it was now working to allow practitioners to "take our rightful place in society." Baja concluded: "We want arrival, like Indian Arrival Day."

A district coordinator spoke next, reaffirming Baja's commentary, and reminding people that "we are our own best solution!" She questioned whether the Orisha Movement wanted an authority structure like that of Catholicism, though there was little conversation about this. A historical introduction to the Council, progress reports, and lively discussions ensued. Information was presented about the Squatter's Land Act, which enables shrines on state lands to apply for deeds. One speaker pled for rising above factionalism and "bickering about leadership." An economic report was given and a brainstorming session was held regarding revenue for the Council. Ideas floated were to produce "anthropologically relevant" CDs or videos (such as of Family Day at Lopinot), a shareholder scheme, the encouragement of entrepreneurship, and a campaign to persuade practitioners to avoid prestige spending.[5]

Another speaker shifted the conversation from revenue raising to more global problems, arguing that devotees suffered worldwide from the same oppression: "Whatever affects our brothers elsewhere affects us." He emphasized the need for direct contact between the Caribbean and West Africa: "Why do we have to fly to London to get to Nigeria?" Yoruba—not English—is "your own language." Along with others, he also called for more, and better, media coverage, advocating that the Orisha Movement apply for its own radio broadcasting license in order to keep pace with the proliferating number of Indian radio stations.

A year later, in 2000, the Council oversaw the systematic registry of all local shrines. A Certificate of Registration was issued to each shrine registered with the Council. I began seeing certificates crop up in shrine complexes throughout Trinidad, representing an unprecedented level of bureaucratization for the tradition.

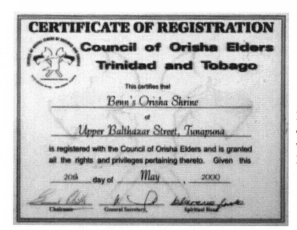

Figure 6.1. Orisha shrine registration displayed prominently on the palais wall of a shrine in northern Trinidad. Photo by author.

Figure 6.2. Orisha shrine registration certificate framed within a painted Christian banner. Orisha Movement reformers want their faith freed of such overt signals of religious syncretism. Photo by author.

Coextensive with these efforts has been a push toward Yorubacentric language and activism. For example, the Traditional Afrikan National Association of Tunapuna circulated a statement in 1999 criticizing capitalist underdevelopment of Africa and oppression of Orisha Worship throughout the diaspora. Claiming that Orisha "predates Hinduism, Christianity, and Islam," it demanded an "Era of Reparation," as well as representation in the National Inter-Religious Organization. The group's antisyncretic position was explicit: "The Africans were forced to camouflage and synchronize their form of worship with that of Christianity in order to cling to their only hope of survival. Against this background, this religion persisted, deeply entrenching itself throughout T and T and creating in the process a spiritual hybrid, 'Shango-Baptist.' Today this most ancient belief system is being practiced throughout the year at different points of our society and a natural instinctive gradual transition signals the return of this great religion to its former glory, free of all Christian encumbrances." The statement concluded by advocating formal legitimation of "the Orisha Faith as a religion of T and T" along with official recognition of the Yoruba language as "the most vital means of communication between African people of T and T." In a similar spirit, "An Introductory Course on Yoruba Culture and Language" was slated to be offered in July of 1999 through the National Institute of Higher Education, Research, Science and Technology (NIHERST) for TT$300. However, it was cancelled due to lack of enrollment.

The high points of 1999 were undoubtedly the passing of the Orisha Marriage Act in Parliament and the government-supported hosting of the Sixth World Congress of Orisha Tradition and Culture in Trinidad and Tobago. Agitation for marriage legislation had been active since the early 1990s. Prime Minister Panday signaled his intention upon taking office of honoring African religions through the establishment of officially recognized marriages performed with their own rites. This development came to pass in 1999 with passing of the Orisha Marriage Act by Parliament. Advance drafts of the legislation were circulated at the local Congress Secretariat in July, just before debate on the bill in the House of Representatives. Several members of the Orisha Movement met with the Ministry of Legal Affairs in order to fine-tune the wording.

The bill was quickly passed, but its implementation was not as swift. Debate emerged as to what constituted requirements for being an official orisha marriage officer, accompanied by sideline controversy over the view of several (male) practitioners who wanted polygamous marriage to be included. Guidelines for candidacy as a marriage officer were finalized and marriages were eventually restricted to monogamous (heterosexual) unions. The first orisha marriage license was granted in 2001 to Babalorisha Songodele Adeleke Kunle and was reported in the major news media. Several others have since received licenses, and some marriages have been performed, but the number has thus far been small. Yet the symbolic and political significance of the Orisha Marriage Act far outweighs the limited demographics of such newly minted "African" marriages.

A concurrent and equally significant development was Trinidad and Tobago's hosting of the Sixth World Congress of Orisha Tradition and Culture on 15–22 August 1999. The first Congress was held in 1981 in Ile-Ife, Nigeria. An International Steering Committee is made up largely of representatives from Nigeria, Brazil, the United States, Cuba, and TT. TT's election as host of the Sixth Congress resulted from deliberations at the Fifth in San Francisco, California, in 1997. The theme for 1999 was "The Orisa, the Ancestors, Family, and Community in the New Millennium—Strategies for Survival." Several hundred, mostly international, delegates attended. Local participation was apparent, but not by the majority of grassroots leaders and devotees. TT's presence at the Congress mainly stemmed from those associated with the local Secretariat, Orisha Movement leaders and activists, some practitioners from shrines most directly affiliated with the movement, and local intellectuals, artists, and professionals interested in or identified with Shango-Orisha.

Glocal disjunctures and class tensions surfaced at the Congress. The cost of attendance was relatively prohibitive, and there was a general lack of communication about it nationally among practitioners. Some grassroots devotees were not even aware of the Congress until I told them about it. Some were uninterested in the talks and politics, though others were critical of the "elite" nature of the event, saying they would not go on principle even if they were able to scrape together the money needed to register. "How can they hold such an event right here in TT and all of us not be able to attend?" a woman queried rhetorically. In the end, attendance was relatively low, and local hosts, as well as the state, incurred debts.

The local Secretariat was mobilized in the offices of a high-profile local businessman, I. T. McCleod, some of whose family members are devotees. These offices were located in the elite neighborhood of St. Clair in Port-of-Spain. Wealthy locals and expatriates have historically inhabited the luxurious homes of this area, some of which have now been converted into offices or other establishments. The Secretariat was staffed by volunteers, most of whom were connected with the McCleod family and associated with the Kenny Cyrus Alkebu Lan Ile Ijebu Shrine in Enterprise, Chaguanas. Local factionalism existed but was not overt, and local internecine conflict was temporarily repressed for the event.

I volunteered part time at the Secretariat for several months to help with preparations and to gain perspective on the Congress from inside its official local epicenter. Much preparation had already been done, but paperwork and a seemingly never-ending series of organizational and logistical matters remained. Given that I was a graduate student at the time, sporting competence with computers, word processing, and the like, I was asked to oversee the effort to organize, edit, and publish the contributions of participants in an official Congress Proceedings. This experience proved to be revealing.

Papers—or sometimes only abstracts of papers—arrived representing a diverse array of personal, historical, political, theological, and practical interests. Foreign contributions ranged from formal addresses by titled Yoruba leaders and Nigerian ruminations on the challenges to Ogun Worship in contemporary West Africa, for example, to literary expressions of the tradition in Latin American literature and the relationship of Ogun to modern digital technologies. A well-respected African-American Babalorisha from the United States presented on therapeutic dimensions of Ifá, to which I was asked to respond on the panel. There were scholarly contributions from home and abroad. Local contributions included a historical reflection on the late Babalorisha Isaac "Sheppy" and "Queen Mother" Pearlie Lindsay's United Brotherhood of Time Spiritual School; a report given by a leading Yoruba revivalist of the local Orisha Movement, who laced her commentary with antisyncretic polemic; an essay criticizing the effects of cultural imperialism, especially on the part of U.S. media; a synopsis of collaborative sociohistorical research carried out by a Trinidadian artist-intellectual and a Nigerian scholar of literature based at the local campus of the University of the West Indies; and a reflection upon educational pedagogy and curricular issues by an expat who was living in the United Kingdom.

Congress Proceedings were published by the Government Printery of Trinidad and Tobago and cost TT$100 over the cost of registration. Leftover copies were later sold at the UWI bookstore. Less overt, but equally symptomatic of class differentiation, were the complex formatting instructions that had been developed for paper submission and publication in the Proceedings, which would have challenged even the most accomplished of computer users and also presupposed access to computers. I found them daunting and, as organizing editor of the Proceedings, experienced considerable difficulty dealing with contributors about them. In the end, almost none of the contributions were submitted as requested; thus we decided to publish them just as they were sent to the Secretariat, making for an eclectic text.

The Congress involved meetings, workshops, plenary sessions, and roundtable discussions in addition to several formal ceremonies held at the upmarket

Holiday Inn (now Crowne Plaza) in downtown Port-of-Spain. A special cultural performance was held off site at the conclusion of the conference. There was also a nighttime fieldtrip to the Cyrus shrine in Enterprise, where a visiting Haitian-American *Mambo*—Vodou priestess—from Philadelphia underwent an intense manifestation of Ogun. Though plans had been drawn up in anticipation of the Ooni of Ife's return visit, he was unable to attend in the end. Sent as emissary in his stead was Chief Omotoso Eluyemi—the *Apena* of Ife—a close ritual and political associate of the Ooni.

The opening ceremony on Monday morning was by far the best attended event, receiving considerable media publicity. It included musical performances accompanied by drumming and was opened by invocation and prayer offered by the leader of Egbe Onisin Eledumare. Nigerian professor Wande Abimbola offered an opening speech on behalf of the International Steering Committee, and Iyalorisha Joan Cyrus of TT welcomed foreign delegates. The Apena of Ife read an address on behalf of the Ooni, emphasizing the "common culture" of the Yoruba diaspora and the need for returning to the Nigerian "source" in this stormy era of globalization.

Official representation included President of the Republic A.N.R. Robinson—who had been bestowed a Yoruba chiefly title by the Ooni in 1988—as well as Prime Minister Basdeo Panday. Panday's comments reiterated his commitment to advancing the cause of African religions and summarized his proactive efforts since early in his administration. Indeed, he took the occasion to formally announce that the Orisha Marriage Act had just been passed and that President Robinson had signed the bill into law that very morning, which was met with thunderous applause. Panday touted TT as "a global village within a global village," "a laboratory of diversity in which we have had remarkable success in creating a note of harmony." He corrected Microsoft's Encarta Encyclopedia's depiction of him as improving the conditions of Indians at the expense of Blacks. Reminding the audience of his move to establish Spiritual Baptist Shouters Liberation Day as well as grant land for an African Religions Spiritual Park, he noted, "What is not recorded is the widespread criticism that I have been favoring Afro-Trinidadians at the expense of Indo-Trinidadians!"

Overall, the opening ceremony privileged the Nigerian delegation and a chronotope of "Africa." No mention was made of hybridity with other religious traditions. As Frances Henry (2003:151) observes, while the inaugural opening event embodied the Afrocentric vision of the movement's transatlantic leaders and activists, this contrasted with some of the most prominent and heated interchanges in the panels, as well as in the hallways of the conference hotel, regarding the politics of syncretism within the religion.

Most vocal in their criticisms and assumption of superiority were representatives from the neo-Yoruba revivalist Oyotunji Village in South Carolina (see
K. Clarke 2004, 2007 on Oyotunji). Many of these North American delegates
claimed lineage with Yorubaland through pilgrimages and initiations in Nigeria. Several times, members of the Oyotunji contingent directly attacked Caribbean practitioners for continued patterns of Afro-Christian and other forms
of spiritual bricolage for their inability to deal with the corrupting legacy of
slavery and colonialism. The critique was accompanied by poorly received offers to help show locals the "true path," though some nonetheless respected
North American expertise. On one occasion, a local Iyalorisha gave a video-
based report on the new tradition of Egungun ancestral masquerade her *ile*
had established in southern Trinidad. One of the Oyotunji priests challenged
her, reminding everyone that only men were traditionally members of Egungun secret societies in Yorubaland. This interchange was especially ironic given
that the local invention of Egungun was in fact a recent Afrocentric innovation
geared toward countering local syncretic patterns.

Yet the critical ire of the North Americans was not reserved solely for the
"taint" of Trinbagonian practices. In a dramatic confrontation after a panel in
one of the main reception areas, a debate arose between the Oyotunji practitioners and a group associated with Gro Mambo Angela Novanyon Idizol, a
Philadelphia-based Vodou priestess mentioned above. Her panel presentation
criticized petty politics and divisiveness and supported the sociosymbolic evolution of Black Atlantic traditions, including incorporation of Christian elements; indeed, she even appealed *Afrocentrically* to the authority of the ancestors whose actions had taken them down such hybrid historical paths. But the
Americans disagreed, arguing that the real problem was people like her who
"confused" the religion with "outside," "impure" elements. For myself and others, this hour-long exchange was one of the most memorable occurrences of the
week.

Such dynamics were difficult for local purists. On the one hand, they agreed
ideologically with Oyotunji sentiment, which demoted syncretism—especially
with Christianity—and espoused returning to African sources. On the other
hand, locals were dismayed by the patronizing arrogance of the Americans and
were defensive about their unique historical experience. All in all, the Congress
dramatized as many tensions as it sought to establish international alliances and
local solidarity.

That year, it also just so happened that the date of the Oshun Festival came
just at the end of the Congress week. Although not part of the official itinerary, a number of delegates traveled to the northeast coast to attend the annual

seaside offering for Oshun. That day the crowd was larger, more fancily dressed, and awash with more cameras and video recorders than usual. Some North American visitors told me they were especially glad to be participating in the "real" scene beyond the conference, unaware of the festival's recency and its unrepresentative ceremonial character vis-à-vis the popular local orisha circuit.

The following year, in 2000, Iyalorisha Melvina Rodney was awarded an Independence Day award by the government in response to nomination from the National Council of Orisha Elders. The award ceremony was covered on national television and was a very special honor for Iya Rodney, who attended in formal African-style attire complete with a head wrap. An op-ed published in the *Trinidad Guardian* on 12 September by Frances Henry and me concerning Iya Rodney's reception pinpoints both the significance and the shortcomings of the event:

> We are very gratified the Government has recognized the contribution of Iyalorisha Melvina Rodney, Spiritual Leader of the Orisha Religion in Trinidad and Tobago, by granting her a Chaconia Silver Medal. In a formal and dignified ceremony, each award recipient's name was called out as the person made their way to shake hands with the President, Prime Minister, and their wives and receive their awards. As this was happening, the television announcer read out their positions and a list of their accomplishments which, although brief, was very informative. However, this procedure was not followed in the presentation made to Iya Rodney. In the first place, her name, followed by the stereotyped designation, "High Priestess," was read out but the religion that she is "High Priestess" of was not identified, much less described. Secondly, there was no mention of any biographical information about her, nor were any of her spiritual achievements presented. This was particularly surprising since Iya Rodney acknowledged the President as a Yoruba chief—Chief Olokun Igbaro—by clasping both his hands and touching foreheads. Because of these omissions, the public, some of whom are not aware of the achievements of this gracious woman, might wonder why she even deserved an award. Moreover, we are led to wonder if the failure to properly identify and recognize Iya Rodney has something to do with the fact that she represents an African-derived religion in a country that is, in some ways, still trying to deny aspects of its past.

This editorial was published several months before the end of my longest period of fieldwork.

That evening we received an e-mail with the subject line "Orisha Priestess" from an expat living in Houston, Texas, saying, "I am writing to commend you for addressing the Trinidad Guardian about the award to Mrs. Rodney. Not being of the Orisha faith, I do not know the appropriate way to address you in reference to her. I too am from Trini and am daily pained by the ignorance African Caribbean people have about themselves, and the members of the media are part of that ignorant group. Keep at it. Enlightenment will come." Then, when I happened to run into one of the country's well-known Carnival artists with whom I am acquainted the following day, he looked at me—chuckling—and commented, "I see you've joined the fray!"

"Africanizing" a Problematically "African" Religion

In order to better understand these postcolonial developments, we must return to colonial ideologies of racial subordination. Because "achievements" were symbolically white in the colonial order and rationalized by the racist mythology of the culturally naked African, their accomplishment by black people may have provisionally contested viewing the "Negro" as inferior but nonetheless also precluded affirming blackness. Any celebration of achievements by black Afro-creoles became a valorization of the European "culture" which "civilized" them. Accomplishments did not make Indians anything other than themselves, by contrast, under the reigning imagery of the "culturally saturated East Indian." "Because 'achievements' did not alter 'Indian identity,' it could possess 'achievements'—which was precisely what the idiom of 'respectability' and the referential shifting of color terms denied 'Africans'" (Segal 1993:103).

These racial ideologies prefigured divergent sociosymbolic pathways for the organization of inequality throughout the colonial era, positioning socially mobile "Blacks" and "Indians" differently—yet not unrelatedly—in time and space. These contrasting colonial ideologies of racial subordination influenced the social differentiation and cultural evolution of religious institutions and ritual practices throughout the colonial period, as we have already seen, and they also account for trends in the multiculturalist politics of religion precipitated by decolonization and the experience of independence. Given the prevailing colonial logic, it made sense to contest ideological inferiority of "Negro" by celebrating the achievements of Afro-creoles in the postcolonial period, especially by affirming their blackness and Africanness. As a corollary, the idealization of whiteness and legacy of Christianity as dominating cultural institution had to be reversed and undone: in with "Africa" and out with "Europe." If colonialism was perverted by imagery of the culturally naked African, whose betterment was premised upon Euro-Christian acculturation, then decolonizing the nation as well as the Afro-creole self-required exorcism of the subjugating "taint" and "false consciousness" of such identifications and institutions.

Much to their frustration, however, Black Power advocates discovered just how difficult it was to transform interpenetrating racial and class hierarchies within the sphere of global capitalism. TT originated as an overseas colonial project, and capitalism—through a series of transmuting iterations—became the only game in town. Playing its cards well, Eric Williams's PNM was able to co-opt much of the critical edge of 1970s radicalism. Yet this is not to say that the so-called Black Power revolution was inconsequential. On the contrary, as I have shown, Black Power stimulated substantial changes in public culture. I see it as the first of four main chapters in the development of TT's postcolonial multiculturalism, the others being the rise and fall of the NAR in the latter half of the 1980s, the Islamist uprising of 1990, and the Indian cultural renaissance and the rise of the UNC in the 1990s. Each challenged the postcolonial state, driving its own nail into the coffin of Afro-creole nationalism.

Building a national Orisha Movement upon the grassroots shoulders of Shango has hardly been straightforward. Whereas Shango embodies the per-sisting subaltern significance of African cultural behavior, it also embodies hybridity with Christianity and other forms of creolization. Framing these as contradictory, the strategy of the Orisha Movement has been twofold: first, raise consciousness about and contest discrimination against African religiosity in politics and national culture; second, reform and revitalize popular ritual praxis through processes of de-Christianization and re-Africanization. A camouflage perspective on syncretism acknowledges the reality of Christianisms while cel-ebrating the cunning of black culture, underwriting an antisyncretic agenda trained on the multiculturalist politics of the postcolonial state. This trend is driven by a desire to "purify" the local tradition of all ostensibly non-"African" elements: "to reorient religious standards to reflect that of Nigerian Yoruba" (Hucks 2001:342), or more precisely, by a particular understanding of what is taken to be precolonial "Yoruba." This perspective frames syncretism as a prob-lem and puts less Afrocentric practitioners on the defensive for their "impuri-ties" of practice.

For Houk (1993, 1995), this so-called Africanization of Orisha Worship is not just a reverberating development resulting from Black Power, but also a response to the influx of Indians and the incorporation of Hindu elements into the practice. The Afrocentric dynamic is a "grassroots" phenomenon in his view (1993:175), but I think it is precisely at this level at which the overtly politicized, Afrocentrically "purifying," antisyncretic trend is in fact *least* salient, especially as compared with the younger, professionally minded, activist-oriented, mid-dle-class recruits at the forefront of the national Orisha Movement.

Frances Henry (1983, 1991, 2003) offers a fuller account of the postcolonial transformation of Shango into Orisha. In the 1960s, older leaders were dying off, and she predicted Shango's rapid demise. At that time, the Catholic Church was still denying known practitioners confession, baptism, and the like. Yet by the 1970s, Henry encountered an "astonishing resurgence" (1983:63). Membership and the number of shrines had increased. There was greater acceptance of the practice accompanied by increasing public appreciation for its significance as an African cultural retention. These developments may be broken down into several interrelated causes.

First, new forms of political consciousness resulting from the Black Power Movement were attractive to younger people and led to increased interest in Shango as the live African cultural past within the nation. Many recruits were attracted for political as much as religious reasons. These developments within the contested and evolving postcolonial context led to de-Christianizing efforts in prayer, praxis, and symbolism, as well as a corollary emphasis upon increased Africanization in language, liturgy, clothing, and so forth.

Second, a change in class composition has been evident, involving an increase in middle-class worshippers and supporters, who have become more public and vocal than ever before. As Henry observed in 1983, "It has become almost a mark of prestige particularly among younger university educated persons to not simply admit to, but brag about, having consulted a Shango healer or attended a feast" (66). Henry estimated that approximately 10 percent of practitioners were hailing from the middle classes by the 1970s, and that recruitment up the class ladder was on the rise. She saw the growth of such "new" members—professionals, entrepreneurs, artists, intellectuals, and students—as the single most important force at work transforming the religion in the postcolonial era, reflected especially in the arts and popular culture, as well as in politics. Though few have commented upon it, we must also appreciate the significance of the oil boom from the mid-1970s through the early 1980s for spurring new patterns of economic mobility and intensifying consumption habits in ways relevant to this story.[6]

Third, Shango cultism has received an influx of Indians into the practice, in some cases even into leadership positions. In the early 1980s, for example, an Indo-Trinidadian—Ralph Frank of Couva—was commonly said to give the largest, best feast in the country. During my fieldwork, there was a prominent Indian shrine leader involved with the Council of Orisha Elders. While increasing Indian involvement may reflect postcolonial recuperation of Shango, which attracted adherents from all ethnic quarters, however, this development stands in an awkward relationship to the ascendant Afrocentrizing paradigm.

Finally, Catholicism and Anglicanism have changed their tune considerably in the wake of decolonization, confronting the counterproductivity of their historical anti-Africanist bias in the era of independence. This is related to the indigenization of church leadership and pedagogy as well. Frances Henry even notes some token inclusion of orisha song-chanting in the services of several progressive urban church congregations in the late 1970s (1983:68).

These are significant changes. Postcolonial Afrocentrists now advocate the exorcism of "Christianisms" (Hucks and Stewart 2003) altogether. In the antisyncretic view of such reformists, popular hybridity and creolizing innovation—known colloquially as the "full-circle approach"—are seen as "local" developments privileging variation and flexibility over purity. Yet this purifying Afrocentric revitalization must be seen as a form of innovation as well, albeit of a culturally and historically specific sort (cf. D. Brown 2003 on Santería). The assumption that hybrid variability is local mystifies the dynamic character of West African religiosity, to some extent reproducing colonial imagery of the culturally naked African in subterfuge. Hybridity is not just diasporic, in other words, and purity not just African. Indeed, preoccupation with purity and the effort to standardize Orisha Worship seems to reflect historically Eurocentric models of what a legitimate "religion" is within the contested political context of postcolonial multiculturalism. In a certain ironic, nontrivial sense, then, what many refer to as "re-Africanization" may also be viewed as a sort of *de*-Africanization.

This is evident in the relative decline of trance performance as focal ritual practice as one ascends structurally from grassroots Shango ceremonialism to the bourgeois spheres of the Orisha Movement. This phenomenon has also been noted by Frances Henry (1983:63–65; 2003:9, 13–14, 118, 140–41). Consider the sentiment of "Auntie Joyce"—a local dancer interviewed on the newly independent television station Gayelle during August of 2005—who uses saraka and nation dance material in her choreographic work but shies away from trance dance, since "catching power" is so "frightening." Bourgeois sensibility is threatened by the conspicuous loss of control in popular mystical forms. Related to this is a trend toward initiations without first having undergone the onset of trance (Babalorisha C. Forde, pers. comm., 2000).

Moreover, middle-class devotees are generally less active on the feast circuit. They turn more toward texts and espouse a more overtly "philosophical" orientation. These are also the practitioners most interested in recuperating Ifá, esoteric divinatory knowledge primarily accessed through printed or online materials in this diasporic neck of the woods. In order to spread knowledge of Ifá as well as Yoruba liturgy, they sponsor educational classes designed to restore and purify. Some are fortunate enough to have made trips abroad to Brazil, North America, or, especially, Nigeria to be initiated and to cultivate relations with foreign mentors. In this regard, they are more similar to the Oyotunji Congress delegates.

These processes reveal a number of ironies and contradictions. Some Afrocentric shrines have not entirely dispensed with all non-African elements. Moreover, the head of EOS—one of the leading Afrocentric innovators—is affiliated with the Ethiopian Orthodox Church. He has adopted the view that all religions—including Judaism, Christianity, and Islam—ultimately derive from "African Sacred Science"; therefore any Christianisms within local practice may be reinterpreted within an Africanist framework. Meanwhile, some politically informed grassroots devotees see the Orisha Movement folks as "Johnny-come-latelies," as one Iyalorisha in central Trinidad put it.

A complex combination of transgenerational and class tensions likewise surfaced in the Carnival controversies of 2001–2002, as two leading movement shrines brought out Carnival bands with orisha-based themes (also see F. Henry 2003:185–91; Hucks and Stewart 2003). Egbe Onisin Eledumare named its band 401 Meets 2001, referring to the number of deities in the traditional Yoruba pantheon according to one influential count. Iyalorisha Patricia "Sangowunmi" McCleod's shrine put on a band called Faces of Oshun the following year, in 2002. These developments stimulated opposition by the Council of Orisha Elders, which—as local, popular-level traditionalists that came up during the colonial era and weathered its many challenges—sees Carnival as a sphere of profane revelry ("bacchanal" is the colloquial term) in which representations or invocations of the orishas do not belong. Afrocentric activists, by contrast, see orisha mas as a fresh and timely contribution to national culture and public revitalization of the tradition. They point to the originally sacred nature of West African masquerade. They not only look more toward foreign connections and inspirations, but also privilege Ifá as the final arbiter on the matter. This rarefied oracle was personally consulted in one case and, in the other, sought, via long-distance, personal connection with a Nigerian *babalawo*. These early-twenty-first-century Carnival controversies were not reconciled at the time, with the activist shrines carrying on with their masquerade and the Council of Elders officially disapproving.

This is not the only way conflict overdetermined by ideology and anachronism bubbles up within the contemporary scene. For example, members of the Orisha Movement seek to raise historical consciousness about African cultural influences and subaltern local resistance. And the mid-twentieth-century Shango king affectionately known as Pa Neezer has been appropriately lionized as one of the local greats who kept the tradition alive under forbidding circumstances. Yet Neezer was not only an avid Shangoist, but also a London

Baptist (F. Henry 1981, 2003:202–10). His healing repertoire consisted of "bush" (herbal) remedies, obi divinatory seeds, *and* the Bible. Warner-Lewis (1996:67) reports that, in addition to possessing copies of Yoruba grammar books—one published by the Christian Missionary Society in 1948—Neezer also acquired a Yoruba Bible in the early 1960s, found after his death earmarked on the page of the Lord's Prayer. Thus commemoration of Pa Neezer by the Orisha Movement turns out to be somewhat tricky, given his Christian involvement.

Indeed, his case shows the possibility of Afro-creoles in the post–World War I colonial period becoming racially self-conscious and even oriented toward Yoruba revitalization in ways not well understood within, or translated into, the cultural politics of the postcolonial period. One of Warner-Lewis's (1991:125–40) informants learned Yoruba devotional ideas from her grandfather, which she practiced until her dying day. She was also influenced by early currents of black nationalism connected with the Garvey Movement of the 1920s, which espoused a "race-conscious" worldview.[7] Yet this third-generation Yoruba-creole was also a Catholic who experienced light trance manifestations in her youth during Mass and who saw the orishas and saints as different sides of the same spiritual coin. For her, the Old and New Testaments were scriptures of African religious history and Jesus, Mary, and the Apostles were all black people. She posited deep interconnections between Yoruba and Hebrew cultures, views not easily translated into the dominant cultural politics of the postcolonial era.

Warner-Lewis's research offers several other valuable cases. One Yoruba-identified woman kept notebooks of transliterated Christian prayers she remembered hearing her grandfather use (1991:67–68). Motivated by fierce racial consciousness, another man conducted evening language classes in Yoruba twice a week in the late 1920s at the old Diego Martin Catholic School, in greater Port-of-Spain (68–71). He lamented ridicule by others, and the class was eventually terminated, presumably because of the church's resistance to his Garveyism. The class had drawn a small number of students, and most instruction—premised upon a colonial primary school methodology developed for English—focused upon rote learning and repetition of phrases and texts, such as the Lord's Prayer and the Apostles' Creed. Indeed, he even composed several Christian hymns in Yoruba (83–84).

A further case involves another Garveyite who first turned to Spiritual Baptism (Warner-Lewis 1991:71–72). He then turned to the North American branch of Garvey's Universal Negro Improvement Association (UNIA) and—through their referral—obtained Yoruba grammar books and probably a Bible from contacts in Nigeria. He spearheaded the teaching of Yoruba language classes throughout Trinidad during the latter half of the 1940s. Warner-Lewis found that the best-remembered tribute among his students was recall of the Lord's Prayer, which they learned through repetitive chanting. At one point, their teacher also teamed up with several other locals to found the Ethiopian Orthodox Church in Trinidad, leading him to launch classes in Amharic and Ge'ez in addition to Yoruba for a time.

Indeed, it is important to remember it was a different African nation—Ethiopia—that captured the early black nationalist imagination among Garveyites in the 1920s and then especially in response to the Italo-Ethiopian War of 1935–36. This upsurge of "Ethiopianism" was characterized by an energized black consciousness that identified events and figures in the Bible as "African" (Yelvington 1999:196–97). The 1930 coronation of Ras Tafari Makonnen, who traced his lineage to David, Solomon, and Queen Sheba of the Old Testament and became known as Haile Selassie I, was taken by many as biblical prophecy coming to fruition. A catechism of the UNIA cited the thirty-first verse of the sixty-eighth psalm to substantiate Ethiopia's sacred status and Haile Selassie's significance. "Ethiopia," then, served as the primary metonym for blackness within this Afrocentric consciousness of the late colonial era, which sought to blacken Christianity rather than to demote or dispense with it. The ascent of "Yoruba" as the premier chronotopic sign of Africa is therefore significant, given that postcolonial Afrocentrism has taken up such an explicitly antisyncretic position vis-à-vis Christianity.

This discussion identifies the ironies and tensions associated with a conceptualization of Africanization specifically as Yorubanization (see Falola and Childs 2004 on the polysemy of both "Yoruba" and "Africa"). We must recall that Trinidad's African heritage is neither exclusively nor overwhelmingly Yoruba, though this cultural stream has been undeniably influential. Moreover, Yoruba-speaking peoples of West Africa never constituted a single political entity, nor did they refer to one another by a common name. Colonial nineteenth-century European missionaries adopted the term "Yoruba" as an overarching moniker based on a double loan translation. Originally a Muslim Hausa xenonym referring specifically to peoples of the Oyo state, it was later adopted by those same peoples as a term of self-reference. Application of Yoruba terminology by colonials and converts to designate a broad ethnolinguistic group inhabiting what is today southwest Nigeria therefore represents a further instance of semantic transposition (Peel 2000). Remember also that the cult of Shango was an integral feature of imperial Oyo, an avid slaving state that sent thousands of war captives into the Middle Passage. These historical realities sit uncomfortably beside the politics of postcolonial Afrocentrism; hence it is unsurprising that they are sidelined by a selective view of "Yoruba" tradition.[8]

Antisyncretic "Africanizing" trends and the politics of the Orisha Movement must be understood in terms of the racial ideology they seek to contest. Yet there is a profound way in which subverting colonial ideology also means allowing it to indirectly frame the terms of engagement. An antisyncretic politics espousing a camouflage view of syncretic incorporations at the level of popular practice may invert, yet also reinscribe, colonial imagery of the culturally naked African, pitting itself against the persisting subaltern Africanity of the grassroots tradition in terms of the latter's transculturating dynamism and less bourgeois orientation. Ironically, then, Afrocentric preoccupation with purity owes something to Eurocentric consciousness and Western models of legitimate religion. Most traditional devotees are not involved in these higher-level developments or politics; indeed, some are quite removed. When a devotee friend accompanied me in 2000 to several feast nights at the shrine of Iyalorisha Rodney, for example, he commented that he did not know much about her. In fact, he was much more concerned with the micro-details of ritual praxis at her feast than her top-down stature. I doubt he would have visited her yard had I not invited him to join me.

The development of more overtly Afrocentric approaches has entailed some decline of feasts as the center of spiritual attention. This is reflected in the diminished emphasis upon trance performance in newer types of ceremonial events and, more generally, as one moves up in socioeconomic status. The more Africanized feasts seem to appeal less to grassroots devotees, reflecting an identity politics that does not preoccupy them as much.

To return to Iyalorisha Rodney's feast: I was surprised by the low attendance despite her national stature. Several of those with whom I discussed the matter believed it was due to her shrine having come under the influence of the more activist-oriented and politically minded within the fold. Thus, it seems that the more one moves from Shango to Orisha, the more the religious field becomes gentrified, taking on increasingly bureaucratized features and bourgeois inflections as a sociopolitical entity and vehicle of postcolonial cultural politics.

One final occasion will suffice to close this discussion. It involves Iyalorisha Valerie "Amoye" Stephenson Lee Chee, Trinidad and Tobago's country representative to the World Orisha Congress at the time. Her shrine in Princes Town has been the sole innovator in bringing local forms of Egungun and Gelede masquerade into being. Iya Amoye delivered the annual sermon for the ceremonial opening of the law courts of TT in December of 2004, the first time any representative of Orisha religion had been granted the honor. Only fifteen years before, as part of the fierce debates over multiculturalism and state policies catalyzed by the NAR's victory in 1986, Hindu activists had criticized the historically dominant Christocentricity of the judicial system's annual ceremonial opening, pointing out that even though the "interfaith" services marking the formal opening of the law term included a Hindu pandit chanting mantras and a Muslim imam offering a prayer, the sermon had always been based on Christian scripture and had taken place in a Christian church (Ryan 1999:40).

The 2004 sermon by Iyalorisha Amoye included Yoruba prayers at the beginning and end (with English translations), reflected upon the spiritually and materially intertwined nature of human existence, and extolled the emphasis in Yoruba tradition upon *iwa pele*: the development of good and noble character. Moreover, Iya Amoye spoke of the orishas in order to reframe the symbolism of law. Most important in this regard is Obatala, characterized as the Divinity of Justice in the Yoruba pantheon, who rules the inner head upon which humans depend for wisdom, judgment, and discretion. To quote from her address:

> The symbol of Obatala is the Scale or the Instrument of Balance, which we notice is also the symbol of the Judiciary. Obatala's number is 8—the symbol of infinity and perfect balance—and Obatala is also described as "the Chief of the White Cloth," a color that symbolizes purity of thought and action. All matters relating to Law and the Courts come under his purview. Obatala's positive attributes are equality, fairness, wisdom, patience, serenity, tranquility, calmness, gentleness, temperance, and sobriety, indeed all the qualities that are supposed to come with old age. In all indigenous traditions, white hair is respected and revered. The Judge's wig is symbolic of white hair—the wisdom of the aged—the *ashé* (spiritual energy) of Obatala.

The sociohistorical significance of the sermon in this context is clear, emblematic of the social transformations and political accomplishments incrementally wrought by those in the vanguard of the Orisha Movement over the preceding three decades.

Yet one must also call attention to the cross weaving of symbolism—dare one call it syncretism?—at work in Iya Amoye's oratory. Not only are Yoruba prayers given in English in order to clarify their meaning, but the sacred symbolism of Obatala is also intertwined with that of the West Indian judiciary. The orisha's color, white, and the wig of the wise judge are poetically explicated in relation to one another. The address illustrates the powerful analogical processes that generate "hybrids" and "bricolage," somewhat ironically so here in having come from the mouth of an Afrocentric reformer. Their transformations proceed by charting conceptual paths through unrealized frontiers of social experience and cultural space. Historically independent sources of symbolism become layered and intertwined without being contradictory or losing their original referents. As Mintz observes, "the culture of a people is like a living fabric, and for those who weave it, origins matter less than the creative acts their behavior involves" (1974a:326).

Hindu Renaissance and the Failure of the National Maha Kali Shakti Temple Association

Having considered the legacy of Black Power for the evolution of the Orisha Movement, we turn now to Shakti Puja to query why Hindu revivalists have not similarly taken it up. This is a revealing fact, since *non*-politicization of Shakti Worship may also be understood in relation to the colonial ideology of racial subordination regarding the culturally saturated Indian, and its continuing influence on the postcolonial politics of alter-nationalist revitalization.

Yet this is an admittedly peculiar discussion, since I am analyzing something that did not happen. The question arose for me as an ethnographer as I contemplated the drastically different political fates each had undergone in the postcolonial era, despite their lateral subaltern histories of transculturation and structurally convergent patterns of practice. Why did Indocentrists turn a blind eye toward Shakti Puja while Afrocentrists so earnestly took up Shango as cause célèbre?

Put succinctly, some dimension of the internally subjugated local past was not taken up by postcolonial Indocentrists because Indians had been positioned as Oriental Outsiders in the colonial period—East not West Indians—and since Hinduism had, accordingly, long represented the quintessentially "Indian." Southern Caribbean Hinduism, as we have seen, had already been consolidated and standardized in counterpoint to sociopolitical threats from Christian evangelization, neo-Hindu missionaries, and the colonial state. Thus it operated as a recuperating vehicle of Indian identity *before* the independence period and ensuing onset of postcolonial multiculturalism. It entered the postcolonial era carrying considerable ideological weight and did not now need to claim any further subalternity in order to recuperate itself from within. Indeed, mainstream West Indian Hinduism has become deeply invested in its own alternative respectability vis-à-vis Christianity and the state. Championing a heterodox, "lower," practice would compromise this well-entrenched political posture.

Put otherwise, the figure of the culturally saturated Indian meant that creolization of Hinduism in the West Indies was culturally hypocognized, despite the fact that the construction of a gentrifying form of Sanatanist Hindu orthodoxy pitched in a conservative, "traditional" direction poignantly reflected its New World experience. Because colonial imagery framed Indo-Trinidadians as a sectarian minority within-but-outside the emergent nation, their social mobility and political recuperation has largely been constructed as a collective ethnic achievement, not the result of intermixture with Europeans. Meeting the colonial challenge meant carving out a socially "respectable" form of Hinduism that progressively gutted itself of "backward" popular practices. In this regard, though Hinduism and African religions have both historically suffered from colonial subjugation and Christian critique, they have nevertheless experienced quite different trajectories as diasporic streams adapting to the constraints and affordances of life in the West Indies.

Of course, this hardly means the machinations of Hinduism in the colonial and postcolonial periods are reducible to one another. The important point is that Hinduism had already taken shape as the essentially diasporic vehicle for "overseas" Indians in the colonial era. The politics of maintaining its viability meant establishing a respectable local orthodoxy, which translated into the progressive marginalization of more heterodox, ostensibly primitive, forms of ritual devotion such as fire walking, animal sacrifice, and trance performance. Though the advent of postcolonial multiculturalism has brought new twists and turns to this story, it has changed neither the class-inflected nature of cultural politics nor the dominating local weight of neotraditional Hindu orthodoxy and associated developments.

A small, formally educated, professionally oriented, Christian-identified group emerged in the years after indentureship to become the vanguard of modernization in the Indian sector. Not far behind, however, was the development of what Kelvin Singh (1996) calls an Indo-Trinidadian "traditional elite" led by Hindu and Muslim leaders. Under the influence of educated emissaries of Indian nationalism, and responding to encroachment by foreign Arya Samaj missionaries, a new sense of diasporic ethnic consciousness emerged after the 1920s, interestingly—and not unrelatedly—paralleling developments among Blacks and Coloreds. This, for example, motivated battles for the formal legitimation of Muslim and Hindu marriages, which were won, respectively, in the 1930s and 1940s.

From World War I to the debut of the PNM in 1956, both of Singh's so-called modernizing and traditionalizing elite groups focused almost exclusively upon primarily Indian matters. Indeed, overcoming intense racial stigma and status deprivation in colonial society prompted cooperation between these groups. In the mid-1940s, the issue of an English-only language test for the exercise of the franchise galvanized Indo-Trinidadians, intensifying a sense of ethnicity and related political struggle. Geographer Colin Clarke's (1986) study of Indians in San Fernando—Trinidad's "Second City" and the "Capital of South"—during the 1930–70 period points to the complexity of mid-century developments. Representing approximately one-quarter of the population of San Fernando, Indians of this era maintained various forms of what Clarke calls "social distance" from other groups despite residential integration.

Singh's traditional elite began coming into its own in the 1930s and became ascendant in local political culture after World War II. The revitalization of Hinduism was a central aim, culminating in a series of political and cultural developments by the 1950s, such as the establishment of the Sanatan Dharma Maha Sabha and an intense wave of school and temple building. Thus the vicissitudes of Hinduism have been anything but static, especially with decolonization and the nationalist struggle. In fact, Vertovec (1992) observes that Hinduism languished throughout the independence era, during which time Pentecostal and Evangelical Christian missionaries made significant inroads among Indians. Then came the national soul searching brought about by the turmoil of Black Power, which alarmed many Hindus and catalyzed an equally confrontational approach by Bhadase Sagan Maraj's Maha Sabha. His death in late 1971 intensified internal power struggles and stimulated factionalism among orthodox groups. On the eve of the oil boom, TT faced dire economic circumstances, which took a severe toll on rural Indians, the majority of whom were Hindus.

Yet, as we have seen, the boom catalyzed far-reaching changes. Most important is the fact that—relative to other groups—Indians experienced the most significant degree of overall mobility, spurring further class differentiation and heightening racial consciousness and political assertiveness in the wake of Black Power. Among the effects of newfound wealth generated by the oil boom were a revitalization of Indian ethnicity and an interrelated "Hindu Renaissance." Vertovec's study of postcolonial Hinduism in Trinidad surveys multifarious institutional and ritual changes and transformations wrought since the 1970s, from consolidation of the multipurpose *yagna* (devotional ritual observance), diversification of the common puja, and elaboration of more intimate satsang devotions to the increasing national prominence of Hindu holidays such as Divali, Nava Ratri, Holi (Phagwa), Shiv Ratri, and Kartik-ke-Nahan. More recent groups have also emerged and now compete, such as the Divine Life Society, Raja Yoga Movement, Sai Baba Satsang, the Hindu Prachar Kendra, and a spectrum of activist Hindu youth groups. The dramatically greater availability of Indian mass media such as Hindi popular music and Bollywood cinema, as well as chromolithographic imagery, has provided mass-mediated avenues of identification with the motherland, facilitating further revitalization. And though Hindu temple activities and ritual observances have maintained their communal symbolism and political significance, a trend toward individualism in devotions and ritual sponsorship has also emerged.

Though the oil boom created new forms of wealth facilitating Indian social mobility and bolstering political and cultural confidence, it was not until the aftermath of the National Alliance for Reconstruction that Indo-Trinidadians sought control of Parliament and the reins of state governance through their own United National Congress, led by former labor activist Basdeo Panday. After a reprise of the PNM in 1991, Panday became the country's first Indian prime minister at the turn of 1996. His early moves included establishing Indian Arrival Day and Spiritual Shouter Baptist Liberation Day as national holidays.

The 1990s also brought a wave of cultural and religious developments in conjunction with the rise of Indo-Trinidadian political power, such as the proliferation of "Indian" radio stations, the introduction of novel Hindu ritual forms such as *pichakaree* music and song competitions associated with religious observance of Phagwa (Holi), and establishment of the new Hindu pilgrimage of Ganga Dashara held in the northern mountain range Blanchisseuse River, which for the duration of the festival becomes ritually transformed into the sacred Ganges River of India. Particularly emblematic of this renaissance during my fieldwork was the holding of Pooja 2000—also known as Millennium Pooja—in the southern town of Debe, in late January of 2000, honoring the dawning of the twenty-first century. It was staged by the Sanatan Dharma Maha Sabha, attended by Prime Minister Panday, President Robinson, and other important political and religious personages and attracted considerable media coverage. Debe is located in the Oropouche political constituency, which—it was noted by Agriculture Minister Trevor Sudama, its parliamentary representative—is home to the largest number of Hindu temples in all of Trinidad. Female devotees predominated under the puja tents and were involved in activities on the main stage and throughout the recreation grounds more generally in terms of organizational and logistical matters.

Temple and school groups simultaneously conducted 108 Hanuman Pujas, led by one main puja on center stage, which was broadcast over loudspeakers. Doing Hanuman Pujas with red jhandis—the color of victory—was a way of starting off the new year and millennium "victoriously." The event foregrounded a decidedly orthodox deity in an entirely nonecstatic fashion, with each puja group seated around its respective bedi altar, and with mainstream pandits at the helm. Hanuman has experienced renewed prominence in India as well, in association with the rise of Hindu nationalism; thus his centrality in Pooja 2000 is significant. At one point during the proceedings, the entire crowd was led in the singing of the "Shri Hanuman Chalisa," the standard Hindi devotional song associated with the deity, also sung during pujas for him in heterodox Kali temples throughout the island. As delineated in chapter 4, Hanuman has in fact recently been charismatically apotheosized as a deota that manifests ecstatically during Shakti Puja services. Hanuman's contemporary importance therefore spans the orthodox to the heterodox within the local West Indian Hindu imagination.

A fellow passing out brochures with whom I spoke made reference to the "Hindu resurgence" taking place. "We are not ashamed of ourselves in a plural society anymore like twenty years ago," he observed. The booklets, entitled *Hinduism: 100 Questions and Answers,* had been printed by the Shakti Sangha, the "Women's Arm of the Maha Sabha." The booklet's foreword, authored by secretary-general of the Maha Sabha, Satnarayan Maharaj, emphasized the "revival of Dharma" currently at work in Trinidad and Tobago.

Pooja 2000 began onstage with a prayer from the now former *Dharmach-ari*—"the Spiritual Head of the Hindu Community"—Pandit Krishna Maharaj, also a noteworthy oil and building contractor. President-general of the Maha Sabha, Thirbhawan Seegobin, then noted the auspiciousness of the day's event being held contemporaneously with Khumba Mela in India. Debe that day was a *tirtha*—spiritual threshold—connected with a "resurgence of divine spirituality." Sat Maharaj's ensuing oratory offered more exegesis of the event.

After the round of collective Hanuman Pujas was completed, jhandis from all of the respective group ceremonies were brought to the main stage and hailed before being taken across the road to the Maha Sabha–affiliated school grounds for planting. Sat Maharaj observed that they could not be planted on public property—Pooja 2000 was carried out at the civic Debe recreation grounds—noting, however, that "I wish we could plant them here!" He then introduced the president, prime minister, and leader of the opposition, commenting that their presence there together "demonstrated ancient civilities in modern Trinidad." As non-Indians, Robinson and Manning adopted secular stances, emphasizing how the event represented a gorgeous tile in TT's efflorescing mosaic constitution; Panday and Sudama each focused upon the day's religious content, drawing upon this symbolism to also speak of multiculturalism and strength in diversity. Panday's "Millennium Message" concluded: "Let us take a pledge for greater clarity and understanding for one another. Our nation needs loyalty more than ever. We must look to Hanuman's example. Let us think of the nation as Lord Rama and we the citizens as Hanuman, as devotees of the nation." He ended by chanting the "Hanuman Chalisa."

Hinduism, then, has been taken up as a political vehicle in public culture. Sponsored by the Maha Sabha, Pooja 2000 foregrounded the most respectable local form of Hinduism, in which any hint of subaltern heterodox Hindu practice was decidedly absent. The significance of this pattern is clear when we consider that any analogously high-profile celebration of African religion would necessarily make recourse to the commemoration and recuperation of the subaltern ecstatic spiritism of Shango. The nonpoliticization of ecstatic Shakti Puja by Indocentrists and Hindu revivalists may be differently grasped by considering the failed attempt at forging a National Maha Kali Shakti Temple Association in the mid-1990s on the inaugural occasion of Indian Arrival Day. With the Hindu Renaissance at the forefront of rising Indian consciousness and political power into the 1990s, the establishment of Indian Arrival Day in 1995–96 represented a sort of climax in terms of the politics of national culture. The holiday stimulated widespread enthusiasm and solidarity among Indo-Trinidadians, and considerable national support. These sentiments were also alive and well in Shakti temples.

Indeed, Pujari Krishna Angad of Chase Village even tried to establish a coalition of mandirs into one unified National Maha Kali Temple Association of Trinidad and Tobago. His efforts were prompted by the fervor around Indian Arrival Day but strove beyond it toward an enduring organization representing the interests of Shakti Worshippers at large. One of the earliest memories I have of his temple comes from my first visit, when I stumbled upon a big, old, four-door Oldsmobile parked outside and painted in the red, white, and yellow colors prominent in local Shakti Puja. It had been painted for the inaugural Arrival Day parade. A scattered contingent of folks from several temples, carrying a large sign with lightbulb-festooned scaffolding spelling out the letters U N C, materialized in order to support the event.

However, this move to confederate as one institutional body was short-lived. For one thing, there is considerable factionalism among Shakti temples; thus collective representation is already challenging. Yet it is also important to appreciate the lack of national appetite among Hindus more broadly for an open and explicit Shakti Temple Association. Pujari Angad and others noted that their reception within the Hindu community in this regard has hardly been warm. Their approach challenges the boundaries of respectable Sanatanist orthodoxy and other, similarly spirited, neo-Hindu approaches, all of which look askance at the practices connected with ecstatic Shakti Puja. Hinduism does the ideological work it does within the politics of national culture, in other words, because it has been wrought in a way that takes Christianity as moral barometer, even while contesting it.

Further illustrating these trends, while showing they are also neither simple nor linear, is the only orthodox local mandir that houses a prominent murti of Kali. It represents an important exception to the characterization developed earlier about Kali Puja being primarily a grassroots phenomenon, since Paschim Kaschi (literally, "West of Kaschi," the sacred city of Varanasi, in India)—located in St. James, Port-of-Spain—is not only orthodox, but also an elite temple. It is therefore an "exception" that does not simply prove the rule, but that might better be seen as manifesting the rule with a twist.

The St. James Hindu Mandir did not originate as a Kali temple, though it now conducts an annual, resolutely antiecstatic Kali Puja at the end of each calendar year. The impressive black marble murti of Mother Kali was imported from Jaipur, India, and installed in its own private sanctuary in 1991, made possible by the benefaction of Simboonath and Indradai Capildeo. Although Mr. Capildeo passed away just before the arrival and installation of the murti, Mrs. Capildeo—family matriarch and a longtime celibate *yogin*, as she refers to herself—had an intense visionary experience at the temple in 1996, in which she fell unconscious for a short time one night during a service being given by a visiting Indian swami and saw Lord Shiva and Mother Kali, her "parents." The experience was considered miraculous and received notable attention in the media.

Figure 6.3. Orthodox Kali Puja at the St. James Hindu temple. Photo by author.

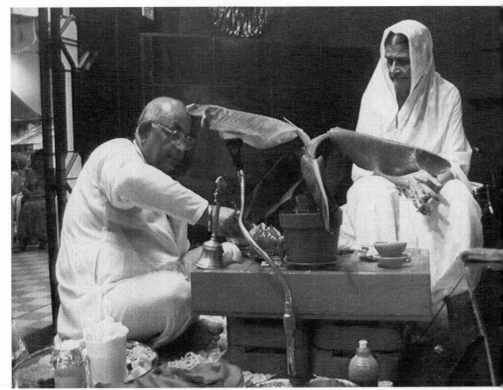

Figure 6.4. The presiding pandit enacts the puja on the bedi next to the St. James Hindu Temple's black marble murti of Kali. Photo by author.

This clear exception to the general profile of contemporary Kali Worship is significant because it concerns the observance of Shakti Puja at a more respectable temple patronized by Hindus of a much higher social echelon and because it reflects a reiterated dialectic of transgression and conformity animating the more popular form of Shakti Worship. Kali Puja at this temple is decidedly *non-ecstatic*, aside, that is, from Mrs. Capildeo's own idiosyncratic visionary experience, and Kali's murti is housed in its own separate, typically locked, mandir structure. Moreover, Mrs. Capildeo and others have observed a relative decline in attendance at temple services and in the number of marriages conducted at the temple since Kali's icon was installed. Thus an ostensibly wayward Hindu deity has become lionized in an orthodox temple, which has in turn pushed it a bit off the more beaten elite path, despite the fact that there is hardly a trace of popular mysticism involved.

The Capildeos took up Kali in a relatively unsympathetic environment for complex reasons—not through any association with local traditions of temple-based ecstatic Shakti Puja, but through their global connections with India supported by their wealth and resources. Kali's reputation in India is not the same as in the Caribbean. Indeed, she even became something of a counter-colonial symbol, especially among Bengali intellectuals and nationalists of yes-teryear. Kali's materialization at the St. James Hindu Mandir therefore shows how complex are the roots and routes of glocal divinities. Whether her two incarnations—an idiosyncratic elite temple iteration or her more pervasive role as a grassroots dominatrix in ecstatic puja—will meet in the future is uncertain but probably doubtful because of the cultural politics elaborated here. Media coverage of one or the other is, revealingly, always separate.

One final case that helps to flesh out these structural contours and patterns of practice concerns Krishna Singh (a pseudonym), since his story encompasses the overarching class-inflected dynamic I am highlighting here. Singh was not raised within the practice but hails from relatively modest roots and held an orthodox view of Kali Worship before coming to it through marriage. His first wife was involved at the Moonsammy temple, and he began to appreciate the enigmatic depth of ecstatic puja through her; he subsequently grew in his own personal devotions. He sometimes experienced baseline vibrations, but these never developed into serious shakti play, much less individuated mediumship for any of the deotas. This continued for some time. At some point, however, dissonance at the temple and conflict with his wife arose, and they eventually split.

Years later—through circuitous research connections—I found myself across his desk at a business research firm associated with the university. He sported a business suit and acted with confidence and grace. He explained how his time at the Moonsammy temple had to end, as he was a "professional" and could not "spend hours and hours or even a whole day" doing puja and prayers. Now he could only afford *one* hour between 7:30 and 8:30 a.m. each Sunday morning for his Kali devotions, conducted at the St. James Hindu Mandir, where he was af-filiated with Mrs. Capildeo. He no longer frequented heterodox temples "at all, at all, at all" (meaning not at all). Mr. Singh repeatedly emphasized that he and his then-fiancée were "professionals" and that he now sought most information about Kali through the Internet.

This story embodies several important dynamics. Singh was brought into the popular local fold of ecstatic Shakti Puja through personal connections and cultivated some degree of devotion within that context. Yet he was also socially mobile, with increasingly professional identifications. Thus it is not surprising he fell out with the shakti mandir and then turned his sights upon the only locally available orthodox temple with a commitment to Kali Puja. That this latter practice was nonecstatic and carried out by a pandit—not a pujari—in an elite Hindu temple is not coincidental to Krishna's life experience. Having a "respectable" temple such as Paschim Kaschi for his recalibrated devotions represents an important compromise, since their observance within the St. James Hindu Mandir allowed him to pursue a profession without giving up Kali Ma, whom he spoke about affectionately.

My argument here is that the framing of Indians and Hinduism as always already East rather than West Indian—an ideology premised upon racialized colonial imagery—has meant that postcolonial assertion of Indo-creole power has not involved itself in the recuperation of lower-status "folk" ritual practices such as trance performance or fire walking. Since Hinduism has always been diasporic in the southern Caribbean, in other words, its revitalization has not looked to the periphery within itself for vehicles of authenticity and self-rediscovery.

Munasinghe's (2001a, 2001b) historical ethnography of Indians in Trinidad explores how they have become creolized—understood in the analytical sense (see Appendix)—while overtly rejecting the explicit identity of "Creole." They have sought to reconcile themselves vis-à-vis the nation by redefining the notion of "Trinidadian" more than that of "Indian," thus in an important sense tacitly reproducing colonial racial ideology rather than transcending it. Similarly, Khan exposes the postcolonial multiethnic state—in which the notion of "mixture" constitutes an ideological good—as a space in which "the boundaries of orthodoxy can safeguard a political constituency and yet veer dangerously close to being 'racial' (racist); on the other hand, the ambiguities of heterodoxy and syncretism ideologically resonate well with the callaloo nation, but ostensibly jeopardize group cohesion" (2004:13). Thus Trinbagonians of Indian descent continue to struggle with the colonial heritage of race and nationalist ideologies of creolization in the postcolonial era in ways that necessarily implicate the cultural politics of religion.

Religion and the Alter-Nationalist Politics of Diaspora

I have considered why two subaltern traditions of popular mysticism, which converged structurally at the grassroots level over the course of more than 150 years, have nonetheless been subject to such different political fates in TT's postcolonial era. My analysis of colonial ideologies of racial subordination in chapter 2 illustrates their influence on religious institutions and cultural politics over the longue durée. Here I have extended that analysis by showing how the logics of these racializing mythologies have not simply conditioned the postcolonial horizon of subsequent religious transformations in general, but have differentially motivated the politics of ecstatic traditions in particular. These ideologies have been transformed by change and crisis, such as decolonization and political independence, giving rise to a succession of challenges to the formerly dominant Creole nationalism of the People's National Movement. It is difficult to precisely date the onset of Trinidad and Tobago's era of postcolonial multiculturalism, but it had certainly materialized by the 1980s.

On the African side, activists and leaders concerned with the subjugation of popular Afro-creole ritual forms took up Shango in relation to the state and public culture, a process characterized by class and ideological conflict. One may only understand why Afrocentrists building an Orisha Movement upon the grassroots shoulders of Shango adopted such a strong antisyncretic position vis-à-vis Christianisms by clarifying the religious implications of the colonial ideology of the culturally naked African they were contesting. This imagery postulated the supposedly civilizationless African as receptacle for Eurocentric acculturation, in which Blacks were compelled to identify with Christianity and adopt respectable ways if they were to "uplift" themselves within the colonial order. African religious forms such as Shango were seen as persisting "holdovers" or survivals that would eventually fade away with progressive black acculturation to colonial institutions and Christian civilization.

Yet it is helpful to remember that, during the interwar period, when Garveyism took hold throughout the hemisphere, black nationalists were *neither* especially critical of Christianity *nor* did they adopt an antisyncretic position on Afro-Christian bricolage. Colonial Ethiopianism of the second quarter of the twentieth century instead sought to blacken or Africanize Christianity. It was not until the postcolonial period—with the dawning of Black Power and the ascent of Yoruba as the privileged Afrocentric paradigm—that an antisyncretic posture took hold, during a time when Creole nationalism's shortcomings became increasingly apparent. The "Afro-Saxon" state was criticized for the "false consciousness" it promulgated. Only by dispensing with Christian identification and Eurocentric norms could a more authentic blackness be forged. For activists, this has meant the "de-Christianization" of Orisha Worship accompanied by a corollary "re-Africanization" of the practice.

Thus postcolonial contestation of the colonial legacy rebuts imagery of the culturally naked African by inverting the hierarchical relationship of Christianity and African religion, rather than by seeing Christianisms and the incorporation of other "foreign" influences into the sphere of Orisha Worship as signs of how culturally African the practice may in fact be. Espousing an antisyncretically oriented camouflage view of Afro-Christian hybridity has meant that colonial ideology continues to recursively condition politics by framing the underlying debate through a degree of separation. If racial mythology posited a culturally naked African with no choice but to clothe himself in Christianity, the postcolonial Afrocentric position inverts the relationship by demoting Christianity and idealizing Africanity. Yet in doing so, Afrocentrists, preoccupied with purity, policing the new boundaries of heterodoxy, and playing by the rules of the liberal capitalist state, have, ironically, adopted a rather Eurocentric model of what makes for a legitimate or authentic religion.

Indocentric activists and revivalists on the Hindu side, by contrast, have not similarly taken up Shakti Puja. Yet this pattern of nonpoliticization within Indo-Caribbean culture must also be understood in relation to the reiterating effects of the colonial ideology of the culturally saturated East Indian in the postcolonial era. Trinidadians of South Asian descent were first positioned as Outsiders to the colony and the early postcolony in turn, and Hinduism has long been taken to be the quintessential Oriental religion, always already diasporic. Though it took awhile to reconstitute and legitimate itself, Hinduism became an increasingly important token of Indian ethnicity and locus of Indocentric assertion in the twentieth century. So, even though it has come to see itself as a bulwark against Christian hegemony, the development of a "mainstream" Hindu orthodoxy has nonetheless involved coming of age within a society saturated by colonial ideology and Eurocentric institutions.

Given the cultural logics and historical forces at work, West Indian Hinduism has therefore incorporated values and biases that take the colonial matrix of respectability as their frame of reference. In order to authenticate their religion, orthodox leaders and their constituencies have sought to "modernize" and purify Hinduism of the more "primitive" aspects of the Indian past, such as animal sacrifice, fire pass, and trance performance. This process had developed considerable momentum by the late colonial period and continues to influence the field of Hindu cultural politics in the postcolonial era. The advent of modern Shakti temples therefore stimulated neither enthusiasm nor support within the national Hindu community at large, making the formation of a National Maha Kali Temple Association a lost cause. Indeed, many find it inscrutable that such "backward" practices continue to flourish among the proletarian and lower classes at all.

Unlike the logic of the culturally naked African—which influences the postcolonial scene in a roundabout way via contested inversion by Afrocentrists—colonial mythology of the culturally saturated Indian continues to more straightforwardly condition the political culture of Hinduism from within as well as without. This means ongoing reification of a respectable (Indo-Trinidadian)

Hinduism on par with (Afro-creole) Christianity, harboring no effort to recuperate any subjugated "folk" practice from within as a vehicle of Indocentric assertion. Revitalization precipitated by the country's oil boom has therefore largely proceeded through intensified diasporic identification with Mother India.

Having now invoked the notion of "diaspora" variously throughout my discussion, I want to clarify two interrelated levels of analysis at work here. Both African and Indian peoples and cultures in the Caribbean are typically seen as diasporic in that they are not indigenous and understand themselves as having historical, cultural, or racial connections with respective homelands abroad. In this regard, my study may be seen as a comparative historical ethnography of diasporic spirits and their transculturation in the southern Caribbean. Their "geopiety" (Tweed 1997) is translocal. Yet "diasporic" consciousness among globally dispersed populations fluctuates in relation to a host of factors. Thus— akin to "syncretism" and "creolization" (see Appendix)—"diaspora" is more of an analytical starting point than an ending point. We must always strive for clarity about how it is being employed.

The present chapter concerns the differential politicization of religions in relation to colonial ideologies and their reiterating effects within the evolving matrix of postcolonial multiculturalism. Ideologies of the culturally naked African versus culturally saturated Indian figure profoundly in the colonial and postcolonial politics of religion, because the African and Indian diasporas have been racialized from the beginning and because religion constitutes a translocal source of imagination and identification and has also been taken up in various ways as a vehicle of ethnic revitalization and political assertion. Thus I am concerned here with ritual evolution and religious transformations within African and Indian diasporic populations at the grassroots level in addition to the ways they gain differential attention as vehicles of a more self-conscious and assertive political voice.

Rogers Brubaker (2005) cautions that scholars and activists alike have become mired in an overly zealous and counterproductive "'diaspora' diaspora," in which the term has become a gloss for almost any sort of experience involving translocal dispersion. "The problem with this latitudinarian, 'let-a-thousand-diasporas-bloom' approach," he writes, "is that the category becomes stretched to the point of uselessness. If everyone is diasporic, then no one is distinctively so. The term loses its discriminating power—its ability to pick out phenomena, to make distinctions. The universalization of diaspora, paradoxically, means the disappearance of diaspora" (3). Thus Brubaker identifies three core conditions as the organizing principles of diaspora as an idiom, stance, claim, or practice: translocal dispersion; some sort of homeland orientation, however symbolic or imagined; and group boundary maintenance vis-à-vis the host context over time. Khachig Tölölyan (1996:19) observes that it is, indeed, often only a small minority of a population that consistently adopts a forthrightly diasporic stance.

This means not taking for granted the identifications or politics of any group in the West Indies. Patterns and degrees of "diasporic" consciousness fluctuate in relation to sociohistorical circumstances. Religion may or may not be taken up within the cultural politics of ethnicity and diaspora, but it does seem to be an especially potent vehicle for the articulation of diasporic identity by postulating omnipotent powers and translocal imaginaries. In Trinidad and Tobago, religion has taken up some political slack in relation to the shortcomings and contradictions of "race" in the context of an ongoing crisis in the nationalist project.[9]

One interesting outcome of this permutating dialectic of diasporic identifications and politics pertinent to this study is the fact that the initial wave of postcolonial Shakti temples established in the late 1970s was conceived by their founders as Madrassi revitalization. I think this development stems as much from the recent experience of Black Power—in which the subjugated, "darker" racial identity within was reclaimed and recuperated—as from the socioeconomic boost of the oil boom, whose time-released effects led to an Indian Renaissance and upsurge of Hindu revitalization. Indeed, it is not incidental that the first two modern Kali mandirs were established quite close to the University of the West Indies, where much of the fervor for Black Power arose and filtered out into society. Thus the evolving logics of racial politics on each side of the ethnic spectrum also influence one another.

Madrassis had long been marginalized as racially inferior within the Indo-creole community. Thus there was better precedent for reclaiming subaltern identity through the recuperation of ritual practices seen as quintessentially Madrassi in relation to the newly circulating currents of Afrocentrism than in the longer-standing politics of Indian revitalization. Of course, as we have seen, the constellation of practices that amalgamated as Kali Puja were hardly Madrassi in any simple sense, and the Madrassocentric posture progressively lost its initial impetus, though the two original temples in the southern St. Augustine areas of Pasea and Streatham Lodge nonetheless still maintain a much stronger degree of Madrassi identification than all the others. I know an assistant pujari, for example, who has reinterpreted his own north Indian background in progressively Madrassocentric terms as a result of his intimate association with the Maha Kali Devi Mandir in Pasea.

Local diasporic dynamics therefore unfold in relation to one another in a complex hall of mirrors. The chair of the Council of Orisha Elders claimed that "we want arrival—like Indian Arrival Day" at the second annual convention of the Orisha Movement in 1999, as noted above. This was several years after the official establishment of Indian Arrival Day by the newly elected UNC government headed by Prime Minister Panday in the context of concurrent debate over Spiritual Baptist Shouters Liberation Day. The fact that the national liturgical cycle has been hammered out in relation to both African and Indian commemorations evidences the degree to which the cultural politics of ethnicity and diaspora play out recursively.

These considerations lead me to concur with James Clifford (1994), who argues that late-modern "diaspora" offers ready-made resources for postcolonialisms. Enabled by global capitalism and the multiculturalist politics of late-modern nation-states, diasporic projects provide alternative counternationalisms in contexts characterized by the crises and contradictions of nationalism in the wake of decolonization. Similarly, Rogers Brubaker (2005) identifies the nation-state and diaspora as alter-egos. Thus, even though diasporas are taken up as alternatives to nationalist essentializations of belonging, they may also represent an ostensibly deterritorialized form of reessentialized belonging characterized by corollary politics of inclusion-exclusion as well as tensions between utopia and dystopia. Intended to counter the nationalist project, late-modern diasporas have nonetheless increasingly developed a teleological language of "awakening," echoing the nationalist ideologies they ostensibly contest (13). Indeed, diasporic alter-nationalisms are conditioned by local politics and subject to the inequalities and tensions of class stratification.

One last example that brings this discussion around full circle is the heated controversy over membership of Orisha Religion in Trinidad and Tobago's Inter-Religious Organization (IRO), which erupted into public consciousness toward the end of 2000. The IRO is a government-supported ecumenical coalition founded in the early 1970s by leaders of the orthodox Catholic, Anglican, Hindu, and Muslim communities. The IRO claims to represent the interests of various religious bodies in relation to the state and orchestrates multifaith ritual management of the ceremonial functions of statecraft, such as the formal opening of Parliament or the Judiciary. Various groups—including Spiritual Baptists—were admitted to the IRO later, after it was founded. Yet at the turn of the twenty-first century, a representative of Orisha had not yet been integrated into the by-then sixteen-member umbrella organization.

So in September of 2000, during celebration of Utsav in honor of Lord Ganesha, the Maha Sabha organized leaders from several organizations in a demonstration of "Non-Christian Unity." Secretary-General Satnarayan Maharaj threatened Maha Sabha withdrawal from the IRO in order to form its own separate "ecumenical" organization if representatives from the Orisha and Ahmadiyya (heterodox Muslim) faiths were not promptly admitted into the IRO. Babalorisha Sam Phills—then chair of the Council of Elders—and Pearl Eintou Springer were in attendance, expressing appreciation and support on behalf of the Orisha Movement. Soon thereafter, Sat Maharaj and Ms. Springer appeared together on one of the main local morning television programs, making the case for more inclusive membership and rebutting the IRO's excuses for delay. After subsequent negotiations, the Orisha Movement was finally accepted into the organization in 2001, which paved the way for Iyalorisha Amoye's sermon for the opening of the law courts in 2004, discussed above.

What I most want to emphasize here is that the Maha Sabha and the Orisha Movement allied with one another in order to leverage their respective power, which reflects the class-inflected postcolonial politics of diasporic religion addressed throughout this chapter. Consider that the Orisha Movement—which champions the cause of popular Afro-creole ecstasy—teamed up with the most orthodox national Hindu organization, one which maintains a resolutely biased posture against any form of ecstatic Hinduism analogous to grassroots Shango. This alliance makes sense in terms of the increasingly convoluted and contested multiculturalist logic of postcolonial politics, yet also embodies the complex intertwining of racial and class stratification in religious forms that has so profoundly influenced the respective historical trajectories and political fates of Orisha Worship and Shakti Puja, the combined focus of this comparative study.

Epilogue

Ecstasy in Exile

Part of being modern is wishing to be otherwise.

Thomas de Zengotita, "Speakers of Being"

Trance and Modernity in the Southern Caribbean

It was only late in the twentieth century that anthropology became less trans-fixed by tribal, ancestral, small-scale, and other localizing religious expressions (Hefner 1998). Flickers of activity beyond this purview emerged after World War II, with interest in translocal "world" religions—the so-called Great Traditions—yet the center of gravity nonetheless remained Little. Things finally changed by the 1980s, with renewed interest in the history and genealogy of culture generating attention to complex civilizations and the proliferating realities of global culture. Budding interest in globalization brought fresh awareness of translocal religious forms and the political economies in which they operate.

Efforts to document and analyze religion in the "global ecumene" (Hannerz 1992a, 1992b, 1996) proceed within the context of an unfolding crisis in secularism, however. Western science and social theory have seen religion as a declining historical force since the nineteenth century. Premised upon an idealized model of the West as prototype for modernization, secularization theory emphasized the disenchanting influence of scientific rationality and secular reason on religion's demise, the dominating and ostensibly marginalizing influence of institutions such as the market and the state, and the rationalizing effects of intensified pluralization of the life-world, inhibiting attempts to project over-arching symbolism or sentiment into public culture (Hefner 1998:85–86).

Yet mainstream secularization theory accounts inadequately for the vicis-situdes of religion in the West. Indeed, vibrant new religious forms emerged throughout the "modern" North Atlantic. Methodism provided opportunities otherwise unavailable in proletarian Britain, for example, promoting emotive piety while also instilling a sense of self-control suited to the demands of an ascendant industrial order (E. Thompson 1963). Disestablishment of a state church in the United States paved the way not for the decline of religion, but for freewheeling competition and lively sectarianism especially benefiting populist groups such as Baptists and, later, Pentecostals. Catholic and Jewish emigration from Europe may have undermined Protestant hegemony, but this encouraged more religious freedom, not less. And now, in a neoliberal era of "remarketized capitalism" (Fulcher 2004), varieties of both Protestantism and Catholicism have in turn become "deprivatized" (Casanova 1994), challenging deeply held Western assumptions about the role of secularism in modernity.

It is also now clear that secularization theory oversimplified not only the fate of religion in the "West" itself, but also that of the West's ostensibly premodern "Other(s)." Robert Hefner (1998) concludes that all religions confront similar predicaments and structural dilemmas in the late-modern period, but that their patterns of response and transformation reflect the resources and experiences each brings to its encounter with modernity and struggles for influence among competing interpreters. The so-called Clash of Civilizations is not so much be-tween the West and the Rest as among rival carriers of tradition within nations and civilizations. Globalization of religion is characterized by dilemmas over-determined by a world of nation-states, mass urbanization, capitalist differen-tiation, migration and displacement, and proliferating technologies that render social borders permeable to transcultural flows and interconnections. Contem-porary religious refigurations thrive by drawing themselves into mass society, generating an intensified and contested dialectic between homogenization and heterogenization. All of which compels reconsideration of conventional wis-dom regarding the progressivist teleological narrative of secularization as yet another "North Atlantic fiction" (Trouillot 2003), concepts projecting Western experience on a universal scale.[1]

This is why the precocious modernity of the Caribbean is so critical, con-founding the West-and-the-Rest dichotomy by being *both* well before this dis-tinction had fully materialized. Grappling with inadequacies stemming from an idealized model of the West as the prototype for modernization, in other words, not only means serious engagement with the West's many Others—the traditional charge of anthropology—but also *de*-idealization of the West itself, for which the Caribbean—the First World's first world—is so instructive. World religions take on striking reformulations throughout the region. New racially inflected forms of West Indian Islam coexist as alternative geopieties within the Sunni Umma (Khan 2004), with late-twentieth-century inroads by Shii missionaries from Canada (Korom 2003). Varieties of Christianity compete with each other and replicate themselves in ways both similar to and different from their metropolitan counterparts and find themselves subject to a kaleidoscopic range of creolizing reconfigurations spanning the gamut from Afro-Catholic syncretism to Afro-Protestant reinterpretation. "Great" West African religious traditions have become "Little" while also globalizing their reach, forging diasporic innovations in black spirituality. They have also done U-turns, generating novel transatlantic conversations and spheres of influence (see, e.g., Matory 2005 on Brazil-Nigeria interconnections) and continue to take new diasporic twists and turns (see, e.g., P. Johnson 2007 on triply diasporic "Black Carib" religion). Despite earlier inclusion in the Eurocentric category of "World Religion" (see Masuzawa 2005), Hinduism has taken on a truly global reach only as a result of modern labor migration and capitalist transculturation (Younger 2010).

And last, but not least, a small but significant indigenous resurgence has taken place in turn-of-the-twenty-first-century Trinidad among Santa Rosa "Caribs," who cannot be distinguished physically from their neighbors, whose ancestry is tied to their Spanish surnames, and many of whose rituals have been borrowed from groups in Central and North America (Forte 2005). Since native Antillean populations are supposed to have disappeared early in the colonial era, this is cultural "reengineering" in unlikely territory, or so one might think.

As the West's original alter-native, conjured yet disavowed in Europe's backyard-on-the-colonial-frontier, the Caribbean reminds us that modernity never was—and never could be—what it claims (Trouillot 2003). The fact that seemingly primitive practices based on popular forms of ecstasy have neither declined nor disappeared in the shadow of modernity surely drives another nail in the coffin of secularization theory. Indeed, as subaltern archetype for the historical anthropology of modernity, the Caribbean may even offer a sort of crystal ball regarding the future of religion under the sign of the modern. Spiritism has not disappeared. It's taken cover.

Even Caribbeanists predicted the decline of subaltern regional spiritisms in an earlier intellectual era (e.g., Jayawardena 1966 on Shakti Puja in Guyana; F. Henry 1983 on Shango in Trinidad). Such infelicitous soothsaying must give us pause. For Shango has not only survived and continued to evolve at the popular level, it has also been taken up by an Afrocentric postcolonial movement bringing new consciousness of "Orisha" in an effort to forge alternative forms of black selfhood. Shakti Worship in Guyana underwent its own revitalization and was also transported to Trinidad, catalyzing an innovative new temple dispensation that embodies the hybridizing confluence of several colonial precursors. Orthodox Indo-Trinidadian Hinduism has hardly embraced Shakti Puja, and yet it too continues to flourish in a subordinate position.

My comparative historical ethnography of Orisha Worship and Shakti Puja in the southern Caribbean shows how they have each undergone both "globalization" and "modernization." Though practices of shamanism and mediumship likely represent the most archaic of human religious experience, this does not make them mere "survivals" of an earlier, less evolved, age. On the contrary, I have shown how West African and South Asian forms of ecstasy adapted to the perverse vicissitudes of the colonial Atlantic system by facing the challenges of transoceanic transfer and resiliently reconstituting themselves within the radically different context of the "New World." I have not only charted the respective genealogies of each tradition, but have also examined patterns of structural convergence and subaltern liberalization experienced by both as a result of lateral adaptation to a shared colonial environment. These processes involved considerable creativity, sacrifice, and accommodation along the way, only some of which are we able to approximate after the fact. Each stream of popular ecstatic mysticism has come to occupy a similar structural position relative to the otherwise divergent Afrocentric and Indocentric postcolonial politics of multiculturalism and diaspora in Trinidad and Tobago.

In this regard, it helps to recall Bourguignon et al.'s central insight that the ritualization of trance as alter-cultural praxis is ubiquitous in human experience (see chapter 1). Over 90 percent of their sample of 488 societies practiced some version of institutionalized dissociation, suggesting that those without such forms are the *exception* rather than the rule, thus presenting the more perplexing puzzle for anthropology! We are dealing with a transculturally vibrant human capacity for playfulness, which finds multifarious expression across space and through time (McNeal Forthcoming b). Practices of ecstasy change in order to be meaningful and responsive to the needs and desires of practitioners. Rather than disenchantment of the world and the disappearance of spirits, we confront the modern proliferation of ecstatic spiritisms (cf. Luig and Behrend 1999 on Africa; Chestnut 2003 on Latin America; Fjelstad and Thi Hien 2006 on Vietnam). Spirits and their adepts are part of global and local cultures, whether their cults be radical or conservative, and whether or not they conceive of themselves as "modern."

Spirits and Transculturation

As arenas of alter-cultural praxis, ecstatic ritual forms reveal areas of deep concern, stress, or ambivalence within society, encompassing a complex mix of opposition and accommodation to cultural norms and conventional sentiments. Their ubiquity is therefore revealing. We have seen how trance-based alter-cultural praxis is highly responsive to patterns of social and cultural change. Recall that the concept of "trance" derives from a Latin root *trans* whose intransitive form means "to pass" or "to go from one condition or state to another," as well as "to cross" or "to go through" something. The transitive form expresses even more the meaning of "to go through" or "to cross over" when speaking of time, place, or condition. This etymological awareness helps us better appreciate the "passage" of history in the cultural experience of trance at both micro- and macrolevels.

I have shown how the ecstatic spirit idiom may operate in terms of personal devotion and transformation as well as a locus of cultural interaction and ritual change at the popular level. I identify the liberalizing spirit idiom itself as a vehicle of transculturation, highlighting the "trans" in trance. My approach has been to examine the transculturating histories of subaltern spirit practices and ecstatic pantheons in order also to broach larger questions concerning modernity and the globalization of religion. We have seen how innovation and change have been afforded by synergy between processes of subaltern liberalization and popular contact with the sacred in an underbelly of the global village. One is reminded of the "laissez-faire attitude toward truth" (M. Brown 1997:44) in late-twentieth-century North American New Age channeling, only it developed much earlier within subaltern West Indian spiritisms.

Yet I utilize the notion of "transculturation" for reasons extending well beyond the sense of "trance-culturation" per se, referring to several dimensions of social action and cultural change concurrently: (a) cultural behavior and social practice through time, that is, the temporal dimension of transculturation; (b) the transfer and reproduction of cultural knowledge and social institutions across space, that is, the translocal dimension; and (c) the original sense proposed by Fernando Ortiz (1947) concerning sociocultural interpenetration and recursive processes of deculturation and neoculturation. For me, "transculturation" better serves scholarship than do "creolization," "syncretism," or "hybridity" (also see Coronil 1995, 2005; Bolland 2005), since it may be framed as more than sociocultural mixture alone and retains in a less reified form the kernel of anthropological insight originally captured by the concept of "culture." Poststructuralist and related critiques of the culture concept prompt not only a nuanced distributive approach to cultural knowledge and action, but also a renewed theorization of the human being (Shore 1996, 2000).

Although it never quite caught on, Ortiz (1947:102–3) introduced the neologism *transculturation* as an alternative to *acculturation* as an assimilationist paradigm, which—ironically, since it was never intended as such—became the received wisdom in anthropology (cf. Redfield, Linton, and Herskovits 1936; Devereux and Loeb 1943; Spicer 1968). Nowadays, if the turn-of-the-twenty-first-century upsurge of interest in creolization stems from having supplanted the conceptual hegemony of acculturation (Palmié 2007b:196), we should not be surprised by a desire for alternatives as creolization's promise as master concept dissipates.

Yet transculturation is hardly without problems. Although he "attempted to create a meaningful place in the national story for Cubans from marginal races and cultures," Patricia Catoira (2005:181) concludes that Ortiz nonetheless "gravitated toward a homogenizing cultural project." Kevin Yelvington also believes Ortiz never lost his nationalist bent: "*transculturación* can be seen as a way of coming to grips with a new dispensation brought about by politically active blacks by imagining Cuba as a *mestizo* (racially and culturally mixed) nation" (2006b:51). Rafael Rojas (2005), by contrast, sees an unfinished relationship between Ortiz's nationalism and his notion of transculturation. And Fernando Coronil similarly observes (1995:xiv), "Formed and transformed through dynamic processes of transculturation, the landscape of the modern world must constantly be stabilized and represented, often violently, in ways that reflect the play of power in society." For the latter two scholars, the scale tips in favor of transculturation.

My task here is not to adjudicate between competing interpretations of Ortiz. The debate is productive. I favor an expanded notion of transculturation not because it is flawless, but because it seems less encumbered by the conceptual baggage of syncretism, creolization, and hybridity, especially as it focuses on *culture* in a more dynamic and distributed way. Yet these terms are all ultimately heuristic, valuable in the context of empirical specificity. Scholarly documentation and analysis must attend not only to sociocultural processes of interpenetration and hybridity, but also to the temporality and proliferating realities of translocal culture, whether or not these involve "mixture" per se. The concept of "transculturation" serves a purpose if it facilitates scholarship in such a way.

Ecstasy in Exile and the Spirits of Globalization

Transborder crossing has been inherent to the expansion of global capitalism. Indeed, elites have speculated on returns from economic exchanges with selective disrespect for geopolitical boundaries since at least the sixteenth century. By the seventeenth, these circuits of exchange had reached planetary dimensions. As Karl Marx put it in 1867, "The discovery of gold and silver in America, the extirpation, enslavement and entombment in mines of the indigenous population of that continent, the beginnings of the conquest and plunder of India, and the conversion of Africa into a preserve for the commercial hunting of blackskins, are all things which characterize the dawn of the era of capitalist production" (1876:915). The centrality of the Atlantic as staging ground for major global flows over more than five centuries compels us to view this half-millennium as the world's first extended moment of globality.

Since the fleet was loaded down not only with the technology of conquest, but also with seeds, plants, crops, animals, goods, commodities, texts, and people—not to mention diseases—destined for reproduction in the Antilles, Trouillot characterizes Columbus's second trip to the New World as a "colonial Noah's Ark" (2003:29–30). This biblical imagery is not trivial. "In the beginning," according to John Locke in the second of his *Two Treatises on Government* (1690), "all the World was America" (quoted in J. Dunn 2003:45). Aníbal Quijano and Immanuel Wallerstein (1992) observe that European conjuring of a "New World"—the constitutive act of the capitalist world-system—was accomplished for all intents and purposes *ex nihilo* throughout the Americas, except in Mesoamerica and the Andes. Coloniality was essential for establishment of a global interstate system, which decolonization then reified by establishing the "stateness" of former colonies: "Independence did not undo coloniality, it merely transformed its outer form" (550). Liberalism became a surrogate faith (Biagini 2003) and, eventually, globalization, a religion (D. Hopkins 2001), guided not just by the market's "Invisible Hand," but also by appeasing the "Animal Spirits" of the economy (E. Martin 2007). In the process, religion itself became a market commodity (Moore 1994).[2]

Just as "modernity" arose in the nineteenth century as the "civilizational" sublime began to wane, "globalization" has now taken prominence as modernity's wrinkles deepen (Kelly 2002; Trouillot 2003). "Globalization" emerges as a neoliberal trope afforded by amnesia about the past and under the sway of a "globalitarist" ideology promoting teleology of the market as trumping metanarrative of modernity. Yet, as Trouillot observes, "if by globalization we mean the massive flow of goods, peoples, information, and capital across huge areas of the earth's surface in ways that make the parts dependent on the whole, then the world has been global since the sixteenth century. To acknowledge these earlier global flows is not to claim there is nothing new under the sun. On the contrary, by helping us screen out that which passes for new and may actually be quite old, the reference to a massive empirical record of five centuries highlights the more profound changes of our present" (47–48). This perspective on "globalization" is the context for my study of subaltern African and Hindu traditions of ecstasy and mediumship in Trinidad and Tobago.

Let us return, then, to how and why Shango and Shakti Puja could have seemed so much like "dying survivals" to an earlier generation of anthropologists and continue to seem as such for so many citizens of the twin-island republic today. I have encountered the view of these traditions as "primitive" holdovers from earlier, less "enlightened" eras and places again and again in the field. Many look upon such practices akin to how the middle-class "mainstream" sees Pentecostal serpent-handling in the United States, as a folkloric curiosity at best or déclassé primitivism at worst. An ostensible anomaly is pushed into the "past" in order to exorcise it from the present. Resisting this modernist impulse, I show southern Caribbean spiritisms to be not only alter-cultural, but also alter-native, as well as subjected to alter-nationalist politics. They are precociously modernized formations operating in the Janus-faced West's own underbelly. And they happen to be spreading rhizomatically throughout the West, recursively crisscrossing the Atlantic and circulating surreptitiously throughout the Americas.

The capitalist organization of social relations and corollary stratification of religious traditions provides the key to understanding how ecstatic cultism may flourish locally at a subordinate level and thus not disappear, but also be seen as "receding" and "backward" from more privileged rungs on the structurally conservative, yet internally dynamic, hierarchy of social status. This substantiates a view of charismatic forms as representing a dialectical counterpoint to the liberal bourgeois ethic of possessive individualism (Lindholm 1990). Analysis of stratification and conflicts stemming from relations of social class also enables us to account for resonant tensions and conflicts within the respective postcolonial politics of Afrocentrism and Indocentrism. This requires seeing the Caribbean as part and parcel of the global village, in which the ideologies and institutions of liberalism have exerted deeply generative effects, however partial and unruly these may actually be. Liberal bourgeois models of self and society operate in complex stratified ways within West Indian experience. I developed the notion of subaltern liberalization in order to identify subordinate processes of capitalist transculturation in the evolution of popular spiritisms.

Shango and Shakti Puja both therefore operate in a sort of double exile. First, they may be seen as diasporic cults resulting from transoceanic maritime colonial transfer in the nineteenth century and their respective orientation toward spiritual homelands in West Africa and South Asia. Of course, they have been protean and their "diasporic" consciousness variable, yet there is no question as to their vernacular sense of geospiritual exile. This is evident, for example, in the symbolism of their pantheons, which respectively anchor each to Africa or India, in relation to which other layers of bricolage have been incorporated. Second, we must also see these traditions as having been locally "exiled"—or structurally marginalized—as well, albeit in ways differentially conditioned by the vicissitudes of racial ideologies.

Popular Orisha Worship developed in recursive relations with other Afro-creole subcultural streams and was subject to visible interlocution with Christianity, embodying multiplex layers of transculturation through time. Despite the significance of Yoruba-creoles as upstanding colonial subjects, their reconstituted form of ecstatic cultism expanded primarily among subaltern black classes. The development of Christian-identified colored and black middle classes served to seal the continued structural fate of Shango well into the twentieth century. It is only with the advent of independence and Black Power in relation to a crisis of Creole nationalism that an "Orisha Movement" has evolved, which seeks to promote the legal and political interests of Shango as well as recuperate black selfhood through antisyncretic reformulations of the tradition. While some of these efforts have been salutary, I have also identified conflicts between popular "Shango" and the "Orisha" vanguard, showing how they must be understood in terms of the stratified vicissitudes of class habitus.

Precursor forms of Kali and Di Puja as well as Madrassi devotionalism seem to have been less initially stigmatized among indentured South Asians, but on the whole, Indians occupied the lowest structural rung of the local hierarchy until well into the twentieth century. A colonially educated, Christian-identified, elite "modernizing" minority emerged early in the twentieth century, followed in turn by an ostensibly "traditionalizing" Indian middle class that buttressed itself with an orthodox form of Hinduism that made increasing strides in education and politics. This class-inflected orthodoxy subordinated "backward" or "primitive" practices from the Indian "past" down the status ladder, where they have been revived and recontextualized under the influence of Guyanese inputs. Sanatanist Hinduism and other neo-Hindu sects look askance at ecstatic Kali Puja in contemporary Shakti temples. It not only ruffles more "respectable" feathers, but also serves little political purpose, since Hinduism has represented the diasporic Other all along, without the need to recuperate a subaltern dimension within in order to burnish its postcolonial credentials.

My point about the doubly exilic character of these traditions is that they have not only been hierarchically marginalized by colonial, Eurocentric, and Christian interests over time and also by orthodox forms of Hinduism in the case of Shakti Puja and even to some extent—albeit ironically—as a result of the more bourgeois orientation of the postcolonial Orisha Movement in the case of Shango. The analysis demonstrates why racial and class stratification and their reiterating dynamics in the postcolonial era are crucial for understanding the overall religious scene in general and these subaltern spiritisms in particular. We are dealing with multifaceted global dynamics related to the subaltern liberalization of religion regarding the structurally convergent paths of Orisha Worship and Shakti Puja in the southern Caribbean.

As a cultural nexus of ideas and institutions, liberalism originated in seventeenth- and eighteenth-century England. Thereafter, liberal parties or views—developing independently or derived from the English model—materialized in continental Europe and beyond. I take "liberalism" less as a discrete ideology or political party than as a powerful culture of autonomous individualism connected with the rise and differentiation of capitalism. Liberalism's cosmology is "possessive individualism" (Macpherson 1962) or what Thomas de Zengotita (2005) calls "proprietorial humanism." Its dominant version privileges an individualist orientation whose realization manifests as the achievement of "independence" or "freedom" exercised through economic power and property ownership. Liberalism is quintessentially modern, associated with the rise and politics of bourgeois capitalism. David Smith characterizes the self-conscious middle class as "the most important vehicle for liberal doctrine" (1968:277), yet liberalism has subordinate variants as well (S. Hall 1986).

Thus we must consider liberalism's moral economy throughout all levels of modern social formations. Bringing this to bear upon the historical anthropology of religion helps us better account for patterns and transformations of both Great and Little traditions over the longue durée in the southern Caribbean. Charting a range of liberal characteristics in each tradition—a lively insistence on religious autonomy, a strong individualist and increasingly psychologized orientation, and capitalist-inflected relationships to property and the private sphere—led me to the notion of "subaltern liberalization" as a way of capturing deeper trends of "structural convergence" in Shango and Shakti Puja. I am aware of the ironic juxtaposition in speaking of "subaltern" and "liberal" in the same breath. However, the tension is productive. If we focus on the subaltern to the exclusion of the liberal, then we risk misrecognizing the ways each tradition has become glocalized. Trends in political and economic culture may find their way into and become incorporated within subordinate strata in unpredictable ways.

Perhaps we should think in terms of orthodox and heterodox liberalisms that are structurally interrelated and subject to cultural change and historical contestation, thus riven by conflict and contradiction. This refracts liberal cosmology into a pantheon of "higher" and "lower" spirits moving "freely" about, casting their spells, doing their work. The subaltern liberalization of African and Hindu spirits in the Caribbean is therefore alter-native testament to capitalist transculturation as much as the class-stratified orientations of postcolonial Afrocentrism and Indocentrism are. A shared bourgeois habitus cross-cuts each local diaspora's otherwise divergent agendas and postures. Thus the dominant spirit of globalization may be "liberal," yet it is flanked by a host of subalter-natives.

Deep Play Revisited

This discussion also helps account for the elusive specter of "play" in the materials examined here. I have, first, shown how the Afro-creole meaning of play extends beyond the region in connection with precedents and cognates in West Africa, where the theological connotations of play are deep and robust. This is an analytical addendum for which Richard Burton (1997) would have not been surprised. However, I also bring into view the significance of play in the Indo-Caribbean materials by emphasizing the centrality of ludic conceptualization in local forms and by tracing transoceanic taproots in line with South Asian philosophy and religious culture as well. Moreover, Shango and Shakti Puja are both now largely practiced utilizing a shared creole Anglophone tongue. Each employs equivalent metapragmatic discourses concerning "play," "work," "power," "manifestation," "possession," and so forth as a result of structural convergence. I have augmented these considerations with a view of ecstasy as a form of alter-cultural praxis afforded by the human capacity for playfulness and imagination. My analysis of the globalization of trance performance has therefore been an excursion in the modern historiography of *homo ludens*.

Europeans were preoccupied by Afro-American play because it departed so distinctly from their own notions of work and play (Abrahams and Szwed 1983:34). Such activity represented what English utilitarian Jeremy Bentham called "deep play": seemingly irrational behavior, such as gambling or dangerous sport, that violates utilitarian social and economic ideals. Deep play is playing with fire, risking oneself by putting one's stakes on the line. Yet taken to its extreme, proprietorial humanism squeezes the life out of life itself, leaving no room for art or religion, science or politics for their own sake. "The *sacra* which bourgeois materialism has set apart from its militantly profane world," Robert Paul and Paul Rabinow observe, "is nothing other than life itself" (1977:134). Indeed, a Protestant ethic possessed by the spirit of capitalism made the Western notion of leisure ergic (work-related) rather than ludic, paving the way for infantilization of playfulness as antiutilitarian and therefore irrational in liberal bourgeois economic and political culture (Turner 1987:37–39).

Yet anthropology prompts us to ask, utilitarian for whom and according to what frame of reference? Cast in terms of class habitus and ideologies of personhood, the liberal bourgeois culture of proprietorial humanism is one that privileges property ownership, personal independence, and self-possession; thus it generally scoffs at trance performance and the ecstasy of mediumship, seen as always just on the cusp of taking their last dying breath. Yet such practices have hardly disappeared. Rather, they may be subordinated, from which position they exist in complex and dynamic tensions with other ritual forms, becoming liberalized, modernized, Westernized—pick your term—at the subaltern level.

Which brings us back to the mischievous North Atlantic fiction of secularization. Charles Lindholm (1990) argues that the dominant rationalizing and secularizing trends of liberal economic modernism may work against the cultivation and elaboration of charisma, but that does not make them necessarily successful in snuffing it out. There seems to be a fundamental paradox at the heart of the modern condition in that the very circumstances that corrode enchantment simultaneously stimulate people's desire for the experience of *communitas* and heighten the intensity of ecstasy when it manifests. Lindholm (85–88) believes the emotionally distancing and role-playing qualities of modern life are indeed conducive to the experience of charisma. All forms of ostensible escape from contemporary alienation and anomie—including the ideology of romantic love, as robust in Trinidad and Tobago as anywhere else—seem to point in the same direction: toward enchanted social relations as a dialectical counterpoint to the liberal bourgeois ethic of possessive individualism. "The question is not whether such moments of selflessness and communion will continue to exist. They are a part of our human condition. The question is what form these moments will take" (189).

I have shown how popular traditions of ecstatic mysticism in the southern Caribbean have adapted and morphed in relation to their experience of modernity. They are not anachronistic primitivisms destined to die out, but subaltern spiritisms reflecting transcultural histories as well as a transculturating human capacity for playfulness. The ludic heart beating at the center of each tradition has made it an obvious target of liberal bourgeois critique in the colony as well as postcolony. Yet they abide, playing deeply into the future.

Appendix

Note on "Creolization" and "Syncretism"

A fuller note on the terms "creolization" and "syncretism" invoked in this study is helpful. They are imperfect analytical concepts, yet it is difficult to avoid them because they are prevalent in both emic and etic discourses and because their meanings have also come to overlap recursively over time. Both concepts arose from complex usage in natural languages, have been contested and mutable through time, and therefore are subject to a dizzying array of meanings and politics. Scholarly critiques of each have mounted, prompting some to advocate abandoning them altogether.

I find the critiques edifying but the terms difficult to wholly abandon. Old wine is not necessarily better in new bottles. My position is the same regarding both: as gatekeeping concepts (Appadurai 1986a), "creolization" and "syncretism" are most valuable as starting—not ending—points for analysis. They are not essences to be revealed but glosses that must operate heuristically in the context of empirically rigorous scholarship. If we cannot entirely avoid using them, we should be as mindful as possible regarding their pitfalls. I favor "transculturation" over both "syncretism" and "creolization," for reasons explicated in the text.

Syncretism generally refers to the hybridizing combination of elements from two or more sociocultural traditions, most often in relation to religion, but not necessarily so. Though the term is widely used, however, uneasiness has arisen in relation to several concerns: pejorative invocations deriding cultural intermixture itself and the corollary tendency to presuppose "purity" or greater "authenticity" among parent traditions that interact to produce "syncretic" off-spring (Lindstrom 1996). These are certainly pitfalls to be avoided.

But it is possible to draw upon the language of syncretism without trafficking in too much bias or false essentialism. Critically informed usage of the concept may, in fact, help focus analysis upon the intertwined cultural politics of religious synthesis and schismogenesis (Shaw and Stewart 1994; C. Stewart 1999). As Shaw and Stewart observe, "syncretism has always been part of the negotiation of identities and hegemonies in situations such as conquest, trade, migration, religious dissemination and marriage" (1994:19–20).

Apprehending its etymology puts things into perspective. Syncretism was originally used positively among ancient Hellenes regarding forms of trans-cultural allegiance or synthesis, the valence of which continued through the Renaissance into the early modern period (Colpe 1987; Shaw and Stewart 1994). During the sixteenth and seventeenth centuries, however, the term's meaning was transposed into a pejorative one by Protestants criticizing the "impure" taint resulting from the "unprincipled" jumbling together of religions (C. Stewart 1999). Such sentiment carried the day until positive reuptake in twentieth-century scholarship.

This genealogy is especially helpful for contextualizing "syncretism" in the Caribbean, since theoretical tendencies regarding what has been taken as the proto-typical form of hybridity—Afro-Catholic syncretism—echo tensions within the term's own history. It also teaches us that, whether we like it or not, those processes and forms dubbed "syncretism" are ever present in social and cultural life.

The term "creolization" has more recently—and revealingly—become popular among scholars, just as mounting critique of "syncretism" began to problematize that term's use. Indeed, given the conceptual labor required of "creolization," it is unsurprising that some actually define it explicitly in terms of syncretism (e.g., Balutansky and Sourieau 1998). Some influential theorists have taken up creolization as emblematic of what is happening in the world at large, in which "the old localizing strategies—by bounded community, by organic culture, by region, by center and periphery—obscure as much as they reveal" (Clifford 1994:303). Taking his cue from creole linguistics in order to depict the "world in creolization," Ulf Hannerz writes, "As languages have different dimensions such as grammar, phonology and lexicon, and as creole languages are formed as unique combinations and creations out of the interaction between languages in these precarious dimensions, so creole cultures come out of multidimensional cultural encounters and can put things together in new ways" (1992a:265). The phenomena once known as "cultures," in other words, are now all becoming "subcultures" in the "global ecumene" (also see Hannerz 1987, 1992b, 1996). "We are all Caribbeans now," wrote James Clifford (1988:173), "living in our urban archipelagos."

However, the genealogy of "creolization" is specific to post-Columbian Atlantic experience and carries a congeries of meanings and ambiguities conditioned by the pressing history of colonialism in the Americas. Caribbeanists have criticized the conceptual fetishism of creolization as a free-floating abstraction in scholarship concerning modernity and the globalization of world cultures at large (see Mintz 1971a, 1996b; Green 1986; Bolland 1992b, 2005; Trouillot 1998; Khan 2001, 2004, 2007a, 2007b; Munasinghe 2001a, 2001b; Price 2001, 2007; Shepherd and Richards 2002; Sheller 2003; Palmié 2006, 2007a, 2007b; C. Stewart 2007a, 2007b). Within regional study, previous treatments of creolization have been taken to task for being inadequately historicized, overly idealized, undertheorized, and not enough subjected to comparative scrutiny, as well as too naïve regarding ideological usages and political motives. Beyond the region, these problems are compounded by a tendency to ignore the specificity of the history giving rise to the terminology of "creole" and concepts related to it.

Though the original meaning of "creole" pertained to people or things of Old World ancestry raised or cultivated in the New World, thereby implying localization and a sense of continuity, it is critical to appreciate that the term's raison d'être necessarily invoked vectors of differentiation as well. Metropolitan Europeans looked down upon Euro-American Creoles, whereas Afro-Creoles came to see themselves as superior to African-born Blacks. Thus, even before coming to take on "mixture" within its semantic range, the notion of "creole" was deeply implicated in power relations and the politics of identity. This has made for an astonishing diversity of referential usage throughout the region (see Lowenthal 1972; Hoetink 1985).

An important historical semantic shift toward "creolization" understood as intermixture occurred with the rise of decolonizing revolutionary Latin American *mestizo* nationalisms in the late eighteenth and early nineteenth centuries (Palmié 2006). This shift must be understood as ideologically motivated in relation to the actions of elites in their efforts to control the apparatus of the state. Something similar transpired in the mid-twentieth-century West Indian cultural nationalisms and decolonization movements, which vaunted creole ethnicity and its popular culture as symbols of the emergent postcolonial nation. The fact that the term "creole" has manifested such remarkably contested diversity has made it a fertile ideological idiom.

I employ the relatively unconventional term "Indo-creole" throughout this study in order to emphasize transformations and processes—including but not limited to intermixture—pertaining to the experience of Indo-Caribbean peoples and West Indian Hinduism. The same applies, *mutatis mutandis*, regarding the term "Afro-creole," though this is a more conventional designation (see, e.g., Burton 1997) for reasons that make social and historical sense. In the case of Trinidad and Tobago, for example, "Creole" refers primarily to people of African and mixed Afro-Euro descent, a regulating discourse positing Indo-Caribbeans as foreign, hence "East" and not ultimately "West" Indian, thus also not "Creole."

I invoke "creolization" in this study in order to explore the layered complexities of "localization" in southern Caribbean cultural history, such as what I have called "structural convergence" and "subaltern liberalization," considering both the African and the Indian experiences equivalently as empirical cases for comparison and contrast. I also refer to "syncretism" in relation to Orisha Worship or Shakti Puja with an awareness of the dynamics of hybridity and antisyncretism in everyday life and political culture. Yet I remind my reader that leaning upon the discourses of creolization and syncretism throughout is but a heuristic move and does not substitute for empirical and comparative analysis. I have taken a middle path in relation to relevant scholarship and related critique.

Notes

Prologue

1. Diacritics are not used since they are largely irrelevant within the discursive consciousness and textual conventions of Trinidad and Tobago's English Creole, including the foreign language–inflected religious subcultures at the heart of this study. See Lise Winer's (1993, 2007) cultural history of language in TT's English and English Creole tongues. There is no standard Creole orthography, and scholars continue to debate the degree to which West Indian discourse should be rendered in transliterated approximation versus translated into standard English. Though creole linguists themselves have become more experimental and moved increasingly toward encoding vernacular speech in published text, the rest of academia remains more conservative and seems to prefer quotations in something closer to standard English. At the risk of pleasing no one, I have taken a middle path by indicating some creole forms of pronunciation and thereby reminding my readers that English Creole and English are not the same thing, even though they overlap in complex and ambiguous ways. I use lowercase for adjectives with racialized "color" terms such as "black" and "white," but capitalize nominal forms such as "Blacks" and "Whites."

2. I use actual names in this text except where noted otherwise. This decision arises from the fact that almost everyone I spoke to or worked with expressed interest in being identified in print, and because so many people have already been named in previous publications, such as Guinee's (1992) dissertation or Houk's (1995) and Henry's (2003) books, in which people take great pride. Thus I have generally respected people's wishes throughout. However, where I mention more personal, possibly compromising, information, I use pseudonyms identified as such.

3. I follow the lead of other specialists such as Stuempfle (1995) and Khan (2004) in utilizing the term "grassroots" to refer broadly to the working, underemployed, and unemployed classes in Trinidad and Tobago. It is not meant pejoratively and likewise not intended to suggest that grassroots people are uninvolved in complex transnational networks of kith and kin. Indeed, many practitioners of spiritism have either lived in or visited the United Kingdom, Canada, or the United States many a time, or else are connected with people "from away" (abroad) in a host

of circuitous ways. I employ the gloss "grassroots" here in relation to proletarian and lower-class socioeconomic status as well as in reference to local ritual processes tied to ceremonial action as it happens in close association with these classes on the ground in the southern Caribbean, despite the fact that this "locality" is by no means insulated from complex, translocal flows of people and paraphernalia, as we shall see. From the early-modern period onward, the "ground" of Trinidad and Tobago has hardly been "local" in any simple or straightforward sense at all. The neologism "glocal" (Robertson 1995) attempts to grasp complexities of this kind. I also employ the term "popular religion" throughout, with a rationale similar to my use of "grassroots." The notion of "popular culture" in contrast with dominant, elite, literate culture is an admittedly imperfect heuristic, since popular cultural imagery and praxis should neither be overly essentialized nor shorn from wider political and economic currents. My own view of popular culture hews closely to that of Fabian (1978, 1981, 1998). See Burke (1981), S. Hall (1981), Droogers and Siebers (1991), and Rostas and Droogers (1993) on the late-eighteenth-century discovery of "popular culture," as well as the pros and cons of this concept for social and cultural analysis. Finally, in speaking generically of "spiritism," I refer broadly to any religious practice involving trance performance and spirit mediumship. This would include, but is not limited to, specific traditions of Latin American *espiritismo*, for example.

Chapter 1. Catching Power, Playing Deep

1. Wallace Zane (1995), for example, calls for analytical categories that do not obscure meaningful cultural differences in the practice of ecstasy and trance, which leads him to argue against the concept of "altered" in favor of "ritual" states of consciousness, based on a view of "altered" as involving a scholarly ethnocentrism predicated on a pathological model of dissociation. Yet practitioners of spiritism see these states of being as distinct *alterations* of consciousness associated with divine agency. I do not see what this terminological change buys us as scholars. In fact, it leaves something important behind. Ironically, Zane utilizes the overly encompassing anthropological concept of "possession," evincing little concern for what I believe is the most problematic term in the comparative study of ecstasy. It is precisely because of the *pathocentric* connotations of "possession" in English that I want to restrict its meaning in anthropology and comparative religious studies.

2. If one follows ethnologist S. M. Shirokogoroff (1935:118) in viewing shamans as those who practice the conscious loss of consciousness, then both baseline players and spirit mediums in Trinbagonian Shakti Puja and Orisha Worship alike might all be called "shamans." However, for the purposes of discussion here, I would limit the purview of shamanism to practices of entrancement conceptualized as mystical flights or journeys of the ecstatic soul. This pattern is especially characteristic of indigenous northeast and southeast Asia as well as the native Americas (Eliade 1964; Vitebsky 1995; Stutley 2003).

Indeed, while mediumship and shamanism both involve the cultivation of trance for sacred purposes, they differ conceptually. The displaced self of the medium becomes a divine vehicle for the action of the gods in the here and now, whereas shamans embark upon noumenal journeys out of and away from the body to interact with the gods. Etymologically derived from the Latin for "passage," *trance* originally referred to the existential transition from life in death. In the contexts of shamanism and mediumship, the shaman's entranced passage is to another world outside the body, whereas the medium's trance makes way for the passage of divinity into the phenomenal world of the ecstatic body.

These are ideal-types used for analysis (see Atkinson 1992 for critique). I am not invested in typologizing except for heuristic assistance here. Of course, these types may coexist or blur together on the ground. I. M. Lewis (1986, 1989) has reexamined Shirokogoroff's material on Siberian Tungus religion—which was taken as the prototypical case of magical-flight shamanism by Mircea Eliade—in order to show that it includes *all* the ecstatic forms, from "shamanistic" to "possession," which Eliade and others excluded from their definition of shamanism.

Yet some broad comparative patterns do seem to emerge in the ethnographic literature. In contrast to the "shamanistic" regions mentioned above, Sub-Saharan Africa has produced many of the most stunning traditions of ceremonial mediumship per se (see de Heusch 1962, 1965; Beattie and Middleton 1969; Walker 1972; Bourguignon and Evascu 1976; Lewis 1989; Kramer 1993; Behrend and Luig 1999), streams that have been rhizomatically dispersed throughout the New World as a result of colonial imperialism and the globalization of capitalism.

3. I take "impersonation" here to be the entranced personification of divinities in the context of ritual performance. Use of this language is hazardous, though, since in English the notion of impersonation is now somewhat pejorative, connoting mere playacting or deceptive mimicry and dissimulation. I want to resuscitate the Latin meaning of *persona* as "mask" (see Carrithers, Collins, and Lukes 1985), recalling that masking traditions the world over have been deeply intertwined with practices of trance and mediumship. John Emigh (1996) observes that the history of Western theater has been characterized by the progressive shedding of masks accompanied by hypercognition of an increasingly expressive individualism. Liberal bourgeois preoccupation with "sincerity" and "authenticity" (Trilling 1972; C. Lindholm 1990, 2008) occludes deeper appreciation of masks as revelatory devices.

The dramaturgical approach is a venerable tradition in the study of trance performance and spirit mediumship. As the late Alfred Métraux wrote about the practice of Haitian Vodou (note his use of the *positive* sense of "possession"), "Every case of possession has its theatrical side. The rooms of the sanctuary are not unlike the wings of a theater where the possessed find the necessary accessories. Unlike the hysteric, who reveals his anguish and his desires through symptoms, the ritual of possession must conform to the classic image of the mythic personage" (1955:24). French ethnologist Roger Bastide (1978) explicitly drew upon the terminology of "persona" when talking about orisha manifestations in Afro-Brazilian religions. Indeed, it is the French (see also Leiris 1958) who have most developed the dramaturgical approach to trance performance, ultimately building upon Aristotle, who, in his *Politics*, treated ancient Greek ecstatic ceremonialism as cultural theater. Andrew Schaeffner (1965) viewed oracular mediumship as a pretheatrical forerunner to the Greek chorus, and Gilbert Rouget (1985) traced influences of Corybantes trance praxis in the development of classical Greek theater. Thus the dramaturgical approach carries considerable vintage.

Care must nonetheless be used in employing the theatrical analogy (see Schechner 1977, 1985, 2002; Wilshire 1982; Schechner and Appel 1990; Blau 1992; Carlson 1996; Emigh 1996; Schieffelin 1998). I utilize the concept of "impersonation" here in order to recuperate a recessive meaning sidelined within the North Atlantic epistemology of liberal bourgeois modernism as reflected in contemporary English. Bourguignon (1970, 1973), Lawal (1977), Àjàyí (1998), and Desmangles (2001) similarly speak of "impersonation" or "personification" with regard to West African and Afro-Atlantic forms of masquerade, trance performance, and spirit mediumship.

4. This accords with Gell's view of generative entrancements arising from vertiginous play within ceremonial contexts, in sharp contrast with organic disturbances of the vestibular system. In other words, the medium's—or shaman's—ability to control his or her trance is a sign of

functional normality, *not* abnormality. They confront chaos in order to control and transform it. Csordas (1987) considers materials from Candomblé and examines a case in which cult initiation was denied to someone because he or she was psychologically unwell, which emphasizes a complex and recursive continuum between positive and negative forms of ecstasy in this context. Sheila Walker (1972) made a similar point regarding African and Afro-American ecstatic traditions, noting the lack of any simple correlation between personality and inclination toward trance.

5. Foucauldian "resistance" would therefore be translated into "opposition" within this scheme.

6. Kenneth Bilby (1999) has brought attention to subaltern "Gumby Play" in Jamaica and uncovered its connections with the ecstatic Myal complex as well as Jonkonnu masquerade. Elsewhere (2005), he examines the role of Kromanti "Play" in Maroon cultural history and ritual tradition. In Haiti, Elizabeth McAlister (2002:31–33) discloses the generative significance of "play" as well as "work" in subversive Rara street processions throughout the Lenten period, festivity that "looks like Carnival, but feels like Vodou" (184). In a post-Katrina scholarly homage to Mardi Gras, Abrahams, Spitzer, Szwed, and Thompson (2006) emphasize the depth and significance of "play" within this tradition so definitive of "America's Creole Soul." Henry Louis Gates (1988) and Theophus Smith (1994) make similar points about the rhetorical, improvisational, and tricksterish playfulness at the heart of African-American religion, vernacular traditions, and literature in the United States.

7. Zammito's (2004) critique of pseudo-antipositivism in the philosophy of science and contemporary science studies shows how problems with positivism provide justification for neither denigrating empirical inquiry nor comparative practice. Closer to home, Bunzl (2008) subverts the "antipositivistic" sign under which so much sociocultural anthropology operates, identifying the demand for ever-increasing complexity as an ironic form of crypto-positivism, which renders anthropology increasingly marginal to intellectual discourse and public debate.

8. I did not know of it at the time of our conversation, but Brereton's view echoed that of Barry Higman (1999), who published an important critique and reconsideration of Caribbean historiography the very same year as our discussion. Higman looks to the future and calls for more inclusive regional scholarship, more comparative inquiry, histories of specific territories and groupings in larger imperial, Atlantic, and globalizing contexts and more innovative ways of representing the past.

9. I credit Todd Ramón Ochoa (pers. comm., 2007) for the felicitous term "African-*inspired*" as an alternative to the more ubiquitous discourse on "African-*derived*" religions. Fetishistic emphasis on "derivation" seems to stem from the prevalent racial ideology concerning Africans and Afro-creoles examined below. My historical anthropology of Shango in the southern Caribbean shows why the dynamic and open-ended language of inspiration is as important as the focus on the past curried by concern with derivation.

10. I additionally came to know several *douglas* of quite varied backgrounds within each sphere, whose participation tended to magnify identification with the dominant ethnoracial profile of the tradition in question. A dougla is someone with mixed African-Indian ancestry recognizable enough to warrant the self-identification. That is, dougla practitioners in Shango seem more inclined to favor their African ancestry, whereas those active in Shakti Puja tend to emphasize their Indianness. Though I did not collect quantitative data in this regard, I think it telling—as well as unsurprising in retrospect—that transracialization of consciousness may take place with especially compelling implications for douglas.

Chapter 2. Hierarchy and Heterodoxy in a Maze of Color

1. I borrow the "maze of color" trope from Albert Gomes's autobiography, *Through a Maze of Colour* (1974). Gomes was an important early-to-mid-twentieth-century Portuguese-creole who entered politics vociferously as a labor leader and public intellectual, then moved more deeply into the central halls of political power as minister of labour, commerce, and industry in the transitional colonial government of 1950–56. My literary invocation of pluralist ideology is just that; I wish only to point to the complex experience and ambiguities of "imagined pluralism" (Segal 1994) among Trinbagonians in public culture, *not* to overly reify that sense of heterogeneity.

2. Constraints of space disallow consideration of other significant minority communities that developed on respective islands as an outcrop of the nineteenth-century emancipation era, such as the "Potagee" (Portuguese) from Madeira, who took up a creolized path not unlike the Chinese, or the "Syrians," those Near Eastern Christians who became upwardly mobile and have tended strongly toward endogamy. See Green (1976) for an overview of postemancipation demographic patterns to and within the British West Indies between 1830 and 1865.

3. It is worth noting that missionaries and planters shared many of the same racial prejudices toward the enslaved, differing mostly on the question of whether Africans were capable of ultimate redemption within the folds of the church. While not foreclosed completely by power and privilege, perhaps, the missionary effort was also never able to truly divorce itself from the material and ideological interests of a transnational English bourgeoisie.

4. Compare with the fact that only 1 percent of the African-born slaves in 1819 were Yorubas (John 1988).

5. Dahomey, from the seventeenth to late nineteenth centuries, was a West African kingdom formed by the Fon ethnic group in the southern third of what is today the independent country of Benin, just west of Nigeria. Its language, Fongbe, is part of a larger family of Gbe languages. Together, Gbe- and Yoruba-speaking peoples were among the main groups exported into the transatlantic slave trade along the Slave Coast. Indeed, a decidedly significant portion of the entire trade left the Slave Coast (the Bight of Benin) between the mid-seventeenth and mid-nineteenth centuries, even rising in significance toward the closing years of the trade (Eltis and Richardson 1997a, 1977b). The religious systems of the Fon and Yoruba are similar, sharing a number of cognate deities and religious concepts that are either identical or quite resonant with one another.

6. The expansion of European colonialism and the march of industrializing capitalism in the nineteenth and early twentieth centuries meant that Indians were not the only Asians swept up into the evolving world-system as transmigrant laborers. These "coolies"—as they were called by their colonial masters—originated in India, China, Indonesia, and Indo-China, as well as Japan and Oceania. Lydia Potts (1990:72–73) writes that "the total number of men, women and children sent abroad as coolies could not have been less than 12 million, and an estimate of 37 million or more would not be entirely without foundation." Jan Breman and E. Valentine Daniel (1992) observe that the Tamil word *kuuli*, from which "coolie" derives, denotes payment for menial work without customary rights, yet never refers to a person—by contrast with *coolie*, a transcultural modification reflecting cooptation into capitalism.

7. Louis Dumont describes caste society in India as "divided into a large number of permanent groups which are at once specialized, hierarchized and separated (in matters of marriage, food, physical contact) in relation to each other. It is sufficient to add that the common basis of

these three features is the opposition of pure and impure, an opposition of its nature hierarchical which implies separation and, on the professional level, specialization of the occupations relevant to the opposition; that this basic opposition can segment itself without limit; finally, if one likes, that the conceptual reality of the system lies in this opposition, and not in the groups which it opposes—this accounts for the structural character of these groups, caste and sub-caste being the same thing seen from different points of view" (1961:34). Given the seemingly essential connection between caste and Hinduism for many commentators (see Appadurai 1986b, 1992 for critique), it is ironic that the institutions often regarded as the most deeply rooted and distinctive in Indian culture have undergone the most radical change abroad. Indeed, in none of the many societies that have received substantial immigration of South Asians (Guyana, Trinidad, Suriname, South Africa, Kenya, Uganda, Tanzania, Mauritius, Fiji) except Sri Lanka—and perhaps Malaysia—was a caste system reproduced in Dumont's sense within the Indian sector (Jayawardena 1968). See Khan (1994) for an examination of how the caste-derived notion of *juthaa* has been transformed in the Caribbean.

8. On the development of orthodox West Indian Hinduism, see Niehoff and Niehoff (1960), Klass (1961), Ramesar (1976, 1994), La Guerre (1974), Haraksingh (1986, 1987, 1988), Samaroo (1987, 1996), Forbes (1987), Guinee (1990, 1992), Maharaj (1991), van der Veer and Vertovec (1991), Vertovec (1992, 1996), Khan (1994, 1995, 2001, 2004), and Munasinghe (2001a).

9. The Legislative Council had been established in 1880, with the governor nominating all of its members until 1925, when constitutional reform following the Wood Commission led to the first elections for several newly constituted representative positions on the council. However, suffrage was highly restricted by property and literacy, with only 6 percent of the total population qualified to vote. Yet, constitutional change and modifications to the colonial Legislative and Executive Councils began accelerating at this time, culminating in the advent of universal adult suffrage in 1946 and a clear majority of electoral representation on both councils by 1950.

10. It was Eric Williams's *Capitalism and Slavery* (1944), published when he was thirty-three years old, which put the critical study of slavery in connection with the development of capitalism on the historiographical map. Williams received a colonial island scholarship and earned his PhD in 1938 at Oxford University, where he not only excelled but also felt the effects of racism in a rarefied intellectual sphere he had previously idealized (see his 1969 autobiography, *Inward Hunger: The Education of a Prime Minister*). Prior to entering politics, Williams was a professor at Howard University in Washington, D.C. His thesis concerning the role of slavery in financing the Industrial Revolution firmly established slavery within the study of economic history, subverting received wisdom about enlightened "progress" in European historiography (see Solow and Engerman 1978; C. Palmer 1994; Cateau and Carrington 2000). Williams argued not only that slavery fueled the rise of capitalism, but also that industrialization in turn destroyed the system which had helped build it, thereby suggesting less than philanthropic motivation for metropolitan abolitionism. Seymour Drescher (1977, 1999) tempers this perspective by showing that abolition of the British slave trade preceded by several decades any general decline in the British West Indian economy. Drescher's challenge to overly economistic accounts of abolition has been elaborated by more recent comparative study across several colonial Atlantic vectors (see Brereton 2002). Still, Williams argued that Britain could *afford* to legislate against the slave trade only after that trade had helped to provide the surplus capital necessary for industrial "take-off." Moreover, Britain had lost much of its slave-owning territory as a result of the American Revolution, and—as the West's leading industrial power—found in abolition a way to work against the interests of its rivals, who were still heavily involved in slavery (Brantlinger 1985:2).

Chapter 3. Serving the Orishas

1. A note on terminology. I often refer to the tradition practiced at the popular level as "Shango," a term deriving from one of the cult's most prominent deities. This is a common vernacular term, though by no means the only one. Shango has also been known historically as "African Work," "Orisha Work," or "Orisha Worship" among practitioners. The active recuperation of Shango as a marginalized practice and its use as a vehicle for Afrocentric cultural politics has developed in the postcolonial era and come to be known as the "Orisha Movement," "Orisha Faith," or simply as "Orisha." While there is no clear-cut distinction between these terms, the terminological spectrum is nonetheless meaningful, reflecting changes related to social class and racial politics. I therefore refer more often to the grassroots practice as "Shango" and the middle-class postcolonial movement more frequently as "Orisha," though they necessarily overlap. The politicized wing of the Orisha Movement criticizes "Shango" as a term bearing too much colonial baggage and social stigma, a critique to which I am not entirely unsympathetic. They point out that Shango is but one among many important local powers and abandon usage of the term in favor of "Orisha." However, I find it equally problematic to privilege postcolonial phraseology when speaking of the tradition's deeper sociohistorical experience. I therefore utilize both "Shango" and "Orisha" to track changes over time and patterns of practice inflected by class, fully acknowledging that there is no perfect strategy in dealing analytically with this revealing terminological heteroglossia and lexical politics.

2. Interestingly, re res may be in the process of becoming less subordinate and more ensconced as a legitimate class of spirits on their own terms, though it is difficult to be definitive without further investigation.

3. In ethnomedical research comparing Trinidad and Grenada, Mischel (1959) revealed an interesting contrast: whereas doctors in Trinidad expressed strong bias against treatment by bush healers and would not send patients to them, doctors in Grenada would in fact refer patients with psychosomatic illnesses—but not obvious organic problems—to folk healers. Mischel attributed this divergence to Trinidad's "medical progress" as compared with the underdeveloped medical infrastructure in Grenada.

4. According to Simpson (1980:131), *peregun* in West Africa refers to a leafy plant used to wash Shango's thunderstones. According to Warner-Lewis (1991:123), the word originally referred to the shrub marking shrines for Ogun. Whatever the case, Trinbagonian "perogun" has undergone transatlantic modification.

5. Houk's (1995:148–49) survey sample of thirty-seven shrine yards in Trinidad produced the following perspective on the incidence of *outside* stools, listed here in decreasing demographic significance and accompanied by their percentage represented in the sample: Ogun (100 percent), Osain (92 percent), Shakpana (86 percent), Mama Lata (59 percent), Oshun, (57 percent), Peter (46 percent), Yemanja (40 percent), Erile (32 percent), Oya (27 percent), Elofa (22 percent), Gurum (19 percent), Anthony (14 percent), Eshu (11 percent), Raphael (11 percent), Shango (5 percent), Ajaja (5 percent), Vigoyana (5 percent). As for *inside* stools, by contrast, Houk (150) surveyed thirty chappelles and generated the following demographic portrait: Shango (100 percent), Oya (89 percent), Yemanja (50 percent), Oshun (43 percent), Obatala (40 percent), Osain (37 percent), Erile (37 percent), Mama Lata (10 percent).

6. Here I paraphrase Robert F. Thompson (1983:89), who makes an insightful remark about a late-nineteenth-century Afro-Cuban image of Changó–Santa Bárbara. My spelling of the

names of deities throughout hews as closely as possible to local pronunciation as well as common renderings in the relevant literature.

7. See R. Thompson (1983), Barnes (1997), Cosentino (2005), and Largey (2005) on the "ever pliant" and "recombinant" mythology of Ogun's iron complex in the Old and New Worlds.

8. It is also relevant to note that Oshun has a special affinity for homosexual men in TT.

9. See Goldwasser (1996) for a folklorist's polyethnic perspective on this Madonna's history and symbolism. One friend of mine active in Spiritual Baptism, Shango, and Kabbalah tells me that, while he has never seen her manifest at any orisha feasts, he once saw La Divin materialize at a Kabba banquet.

10. It is not only noteworthy that all scholars of Shango have reported an ideal among practitioners of a fixed night-by-night sequence in feasts, but also important to observe that they all differ from one another in their reporting of this rotation aside from beginning with Ogun on opening night, which testifies to the variability encountered on the ground (cf. F. Mischel 1957; Houk 1995; Aiyejina and Gibbons 1999; Lum 2000).

11. *Hoosi* derives from the Fon *hounsi*, which refers to an initiate, literally, "wife of the spirit," terminology salient in Haitian Vodou as well.

Chapter 4. Doing the Mother's Work

1. Consider Seepersad Naipaul's (1976:163–71) short story "Obeah," which appeared in 1943, describing the trials and tribulations of a love-struck canefield worker who solicits the services of a local obeah-man for his love magic. The healer's *devi puja* (*devi* means goddess) involves the offering of a goat as well as the ecstatic conjuring of the goddess upon his wife as an oracle. However, it turns out that the story's protagonist falls in love with the obeah-man's married daughter, and once the truth comes out, the interaction ends in fisticuffs. Naipaul was a civil servant, and his treatment is ironic and patronizing, producing a humorous underside to the plot. The point is that Shakti Puja is talked about explicitly as "obeah," originally an African-derived term used for heterodox African religious and healing practices that fall beyond the mainstream threshold of respectability.

2. The owner of the paper—*The Bomb*—is also the secretary-general of the Maha Sabha. By the time of my own fieldwork a decade later, the temple had recovered and held popular Saturday puja services.

3. According to Guinee (1990:48), the word *jharay* probably comes from the transitive Hindi verb *jhalna*, which means "to flap or fan." Khan (1999:265) consults the *Standard Illustrated Dictionary of the Hindi Language* (1977) and derives the Indo-Caribbean word *jharay* from *jharna*, meaning "to brush, sweep, clean, remove, snatch away by force, or repeat spells for exorcising." In Trinidad, the term is used as both a verb and a noun, for example, "The pujari jharays" or "I got a jharay." By extension, *jharay* may also be used to refer to the entire encounter with a deota through a manifesting medium, since the encounter typically begins with the preliminary jharaying of the supplicant. Pandits and other Indian folk healers—including Muslims—also practice jharaying, but they use dried cocoyea palm-frond spines or peacock feathers. Only manjatani-soaked neem leaves are used to jharay in Shakti temples. Though jharaying by manifesting mediums using ritually prepared neem leaves soaked in manjatani—called "saffron water," but actually turmeric-based—is considered the most potent form of healing power in these temples, sacred ash from the temple puja—called *vibhuti* or *babhoot*—is also an important substance used for therapeutic treatment as well as spiritual cleansing. A temple leader in

Moruga, deep in southern Trinidad, claimed babhoot was "one of the greatest cures we have" as he applied it to a wound on my neck from a Jack Spaniard wasp sting received while hanging out in the bush behind their temple one day. I was agitated yet trying not to show it, since I had heard repeatedly that Jack Spaniard stings are not only painful, but may also elicit very serious allergic reactions in some. The "old head" of the temple assured me I shouldn't worry once he applied ash from the Shakti Puja to my neck, calling it a "jharay." "The Mother will protect you," he soothed. The pain rapidly dissipated, in fact, although the wound took a few days to heal.

4. Guinee's survey of 132 people attending the Maha Kali Mata Devi Mandir in Pasea, Tuna-puna, on a Sunday in October 1988 provided the following demographic profile (23–45). Temple members and visitors were generally less well educated and more illiterate than the national average. Half of those present were very new to the temple, whereas the remaining half had considerably more experience under their belt. People came to the temple from rural village areas more often than not. Some 23.5 percent considered themselves as coming from higher "nations," that is, ostensibly from higher-caste backgrounds; 12.8 percent identified themselves as Chamars; 10.6 percent as Madrassi; and 11.4 percent as Ahir (a demographically large mid-dling "caste" in Trinidad). Of the survey respondents, 14.4 percent were non-Hindu, including 4 Muslims, 1 Open Bible Christian, 2 Pentecostals, 1 Presbyterian, 3 Roman Catholics, 2 other nonspecified "Christians," 1 generic "non-Hindu," 3 "Spanish" (probably Catholic, but unclear), and 3 blanks left unfilled by Afro-Trinidadians. Most in the temple community were of Indian descent; however, 6 (4.5 percent) identified as either "Negro" or "Creole," 2 claimed "Spanish" descent (i.e., of mixed Afro-Latin-Creole descent), 1 identified as "Spanish Negro," another as "Indian, Negro, Spanish, French," another as "Indian and White," and another as "Indian and Venezuelan."

Temple attendees were characterized by a considerable degree of un- or underemployment, and those employed were largely occupied in labor and craftwork. In general, therefore, most Kali temple patrons are economically poor and financially strapped. Reasons for seeking out the temple vary, but most initially come for assistance with problems, the three most prevalent cat-egories of which are physical or medical, domestic (familial, marital, and sexual), and financial, in decreasing order of statistical significance. Most attendees had previously tried seeking help through other routes, such as with biomedical doctors or in more orthodox religious contexts; thus many newcomers seek Kali Puja as an avenue of last resort.

Though one might be tempted to see these figures for non-Indian participation as low, it is important to emphasize that Shakti temples draw many more non-Indians than orthodox forms of Hinduism, relatively speaking. Pujari Mootoo Brown (discussed below) is reported to have said on more than one occasion that non-Hindus "get through" quicker doing the Mother's puja than Hindus because they come with fresh minds ready to learn. Afro-creole participation in temple-based Kali Puja in Trinidad is apparently not as significant as it is in Guyana, however. Furthermore, despite the antiracist ideology that "all o' we is de Mudda children" in Shakti temples, they are certainly not racial utopias in that antiblack Indian racism may be found to exist to some degree and, in some contexts, just under the surface. Guinee (1990, 1992) has also made this observation.

5. I am dependent upon the account of Guinee (1992:175–79) here, since the pragmatic constraints of comparative fieldwork kept me from becoming deeply involved with the Maha Kali Shakti Mandir. I became acquainted with Pujari Angad and intermittently attended the temple's weekly pujas. He also permitted me to videotape several ecstatic services. We addi-tionally interfaced several times at the Moruga temple in the deep south, which got its start

under Krishna's tutelage. The Joyce Road temple is also where I once took my black spiritist friend Dexter after he had repeatedly expressed interest in attending an ecstatic Shakti Puja (see chapter 5). Guinee reports that, early on, Angad would himself manifest for considerable periods of time during the weekly puja (1992:205). However, during my own time in the field, I never once saw Krishna involved in an ecstatic manifestation of any kind. Like so many Kali temple leaders as well as orisha shrine heads, Pujari Angad cut his teeth as a trance medium and then became an overall orchestrator of ecstasy, leaving mediumship to others under his purview.

6. The significance of this Caribbean conjunction is thrown into relief when compared with the scenario on Mauritius, in the Indian Ocean, where the temples and iconographic traditions of Kali and Mariyamman are generally independently operative vis-à-vis one another (field observations, June 2004).

7. In Guyana, Di is not only venerated and known as the Dutchman in Kali Mai Puja (Younger 2002:175), but he has also been appropriated by Afro-Guyanese spiritism as the head of a phalanx of Dutch ghosts, reflecting the contingencies of mythistory in the Guianas (B. Williams 1990).

8. Again, a comparison with other areas of the Indian diaspora is instructive: Munisvaran and Maduraiviran's very different coupling among Tamil Hindus in Malaysia, where Maduraiviran's iconographic persona is still very much connected with predominant south Indian traditions. In this region, Maduraiviran is certainly not syncretized with the Bhairo form of Shiva, as in Trinidad. And in Malaysia, his murtis are most often found outside shrines for Munisvaran, also in more direct line with prevailing, south Indian–based, Tamil practices, where he dutifully guards Munisvaran's sanctums (field observations, June 2005).

Chapter 5. Sides and Paths

1. The late Babalorisha Sam "Baja" Phills (he passed away in 2005) is another exception. He maintained relations with a Hindu temple in Gonzales, Belmont, Port-of-Spain, where he grew up "like brothers" with the temple's lay pandit. However, Baja's Hindu connection here is with a mainstream mandir, not a shakti temple. I also know one case of "Shango Baptists" who established contact with a Kali temple in Pasea as a result of visions experienced by two leaders near Trincity, encouraging them to connect with "Mother India." I was never around when they visited the temple on non-puja days. When one of the assistant pujaris and I went to find them for me to speak with them one day, we learned they had gone to Florida for several months in order to pursue spiritual work in the United States. To my knowledge, the connection has never been revived on either side. Relatedly, I know of one case in which an avid Shango woman sponsored a visit by a shakti medium from a nearby Kali temple for special "Indian Prayers" in Tunapuna. The event was attended by a small gathering of women, the male medium, and an anthropologist (Vincent Goldberg, pers. comm., 2000). A single orisha drum was played, and the shakti medium manifested Nag Deota—the spirit of Shiva's serpent protector—in the chappelle, which contained several chromolithographic images of Hindu deities. The ceremony did not last long, consisting of consultations with the manifesting medium. This idiosyncratic engagement came about because of another woman's having sought out healing power at the medium's home temple for her battle with cancer. Contrariwise, I know of no cases of shakti leaders or devotees who have cultivated experience with Shango praxis in any significant manner. This does not mean that such people do not exist, but if they do, I did not cross paths with

any of them. I think I would probably have either heard about or run into them within the relatively smaller demographic matrix of Kali Puja.

2. Note that even though he finds the general term "possession" problematic, Smith retains its usage, since "the broad semantic boundaries of the terms under study here provide no attractive alternative" (2006:10).

3. Also see the introduction and case studies in Apter and Derby's *Activating the Past* (2010) on "fetishized forms of history" throughout the Black Atlantic. J. Lorand Matory (2009:257) puts the matter similarly: "First, while the qualitative protocol of constructing the self in transaction with the foreign is fundamental to all the Yoruba-Atlantic traditions, the Other Places and the sacred technology of transaction with them have been meticulously elaborated and synthesized in the American traditions of orisha worship. Thus the difference between these West African religions and their American counterparts strikes me not as qualitative—as recent transnationalist models might lead us to suspect—but as quantitative. The New World devotees construct themselves at the convergence of a quantitatively far more diverse set of nations and, quantitatively, a far more plural sense of the self than do the West African devotees. Second, and also quantitatively, the number of people who dramatize their penetration by multiple nations has increased exponentially, and the imagery of involuntarism has grown."

4. Though Holland and Crane's (1987) argument that Shango provides an institutional training ground for middle-class life is overstated in my view, they are on the right track in attending to wider industrializing effects upon the religious system in the twentieth century and the ways bourgeois values and institutions have in fact impacted ritual practices at the subaltern level.

Chapter 6. Religion and the Politics of Diaspora in an Era of Postcolonial Multiculturalism

1. The spelling of "Orisa" here is not an error, since many of the more intellectual activists and socially mobile recruits have adopted their own orthography in which the pronunciation of 'sh' is understood as implied by the letter 's' in Orisa. This is an invisible sort of diacritical practice indexing involvement by a more privileged, intellectualized, textually oriented, Afrocentric vanguard.

2. The title of Ooni refers to the living representative of Oduduwa, the cosmic progenitor of the Yoruba peoples and first king of ancient Ife, the archaic locus of creation where Oduduwa descended to the land and proclaimed himself the first Ooni. The Ooni is *primus inter pares* among Yoruba kings, his crown the most ancient and therefore the most sacred. According to the Nigerian High Commission in Port-of-Spain, the Ooni of Ife is "the ultimate authority of the Yoruba race in both spiritual and political matters," "the head custodian of all that is traditional and cultural in Yoruba Land" (information provided in 1999).

3. The Little Carib Theatre was founded by Trinidadian dancer and folklore researcher Beryl McBurnie in the middle-class Port-of-Spain suburb of Woodbrook in 1948. McBurnie was among the vanguard of artists and intellectuals whose work and creativity contributed to a remarkable cultural renaissance accompanying the Afro-creole nationalist awakening associated with political decolonization after World War II. According to Brereton (1981:223), "she organized and presented folk dances based on Trinidad and Tobago's rich multi-cultural heritage, jeopardizing her standing in the city's colored middle class (to which she belonged by birth) by her active participation in African dances and her cooperation with young dancers of all ethnic backgrounds. For this was a time when most middle-class blacks were still ashamed

of African-derived cultural forms and the music and dance of working-class West Indians" (see Ahye 1983 on McBurnie's life, including her formative years in New York City).

4. EOS has additionally launched an annual ceremony for a locally little-known orisha, Olokun, held "down the islands," that is, at a relatively inaccessible seaside cave on one of the small islands stretching westward from one tip of Trinidad toward Venezuela, islands most often frequented by middle- and upper-class people from Port-of-Spain as a weekend getaway. Olokun is not commonly encountered within the sphere of grassroots orisha praxis, but was learned about and focused upon by the group's well-educated leader.

5. I was not the only anthropologist in the audience that day, as another graduate student was present. One has to wonder about whether our presence influenced the proposal to generate documentary items of scholarly interest. It is also important to note, however, that one southern shrine leader strongly contested the idea, criticizing Houk's (1995) ethnography for having published diagrams of various shrine layouts.

6. Indeed, this is the same globally distributed oil boom experienced by the independent Nigerian state, which spawned a nationalistic upsurge in state capitalism and underwrote Nigeria's hosting of the Second World Black and African Festival of Arts and Culture (FESTAC) in 1977, a pan-Africanist extravaganza heralding the country's rebirth as a rapidly developing petro-state (see Apter 2005). Though difficult to substantiate, I think it likely that reverberations of FESTAC's Nigerian pan-African nationalism found their way across the Atlantic in the late 1970s and synergized with what was happening in Trinidad and Tobago.

7. Marcus Garvey (1887–1940) was born in Jamaica and immigrated to the United States. His Universal Negro Improvement Association peaked in the 1920s. Garveyism espoused black self-reliance and African decolonization. Colonial authorities took repressive measures against Garveyism in Trinidad, though they eventually allowed him entry to the island in 1937. Many working-class West Indian activists and labor union leaders during the unrest of 1937–38 were Garveyites (see T. Martin 1994).

8. An "Africanizing" impulse conceived as "Yorubanization" has also emerged in relation to Spiritual Baptism (see, e.g., E. Thomas 1987; Glazier 2001), but this is even dicier given the religion's decidedly Christian orientation as well as its relative lack of Yoruba conceptualization as compared with Orisha Worship (see Shemer 2006). Despite the reality of their overlapping populations, Shango and Spiritual Baptism make even less comfortable bedfellows in recent times, given the shifting and contested ambiguities of Africanity in relation to each. For example, one usually hears little about the struggle of Spiritual Baptists during events sponsored by the Orisha Movement, even though the earlier Baptist struggle paved the way in a most crucial sense. Contrariwise, there was no Orisha presence at the celebrations of Spiritual Baptist Shouter Liberation Day at the African Religions Spiritual Park in 1999 and 2000. The 1999 event was attended by then–prime minister Panday, who presented a Memorandum of Understanding pursuant to transferring legal deed for the land to each of the Baptist and Orisha organizations involved (though the final transfer of title was not granted until 2002). By this point, and despite the fact that the holiday had been established only a few years earlier, in 1996, the celebration held in honor of the day had fractionated from a single, unified one in 1996 to two the following year, and then three by 1999, the year I first began attending. Glazier also documents a telling shift in interrelations between Shango and Spiritual Baptism after a trajectory in which they had begun to overlap and coexist. Rituals "once practiced in close proximity," he writes, "are now carried out in different buildings, and whenever possible, in different communities" (1983:8).

9. See Tweed's (1997) study of devotions to Our Lady of Charity at a Cuban Catholic shrine in Miami for a differently positioned, yet similarly spirited, examination of religion as an alternationalist vehicle of diasporic memory and desire.

Epilogue

1. Also see Bauman and Briggs (2003) for resonant analysis of how modernist ideologies and their metadiscursive regimes enabled Europe to ostensibly "deprovincialize" itself. Their examination of Franz Boas demonstrates that, despite invaluable critiques of evolutionary racism and militant nationalism, his liberal bourgeois modernist assumptions about language and tradition led him—ironically—to an anticulturalist "culturalist" position that continues to bedevil anthropology and social theory to this day.

2. Identifying "Americanity" as root concept, Quijano and Wallerstein (1992) characterize "newness" as the "collective super-ego of the world-system" overall. Naomi Klein (2007) also explicates ideological undertones of creation ex nihilo at work in the neoliberalizing "Shock Doctrine" of the late twentieth and early twenty-first centuries. Yet her analysis only raises much deeper, more poignant, and intractable questions about capitalism's strategies over the longue durée, such as colonial slavery as well as early liberal notions of *tabula rasa* among Enlightenment thinkers such as John Locke.

Bibliography

Abrahams, Roger D., N. Spitzer, J. F. Szwed, and R. F. Thompson. 2006. *Blues for New Orleans: Mardi Gras and America's Creole Soul*. Philadelphia: University of Pennsylvania Press.

Abrahams, Roger D., and John F. Szwed. 1983. *After Africa: Extracts from British Travel Accounts and Journals of the 17th, 18th, and 19th Centuries concerning the Slaves, Their Manners, and Customs in the British West Indies*. New Haven: Yale University Press.

Ahye, Molly. 1978. *Golden Heritage: The Dance in Trinidad and Tobago*. Petit Valley, Trinidad and Tobago: Heritage Cultures Ltd.

———. 1983. *Cradle of Caribbean Dance: Beryl McBurnie and the Little Carib Theatre*. Petit Valley, Trinidad and Tobago: Heritage Cultures Ltd.

Aiyejina, Funso. 2002. Voicing the African Soul: Orisha Songs in Trinidad and Tobago. Paper given at International Conference on New World Religions, St. Augustine, Trinidad and Tobago, University of the West Indies.

Aiyejina, Funso, and Rawle Gibbons. 1999. Orisa (Orisha) Tradition in Trinidad. *Caribbean Quarterly* 45(4): 35–50.

Àjàyí, Omofolabo S. 1998. *Yoruba Dance: The Semiotics of Movement and Body Attitude in a Nigerian Culture*. Trenton, N.J.: Africa World Press.

Allen, Carolyn. 2002. Creole: The Problem of Definition. In *Questioning Creole: Creolisation Discourses in Caribbean Culture*, ed. V. A. Shepherd and G. L. Richards, 47–63. Kingston, Jamaica: Ian Randle Publishers.

Anthony, Michael. 1989. *Parade of the Carnival Bands, 1839–1989*. Port-of-Spain, Trinidad & Tobago: Circle Press.

Appadurai, Arjun. 1986a. Theory in Anthropology: Center and Periphery. *Comparative Studies in Society and History* 28(3): 356–61.

———. 1986b. Is Homo Hierarchicus? Review article. *American Ethnologist* 13(4): 745–61.

———. 1992. Putting Hierarchy in Its Place. In *Rereading Cultural Anthropology*, ed. G. Marcus. Durham, N.C.: Duke University Press.

Apter, Andrew. 1991. Herskovits's Heritage: Rethinking Syncretism in the African Diaspora. *Diaspora* 1(3): 235–60.

———. 1992. *Black Critics and Kings: The Hermeneutics of Power in Yoruba Society*. Chicago: University of Chicago Press.

———. 1995. Notes on Orisha Cults in the Ekiti Yoruba Highlands. *Cahiers d'Études Africaines* 35(2–3): 369–401.

———. 1997. Review of G. Brandon, *Santería from Africa to the New World: The Dead Sell Memories*. *Bulletin of Latin American Research* 16(2): 234–36.

———. 2002. On African Origins: Creolization and *Connaissance* in Haitian Vodou. *American Ethnologist* 29(2): 233–60.

———. 2005. *The Pan-African Nation: Oil and the Spectacle of Culture in Nigeria*. Chicago: University of Chicago Press.

Apter, Andrew, and Lauren Derby, eds. 2010. *Activating the Past: History and Memory in the Black Atlantic*. Oxford: Cambridge Scholars Publishing.

Asad, Talal. 1993. *Genealogies of Religion: Discipline and Reasons of Power in Christianity and Islam*. Baltimore: Johns Hopkins University Press.

———. 2003. *Formations of the Secular: Christianity, Islam, Modernity*. Stanford: Stanford University Press.

Atkinson, Jane Monnig. 1992. Shamanisms Today. *Annual Review of Anthropology* 21: 307–30.

Austin-Broos, Diane. 1992. Redefining the Moral Order: Interpretations of Christianity in Postemancipation Jamaica. In *The Meaning of Freedom*, ed. F. McGlynn and S. Drescher, 221–24. Pittsburgh: University of Pittsburgh Press.

Bahadoorsingh, Krishna. 1968. *Trinidad Electoral Politics: The Persistence of the Race Factor*. London: Institute of Race Relations.

Balutansky, Kathleen M. 1997. Appreciating C.L.R. James, a Model of Modernity and Creolization. *Latin American Research Review* 32(2): 233–43.

Balutansky, Kathleen M., and Marie-Agnès Sourieau. 1998. Introduction. In *Caribbean Creolization: Reflections on the Cultural Dynamics of Language, Literacy, and Identity*, ed. K. M. Balutansky and M-A. Sourieau, 1–12. Gainesville: University Press of Florida.

Barber, Karin. 1981. How Man Makes God in West Africa: Yoruba Attitudes towards the Òrìsà. *Africa* 51(3): 724–45.

———. 1990. Oríkì, Women and the Proliferation and Merging of Òrìsà. *Africa* 60(3): 313–37.

Barnes, Sandra T. 1997. *Africa's Ogun: Old World and New*, 2nd ed. Bloomington: Indiana University Press.

Barrett, Leonard. 1974. *Soul-Force: African Heritage in Afro-American Religion*. New York: Anchor.

Basch, Michael F. 1988. *Understanding Psychotherapy: The Science Behind the Art*. New York: Basic Books.

Bascom, William R. 1944. *The Sociological Role of the Yoruba Cult Group*. Memoir 63. Washington, DC: American Anthropological Association.

———. 1969. *Ifa Divination: Communication between Gods and Men in West Africa*. Bloomington: Indiana University Press.

———. 1972. *Shango in the New World*. Austin: University of Texas Press.

Bassier, Dennis W.M.Z. 1987. Kali Mai Worship in Guyana: A Quest for a New identity. In *Indians in the Caribbean*, ed. I. J. Bahadur Singh, 269–93. New Delhi: Sterling.

Bastide, Roger. 1958. *Le Candomblé de Bahia (rite Nagô)*. Paris: Mouton.

———. 1972. *African Civilizations in the New World*, trans. P. Green. New York: Harper & Row.

———. 1978. *The African Religions of Brazil: Towards a Sociology of the Interpenetration of Civilizations*, trans. H. Sebba. Baltimore: Johns Hopkins University Press.

Baucom, Ian. 2005. *Spectres of the Atlantic: Finance Capital, Slavery, and the Philosophy of History*. Durham, N.C.: Duke University Press.

Bauman, Richard, and Charles Briggs. 2003. *Voices of Modernity: Language Ideologies and the Politics of Inequality*. Cambridge: Cambridge University Press.

Beattie, John, and John Middleton, eds. 1969. *Spirit Mediumship and Society in Africa*. London: Routledge & Kegan Paul.

Behrend, Heike, and Ute Luig, eds. 1999. *Spirit Possession, Modernity, and Power in Africa*. Oxford: James Currey.

Bennett, Herman L. 1989. The Challenge to the Post-Colonial State: A Case Study of the February Revolution in Trinidad. In *The Modern Caribbean*, ed. F. W. Knight and C. A. Palmer, 128–46. Chapel Hill: University of North Carolina Press.

Benítez Rojo, Antonio. 1992. *The Repeating Island: The Caribbean and the Postmodern Perspective*, trans. J. Maraniss. Durham, N.C.: Duke University Press.

Besson, Jean. 1992. Freedom and Community: The British West Indies. In *The Meaning of Freedom*, ed. F. McGlynn and S. Drescher, 183–220. Pittsburgh: University of Pittsburgh Press.

———. 1995. The Legacy of George L. Beckford's Plantation Economy Thesis in Jamaica. *New West Indian Guide* 69(1–2): 111–19.

Best, Lloyd. 1985. West Indian Society 150 Years after Abolition: A Reexamination of Some Classic Theories. In *Out of Slavery: Abolition and After*, ed. J. Hayward, 132–58. London: Frank & Cass Co.

Biagini, E. F. 2003. Neo-Roman Liberalism: "Republican" Values and British Liberalism, ca. 1860–1875. *History of European Ideas* 29: 55–72.

Biardeau, Madeleine. 1981. *Hinduism: The Anthropology of a Great Civilization*. Delhi: Oxford University Press.

Bilby, Kenneth M. 1999. Gumbay, Myal, and the Great House: New Evidence on the Religious Background of Jonkonnu in Jamaica. *African Caribbean Institute of Jamaica Research Review* 4: 41–70.

———. 2005. *True-Born Maroons*. Gainesville: University Press of Florida.

Birbalsingh, Frank, ed. 1989. *Indenture and Exile: The Indo-Caribbean Experience*. Toronto: TSAR.

Blackburn, Robin. 1998. Emancipation in the Americas. In *Historical Guide to World Slavery*, ed. S. Drescher and S. L. Engerman, 184–88. New York: Oxford University Press.

Blau, Herbert. 1992. *To All Appearances: Ideology and Performance*. New York: Routledge.

Boas, Franz. 1896. The Limitations of the Comparative Method in Anthropology. *Science* 4: 901–908.

———. 1940. *Race, Language, and Culture*. New York: Macmillan.

Boddy, Janice. 1988. Spirits and Selves in Northern Sudan: The Cultural Therapeutics of Possession and Trance. *American Ethnologist* 15(1): 4–27.

———. 1989. *Wombs and Alien Spirits: Women, Men, and the Zar Cult in Northern Sudan*. Madison: University of Wisconsin Press.

———. 1993. Subversive Kinship: The Role of Spirit Possession in Negotiating Social Place in Rural Northern Sudan. *Political and Legal Anthropology Review* 16(2): 29–37.

———. 1994. Spirit Possession Revisited: Beyond Instrumentality. *Annual Review of Anthropology* 23: 407–34.

Bolland, Nigel O. 1992a. The Politics of Freedom in the British Caribbean. In *The Meaning of Freedom*, ed. F. McGlynn and S. Drescher, 113–46. Pittsburgh: University of Pittsburgh Press.

———. 1992b. Creolization and Creole Societies: A Cultural Nationalist View of Caribbean Social History. In *Intellectuals in the Twentieth-century Caribbean*, vol. 1, *Spectre of the New Class: The Commonwealth Caribbean*, ed. A. Hennessey, 50–79. London: Macmillan.

———. 2005. Reconsidering Creolization and Creole Societies. In *Contesting Freedom: Control and Resistance in the Post-Emancipation Caribbean*, ed. G. Heuman and D. V. Trotman, 179–96. London: Macmillan.

Bourguignon, Erika. 1965. The Self, the Behavioral Environment, and the Theory of Spirit Possession. In *Context and Meaning in Cultural Anthropology*, ed. M. E. Spiro, 39–60. New York: Free Press.

———. 1970. Ritual Dissociation and Possession Belief in Caribbean Negro Religion. In *Afro-American Anthropology: Contemporary Perspectives*, ed. N. E. Whitten Jr. and J. F. Szwed, 87–103. New York: Free Press.

———. 1973. "Introduction: A Framework for the Comparative Study of Altered States of Consciousness." In *Religion, Altered States of Consciousness and Social Change*, ed. E. Bourguignon, 3–35. Columbus: Ohio State University Press.

———. 1976. *Possession*. San Francisco: Chandler and Sharp.

———. 1978. Spirit Possession and Altered States of Consciousness: The Evolution of an Inquiry. In *The making of Psychological Anthropology*, ed. G. Spindler, 477–515. Berkeley: University of California Press.

———. 1989. Multiple Personality, Possession Trance, and the Psychic Unity of Mankind. *Ethos* 17(3): 371–84.

———. 1991. A. Irving Hallowell, the Foundations of Psychological Anthropology, and Altered States of Consciousness. *Psychoanalytic Study of Society*, vol. 16, ed. L. B. Boyer and R. M. Boyer, 17–41. Hillsdale, N.J.: Analytic Press.

———. 1994a. Trance and Meditation. In *Handbook of Psychological Anthropology*, ed. P. K. Bock, 297–313. Westport, Conn.: Greenwood Press.

———. 1994b. Identity and the Constant Self. *Psychoanalytic Study of Society*, vol. 19, ed. L. B. Boyer, R. M. Boyer, and H. F. Stein, 181–212. Hillsdale, N.J.: Analytic Press.

———. 2004. Suffering and Healing, Subordination and Power: Women and Possession Trance. *Ethos* 32(4): 557–74.

Bourguignon, Erika, ed. 1973. *Religion, Altered States of Consciousness, and Social Change*. Columbus: Ohio State University Press.

Bourguignon, Erika, and T. L. Evascu. 1976. Altered States of Consciousness within a General Evolutionary Perspective: A Holocultural Analysis. *Behavioral Science Research* 12: 197–216.

Bourguignon, Erika, and Louanna Pettay. 1964. Spirit Possession, Trance and Cross-Cultural Research. In *Symposium on New Approaches to the Study of Religion*, ed. M. E. Spiro, 38–49. Seattle: University of Washington Press (American Ethnological Society).

Braithwaite, Lloyd. 1953 (1975). *Social Stratification in Trinidad*. Mona, Jamaica: Institute of Social and Economic Research, University of the West Indies.

Brantlinger, Patrick. 1985. Victorians and Africans: The Genealogy of the Myth of the Dark Continent. *Victorian Studies* 12: 166–203.

Breman, Jan, and E. Valentine Daniel. 1992. The Making of a Coolie. *Journal of Peasant Studies* 19(3–4): 268–95.

Brereton, Bridget. 1974a. The Foundations of Prejudice: Indians and Africans in Nineteenth Century Trinidad. *Caribbean Issues* 1(1): 15–28.

———. 1974b (1985). The Experience of Indentureship: 1845–1917. In *Calcutta to Caroni: The East Indians of Trinidad*, ed. J. La Guerre, 21–32. St. Augustine, Trinidad: University of the West Indies Press.

———. 1979. *Race Relations in Colonial Trinidad, 1870–1900*. Cambridge: Cambridge University Press.

———. 1981. *A History of Modern Trinidad, 1783–1962*. London: Heinemann.

———. 1983. The Birthday of Our Race: A Social History of Emancipation Day in Trinidad, 1838–88. In *Trade, Government and Society in Caribbean History*, ed. B. W. Higman, 69–84. Kingston, Jamaica: Heinemann Education Books.

———. 1989. Society and Culture in the Caribbean: The British and French West Indies, 1870–1980. In *The Modern Caribbean*, ed. F. W. Knight and C. A. Palmer, 85–110. Chapel Hill: University of North Carolina Press.

———. 1993. Social Organization and Class, Racial and Cultural Conflict in Nineteenth Century Trinidad. In *Trinidad Ethnicity*, ed. K. Yelvington, 33–55. Knoxville: University of Tennessee Press.

———. 2002. Slavery, Antislavery, Freedom: A Book Review. *New West Indian Guide* 76(1 and 2): 97–103.

Brereton, Bridget, and Winston Dookeran, eds. 1982. *East Indians in the Caribbean: Colonialism and the Struggle for Identity*. Millwood, N.Y.: Kraus.

Brereton, Bridget, and Kevin A. Yelvington. 1999. The Promise of Emancipation. In *The Colonial Caribbean in Transition: Essays on Postemancipation Social and Cultural History*, ed. B. Brereton and K. Yelvington, 1–25. Gainesville: University Press of Florida.

Breuer, Josef, and Sigmund Freud. 1895 (1955). Studies on Hysteria. *The Standard Edition of the Complete Psychological Works of Sigmund Freud*. London: Hogarth Press.

Brown, David H. 2003. *Santería Enthroned: Art, Ritual, and Innovation in an Afro-Cuban Religion*. Chicago: University of Chicago Press.

Brown, Karen McCarthy. 1991. *Mama Lola: A Vodou Priestess in Brooklyn*. Berkeley: University of California Press.

Brown, Michael F. 1997. *The Channeling Zone*. Cambridge: Harvard University Press.

Brubaker, Richard L. 1983. The Untamed Goddesses of Village India. In *The Book of the Goddess, Past and Present*, ed. C. Olson, 145–160. New York: Crossroad.

Brubaker, Rogers. 2005. The "Diaspora" Diaspora. *Ethnic and Racial Studies* 28(1): 1–19.

Bunzl, Matti. 2008. The Quest for Anthropological Relevance: Borgesian Maps and Epistemological Pitfalls. *American Anthropologist* 110(1): 53–60.

Burke, Peter. 1981. The "Discovery" of Popular Culture. In *People's History and Socialist Theory*, ed. R. Samuel, 216–26. London: Routledge & Kegan Paul.

Burton, Richard D. E. 1993. *Ki moun nou ye?*: The Idea of Difference in Contemporary French West Indian Thought. *New West Indian Guide* 67(1–2): 5–32.

———. 1997. *Afro-Creole: Power, Opposition, and Play in the Caribbean*. Ithaca, N.Y.: Cornell University Press.

Caillois, Roger. 1961. *Man, Play, and Games*. New York: Glencoe Press.

Campbell, Carl. 1974 (1985). The East Indian Revolt against Missionary Education, 1928–1939.

In *Calcutta to Caroni: The East Indians of Trinidad*, ed. J. La Guerre, 117–34. St. Augustine, Trinidad: University of the West Indies Press.

———. 1992. *Colony and Nation: A Short History of Education in Trinidad and Tobago, 1834–1986*. Kingston, Jamaica: Ian Randle.

Carlson, Marvin. 1996. *Performance: A Critical Introduction*. New York: Routledge.

Carmichael, Gertrude. 1961. *A History of the West Indian Islands of Trinidad and Tobago, 1497–1900*. London: Alvin Redman.

Carr, Andrew. 1953. A Rada Community in Trinidad. *Caribbean Quarterly* 3(1): 35–54.

Carrithers, Michael, Steven Collins, and Steven Lukes, eds. 1985. *The Category of the Person: Anthropology, Philosophy, History*. Cambridge: Cambridge University Press.

Casanova, José. 1994. *Public Religions in the Modern World*. Chicago: University of Chicago Press.

Case, Frederick Ivor. 2001. The Intersemiotics of Obeah and Kali Mai in Guyana. In *Nation Dance: Religion, Identity, and Difference in the Caribbean*, ed. P. Taylor, 40–53. Bloomington: University of Indiana Press.

Cashmore, E. 1996. Creole. In *Dictionary of Race and Ethnic Relations*, ed. E. Cashmore, 90–91. New York: Routledge.

Cateau, Heather, and S.H.H. Carrington, eds. 2000. *Capitalism and Slavery Fifty Years Later: Eric Eustace Williams—A Reassessment of the Man and His Work*. New York: Peter Lang.

Catoira, Patricia. 2005. Transculturation à la *Ajiaco*. In *Cuban Counterpoints: The Legacy of Fernando Ortiz*, ed. M. A. Font and A. W. Quiroz, 181–91. Lanham, Md.: Lexington Books.

Chestnut, R. Andrew. 2003. *Competitive Spirits: Latin America's New Religious Economy*. New York: Oxford University Press.

Childs, Matt D., and Toyin Falola. 2004. The Yoruba Diaspora in the Atlantic World: Methodology and Research. In *The Yoruba Diaspora in the Atlantic World*, ed. T. Falola and M. D. Childs, 1–16. Bloomington: Indiana University Press.

Clarke, Colin G. 1986. *East Indians in a West Indian Town: San Fernando, Trinidad, 1930–1970*. London: Allen & Unwin.

Clarke, Kamari M. 2004. *Mapping Yorùbá Networks: Power and Agency in the Making of Transnational Communities*. Durham, N.C.: Duke University Press.

———. 2007. Transnational Yoruba Revivalism and the Diasporic Politics of Heritage. *American Ethnologist* 34(4): 721–34.

Claus, Peter J. 1979. Spirit Possession and Spirit Mediumship from the Perspective of Tulu Oral Traditions. *Culture, Medicine, and Psychiatry* 3(1): 29–52.

Clifford, James. 1988. *The Predicament of Culture*. Cambridge: Harvard University Press.

———. 1994. Diasporas. *Cultural Anthropology* 9(3): 302–38.

———. 1997. *Routes: Travel and Translation in the Late 20th Century*. Cambridge: Harvard University Press.

Cohen, Peter F. 2002. Orìsà Journeys: The Role of Travel in the Birth of Yorùbá-Atlantic Religions. *Archives de Sciences Sociales des Religions*. 117: 17–36.

———. 2009. The Orisha Atlantic: Historicizing the Roots of a Global Religion. In *Transnational Transcendence: Essays on Religion and Globalization*, ed. T. J. Csordas, 205–30. Berkeley: University of California Press.

Collens, J. H. 1888. *Guide to Trinidad*. London: Eliot Stock.

Collins, Elizabeth F. 1997. *Pierced by Murugan's Lance: Ritual, Power, and Moral Redemption among Malaysian Hindus*. DeKalb: Northern Illinois University Press.

Colpe, C. 1987. Syncretism. In *Encyclopedia of Religion*, ed. M. Eliade, 218–27. New York: Macmillan.

Coronil, Fernando. 1995. Transculturation and the Politics of Theory: Countering the Center, Cuban Counterpoint (introduction to Duke University Press edition). In *Cuban Counterpoint* by F. Ortiz, iv–lvi. Durham, N.C.: Duke University Press.

———. 2005. Transcultural Anthropology in the Américas (with an Accent): The Uses of Fernando Ortiz. In *Cuban Counterpoints: The Legacy of Fernando Ortiz*, ed. M. A. Font and A. W. Quiroz, 139–56. Lanham, Md.: Lexington Books.

Cosentino, Donald. 2005. Vodou in the Age of Mechanical Reproduction. *Res* 47(Spring): 231–46.

Cothonay, R.P.M. Bertrand, O.P. 1893. *Trinidad: Journal d'un missionaire dominicain des Antilles Anglaises*. Paris: Victor Retaux et fils.

Crapanzano, Vincent. 1973. *The Hamadsha: A Study in Moroccan Ethnopsychiatry*. Berkeley: University of California Press.

———. 1975. Saints, *Jnun*, and Dreams. *Psychiatry* 38: 145–59.

———. 1977a. Introduction. In *Case Studies in Spirit Possession*, ed. V. Crapanzano and V. Garrison, 1–39. New York: Wiley.

———. 1977b. Mohammed and Dawia: Possession in Morocco. In *Case Studies in Spirit Possession*, ed. V. Crapanzano and V. Garrison, 141–76. New York: Wiley.

———. 1987. Spirit Possession. In *Encyclopedia of Religion*, vol. 14, ed. M. Eliade, 12–19. New York: Macmillan.

———. 1994. Rethinking Psychological Anthropology: A Critical View. In *The Making of Psychological Anthropology II*, ed. M. M. Suárez-Orozco, G. Spindler, and L. Spindler, 223–43. San Diego: Harcourt Brace.

Craton, Michael. 1997. *Empire, Enslavement and Freedom in the Caribbean*. Princeton, N.J.: Markus Wiener.

Crowley, Daniel J. 1957. Plural and Differential Acculturation in Trinidad. *American Anthropologist* 59(4): 817–24.

Csordas, Thomas J. 1985. Medical and Sacred Realities: Between Comparative Religion and Transcultural Psychiatry. *Culture, Medicine, and Psychiatry* 9: 103–16.

———. 1987. Health and the Holy in African and Afro-American Spirit Possession. *Social Science and Medicine* 24(1): 1–11.

———. 1993. Somatic Modes of Attention. *Cultural Anthropology* 8(2): 135–56.

Dabydeen, David, and Brinsley Samaroo, eds. 1987. *India in the Caribbean*. London: Hansib.

———. 1996. *Across the Dark Waters: Ethnicity and Indian Identity in the Caribbean*. London: Macmillan.

Davis, David B. 1970. *The Problem of Slavery in Western Culture*. Ithaca, N.Y.: Cornell University Press.

———. 1998. Introduction: The Problem of Slavery. In *Historical Guide to World Slavery*, ed. S. Drescher and S. L. Engerman, ix–xviii. New York: Oxford University Press.

Dayfoot, Arthur C. 1999. *The Shaping of the West Indian Church, 1492–1962*. Gainesville: University Press of Florida.

———. 2001. Themes from West Indian Church History in Colonial and Post-Colonial Times. In *Nation Dance: Religion, Identity, and Difference in the Caribbean*, ed. P. Taylor, 79–88. Bloomington: Indiana University Press.

de Certeau, Michel. 1980. On the Oppositional Practices of Everyday Life. *Social Text* 3: 3–43.

de Heusch, Luc. 1962. Cultes de possession et religions initiatiques de salut en Afrique. In *Religions de salut*, vol. 2. Brussels: Université Libre de Bruxelles, Centre d'Études des Religions.

———. 1965. Possession et chamanisme: Essai d'analyse structurale. In *Les religions traditionelles africaines*. Paris: Editions du Seuil.

Desmangles, Leslie. 2001. Caribbean: African-Derived Religions. In *Encyclopedia of African and African-American Religions*, ed. S. Glazier, 77–81. New York: Routledge.

Devereux, George, and Edwin M. Loeb. 1943. Antagonistic Acculturation. *American Sociological Review* 8(2): 133–47.

de Verteuil, Fr. Anthony. 1990. Madrassi Emigration to Trinidad, 1846–1916. *Conference of Caribbean Historians*, 22: 1–21. St. Augustine, Trinidad and Tobago: University of the West Indies.

de Verteuil, Louis A. A. 1858 (1884). *Trinidad: Its Geography, Natural Resources, Administration, Present Condition, and Prospects*. London: Ward & Lock.

de Zengotita, Thomas. 1989. Speakers of Being: Romantic Refusion and Cultural Anthropology. In *Romantic Motives: Essays in Anthropological Sensibility*, ed. G.W.S. Stocking Jr., 74–123. Madison: University of Wisconsin Press.

———. 2005. *Mediated: How the Media Shapes Your World and the Way You Live In It*. New York: Bloomsbury.

Dhanda, Karen S. 2002. Labor and Place in Barbados, Jamaica, and Trinidad: Search for a Comparative Unified Field Theory Revisited. *New West Indian Guide* 75(3 and 4): 229–56.

Donham, Donald L. 1990. *History, Power, Ideology*. Cambridge: Cambridge University Press.

Drescher, Seymour. 1977. *Econocide: British Slavery in the Era of Abolition*. Pittsburgh: University of Pittsburgh Press.

———. 1999. *From Slavery to Freedom: Comparative Studies in the Rise and Fall of Atlantic Slavery*. New York: New York University Press.

Drewal, Henry J., John Pemberton III, and Rowland Abiodun. 1989. *Yoruba: Nine Centuries of African Art and Thought*. New York: Center for African Art.

Drewal, Margaret T. 1975. Symbols of Possession: A Study of Movement and Regalia in an Anago-Yoruba Ceremony. *Dance Research Journal* 7(2): 15–24.

———. 1986. Art and Trance among Yoruba Shango Devotees. *African Arts* 20(1): 60–67.

———. 1989 (1997). Dancing for Ogun in Yorubaland and Brazil. In *Africa's Ogun: Old World and New*, ed. S. T. Barnes, 199–234. Bloomington: Indiana University Press.

———. 1992. *Yoruba Ritual: Performers, Play, Agency*. Bloomington: Indiana University Press.

Droogers, André, and Hans Siebers. 1991. Popular Religion and Power in Latin America: An Introduction. In *Popular Power in Latin American Religions*, ed. A. Droogers et al., 1–25. Fort Lauderdale, Fla.: Breitenbach.

Drummond, Lee. 1980. The Cultural Continuum: A Theory of Intersystems. *Man* 15(2): 352–74.

Dumont, Louis. 1961. Caste, Racism and "Stratification": Reflections of a Social Anthropologist. *Contributions to Indian Sociology* 5: 20–41.

Dunn, John. 2003. *Locke: A Very Short Introduction*. New York: Oxford University Press.

Dunn, Richard S. 1972. *Sugar and Slaves: The Rise of the Planter Class in the English West Indies, 1624–1713*. New York: Norton.

Eastman, Rudolph, and Maureen Warner-Lewis. 2000. Forms of African Spirituality in Trinidad and Tobago. In *African Spirituality: Forms, Meanings, Expressions*, ed. J. K. Olupona. New York: Crossroad.

Eggan, Fred. 1937. The Cheyenne and Arapaho Kinship System. In *Social Anthropology of North American Tribes*, ed. F. Eggan. Chicago: University of Chicago Press.

———. 1954. Social Anthropology and the Method of Controlled Comparison. *American Anthropologist* 56(5): 743–63.

Eigen, Michael. 2001. *Ecstasy*. Middletown, Conn.: Wesleyan University Press.

Elder, J. D. 1970. The Yoruba Ancestor Cult in Gasparillo: Its Structure, Organization, and Social Function in Community Life. *Caribbean Quarterly* 16(3): 5–20.

———. 1976. Morality in a Yoruba Ritual in Trinidad. *American Folklife*, ed. D. Yoder, 281–91. Austin: University of Texas Press.

———. 1996. The Orisha Religion (Shango) as Resistance and Social Protest. In *Ay BoBo: Afro-Caribbean Religions, Part One—Cults*, ed. Manfred Kremser, 25–40. Austria: Wuv Universitätsverlag.

Eliade, Mircea. 1964. *Shamanism: Archaic Techniques of Ecstasy*, trans. W. R. Trask. Princeton: Princeton University Press.

Eltis, David. 1995. The Volume and Origins of the British Slave Trade Before 1714. *Cahiers d'Études Africaines* 35(2–3): 617–27.

———. 1998. Trans-Atlantic Trade. In *Historical Guide to World Slavery*, ed. S. Drescher and S. L. Engerman, 370–75. New York: Oxford University Press.

Eltis, David, and David Richardson. 1997a. The "Numbers Game" and Routes to Slavery. *Slavery and Abolition* 18(1): 1–15.

———. 1997b. West Africa and the Transatlantic Slave Trade: New Evidence of Long-Run Trade. *Slavery and Abolition* 18(1): 16–35.

Emigh, John. 1996. *Masked Performance*. Philadelphia: University of Pennsylvania Press.

Fabian, Johannes. 1978. Popular Culture in Africa: Findings and Conjectures. *Africa* 48(4): 315–34.

———. 1981. Six Theses Regarding the Anthropology of African Religious Movements. *Religion* 11: 109–26.

———. 1998. *Moments of Freedom: Anthropology and Popular Culture*. Charlottesville: University Press of Virginia.

Falola, Toyin, and Matt D. Childs, ed. 2004. *The Yoruba Diaspora in the Atlantic World*. Bloomington: Indiana University Press.

Fernandez, Ronald. 1994. *Cruising the Caribbean: U.S. Influence and Intervention in the 20th Century*. Monroe, Maine: Common Courage Press.

Fjelstad, Karen, and Nguyen Thi Hien, eds. 2006. *Possessed by the Spirits: Mediumship in Contemporary Vietnamese Communities*. Ithaca, N.Y.: Cornell University Southeast Asia Program Publications.

Forbes, Richard H. 1987. Hindu Organizational Process in Acculturative Conditions: Significance of the Arya Samaj Experience in Trinidad. In *Indians in the Caribbean*, ed. I. J. Bahadur Singh, 193–216. New Delhi: Sterling.

Forte, Maximilian C. 1995a. *Against the Trinity: An Insurgent Imam Tells His Story*. Binghamton, N.Y.: Polaris-Australis.

———. 1995b. The Crisis in Creolization in Trinidad and Tobago: Globalized Revitalizations, Systemic Ethno-Politics, and Alter-Nationalisms. *International Third World Studies Journal and Review* 7: 41–53.

———. 2005. *Ruins of Absence, Presence of Caribs: (Post)Colonial Representations of Aboriginality in Trinidad and Tobago*. Gainesville: University Press of Florida.

Freud, Sigmund. 1900. The Interpretation of Dreams. In *Standard Edition of the Complete Psychological Works of Sigmund Freud*, vols. 4 & 5, trans. J. Strachey. London: Hogarth.

———. 1910. Leonardo da Vinci and a Memory of His Childhood. In *Standard Edition of the Complete Psychological Works of Sigmund Freud*, vol. 11, trans. J. Strachey, 63–137. London: Hogarth.

Friedrich, Paul. 1991. Polytropy. In *Beyond Metaphor: The Theory of Tropes in Anthropology*, ed. J. Fernandez, 17–55. Stanford, Calif.: Stanford University Press.

Fulcher, James. 2004. *Capitalism: A Very Short Introduction*. New York: Oxford University Press.

Fuller, C. J. 1992. *The Camphor Flame: Popular Hinduism and Society in India*. Princeton, N.J.: Princeton University Press.

Galenson, David W. 1998. Indentured Servitude. In *Historical Guide to World Slavery*, ed. S. Drescher and S. L. Engerman, 239–42. New York: Oxford University Press.

Gamble, W. H. 1866. *Trinidad: Historical and Descriptive: Being a Narrative of Nine Years Residence in the Island*. London: Yates & Alexander.

Gates, Henry Louis. 1988. *The Signifyin' Monkey: A Theory of African-American Literary Criticism*. New York: Oxford University Press.

Geertz, Clifford. 1973. Deep Play: Notes on the Balinese Cockfight. In *The Interpretation of Cultures*, 412–54. New York: Basic Books.

Gell, Alfred. 1978. The Gods at Play: Vertigo and Possession in Muria Religion. *Man* 15(2): 219–48.

Gibbons, Rawle. 1979. *Traditional Enactments of Trinidad: Towards a Third Theatre*. M.Phil. thesis, University of the West Indies.

Glazier, Stephen D. 1983 (1991). *Marchin' the Pilgrims Home: A Study of the Spiritual Baptists of Trinidad*. Salem, West Indies: Sheffield Press.

———. 2001. Spiritual Baptists. In *Encyclopedia of African and African-American Religions*, ed. S. D. Glazier, 315–19. New York: Routledge.

Glissant, Édouard. 1989. *Caribbean Discourse*, trans. J. M. Dash. Charlottesville: University Press of Virginia.

Goldwasser, Michele. 1996. *The Rainbow Madonna of Trinidad: A Study of Belief in Trinidadian Religious Life*. Ph.D. dissertation, University of California.

Gomes, Albert. 1974. *Through a Maze of Colour*. Port-of-Spain, Trinidad and Tobago: Key Caribbean.

Green, William A. 1976. *British Slave Emancipation: The Sugar Colonies and the Great Experiment, 1830–1865*. Oxford: Clarendon Press.

———. 1986. The Creolization of Caribbean History: The Emancipation Era and a Critique of Dialectical Analysis. *Journal of Imperial and Commonwealth History* 14(3): 149–69.

Guha, Ranajit, and Gayatri Chakravorty Spivak, eds. 1988. *Selected Subaltern Studies*. New York: Oxford University Press.

Guinee, William. 1990. *Ritual and Devotion in a Trinidadian Kali Temple*. Master's thesis, Indiana University.

———. 1992. *Suffering and Healing in a Trinidadian Kali Temple*. Ph.D. dissertation, Indiana University.

Habermas, Jürgen. 1971. *Knowledge and Human Interests*, trans. J. Shapiro. Boston: Beacon.

Hagelberg, G. B. 1985. Sugar in the Caribbean: Turning Sunshine into Money. In *Caribbean Contours*, ed. S. W. Mintz and S. Price, 85–126. Baltimore, Md.: Johns Hopkins University Press.

Hall, Douglas. 1978. The Flight from the Estates Reconsidered: The British West Indies, 1828–42. *Journal of Caribbean History* 10–11: 7–24.

Hall, Stuart. 1981. Notes on Deconstructing "the Popular." In *People's History and Socialist Theory*, ed. R. Samuel, 216–26. London: Routledge & Kegan Paul.

———. 1986. Variants of Liberalism. In *Politics and Ideology*, ed. J. Donald and S. Hall, 34–69. Milton Keynes, Eng.: Open University Press.

Hallowell, A. I. 1942. *The Role of Conjuring in Salteaux Society*. Philadelphia: University of Pennsylvania Press.

———. 1955. *Culture and Experience*. Philadelphia: University of Pennsylvania Press.

———. 1966. The Role of Dreams in Ojibwa Culture. In *The Dream in Human Societies*, ed. G. E. von Grunebaum and R. Caillois, 267–92. Berkeley: University of California Press.

———. 1972. On Being an Anthropologist. In *Crossing Cultural Boundaries*, ed. S. T. Kimball and J. B. Watson, 51–62. New York: Chandler.

Handler, Richard, and Daniel Segal. 1990. *Jane Austen and the Fiction of Culture*. Tucson: University of Arizona Press.

———. 1993. Nations, Colonies, and Metropoles. *Social Analysis* 33: 3–8.

Hannerz, Ulf. 1987. The World in Creolization. *Africa* 57(4): 546–59.

———. 1992a. *Cultural Complexity: Studies in the Social Organization of Meaning*. New York: Columbia University Press.

———. 1992b. The Global Ecumene as a Network of Networks. In *Conceptualizing Society*, ed. A. Kuper, 34–56. London: Routledge.

———. 1996. *Transnational Connections: Culture, People, Places*. London: Routledge.

Haraksingh, Kusha. 1985. Aspects of the Indian experience in the Caribbean. In *Calcutta to Caroni: The East Indians of Trinidad*, ed. J. La Guerre, 155–72. St. Augustine, Trinidad: University of the West Indies Press.

———. 1986. Culture, religion and resistance among Indians in the Caribbean. In *Indian Labour Immigration*, ed. U. Bissoondoyal and S.B.C. Servansing, 223–37. Mauritius: Mahatma Gandhi Institute.

———. 1987. The Hindu Experience in Trinidad. In *Indians in the Caribbean*, ed. I. J. Bahadur Singh, 167–84. New Delhi: Sterling.

———. 1988. Structure, Process and Indian Culture in Trinidad. *Immigrants and Minorities* 7(1): 113–22.

Harricharan, Fr. John T. 1981a. *The Feast of La Divina Pastora, Holy Shepherdess: Its Origins, Historical Development and Future Perspectives*. San Juan, Trinidad and Tobago: General Printers.

———. 1981b. *The Catholic Church in Trinidad, Vol. 1: 1498–1852*. Port-of-Spain, Trinidad: Inprint Caribbean.

———. 1993. *History of the Catholic Church in Trinidad, Vol. 2: 1853–1863*. Barataria, Trinidad and Tobago: Hitlal's Printery.

Hawley, John Stratton. 1981. *At Play with Krishna: Pilgrimage Dramas from Brindavan*. Princeton, N.J.: Princeton University Press.

Hawley, John S., and Donna M. Wulff, eds. 1982. *The Divine Consort: Radha and the Goddesses of India*. Boston: Beacon Press.

Hefner, Robert W. 1998. Multiple Modernities: Christianity, Islam, and Hinduism in a Globalizing Age. *Annual Review of Anthropology* 27: 83–104.

Henry, Edward O. 1983. The Mother Goddess Cult and Interaction between Little and Great Religious Traditions. In *Religion in Modern India*, ed. G. R. Gupta, 174–97. Delhi: Vikas Publishing House Ltd.

Henry, Frances. 1965. Social Stratification in an Afro-American Cult. *Anthropological Quarterly* 38(1): 72–78.

———. 1981. Frances Henry Recalls Her Three Months with 'Pa Neezer,' the Shango King. *People* (November). Trinidad and Tobago.

———. 1983. Religion and Ideology in Trinidad: The Resurgence of the Shango Religion. *Caribbean Quarterly* 29(3–4): 63–69.

———. 1991. The Changing Functions of the Shango Religion in Trinidad. In *African Creative Expressions of the Divine*, ed. K. Davis and E. Farajaje-Jones, 53–62. Washington, D.C.: Howard University School of Divinity.

———. 2001. The Orisha (Shango) Movement in Trinidad. In *Encyclopedia of African and African-American Religions*, ed. S. Glazier, 221–23. New York: Routledge.

———. 2003. *Reclaiming African Religions in Trinidad: The Socio-Political Legitimation of the Orisha and Spiritual Baptist Faiths*. Mona, Jamaica: University of the West Indies Press.

Herskovits, Melville. 1937a. The Significance of the Study of Acculturation for Anthropology. *American Anthropologist* 39(2): 259–64.

———. 1937b. African Gods and Catholic Saints in New World Negro Belief. *American Anthropologist* 39(4): 635–43.

———. 1938. *Acculturation: The Study of Culture Contact*. New York: Knopf.

———. 1941 (1958). *The Myth of the Negro Past*. New York: Harper & Row.

———. 1944. Drums and Drummers in Afro-Brazilian Cult Life. *Musical Quarterly* 30: 477–92.

———. 1948. The Contribution of Afroamerican Studies to Africanist Research. *American Anthropologist* 50: 1–10.

———. 1952. Some Psychological Implications of Afroamerican Studies. In *Acculturation in the Americas*, ed. S. Tax, 152–60. Chicago: University of Chicago Press.

———. 1966. *The New World Negro: Selected Papers in Afroamerican Studies*. Bloomington: Indiana University Press.

Herskovits, Melville J., and Frances S. Herskovits. 1947 (1964). *Trinidad Village*. New York: Alfred A. Knopf.

Heywood, Linda M., ed. 2002. *Central Africans and Cultural Transformations in the American Diaspora*. Cambridge: Cambridge University Press.

Higman, B. W. 1978. African and Creole Slave Family Patterns in Trinidad. *Journal of Family History* 3: 163–78.

———. 1999. *Writing West Indian Histories*. London: Macmillan.

———. 2000. The Sugar Revolution. *Economic History Review* 53(2): 213–36.

Hiltebeitel, Alf. 1988. *The Cult of Draupadi*. Vol. 1: *Mythologies: From Gingee to Kurukshetra*. Chicago: University of Chicago Press.

———. 1989. Draupadi's Two Guardians: The Buffalo King and the Muslim Devotee. In *Criminal Gods and Demon Devotees*, ed. A. Hiltebeitel, 339–71. Albany: State University of New York Press.

———. 1991. *The Cult of Draupadi*. Vol. 2: *On Hindu Ritual and the Goddess*. Chicago: University of Chicago Press.

Hoetink, H. 1985. "Race" and Color in the Caribbean. In *Caribbean Contours*, ed. S. W. Mintz and S. Price, 55–84. Baltimore, Md.: Johns Hopkins University Press.

Hollan, Douglas. 2000a. Culture and Dissociation in Toraja. *Transcultural Psychiatry* 37(4): 545–59.

———. 2000b. Constructivist Models of Mind, Contemporary Psychoanalysis, and the Development of Culture Theory. *American Anthropologist* 102(3): 538–50.

Holland, Dorothy, and Julia Crane. 1987. Adapting to an Industrializing Nation: The Shango Cult in Trinidad. *Social and Economic Studies* 36(4): 41–66.

Hopkins, Dwight N. 2001. The Religion of Globalization. In *Religions/Globalizations: Theories and Cases*, ed. D. Hopkins, L. Lorentzen, E. Mendieta, and D. Batstone, 7–32. Durham, N.C.: Duke University Press.

Hopkins, Thomas J. 1971. *The Hindu Religious Tradition*. Encino, Calif.: Dickenson.

Horowitz. 1971. Introductory Essay. In *Peoples and Cultures of the Caribbean*, ed. M. Horowitz, 1–13. Garden City, N.Y.: Natural History Press.

Houk, James T. 1993. Afro-Trinidadian Identity and the Africanization of the *Orisha* Religion. In *Trinidad Ethnicity*, ed. K. Y. Yelvington, 161–79. London: Macmillan.

———. 1995. *Spirits, Blood, and Drums: The Orisha Religion in Trinidad*. Philadelphia: Temple University Press.

Hucks, Tracey E. 2001. Trinidad, African-derived Religions. In *Encyclopedia of African and African-American Religions*, ed. S. D. Glazier, 338–43. New York: Routledge.

———. 2006. "I Smoothed the Way, I Opened Doors": Women in the Yoruba-Orisha Tradition of Trinidad. In *Women and Religion in the African Diaspora: Knowledge, Power, and Performance*, ed. R. M. Griffith and B. D. Savage, 19–36. Baltimore, Md.: Johns Hopkins University Press.

Hucks, Tracey E., and Dianne M. Stewart. 2003. Authenticity and Authority in the Shaping of the Trinidad Orisha Identity: Toward an African-Derived Religious Theory. *Western Journal of Black Studies* 27(3): 176–85.

Ingham, John M. 1996. *Psychological Anthropology Reconsidered*. New York: Cambridge University Press.

Inglis, Stephen. 1985. Possession and Pottery: Serving the Divine in a South Indian Community. In *Gods of Flesh/Gods of Stone*, ed. J. Waghorne and N. Cutler, 89–102. Chambersburg, Penn.: Anima.

Inikori, Joseph. 1992. Slavery and Atlantic Commerce, 1650–1800. *American Economic Review* 82: 151–57.

———. 1998. Capitalism and Slavery. In *A Historical Guide to World Slavery*, ed. S. Drescher and S. L. Engerman, 107–10. New York: Oxford University Press.

Jackson, Walter. 1986. Melville Herskovits and the Search for Afro-American Culture. In *Malinowski, Rivers, Benedict, and Others: Essays on Culture and Personality*, ed. G. W. Stocking Jr., 95–126. Madison: University of Wisconsin Press.

James, C.L.R. 1963. Appendix: From Toussaint L'Ouverture to Fidel Castro. *The Black Jacobins: Toussaint L'Ouverture and the San Domingo Revolution*, 2nd rev. ed. New York: Vintage Books.

Janzen, John M. 1992. *Ngoma: Discourses of Healing in Central and Southern Africa*. Berkeley: University of California Press.

Jayawardena, Chandra. 1966. Religious Belief and Social Change: Aspects of the Development of Hinduism in British Guiana. *Comparative Studies in Society and History* 8: 210–40.

———. 1968. Migration and Social Change: A Survey of Indian Communities Overseas. *Geographical Review* 58: 426–49.

Jha, J. C. 1974 (1985). The Indian Heritage of Trinidad. In *Calcutta to Caroni: The East Indians of Trinidad*, ed. J. La Guerre, 1–20. St. Augustine, Trinidad and Tobago: University of the West Indies Press.

Jilek, W. G. 1971. From Crazy Witch Doctor to Auxiliary Psychotherapist: The Changing Image of the Medicine Man. *Psychiatrica Clinica* 4: 200–20.

———. 1974. *Salish Indian Mental Health and Culture Change: Psychohygienic and Therapeutic Aspects of the Guardian Spirit Ceremonial*. Toronto: Holt, Rinehart & Winston.

———. 1982. Altered States of Consciousness in North American Ceremonials. *Ethos* 10(3): 326–43.

John, A. Meredith. 1988. *The Plantation Slaves of Trinidad, 1783–1816: A Mathematical and Demographic Inquiry*. Cambridge: Cambridge University Press.

Johnson, Howard. 1987. The Chinese in Trinidad in the Late Nineteenth Century. *Ethnic and Racial Studies* 10(1): 82–95.

Johnson, Paul Christopher. 2005. Three Paths to Legal Legitimacy: African Diaspora Religions and the State. *Culture and Religion* 6(1): 79–105.

———. 2007. *Diaspora Conversions: Black Carib Religion and the Recovery of Africa*. Berkeley: University of California Press.

Joseph, E. L. 1838 (1870). *History of Trinidad*. London: Frank Cass.

Kakar, Sudhir. 1991. *The Analyst and the Mystic: Psychoanalytic Reflections on Religion and Mysticism*. Chicago: University of Chicago Press.

Kapadia, Karin. 2000. Pierced by Love: Tamil Possession, Gender and Caste. In *Invented Identities: The Interplay of Gender, Religion and Politics in India*, ed. J. Leslie and M. McGee, 181–202. Delhi: Oxford University Press.

Kelly, John. 2002. Alternative Modernities or an Alternative to "Modernity": Getting Out of the Modernist Sublime. In *Critically Modern: Alternatives, Alterities, Anthropologies*, ed. B. M. Knauft, 258–86. Bloomington: Indiana University Press.

Khan, Aisha. 1993. What Is a "Spanish"?: Ambiguity and "Mixed" Ethnicity in Trinidad. In *Trinidad Ethnicity*, ed. K. Yelvington, 180–207. Knoxville: University of Tennessee Press.

———. 1994. *Juthaa* in Trinidad: Food, Pollution, and Hierarchy in a Caribbean Diaspora Community. *American Ethnologist* 21(2): 245–69.

———. 1995. *Purity, Piety, and Power: Culture and Identity among Hindus and Muslims in Trinidad*. Ph.D. dissertation, City University of New York.

———. 1996. Untold Stories of Unfree Labor: Asians in the Americas. *New West Indian Guide* 70(1–2): 91–99.

———. 1999. On the "Right Path": Interpolating Religion in Trinidad. In *Religion, Diaspora, and Cultural Identity: A Reader in the Anglophone Caribbean*, ed. J. W. Pulis, 247–76. Amsterdam: Gordon and Breach.

———. 2001. Journey to the Center of the Earth: The Caribbean as Master Symbol. *Cultural Anthropology* 16(3): 271–302.

———. 2004. *Callaloo Nation: Metaphors of Race and Religious Identity among South Asians in Trinidad*. Durham, N.C.: Duke University Press.

———. 2007a. Good to Think? Creolization, Optimism, and Agency. *Current Anthropology* 48(5): 653–73.

———. 2007b. Creolization Moments. In *Creolization: History, Ethnography, Theory*, ed. C. Stewart, 237–53. Walnut Creek, Calif.: Left Coast Press.

Kingsley, Charles. 1892. *At Last, a Christmas in the West Indies*, 3rd ed. London: Macmillan.

Kinsley, David R. 1975. *The Sword and the Flute: Kali and Krishna, Dark Visions of the Terrible and the Sublime in Hindu Mythology*. Berkeley: University of California Press.

Klass, Morton. 1961 (1988). *East Indians in Trinidad: A Study of Cultural Persistence.* Prospect Heights, Ill.: Waveland Press.

———. 1991. *Singing with Sai Baba: The Politics of Revitalization.* Prospect Heights, Ill.: Waveland Press.

———. 1995. *Ordered Universes: Approaches to the Anthropology of Religion.* Boulder, Colo.: Westview Press.

———. 2003. *Mind over Mind: The Anthropology and Psychology of Spirit Possession.* Prospect Heights, Ill.: Waveland Press.

Klein, Naomi. 2007. *The Shock Doctrine: The Rise of Disaster Capitalism.* New York: Metropolitan.

Kleinman, Arthur. 1980. *Patients and Healers in the Context of Culture.* Berkeley: University of California Press.

———. 1986. *Social Origins of Distress and Disease: Depression, Neurasthenia, and Pain in Modern China.* New Haven: Yale University Press.

———. 1988. *Rethinking Psychiatry: From Cultural Category to Personal Experience.* New York: Free Press.

Knight, Franklin W., and Colin A. Palmer. 1989. The Caribbean: A Regional Overview. In *The Modern Caribbean*, ed. F. W. Knight and C. A. Palmer, 1–20. Chapel Hill: University of North Carolina Press.

Knipe, David M. 1991. *Hinduism: Experiments in the Sacred.* New York: Harper Collins.

Kolenda, Pauline M. 1968. The Functional Relations of a Bhangi Cult. *The Anthropologist* 2: 22–35.

———. 1983. The Mother-Goddess Complex among North Indian Sweepers. In *Religion in Modern India*, ed. G. R. Gupta, 215–28. Delhi: Vikas Publishing House Ltd.

Korom, Frank J. 1994. Memory, Innovation, and Emergent Ethnicity: The Creolization of an Indo-Trinidadian Performance. *Diaspora* 3(2): 135–55.

———. 2003. *Hosay Trinidad: Muharrum Performances in an Indo-Caribbean Diaspora.* Philadelphia: University of Pennsylvania Press.

Kramer, Fritz. 1993. *The Red Fez: Art and Spirit Possession in Africa*, trans. M. Green. London: Verso.

Kroeber, Alfred L. 1935. History and Science in Anthropology. *American Anthropologist* 37: 539–69.

La Guerre, John. 1974 (1985). *Calcutta to Caroni: The East Indians of Trinidad.* St. Augustine, Trinidad and Tobago: University of the West Indies Press.

Laguerre, Michel S. 1980. *Voodoo Heritage.* Beverly Hills, Calif.: Sage.

Laitinen, Maarit. 2002a. *Marching to Zion: Creolisation in Spiritual Baptist Rituals and Cosmology.* Helsinki: University of Helsinki, Research Series in Anthropology.

———. 2002b. Spiritual Baptist and Orisha Religions. Unpublished manuscript, University of Helsinki.

Lambek, Michael. 1981. *Human Spirits: A Cultural Account of Trance in Mayotte.* Cambridge: Cambridge University Press.

———. 1988. Graceful Exits: Spirit Possession as Personal Performance. *Culture* 8(1): 59–70.

———. 1989. From Disease to Discourse: Remarks on the Conceptualization of Trance and Spirit Possession. In *Altered States of Consciousness and Mental Health: A Cross-cultural Perspective*, ed. C. A. Ward, 36–62. Newbury Park, Calif.: Sage.

———. 1996. Afterword: Spirits and Their Histories. In *Spirits in Culture, History, and Mind*, ed. J. M. Mageo and A. Howard, 237–50. New York: Routledge.

———. 2002. Fantasy in Practice: Projection and Introjection, or the Witch and the Spirit-Medium. *Social Analysis* 46(3): 198–214.

Langer, Suzanne. 1953. *Feeling and Form: A Theory of Art*. New York: Scribner.

Largey, Michael. 2005. Recombinant Mythology and the Alchemy of Memory: Occide Jeanty, Ogou, and Jean-Jacques Dessalines in Haiti. *Journal of American Folklore* 118(469): 327–53.

Lawal, Babatunde. 1977. The Living Dead: Art and Immortality among the Yoruba of Nigeria. *Africa* 47(1): 50–60.

Leach, Robert. 1996. *British Political Ideologies*, 2nd ed. London: Prentice Hall.

Leder, Drew. 1990. *The Absent Body*. Chicago: University of Chicago Press.

Leiris, Michel. 1958. *La possession et ses aspects theatraux chez les Ethiopiens de Gondar*. Paris: Le Sycamore.

Levine, Cheryl A. 2003. *Mediating the Model: Women's Microenterprise and Microcredit in Tobago, West Indies*. Ph.D. dissertation, University of South Florida.

Levitt, Kari, and Michael Witter, eds. 1996. *The Critical Tradition of Caribbean Political Economy: The Legacy of George Beckford*. Kingston, Jamaica: Ian Randle.

Levy, Jerrold, Raymond Neutra, and Dennis Parker. 1979. Life Careers of Navajo Epileptics and Convulsive Hysterics. *Social Science and Medicine* 13: 53–66.

Levy, Robert I., Jeannette M. Mageo, and A. Howard. 1996. Gods, Spirits, and History: A Theoretical Perspective. In *Spirits in Culture, History, and Mind*, ed. J. M. Mageo and A. Howard, 11–27. New York: Routledge.

Lewis, Gordon K. 1968. *The Growth of the Modern West Indies*. New York: Monthly Review Press.

———. 1985. The Contemporary Caribbean: A General Overview. In *Caribbean Contours*, ed. S. W. Mintz and S. Price, 219–50. Baltimore, Md.: Johns Hopkins University Press.

Lewis, Ioan M. 1986. *Religion in Contest: Cults and Charisma*. Cambridge: Cambridge University Press.

———. 1989. *Ecstatic Religion: A Study of Shamanism and Spirit Possession*, 2nd & rev. ed. New York: Routledge.

Lewis, Oscar. 1958. *Village Life in Northern India: Studies in a Delhi Village*. New York: Vintage Books.

Lewis, W. Arthur. 1950. The Industrialization of the British West Indies. *Caribbean Economic Review* 2(1): 1–61.

Lex, Barbara. 1979. The Neurobiology of Ritual Trance. In *The Spectrum of Ritual*, ed. E. D'Aquili, C. Laughlin, and J. McManus, 117–51. New York: Columbia University Press.

Lieber, Michael. 1981. Harmony in Shango Ceremonies. In *Play as Context*, ed. A. T. Cheska, 126–34. West Point, N.Y.: Leisure Press.

Lindholm, Charles. 1990. *Charisma*. Oxford: Basil Blackwell.

———. 2008. *Culture and Authenticity*. Oxford: Basil Blackwell.

Lindstrom, Lamont. 1996. Syncretism. In *Encyclopedia of Social and Cultural Anthropology*, ed. A. Barnard and J. Spencer, 539–41.

Littlewood, Roland. 1993. *Pathology and Identity: The Work of Mother Earth in Trinidad*. Cambridge: Cambridge University Press.

Locke, John. 1690 (1960). *Two Treatises of Government*. Cambridge: Cambridge University Press.

Look Lai, Walton. 1993. *Indentured Labor, Caribbean Sugar: Chinese and Indian Migrants to the British West Indies, 1838–1918*. Baltimore, Md.: Johns Hopkins University Press.

———. 1998. *The Chinese in the West Indies, 1806–1995*. Mona, Jamaica: University of the West Indies Press.

Lowenthal, David. 1972. *West Indian Societies*. New York: Oxford University Press.

Ludwig, A. 1972. Altered States of Consciousness. *Archives of General Psychiatry* 15: 225–34.

Lukes, Steven. 1973. *Individualism*. Oxford: Blackwell.

Lum, Kenneth A. 2000. *Praising His Name in the Dance: Spirit Possession in the Spiritual Baptist Faith and Orisha Work in Trinidad, West Indies*. Amsterdam: Harwood Academic Publishers.

Macpherson, C. B. 1962. *The Political Theory of Possessive Individualism: Hobbes to Locke*. Oxford: Clarendon Press.

Magid, Alvin. 1988. *Urban Nationalism: A Study of Political Development in Trinidad*. Gainesville: University Press of Florida.

Mahabir, Noor Kumar. 1987. The Indian Fire-walking Ceremony in Trinidad. In *Divali Nagar*. Trinidad: National Council of Indian Culture.

Mahabir, Noor Kumar, and Ashram Maharaj. 1985. Kali-Mai: The Cult of the Black Mother in Trinidad. Unpublished paper, West Indiana Division, University of the West Indies, St. Augustine, Trinidad and Tobago.

———. 1996. Hindu Elements in the Shango/Orisha Cult of Trinidad. In *Across the Dark Waters: Ethnicity and Indian Identity in the Caribbean*, ed. D. Dabydeen and B. Samaroo, 90–107. London: Macmillan.

Maharaj, Ashram. 1991. *The Pandits in Trinidad: A Study of a Hindu Institution*. Couva, Trinidad and Tobago: Indian Review Press.

Maingot, Anthony P. 1998. The Caribbean: The Structure of Modern-Conservative Societies. In *Latin America: Its Problems and Its Promises*, ed. J. Knippers Black, 436–54. Boulder, Colo.: Westview Press.

Malik, Yogendra K. 1971. *East Indians in Trinidad: A Study in Minority Politics*. London: Institute of Race Relations.

Martin, Emily. 2007. *Bipolar Expeditions: Mania and Depression in American Culture*. Princeton: Princeton University Press.

Martin, Tony. 1994. Marcus Garvey and Trinidad, 1912–1947. In *Garvey: Africa, Europe, the Americas*, ed. R. Lewis and M. Warner-Lewis, 47–79. Trenton, N.J.: Africa World Press.

Marx, Karl. 1876 (1976). *Capital: A Critique of Political Economy*. New York: Penguin.

Masuzawa, Tomoko. 2005. *The Invention of World Religions; or, How European Universalism Was Preserved in the Language of Pluralism*. Chicago: University of Chicago Press.

Matory, J. Lorand. 1994. *Sex and the Empire That Is No More*. Minneapolis: University of Minnesota Press.

———. 2005. *Black Atlantic Religion: Tradition, Transnationalism, and Matriarchy in the Afro-Brazilian Candomblé*. Princeton: Princeton University Press.

———. 2009. The Many Who Dance in Me: Afro-Atlantic Ontology and the Problem with "Transnationalism." In *Transnational Transcendence: Essays on Religion and Globalization*, ed. T. J. Csordas, 231–62. Berkeley: University of California Press.

Maurer, Bill. 1997. Creolization Redux: The Plural Society Thesis and Offshore Financial Services in the British Caribbean. *New West Indian Guide* 71(3–4): 249–64.

Mauss, Marcel. 1950. Les techniques du corps. In *Sociologie et anthropologie*, 364–86. Paris: Presses Universitaires de France.

McAlister, Elizabeth. 2002. *Rara! Vodou, Power, and Performance in Haiti and Its Diaspora.* Berkeley: University of California Press.

McDaniel, June. 1998. *The Madness of the Saints: Ecstatic Religion in Bengal.* Chicago: University of Chicago Press.

———. 2004. *Offering Flowers, Feeding Skulls: Popular Goddess Worship in West Bengal.* New York: Oxford University Press.

McDermott, Rachel Fell. 2001. *Mother of My Heart, Daughter of My Dreams: Kali and Uma in the Devotional Poetry of Bengal.* New York: Oxford University Press.

McDermott, Rachel Fell, and Jeffrey J. Kripal, eds. 2003. *Encountering Kali: In the Margins, at the Center, in the West.* Berkeley: University of California Press.

McKenzie, Peter. 1997. *Hail Orisha! A Phenomenology of a West African Religion in the Mid-Nineteenth Century.* Leiden: Brill.

McNeal, Keith E. 2000. "This Is History That Was Handed Down, We Don't Know How True It Is": On the Ambiguities of History in Trinidadian Kali Worship. *Oral and Pictorial Records Programme (OPReP) Newsletter* 39(June): 1, 3–5.

———. 2003. Doing the Mother's Caribbean Work: On *Shakti* and Society in Contemporary Trinidad. In *Encountering Kali: In the Margins, at the Center, in the West,* ed. R. F. McDermott and J. Kripal, 223–48. Berkeley: University of California Press.

———. 2010. Pantheons as Mythistorical Archives: Pantheonization and Remodeled Iconographies in Two Southern Caribbean Possession Religions. In *Activating the Past: History and Memory in the Black Atlantic,* ed. A. Apter and L. Derby, 185–244. Cambridge: Scholars Press.

———. 2011a. Firepass Ceremony—Trinidad. In *Encyclopedia of Caribbean Religions,* ed. P. Taylor. Bloomington: Indiana University Press.

———. 2011b. Shakti Puja (Kali Puja, Kali Ma Puja, Kali Mai Puja)—Trinidad. In *Encyclopedia of Caribbean Religions,* ed. P. Taylor. Bloomington: Indiana University Press.

———. Forthcoming a. Seeing the Eyes of God in Human Form: Iconography and Impersonation in African and Hindu Traditions of Trance Performance in the Southern Caribbean. *Material Religion.*

———. Forthcoming b. Trance and the Play of Ecstasy: On Spirits and Self-Objects in the Southern Caribbean. Paper in progress.

———. Forthcoming c. The Arts of Trance and the Problem with Possession. Paper in progress.

Métraux, Alfred. 1955. Dramatic Elements in Ritual Possession. *Diogenes* 11: 18–36.

Mill, John Stuart. 1859 (1963). *On Liberty.* Indianapolis, Ind.: Bobbs-Merrill.

Miller, Daniel. 1994. *Modernity, an Ethnographic Approach: Dualism and Mass Consumption in Trinidad.* Oxford: Berg.

———. 1997. *Capitalism: An Ethnographic Approach.* Oxford: Berg.

Millette, James. 1970 (1985). *Society and Politics in Colonial Trinidad.* London: Zed.

Mintz, Sidney W. 1953. The Folk-Urban Continuum and the Rural Proletarian Community. *American Journal of Sociology* 59: 136–43.

———. 1960. Houses and Yards among Caribbean Peasantries. *VI Congrès International des Sciences Anthropologiques et Ethnologiques,* vol. 2, 591–96. Paris.

———. 1964. Melville J. Herskovits and Caribbean Studies: A Retrospective Tribute. *Caribbean Studies* 4(2): 42–51.

———. 1971a. The Caribbean as a Sociocultural Area. In *Peoples and Cultures of the Caribbean,* ed. M. Horowitz, 17–46. Garden City, N.Y.: Natural History Press.

———. 1971b. The Socio-Historical Background to Pidginization and Creolization. In *Pidginization and Creolization of Languages*, ed. D. Hymes, 481–98. Cambridge: Cambridge University Press.

———. 1974a (1989). *Caribbean Transformations*. New York: Columbia University Press.

———. 1974b. The Rural Proletariat and the Problem of Rural Proletarian Consciousness. *Journal of Peasant Studies* 1(3): 291–325.

———. 1977. The So-called World System: Local Initiative and Local Response. *Dialectical Anthropology* 2: 253–70.

———. 1985a. From Plantations to Peasantries in the Caribbean. In *Caribbean Contours*, ed. S. W. Mintz and S. Price, 127–53. Baltimore, Md.: Johns Hopkins University Press.

———. 1985b. *Sweetness and Power: The Place of Sugar in Modern History*. New York: Penguin.

———. 1987. Labor and Ethnicity: The Caribbean Conjuncture. In *Crises in the Caribbean Basin*, ed. R. Tardanico, 47–58. Newbury Park, Calif.: Sage.

———. 1992. Panglosses and Pollyannas; or, Whose Reality Are We Talking About? In *The Meaning of Freedom*, ed. F. McGlynn and S. Drescher, 245–56. Pittsburgh: University of Pittsburgh Press.

———. 1996a. Ethnic Difference, Plantation Sameness. In *Ethnicity in the Caribbean*, ed. G. Oostindie, 39–52. London: Macmillan.

———. 1996b. Enduring Substances, Trying Theories: The Caribbean Region as Oikoumene. *Journal of the Royal Anthropological Institute* 2(2): 289–311.

———. 1998. Routes to the Caribbean: An Interview with Sidney W. Mintz (by Ashraf Ghani). *Plantation Society in the Americas* 5(1): 103–34.

Mintz, Sidney W., and Richard Price. 1976. *An Anthropological Approach to the Afro-American Past: A Caribbean Perspective*. Philadelphia: Institute for the Study of Human Issues.

Mintz, Sidney W., and Sally Price. 1985. Introduction. In *Caribbean Contours*, ed. S. W. Mintz and S. Price, 3–12. Baltimore, Md.: Johns Hopkins University Press.

Mischel, Frances. 1957. African "Powers" in Trinidad: The Shango Cult. *Anthropological Quarterly* 30(2): 45–59.

———. 1959. Faith Healing and Medical Practice in the Southern Caribbean. *Southwestern Journal of Anthropology* 15: 407–17.

Mischel, Frances, and Walter Mischel 1958. Psychological Aspects of Spirit Possession. *American Anthropologist* 60(2): 249–60.

Mookerjee, Ajit. 1988. *Kali: The Feminine Force*. Rochester, Vt.: Destiny Books.

Moore, R. Laurence. 1994. *Selling God: American Religion in the Marketplace of Culture*. New York: Oxford University Press.

Munasinghe, Viranjini. 1997. Culture Creators and Culture Bearers: The Interface between Race and Ethnicity in Trinidad. *Transforming Anthropology* 6(1–2): 72–86.

———. 2001a. *Callaloo or Tossed Salad? East Indians and the Cultural Politics of Identity in Trinidad*. Ithaca, N.Y.: Cornell University Press.

———. 2001b. Redefining the Nation: The East Indian Struggle for Inclusion in Trinidad. *Journal of Asian American Studies* 4(1): 1–34.

Murrell, Nathaniel Samuel. 2010. *Afro-Caribbean Religions*. Philadelphia: Temple University Press.

Nabokov, Isabelle. 2000. *Religion against the Self: An Ethnography of Tamil Rituals*. New York: Oxford University Press.

Naipaul, Seepersad. 1976 (1995). *The Adventures of Gurudeva*. London: Heinemann.

Naipaul, Vidia S. 1984. Prologue to an Autobiography. In *Finding the Centre*, 13–72. New York: Penguin.

Newson, Linda A. 1976. *Aboriginal and Spanish Colonial Trinidad*. New York: Academic Press.

Niehoff, Arthur, and Juanita Niehoff. 1960. *East Indians in the West Indies*. Milwaukee, Wis.: Milwaukee Public Museum Publications in Anthropology, no. 6.

Obeyesekere, Gananath. 1970. The Idiom of Demonic Possession: A Case Study. *Social Science and Medicine* 4: 97–111.

———. 1977. Psychocultural Exegesis of a Case of Spirit Possession in Sri Lanka. In *Case Studies in Spirit Possession*, ed. V. Crapanzano and V. Garrison, 235–94. New York: Wiley.

———. 1981. *Medusa's Hair: An Essay on Personal Symbols and Religious Experience*. Chicago: University of Chicago Press.

———. 1990. *The Work of Culture: Symbolic Transformation in Psychoanalysis and Anthropology*. Chicago: University of Chicago Press.

Oesterreich, T. G. 1930. *Possession, Demonical and Other*, trans. D. Ibberson. London: Kegan Paul, Trench, Trubner & Co.

O'Flaherty, Wendy Doniger. 1984. *Dreams, Illusions, and Other Realities*. Chicago: University of Chicago Press.

Ohnuki-Tierney, Emiko. 1991. Embedding and Transforming Polytrope: The Monkey as Self in Japanese Culture. In *Beyond Metaphor: The Theory of Tropes in Anthropology*, ed. J. Fernandez, 159–89. Stanford, Calif.: Stanford University Press.

Olawaiye, James Adeyina. 1980. *Yoruba Religious and Social Traditions in Ekiti, Nigeria and Three Caribbean Countries: Trinidad-Tobago, Guyana, and Belize*. Ph.D. dissertation, University of Missouri at Kansas City.

Olupona, Jacob K. 1993. The Study of Yoruba Religious Tradition in Historical Perspective. *Numen* 40(2): 240–73.

Olwig, Karen Fog. 1993. Between Tradition and Modernity: National Development in the Caribbean. *Social Analysis* 33(1): 89–104.

Olwig, Karen Fog, ed. 1995. *Small Islands, Big Questions: Society, Culture and Resistance in the Post-Emancipation Caribbean*. London: Frank Cass.

Oostindie, Gert. 1996a. Introduction: Ethnicity, as Ever? In *Ethnicity in the Caribbean*, ed. G. Oostindie, 1–21. London: Macmillan.

———. 1996b. Ethnicity, Nationalism and the Exodus: The Dutch Caribbean Predicament. In *Ethnicity in the Caribbean*, ed. G. Oostindie, 206–31. London: Macmillan.

Ortiz, Fernando. 1947 (1995). *Cuban Counterpoint: Tobacco and Sugar*, trans. H de Onís. Durham, N.C.: Duke University Press.

O'Shaughnessy, Andrew J. 2000. *An Empire Divided: The American Revolution and the British Caribbean*. Philadelphia: University of Pennsylvania Press.

Oxaal, Ivar. 1982. *Black Intellectuals and the Dilemmas of Race and Class in Trinidad*. Rochester, Vt.: Schenkman.

Padilla, Mark. 2007. *Caribbean Pleasure Industry: Tourism, Sexuality, and AIDS in the Dominican Republic*. Chicago: University of Chicago Press.

Palmer, Annette. 1986. Black American Soldiers in Trinidad, 1942–44: Wartime Politics in a Colonial Society. *Journal of Imperial and Commonwealth History* 14(3): 203–18.

Palmer, Colin A. 1994. Introduction. In *Capitalism and Slavery* by Eric Williams. Chapel Hill: University of North Carolina Press.

Palmié, Stephan. 1993. Ethnogenetic Processes and Cultural Transfer in Afro-American Slave Populations. In *Slavery in the Americas*, ed. W. Binder, 337–63. Würzburg, Germany: Königshausen & Neumann.

———. 1995. Against Syncretism: "Africanizing" and "Cubanizing" Discourses in North American *Orísá* Worship. In *Counterworks: Managing the Diversity of Knowledge*, ed. R. Fardon, 73–104. London: Routledge.

———. 2006. Creolization and Its Discontents. *Annual Review of Anthropology* 35: 433–56.

———. 2007a. The "C-Word" Again: From Colonial to Postcolonial Semantics. In *Creolization: History, Ethnography, Theory*, ed. C. Stewart, 66–83. Walnut Creek, Calif.: Left Coast Press.

———. 2007b. Is There a Model in the Muddle? "Creolization" in African Americanist History and Anthropology. In *Creolization: History, Ethnography, Theory*, ed. C. Stewart, 178–200. Walnut Creek, Calif.: Left Coast Press.

———. 2007c. Introduction: Out of Africa? *Journal of Religion in Africa* 37: 159–73.

———. 2007d. *Ecué's* Atlantic: An Essay in Methodology. *Journal of Religion in Africa* 37: 275–315.

Palmisano, Antonio L. 2003. Trance and Translation in the *Zar* Cult of Ethiopia. In *Translation and Ethnography: The Anthropological Challenge of Intercultural Understanding*, ed. T. Maranhão and B. Streck, 135–51. Tucson: University of Arizona Press.

Parrinder, Geoffrey. 1953. *Religion in an African City*. London: Oxford University Press.

Paton, Diana. 2009. Obeah Acts: Producing and Policing the Boundaries of Religion in the Caribbean. *Small Axe* 28(1): 1–18.

Patterson, Orlando. 1967. *The Sociology of Slavery*. Rutherford, N.J.: Farleigh Dickinson University Press.

Pattullo, Polly. 1996. *Last Resorts: The Cost of Tourism in the Caribbean*. London: Cassell.

Paul, Robert, and Paul Rabinow. 1976. Bourgeois Materialism Revisited. *Dialectical Anthropology* 1: 121–34.

Payne, Anthony. 1993. Westminster Adapted: The Political Order of the Commonwealth Caribbean. In *Democracy in the Caribbean*, ed. J. Domínguez, R. Pastor, and R. Worrell, 57–73. Baltimore, Md.: Johns Hopkins University Press.

Peel, J.D.Y. 1968. Syncretism and Religious Change. *Comparative Studies in Society and History* 10(2): 121–41.

———. 2000. *Religious Encounter and the Making of the Yoruba*. Bloomington: Indiana University Press.

Pemberton III, John. 1987. Yoruba Religion. In *Encyclopedia of Religion*, ed. M. Eliade, 535–38. New York: Macmillan.

Phillips, Leslie H. C. 1960. Kali-Mai Puja. *Timehri: Journal of the Guyana Society* 11: 136–46.

Polk, Patrick A. 1997. *Haitian Vodou Flags*. Jackson: University Press of Mississippi.

———. 2001. Obeah in the West Indies. In *Encyclopedia of African and African-American Religions*, ed. S. D. Glazier, 216–17. New York: Routledge.

Pollak-Eltz, Angelina. 1968. The Yoruba Religion and Its Decline in the Americas. *International Congress of Americanists* 38(3): 423–27.

———. 1993. The Shango Cult and Other African Rituals in Trinidad, Grenada, and Carriacou and Their Possible Influence on the Spiritual Baptist Faith. *Caribbean Quarterly* 39(3–4): 12–26.

Potts, Lydia. 1990. *The World Labour Market: A History of Migration*. London: Zed.

Premdas, Ralph, and Harold Sitahal. 1991. Religion and Culture: The Case of Presbyterians in Trinidad's Stratified System. In *Social and Occupational Stratification in Contemporary Trinidad and Tobago*, ed. S. Ryan, 335–55. Trinidad: Institute of Social and Economic Research.

Price, Richard. 2001. The Miracle of Creolization. *New West Indian Guide* 75(1 and 2): 35–64.

———. 2007. Some Anthropological Musings on Creolization. *Journal of Pidgin and Creole Languages* 22(1): 17–36.

Procope, Judith. 1980. *A Historical Survey of Boissiere Village No. 1, Maraval, with Particular Reference to the Year 1917*. Caribbean Studies thesis, University of the West Indies.

Quijano, Aníbal, and Immanuel Wallerstein. 1992. Americanity as a Concept, or the Americas in the Modern World-System. *International Social Sciences Journal* 134: 549–57.

Ramesar, Marianne D. S. 1976. The Integration of Indian Settlers in Trinidad after Indenture, 1921–1946. *Caribbean Issues* 2(3): 52–70.

———. 1994. *Survivors of Another Crossing: A History of East Indians in Trinidad, 1880–1946*. St. Augustine, Trinidad and Tobago: University of the West Indies Press.

Rawls, John. 1972. *A Theory of Justice*. Cambridge: Harvard University Press.

Reddock, Rhoda. 1991. Social Mobility in Trinidad and Tobago, 1960–1980. In *Social and Occupational Stratification in Contemporary Trinidad and Tobago*, ed. S. Ryan, 210–33. Trinidad: Institute of Social and Economic Research.

———. 1998. Contestations over Culture, Class, Gender and Identity in Trinidad and Tobago. *Caribbean Quarterly* 44(1 and 2): 62–80.

Redfield, Robert, Ralph Linton, and Melville J. Herskovits. 1936. Memorandum for the Study of Acculturation. *American Anthropologist* 38: 149–52.

Richardson, Alan. 1997. Romantic Voodoo: Obeah and British Culture, 1797–1807. In *Sacred Possessions: Vodou, Santería, Obeah, and the Caribbean*, ed. M. Fernández Olmos and L. Paravisini-Gebert, 171–94. New Brunswick, N.J.: Rutgers University Press.

Richardson, Bonham. 1983. *Caribbean Migrants: Environment and Human Survival on St. Kitts and Nevis*. Knoxville: University of Tennessee Press.

———. 1989. Caribbean Migrations, 1838–1985. In *The Modern Caribbean*, ed. F. W. Knight and C. A. Palmer, 203–28. Chapel Hill: University of North Carolina Press.

———. 1992. *The Caribbean in the Wider World, 1492–1992: A Regional Geography*. New York: Cambridge University Press.

Richardson, David, and Stephen D. Behrendt. 1995. Inikori's Odyssey: Measuring the British Slave Trade, 1655–1807. *Cahiers d'Études Africaines* 35(2–3): 599–615.

Rieff, Philip. 1966. *The Triumph of the Therapeutic: Uses of Faith after Freud*. Chicago: University of Chicago Press.

Robertson, Roland. 1995. Glocalization: Time-Space and Homogeneity-Heterogeneity. In *Global Modernities*, ed. M. Featherstone, S. Lash, and R. Robertson, 25–44. London: Sage.

Rojas, Rafael. 2005. Transculturation and Nationalism. In *Cuban Counterpoints: The Legacy of Fernando Ortiz*, ed. M. A. Font and A. W. Quiroz, 65–71. Lanham, Md.: Lexington Books.

Rommen, Timothy. 2007. *"Mek Some Noise": Gospel Music and the Ethics of Style in Trinidad*. Berkeley: University of California Press.

Rostas, Susanna, and André Droogers. 1993. The Popular Use of Popular Religion in Latin America: An Introduction. In *The Popular Use of Popular Religion in Latin America*, ed. S. Rostas and A. Droogers, 1–16. Amsterdam: Centre for Latin American Research and Documentation.

Rouget, Gilbert. 1985. *Music and Trance: A Theory of the Relations between Music and Possession*, trans. B. Biebuyck. Chicago: University of Chicago Press.

Ruesch, Jurgen, and Gregory Bateson. 1968. *Communication: The Social Matrix of Psychiatry*. New York: Norton.

Russell, Horace O. 1983. The Emergence of the Christian Black: The Making of a Stereotype. *Jamaica Journal* 16: 51–58.

Ryan, Selwyn D. 1972. *Race and Nationalism in Trinidad and Tobago*. Toronto: University of Toronto Press.

———. 1991. *The Muslimeen Grab for Power: Race, Religion, and Revolution in Trinidad and Tobago*. Trinidad: Inprint.

———, ed. 1995a. *The Black Power Revolution, 1970: A Retrospective*. St. Augustine, Trinidad and Tobago: Sir Arthur Lewis Institute of Social and Economic Research.

———. 1995b. 1970: Revolution or Rebellion? In *The Black Power Revolution, 1970: A Retrospective*, ed. S. D. Ryan, 691–708. St. Augustine, Trinidad and Tobago: Sir Arthur Lewis Institute of Social and Economic Research.

———. 1996. *Pathways to Power: Indians and the Politics of National Unity in Trinidad and Tobago*. St. Augustine, Trinidad and Tobago: Sir Arthur Lewis Institute of Social and Economic Research.

———. 1999. *The Jhandi and the Cross: The Clash of Cultures in Post-Creole Trinidad and Tobago*. St. Augustine, Trinidad and Tobago: Sir Arthur Lewis Institute of Social and Economic Research.

Samaroo, Brinsley. 1974 (1985). Politics and Afro-Indian Relations in Trinidad. In *Calcutta to Caroni: The East Indians of Trinidad*, ed. J. La Guerre, 77–94. St. Augustine, Trinidad: University of the West Indies Press.

———. 1987. The Indian Connection: The Influence of Indian Thought and Ideas on East Indians in the Caribbean. In *India in the Caribbean*, ed. D. Dabydeen and B. Samaroo, 43–60. London: Hansib.

———. 1996. Animal Images in Caribbean Hindu Mythology. In *Monsters, Tricksters, and Sacred Cows: Animal Tales and American Identities*, ed. A. J. Arnold, 185–203. Charlottesville: University of Virginia Press.

Sax, William, ed. 1995. *The Gods at Play: Lila in South Asia*. New York: Oxford University Press.

Scarano, Frank A. 1989. Labor and Society in the Nineteenth Century. In *The Modern Caribbean*, ed. F. W. Knight and C. A. Palmer, 51–84. Chapel Hill: University of North Carolina Press.

Schaeffner, Andrew. 1965. Rituel et pre-theatre. In *Histoire des spectacles*, 21–54. Paris: Gallimard.

Schechner, Richard. 1977. *Performance Theory*. New York: Routledge.

———. 1985. *Between Theater and Anthropology*. Philadelphia: University of Pennsylvania Press.

———. 2002. *Performance Studies: An Introduction*. New York: Routledge.

Schechner, Richard, and Willa Appel, eds. 1990. *By Means of Performance: Intercultural Studies of Theatre and Ritual*. New York: Cambridge University Press.

Scheper-Hughes, Nancy. 1992. *Death without Weeping: The Violence of Everyday Life in Brazil*. Berkeley: University of California Press.

Scheper-Hughes, Nancy, and Margaret Lock. 1987. The Mindful Body: Prolegomenon to Future Work in Medical Anthropology. *Medical Anthropological Quarterly* 1(1): 6–41.

———. 1991. The Message in the Bottle: Illness and the Micropolitics of Resistance. *Journal of Psychohistory* 18(4): 409–32.

Scher, Philip W. 1997. Unveiling the Orisha. In *Africa's Ogun: Old World and New*, ed. S. Barnes, 315–31. Bloomington: Indiana University Press.

Schieffelin, Edward L. 1998. Problematizing Performance. In *Ritual, Performance, Media*, ed. P. Hughes-Freeland, 194–207. New York: Routledge.

Schwartz, Barton M. 1964. Ritual Aspects of Caste in Trinidad. *Anthropological Quarterly* 37(1): 1–15.

Schwartz, Theodore. 1976. The Cargo Cult: A Melanesian Type-Response to Change. In *Responses to Change: Society, Culture, and Personality*, ed. G. A. De Vos, 157–206. New York: Van Nostrand.

Schwartzman, John. 1982. Symptoms and Rituals: Paradoxical Modes and Social Organization. *Ethos* 10(1): 3–25.

Scott, David. 2004. Modernity That Predated the Modern: Sidney Mintz's Caribbean. *History Workshop Journal* 58: 191–210.

Sedgwick, Peter. 2002. Liberalism. In *Key Concepts in Cultural Theory*, ed. A. Edgar and P. Sedgwick, 208–15. London: Routledge.

Seesaran, E. B. Rosabelle. 2002. *From Caste to Class: The Social Mobility of the Indo-Trinidadian Community, 1870–1917*. Trinidad: Rosaac Publishing House.

Segal, Daniel A. 1988. Nationalism, Comparatively Speaking. *Journal of Historical Sociology* 1(3): 301–21.

———. 1989. *Nationalism in a Colonial State: A Study of Trinidad and Tobago*. Ph.D. dissertation, University of Chicago.

———. 1991. "The European": Allegories of Racial Purity. *Anthropology Today* 7(5): 7–9.

———. 1993. Race and "Color" in Pre-Independence Trinidad and Tobago. In *Trinidad Ethnicity*, ed. K. Yelvington, 81–115. Knoxville: University of Tennessee Press.

———. 1994. Living Ancestors: Nationalism and the Past in Postcolonial Trinidad and Tobago. In *Remapping Memory: The Politics of Timespace*, ed. J. Boyarin, 221–39. Minneapolis: University of Minnesota Press.

Segal, Daniel A., and Richard Handler. 1992. How European Is Nationalism? *Social Analysis* 32: 1–15.

Shaw, Thomas A. 1985. To Be or Not to Be Chinese: Differential Expressions of Chinese Culture and Solidarity in the British West Indies. *Ethnic Groups*: 6(2–3): 155–85.

Shaw, Rosalind, and Charles Stewart. 1994. Introduction: Problematizing Syncretism. In *Syncretism/Anti-Syncretism: The Politics of Religious Synthesis*, ed. C. Stewart and R. Shaw, 1–26. London: Routledge.

Sheller, Mimi. 2003. *Consuming the Caribbean*. London: Routledge.

Shemer, Noga. 2006. *Spiritual Baptism: Meta-Analysis of a Caribbean Discourse*. M.A. thesis, University of California at San Diego.

Shepherd, Verene A., and Glen L. Richards, eds. 2002. *Questioning Creole: Creolisation Discourses in Caribbean Culture*. Kingston, Jamaica: Ian Randle.

Sheridan, Richard B. 1974. *Sugar and Slavery: An Economic History of the British West Indies, 1623–1775*. Baltimore, Md.: Johns Hopkins University Press.

Shirokogoroff, Sergei M. 1935. *The Psychomental Complex of the Tungus*. London: Kegan Paul, Trench, Trubner & Co.

Shore, Bradd. 1996. *Culture in Mind: Cognition, Culture, and the Problem of Meaning*. New York: Oxford University Press.

———. 2000. Human Diversity and Human Nature: The Life and Times of a False Dichotomy. In *Being Humans: Anthropological Universality and Particularity in Transdisciplinary Perspectives*, ed. N. Roughley, 81–103. New York: Walter de Gruyter.

Simpson, George E. 1973. *Melville J. Herskovits*. Leaders of Modern Anthropology Series. New York: Columbia University Press.

———. 1976. Religions of the Caribbean. In *The African Diaspora: Interpretive Essays*, ed. M. L. Kilson and R. I. Rotberg, 280–311. Cambridge: Harvard University Press.

———. 1978. *Black Religions in the New World*. New York: Columbia University Press.

———. 1980. *Religious Cults of the Caribbean: Trinidad, Jamaica, and Haiti*, 3rd ed. Río Piedras: Institute of Caribbean Studies, University of Puerto Rico.

Singer, Philip, Enrique Araneta, and Jamsie Naidoo. 1976. Learning of Psychodynamics, History, and Diagnosis Management Therapy by a Kali Cult Indigenous Healer in Guiana. In *The Realm of the Extra-Human: Agents and Audiences*, ed. A. Bharati, 345–70. The Hague: Mouton de Gruyter.

Singh, Kelvin. 1994. *Race and Class Struggles in a Colonial State: Trinidad, 1917–1945*. Jamaica: University of the West Indies Press.

———. 1996. Conflict and Collaboration: Tradition and Modernizing Indo-Trinidadian Elites (1917–1956). *New West Indian Guide* 70(3 and 4): 229–53.

Singh, Odaipaul. 1993. *Hinduism in Guyana: A Study in Traditions of Worship*. Ph.D. dissertation, University of Wisconsin.

Sirju, Martin. 1990. *The Practice of Kali-Puja at Bharat's Kali Temple, Lower Streatham Lodge, St. Augustine: A Theological Appraisal*. Caribbean Studies thesis, University of the West Indies.

Smith, David G. 1968. Liberalism. In *International Encyclopedia of the Social Sciences*, vol. 9, ed. D. Sills, 276–82. New York: Macmillan.

Smith, Frederick M. 2006. *The Self Possessed: Deity and Spirit Possession in South Asian Literature and Civilization*. New York: Columbia University Press.

Smith, Maynard G. 1965. *The Plural Society in the British West Indies*. Berkeley: University of California Press.

Smith, Raymond T. 1959. Family Structure and Plantation Systems in the New World. In *Plantation Systems of the World*. Social Science Monograph no. 7. Washington, D.C.: Pan American Union.

———. 1976. Religion and the Formation of West Indian Society: Guyana and Jamaica. In *The African Diaspora: Interpretive Essays*, ed. M. L. Kilson and R. I. Rotberg, 312–41. Cambridge: Harvard University Press.

———. 1982 (1996). Race and Class in the Post-Emancipation Caribbean. In *The Matrifocal Family*, 143–64.

———. 1988. *Kinship and Class in the West Indies: A Genealogical Study of Jamaica and Guyana*. Cambridge: Cambridge University Press.

———. 1992. Race, Class, and Gender in the Transition to Freedom. In *The Meaning of Freedom*, ed. F. McGlynn and S. Drescher, 257–90. Pittsburgh: University of Pittsburgh Press.

———. 1996. *The Matrifocal Family: Power, Pluralism, and Politics*. New York: Routledge.

Smith, Raymond T., and Chandra Jayawardena. 1967. Caste and Social Status among the Indians of Guyana. In *Caste among Overseas Indians*, ed. B. Schwartz. San Francisco: Chandler.

Smith, Theophus H. 1994. *Conjuring Culture: Biblical Formations of Black America.* New York: Oxford University Press.

Smith, Wilfred Cantwell. 1998. *Believing: An Historical Perspective.* Oxford: Oneworld.

Solow, Barbara L., ed. 1991. *Slavery and the Rise of the Atlantic System.* Cambridge: Cambridge University Press.

Solow, Barbara L., and Stanley L. Engerman, eds. 1987. *British Capitalism and Slavery: The Legacy of Eric Williams.* Cambridge: Cambridge University Press.

Spicer, Edward H. 1968. Acculturation. *International Encyclopedia of the Social Sciences,* vol. 1, ed. D. Sills, 21–27. New York: Macmillan.

Spiro, Melford E. 1961. Culture and Personality: An Overview and Suggested Reorientation. In *Psychological Anthropology,* ed. F.L.K. Hsu, 459–93. Homewood, Ill.: Dorsey.

———. 1965. Religious Systems as Culturally Constituted Defense Mechanisms. In *Context and Meaning in Cultural Anthropology,* ed. M. E. Spiro, 100–13. Glencoe, Ill.: Free Press.

———. 1967. *Burmese Supernaturalism: A Study in the Explanation and Resolution of Suffering.* Englewood Cliffs, N.J.: Prentice Hall.

———. 1970. *Buddhism and Society: A Great Tradition and Its Burmese Vicissitudes.* New York: Harper & Row.

———. 1982. Collective Representations and Mental Representations in Religious Symbol Systems. In *Symbols in Anthropology,* ed. J. Macquet, 45–72. Malibu, Calif.: Undena.

Springer, Pearl Eintou. 1994. Orisa and the Spiritual Baptist Religion in Trinidad and Tobago. In *At the Crossroads: African Caribbean Religion and Christianity,* ed. B. Sankeralli, 85–108. Trinidad and Tobago: Cariflex.

Stark, James H. 1897. *Stark's Guide Book and History of Trinidad.* Boston: James H. Stark.

Stewart, Charles. 1999. Syncretism and Its Synonyms: Reflections on Cultural Mixture. *Diacritics* 29(3): 40–62.

———. 2007a. Creolization: History, Ethnography, Theory. In *Creolization: History, Ethnography, Theory,* ed. C. Stewart, 1–25. Walnut Creek, Calif.: Left Coast Press.

Stewart, Charles, ed. 2007b. *Creolization: History, Ethnography, Theory.* Walnut Creek, Calif.: Left Coast Press.

Stewart, Dianne M. 2001. African-derived Religions. In *Encyclopedia of African and African-American Religions,* ed. S. D. Glazier, 21–22. New York: Routledge.

———. 2005. *Three Eyes for the Journey: African Dimensions of the Jamaican Religious Experience.* New York: Oxford University Press.

Stewart, John. 1976. Mission and Leadership among the "Merikin" Baptists of Trinidad. *Latin American Anthropology Group Contributions to Afro-American Ethnohistory,* vol. 1, 17–25. Washington, D.C.: Latin American Anthropology Group.

Stone, Carl. 1985. A Profile of the Caribbean. In *Caribbean Contours,* ed. S. W. Mintz and S. Price, 13–53. Baltimore, Md.: Johns Hopkins University Press.

Stuempfle, Steven. 1995. *The Steelband Movement: The Forging of a National Art in Trinidad and Tobago.* Philadelphia: University of Pennsylvania Press.

Stutley, Margaret. 2003. *Shamanism: An Introduction.* London: Routledge.

Sullivan, Harry Stack. 1953. *The Interpersonal Theory of Psychiatry.* New York: Norton.

Sutton, Paul. 1983. Black Power in Trinidad and Tobago: The "Crisis" of 1970. *Journal of Commonwealth and Comparative Politics* 21(2): 115–32.

———. 1984. Oil Capitalism and the "Presidential Power" of Eric Williams in Trinidad and

Tobago. In *Dependency under Challenge: The Political Economy of the Commonwealth Carib-bean*, ed. A. Payne and P. Sutton, 43–76. Manchester, U.K.: Manchester University Press.

———. 1991. Constancy, Change and Accommodation: The Distinct Tradition of the Common-wealth Caribbean. In *The Fallacies of Hope: The Postcolonial Record of the Commonwealth Third World*, ed. J. Mayall and A. Payne, 106–28. Manchester, U.K.: Manchester University Press.

Temperley, Howard. 1998. Abolition and Anti-Slavery in Britain. In *Historical Guide to World Slavery*, ed. S. Drescher and S. L. Engerman, 10–15. New York: Oxford University Press.

Thomas, Rt. Rev. Eudora. 1987. *A History of the Shouter Baptists in Trinidad and Tobago*. Ta-carigua, Trinidad: Calaloux Publications.

Thompson, E. P. 1963. *The Making of the English Working Class*. New York: Vintage.

Thompson, Robert Farris. 1983. *Flash of the Spirit: African and Afro-American Art and Philoso-phy*. New York: Random House.

———. 1993. *Faces of the Gods: Art and Altars of Africa and the African Americas*. New York: Museum for African Art.

Tikasingh, Gerad. 1973. *The Establishment of the Indians in Trinidad, 1870–1900*. Ph.D. disserta-tion, University of the West Indies.

Tindall, David. 2000. Drums and Colours. *Caribbean Beat* (November). Port-of-Spain, Trini-dad and Tobago: MEP.

Tinker, Hugh. 1974. *A New System of Slavery*. London: Hansib.

Tölölyan, Khachig. 1996. Rethinking Diaspora(s): Stateless Power in the Transnational Mo-ment. *Diaspora* 5(1): 3–36.

Trilling, Lionel. 1972. *Sincerity and Authenticity*. Cambridge: Harvard University Press.

Trotman, David V. 1976. The Yoruba and Orisha Worship in Trinidad and British Guiana: 1838–1870. *African Studies Review* 19(2): 1–17.

———. 1986. *Crime in Trinidad: Conflict and Control in a Plantation Society, 1838–1900*. Knox-ville: University of Tennessee Press.

———. 2007. Reflections on the Children of Shango: An Essay on a History of Orisa Worship in Trinidad. *Slavery and Abolition* 28(2): 211–34.

Trouillot, Michel-Rolph. 1992a. The Caribbean Region: An Open Frontier in Anthropological Theory. *Annual Review of Anthropology* 21: 19–42.

———. 1992b. The Inconvenience of Freedom: Free People of Color and the Political Aftermath of Slavery in Dominica and Saint-Domingue/Haiti. In *The Meaning of Freedom*, ed. F. Mc-Glynn and S. Drescher, 147–82. Pittsburgh: University of Pittsburgh Press.

———. 1998. Culture on the Edges: Creolization in the Plantation Context. *Plantation Society in the Americas* 5(1): 8–27.

———. 2003. *Global Transformations: Anthropology and the Modern World*. New York: Palgrave Macmillan.

Turner, Mary. 1997. Religious Beliefs. In *General History of the Caribbean*, Vol. 3: *The Slave Societies of the Caribbean*, ed. F. W. Knight. London: UNESCO.

Turner, Mary, ed. 1995. *From Chattel Slaves to Wage Slaves: The Dynamics of Labor Bargaining in the Americas*. Bloomington: Indiana University Press.

Turner, Victor W. 1987. *The Anthropology of Performance*. New York: PAJ.

Tuzin, Donald F. 2002. Art, Ritual, and the Crafting of Illusion. *Asia Pacific Journal of Anthro-pology* 3(1): 1–23.

Tweed, Thomas A. 1997. *Our Lady of the Exile: Diasporic Religion at a Cuban Catholic Shrine in Miami*. New York: Oxford University Press.

van der Veer, Peter, and Steven Vertovec. 1991. Brahmanism Abroad: On Caribbean Hinduism as an Ethnic Religion. *Ethnology* 30(2): 149–66.

Verger, Pierre. 1957. *Notes sur le culte des Orisa et Vodun à Bahia, la Baie de Tous les Saints au Brésil et à l'Ancienne Côte d'Esclaves en Afrique*. Mémoire 51. Dakar: Institut Français d'Afrique Noire.

———. 1969. Trance and Convention in Nago-Yoruba Spirit Mediumship. In *Spirit Mediumship and Society in Africa*, ed. J. Beattie and J. Middleton, 50–66. London: Routledge & Kegan Paul.

———. 1982. *Orisha: Les dieux yorouba en Afrique et au Nouveau Monde*. Paris: A. M. Metailie.

Vertovec, Steven. 1992. *Hindu Trinidad: Religion, Ethnicity and Socio-economic Change*. London: Macmillan.

———. 1996. "Official" and "Popular" Hinduism in the Caribbean. In *Across the Dark Waters: Ethnicity and Indian Identity in the Caribbean*, ed. D. Dabydeen and B. Samaroo, 108–30. London: Macmillan.

———. 1998. Ethnic Distance and Religious Convergence: Shango, Spiritual Baptist, and Kali Mai Traditions in Trinidad. *Social Compass* 45(2): 247–63.

Vitebsky, Piers. 1995. *The Shaman: Voyages of the Soul: Trance, Ecstasy, and Healing from Siberia to the Amazon*. Boston: Little, Brown.

Wacquant, Loïc J. D. 1989. Towards a Reflexive Sociology: A Workshop with Pierre Bourdieu. *Sociological Theory* 7: 26–63.

Walker, Sheila S. 1972. *Ceremonial Spirit Possession in Africa and Afro-America*. Leiden, Netherlands: E. J. Brill.

———. 1980. African Gods in the Americas: The Black Religious Continuum. *Black Scholar* 11(8): 25–36.

Wallerstein, Immanuel. 1995. *After Liberalism*. New York: New Press.

Warner-Lewis, Maureen. 1991. *Guinea's Other Suns: The African Dynamic in Trinidad Culture*. Dover, Mass.: Majority Press.

———. 1994. *Yoruba Songs of Trinidad*. London: Karnak House.

———. 1996. *Trinidad Yoruba: From Mother Tongue to Memory*. Tuscaloosa: University of Alabama Press.

Wedenoja, William. 1990. Ritual Trance and Catharsis: A Psychobiological and Evolutionary Perspective. In *Personality and the Cultural Construction of Society*, ed. D. K. Jordan and M.J. Swartz, 308–28. Tuscaloosa: University of Alabama Press.

Wheatley, Paul. 1970. The Significance of Traditional Yoruba Urbanism. *Comparative Studies in Society and History* 12(4): 393–423.

Williams, Brackette F. 1990. Dutchman Ghosts and the History Mystery: Ritual, Colonizer, and Colonized Interpretations of the 1763 Berbice Slave Rebellion. *Journal of Historical Sociology* 3(2): 133–65.

Williams, Eric E. 1942. *The Negro in the Caribbean*. Austin: Associates in Negro Folk Education, University of Texas.

———. 1944 (1994). *Capitalism and Slavery*. Chapel Hill: University of North Carolina Press.

———. 1962. *History of the People of Trinidad and Tobago*. London: André Deutsch.

———. 1969. *Inward Hunger: The Education of a Prime Minister*. London: André Deutsch.

——. 1970 (1984). *From Columbus to Castro: The History of the Caribbean, 1492–1969*. New York: Vintage Books.

Williams, Raymond. 1983. *Keywords: A Vocabulary of Culture and Society*, rev. ed. New York: Oxford University Press.

Wilshire, Bruce. 1982. *Role Playing and Identity: The Limits of Theatre as Metaphor*. Bloomington: Indiana University Press.

Wilson, Peter J. 1973. *Crab Antics: A Caribbean Case Study of the Conflict between Reputation and Respectability*. Prospect Heights, Ill.: Waveland Press.

Winer, Lise. 1993. *Trinidad and Tobago*. Varieties of English around the World Series. Amsterdam: John Benjamins.

——. 2007. *Badjohns, Bhaaji, and Banknote Blue: Essays on the Social History of Language in Trinidad and Tobago*. St. Augustine, Trinidad and Tobago: University of the West Indies School of Continuing Studies.

Winnicott, D. W. 1971. *Playing and Reality*. New York: Routledge.

Wolf, Eric R. 1982. *Europe and the People without History*. Berkeley: University of California Press.

Wood, Donald. 1968. *Trinidad in Transition: The Years after Slavery*. San Fernando, Trinidad: Caribbean Educational Publishers Ltd.

Yelvington, Kevin A. 1995. *Producing Power: Ethnicity, Gender, and Class in a Caribbean Workplace*. Philadelphia: Temple University Press.

——. 1999. The War in Ethiopia and Trinidad, 1935–1936. In *The Colonial Caribbean in Transition: Essays on Postemancipation Social and Cultural History*, ed. B. Brereton and K. Yelvington, 189–225. Gainesville: University Press of Florida.

——. 2006a. Introduction. In *Afro-Atlantic Dialogues: Anthropology in the Diaspora*, ed. K. Y. Yelvington, 3–32. Santa Fe, N.M.: School of American Research Press.

——. 2006b. The Invention of Africa in Latin America and the Caribbean: Political Discourse and Anthropological Praxis, 1920–40. In *Afro-Atlantic Dialogues: Anthropology in the Diaspora*, ed. K. A. Yelvington, 35–70. Santa Fe, N.M.: School of American Research Press.

Yengoyan, Aram, ed. 2006. *Modes of Comparison: Theory and Practice*. Ann Arbor: University of Michigan Press.

Younger, Paul. 2002. *Playing Host to Deity: Festival Religion in the South Indian Tradition*. New York: Oxford University Press.

——. 2010. *New Homelands: Hindu Communities in Mauritius, Guyana, Trinidad, South Africa, Fiji, and East Africa*. New York: Oxford University Press.

Zammito, John H. 2004. *A Nice Derangement of Epistemes: Post-Positivism in the Study of Science from Quine to Latour*. Chicago: University of Chicago Press.

Zane, Wallace W. 1995. Ritual States of Consciousness: A Way of Accounting for Anomalies in the Observation and Explanation of Spirit Possession. *Anthropology of Consciousness* 6(4): 18–29.

——. 1999. *Journeys to the Spiritual Lands: The Natural History of a West Indian Religion*. New York: Oxford University Press.

Index

Page numbers in italics refer to illustrations.

Keith E. McNeal is a Fulbright Scholar with the Institute for Gender and Development Studies at the University of the West Indies in Trinidad and Tobago. His work has been published in a number of venues, including *Activating the Past: Historical Memory in the Black Atlantic*; *Encountering Kali: In the Margins, at the Center, in the West*; and the *Encyclopedia of Caribbean Religions*.

New World Diasporas

More Than Black: Afro-Cubans in Tampa, by Susan D. Greenbaum (2002)
Carnival and the Formation of a Caribbean Transnation, by Philip W. Scher (2003)
Dominican Migration: Transnational Perspectives, edited by Ernesto Sagás and Sintia E. Molina (2004)
Salvadoran Migration to Southern California: Redefining El Hermano Lejano, by Beth Baker-Cristales (2004)
The Chrysanthemum and the Song: Music, Memory, and Identity in the South American Japanese Diaspora, by Dale A. Olsen (2004)
Andean Diaspora: The Tiwanaku Colonies and the Origins of South American Empire, by Paul S. Goldstein (2005)
Migration and Vodou, by Karen E. Richman (2005)
True-Born Maroons, by Kenneth M. Bilby (2005)
The Tears of Hispaniola: Haitian and Dominican Diaspora Memory, by Lucía M. Suárez (2006)
Dominican-Americans and the Politics of Empowerment, by Ana Aparicio (2006)
Nuer-American Passages: Globalizing Sudanese Migration, by Dianna J. Shandy (2006)